SS SL
INLP
CAR

Freedom of Information Handbook

The College of Law
believing in your future

D1374412

Birmingham ⏐ Bristol ⏐ Chester ⏐ Guildford ⏐ London ⏐ Manchester ⏐ York

Other titles available from Law Society Publishing:

Data Protection Handbook (2nd edn)
General Editor: Peter Carey

Email: Law, Practice and Compliance
Stewart Room

Information Sharing Handbook
Edited by Claire Bessant; Consultant Editor: Phil Tompkins

Knowledge Management Handbook
Hélène Russell

Privacy Law Handbook
Edited by Keith Mathieson

Titles from Law Society Publishing can be ordered from all good bookshops or direct (telephone 0870 850 1422, email **lawsociety@prolog.uk.com** or visit our online shop at **bookshop.lawsociety.org.uk**).

FREEDOM OF INFORMATION HANDBOOK

THIRD EDITION

General Editors: Peter Carey and Robin Hopkins

The Law Society

Crown copyright material is reproduced with the permission of the
Controller of Her Majesty's Stationery Office. The material in Appendix A
is reproduced with the permission of the Financial Services Authority.

ISBN- 978-1-907698-18-7

First published in 2006
Second edition published in 2008
This third edition published in 2012 by the Law Society
113 Chancery Lane, London WC2A 1PL

Typeset by Columns Design Ltd, Reading
Printed by CPI Group (UK) Ltd, Croydon, CR0 4YY

FSC
www.fsc.org
MIX
Paper from
responsible sources
FSC® C013604

The paper used for the text pages of this book is FSC® certified. FSC (the
Forest Stewardship Council®) is an international network to promote
responsible management of the world's forests.

Contents

CONTENTS

APPENDICES

Foreword

Transparent and open government is an important feature of a mature democracy. The freedom of information (FOI) regime is now established as an enforceable legal framework which ensures the rights of citizens to information on how public money is spent and how decisions about public service provision are made.

The Freedom of Information Act 2000 (FOIA) and the Environmental Information Regulations 2004 have been in force for eight years, but they continue to have a significant impact, as the information disclosed can sometimes not just raise an eyebrow or two but provoke an outrage. The right to know complements the emerging right to open data, drawing out information which can be awkward or embarrassing. No one would seriously suggest that we should have less openness and transparency, but the precise limits of legitimate access to information in the public interest remain the subject of debate, at least in individual cases.

A review by the House of Commons Justice Committee in 2012 concluded that, with a couple of exceptions, there was 'no pressing need for legislative change to an Act which is serving the nation well'. Nevertheless, concerns have been expressed about the burden which FOI can place on public authorities receiving large numbers of complex requests. The question whether a particular request for information is vexatious is one which frequently has to be addressed by public authorities, the Information Commissioner and the Information Rights Tribunal. Meanwhile, many services traditionally provided by public authorities are being delivered via novel arrangements involving new bodies and partnerships which are not subject to the FOIA. There is a real risk of reduced transparency as a result.

So as the law evolves, through jurisprudence and some specific statutory changes, there is a clear need for a comprehensive practical guide to the FOIA and its associated regulations, codes of practice and guidance. This Handbook meets that need. The third edition comes at a time when FOI has become well established in our public life and most of the initial teething problems of implementing the Act have been overcome. Being open and transparent may sometimes still be inconvenient or uncomfortable, but in my view the benefits far outweigh any drawbacks and upholding the right to know is the right thing to do.

Graham Smith
Deputy Information Commissioner and Director of Freedom of Information, Information Commissioner's Office
October 2012

About the authors

Patricia Barratt graduated from Jesus College, Cambridge with a degree in Classics in 1984. She trained in law at Chancery Lane College of Law, and qualified as a solicitor with Clifford Chance in 1991. She worked closely with Richard Thomas (the former Information Commissioner) for 10 years in Clifford Chance's public policy practice area, and is now a senior associate in the litigation and dispute resolution practice area. She has extensive experience of advising on all aspects of parliamentary and public policy related work with particular expertise in parliamentary procedure, freedom of information and standards of conduct in public life, including providing advice on corruption and political donations. She regularly advises public and private sector organisations on freedom of information law, and is on the Editorial Board of the *Freedom of Information* journal, to which she is a regular contributor. She has spoken frequently on freedom of information and is the co-author of the Clifford Chance *Guide to the Freedom of Information Act*. Patricia is a member of the Examination Board for the Practitioner Certificate in Freedom of Information.

Peter Carey is a consultant solicitor with Charles Russell in London, where he is head of the Information Law Team. After gaining a Masters degree in International Business Law in the United States in 1993, Peter spent six years as a senior lecturer at the College of Law, the UK's leading legal education provider. Peter has established a reputation as one of the UK's leading data protection and privacy experts. He has written the UK's leading book on data protection (*Data Protection: A Practical Guide to UK and EU Law*, Oxford University Press) and is the founder of the journal *Privacy & Data Protection*. Peter advises commercial and public sector organisations of varying sizes on all aspects of information law compliance. Peter is head of the Examination Board for the Practitioner Certificate in Data Protection.

Anna Condliffe joined Herbert Smith in 2006, having previously been the senior associate in the public law team at another City firm. Anna specialises in all aspects of public law including judicial review, human rights and information law. As a senior professional support lawyer, Anna regularly provides training to clients in the public and private sectors on developments in freedom of information law and other public law issues. She is also responsible for drafting client publications on public law issues and recently co-authored Herbert Smith's

Freedom of Information: A Guide for Business. Anna has written a number of articles on freedom of information for publications including *Judicial Review*, *Freedom of Information*, *Complinet*, *Business Law Review* and *Utility Week*.

Claire Darwin practises at Matrix Chambers, and is described in Chambers and Partners 2012 as 'a real star in the making'. She specialises in employment, discrimination, public, information and commercial law, and has a broad advisory practice. Her information law practice spans the full range of privacy and information law matters, including the Freedom of Information Act 2000, the Data Protection Act 1998, restrictive covenants, human rights, injunctions, privacy, protection from harassment and breach of confidence actions. In addition to her advisory work, she frequently appears in the specialist tribunals and ordinary courts. Claire has a particular interest in and experience of advising and acting for individuals and employers in cases involving the application of information law in the workplace.

Liz Fitzsimons is a legal director with Eversheds LLP, specialising in information law. She has advised on the Freedom of Information Act and the Environmental Information Regulations since their introduction as well as helping clients with national and international data protection. Her practice includes assisting clients with publication scheme issues, information requests (particularly where sensitive or complex), advising on their interaction with data protection and confidentiality law, selection of and proper use of exemptions and application of the public interest test, as well as helping with redactions, the use of costs grounds and cases involving vexatious or repeated requests. Liz also helps clients deal with internal reviews, the investigation of complaints by the Information Commissioner and appeals. Liz supports clients dealing with third party consultations, has successfully helped clients to avoid FOI related breach of confidence actions and has also persuaded authorities not to disclose third party confidential and sensitive information. Liz regularly speaks, and provides training courses, on this topic, including presenting the FOI Level 2 Advanced Exemptions training course for the leading training provider PDP.

Jackie Gray is a director at Dickinson Dees LLP specialising in public sector projects and information law. She has advised on a wide variety of public private partnership projects, including PFI and outsourcing projects, public sector procurements and general commercial contracts. Jackie also specialises in freedom of information, environmental information and data protection. She has worked with public authorities on the implementation of FOI, providing training and guidance on FOI issues, policy and procedures and regularly provides advice on complex information requests, including on the application of exemptions and exceptions. She also advises clients on internal reviews, complaints to the Information Commissioner and appeals to the Information Rights Tribunal. Jackie has presented FOI practical training courses for the leading training provider PDP, is the former head of the Examination Board for the Practitioner Certificate in Freedom of Information and is an Editorial Board member of *Freedom of Information* journal.

Robin Hopkins is a barrister at 11KBW chambers in London, specialising in information law. He regularly appears in the First-Tier and Upper Tribunals in freedom of information and environmental information litigation, and is one of the most experienced junior counsel in those areas of law. His notable cases include *Bruton* v. *Information Commissioner and the Duchy of Cornwall, All Party Parliamentary Group on Extraordinary Rendition* v. *Information Commissioner and Foreign and Commonwealth Office and Plowden* and *FCO* v. *Information Commissioner.* He edits the Information Law Reports and 11KBW's Panopticon blog. He is the resident 'expert commentator' for the journal *Freedom of Information* and a member of the board of Request Initiative. He frequently speaks and writes on information law matters. He also advises on issues under the Data Protection Act 1998 and the Regulation of Investigatory Powers Act 2000 and e-commerce, privacy and confidentiality issues.

Jeremy Ison wrote the chapter on enforcement and appeals for the first two editions of this book when he was a commercial litigator at Clifford Chance, where he qualified in 1997. In that role, as well as general disputes work, he brought and defended complaints for clients before various regulators, including the Advertising Standards Authority and the Broadcasting Standards Commission. He is now a senior counsel at Deutsche Bank AG, London and is the bank's UK data protection officer. He advises on freedom of information issues from the point of view of a private sector organisation that is affected by the Freedom of Information Act because it does business with central and local government and because it is regulated by bodies which are subject to the Act.

Keith Mathieson is a partner specialising in media law at London solicitors Reynolds Porter Chamberlain. RPC is well known for its representation of media organisations in the defence of libel and other claims. Its clients include national and regional newspaper publishers, magazine publishers, book publishers, broadcasters, independent production companies, journalists and media liability insurers. As well as advice on freedom of information issues, Keith's practice encompasses all legal aspects of free speech, including defamation, copyright, privacy and reporting restrictions. Keith is a member of the Editorial Board of the *Freedom of Information* journal.

Antony White QC of Matrix Chambers practises in media and information law, commercial law and arbitration, employment law and public law. He appeared for the claimant in *Campbell* v. *MGN Ltd* [2003] QB 633 (CA) and [2004] 2 AC 457 (HL) which was the first successful High Court claim against a media defendant under the Data Protection Act 1998. He has appeared in several leading cases in the areas of privacy, data protection and breach of confidence, and before the Information Tribunal in FOIA appeals.

Nick Wilcox is a senior associate in the media team at Reynolds Porter Chamberlain (RPC). His areas of experience include defamation, privacy/confidence, contempt, freedom of information, pre-publication advice and commercial litigation. He works for a variety of clients such as newspapers, broadcasters, publishers, internet service providers and insurers. Nick joined RPC from the BBC litigation department where he worked for three and a half years. His work at the BBC included advising on defamation claims, commercial litigation and the Freedom of Information Act 2000. He acted on the first FOIA case to reach (on separate issues) the House of Lords, and subsequently the Supreme Court, *Sugar* v. *British Broadcasting Corporation*. He also represented the BBC on numerous cases before the Information Tribunal, and on the subsequent successful appeal to the High Court, in respect of the application of the FOIA to various categories of requested financial information, *British Broadcasting Corporation* v. *Information Commissioner* [2009] EWHC 2348 (Admin). Prior to the BBC, Nick worked as a commercial litigator at Herbert Smith.

Nusrat Zar is a partner and solicitor advocate in the Litigation Division of Herbert Smith LLP. Nusrat advises on a range of public and administrative law matters including freedom of information, judicial review, and the European Convention on Human Rights. Nusrat has written various articles for journals including *Judicial Review*. She has advised companies and public authorities on numerous aspects of freedom of information legislation and lectures widely on freedom of information issues. Nusrat is listed as a leading practitioner in administrative and public law in Chambers, the Legal 500 and Legal Experts. Nusrat studied Jurisprudence at St Hilda's College, Oxford and qualified as a solicitor in 1997.

Table of cases

Table of statutes

Table of statutory instruments

Table of international instruments

Abbreviations

ACAS	Advisory, Conciliation and Arbitration Service
ACPO	Association of Chief Police Officers
CCC	criminal conviction certificate
CDPA	Copyright, Designs and Patents Act 1988
CJEU	Court of Justice of the European Union
CPR	Civil Procedure Rules 1998
CRAGA	Constitutional Reform and Governance Act 2010
CRB	Criminal Records Bureau
CRC	criminal record certificate
DCA	Department for Constitutional Affairs
Defra	Department for Environment, Food and Rural Affairs
DMI	Development and Maintenance Initiative
DPA	Data Protection Act 1998
ECGD	Export Credits Guarantee Department
ECHR	European Convention on Human Rights
ECJ	European Court of Justice
ECRC	enhanced criminal record certificate
ECtHR	European Court of Human Rights
EEA	European Economic Area
EIR	Environmental Information Regulations 2004, SI 2004/3391
ERG	Efficiency and Reform Group
Fees Regulations	Freedom of Information and Data Protection (Appropriate Limit and Fees) Regulations 2004, SI 2004/3244
FOI	freedom of information
FOIA	Freedom of Information Act 2000
FTT Rules 2009	Tribunal Procedure (First-tier Tribunal) (General Regulatory Chamber) Rules 2009, SI 2009/1976
GCHQ	Government Communications Headquarters
HFEA	Human Fertilisation and Embryology Act 1990
IAR	information asset register
ICO	Information Commissioner's Office
INSPIRE Regulations	INSPIRE Regulations 2009, SI 2009/3157

LPP	legal professional privilege
MoJ	Ministry of Justice
MoU	Memorandum of Understanding
NAO	National Audit Office
NCND	neither confirm nor deny
OCG	Office of Government Commerce
Open Government Code	Code of Practice on Access to Government Information
PA	Police Act 1997
PCA	Parliamentary Commissioner for Administration
PCA MoU	Memorandum of Understanding on co-operation between government Departments and the Parliamentary Commissioner for Administration of the Code of Practice on Access to Government Information
PFA	Protection of Freedoms Act 2012
PSI	public sector information regime
PSI Regulations	Re-use of Public Sector Information Regulations 2005, SI 2005/1515
Regulation 16 Code of Practice	Code of Practice on the Discharge of the Obligations of Public Authorities under the Environmental Information Regulations 2004
Section 45 Code of Practice	Secretary of State for Constitutional Affairs' Code of Practice on the Discharge of Public Authorities' Functions under Part I of the Freedom of Information Act 2000
Section 46 Code of Practice	Lord Chancellor's Code of Practice on the Management of Records Issued under Section 46 of the Freedom of Information Act 2000
SOCA	Serious Organised Crime Agency
Time Regulations	Freedom of Information (Time for Compliance with Request) Regulations 2004, SI 2004/3364
UT Rules 2008	Tribunal Procedure (Upper Tribunal) Rules 2008, SI 2008/2698
V&B	vetting and barring (scheme)

CHAPTER 1

Introduction and background to the law

Patricia Barratt, Clifford Chance LLP

1.1 INTRODUCTION

> Freedom of information. Three harmless words. I look at those words as I write them, and feel like shaking my head till it drops off my shoulders. You idiot. You naive, foolish, irresponsible nincompoop. There is really no description of stupidity, no matter how vivid, that is adequate. I quake at the imbecility of it.

Tony Blair, whose government introduced the Freedom of Information Act (FOIA) in 2000, wrote these words in his memoirs[1] 10 years after the Act was passed, also calling it one of the two domestic legislative measures he most regretted (the other was the ban on fox hunting).

Is his reaction simply a measure of how successful the FOIA has been in opening up areas which the government would prefer remain hidden, or are there valid concerns that the Act has damaged delicate internal mechanisms for taking public decisions, or introduced a charter for lazy journalists and the green ink brigade?

In the years since the Act came into force, we have seen a revolution in the amount of public sector information published, but this has not created, as a younger Tony Blair had hoped, a position in which people's trust in government was restored.[2] Instead, arguably, public confidence in government and Parliamentarians is at an all time low.

Freedom of information has undeniably played a role in this. It was a series of FOIA requests that led to revelations of scandalous expenses claims by MPs (though the full details were leaked rather than being disclosed under the Act). It was also a FOIA request that led to the disclosure of the Attorney General's opinion on the legality of the war with Iraq, though, yet again, the opinion was leaked before being disclosed.

---

[1] See Blair, T. *A Journey* (2010, Hutchinson), p.516.
[2] 'The only way to begin to restore people's trust is therefore to be completely open about what the risks are and to take whatever action is necessary to restore and renew confidence in our beef industry,' Tony Blair, then Leader of the Labour Party, speaking at the Campaign for Freedom of Information Annual Award Ceremony on 25 March 1996, in the wake of the bovine spongiform encephalopathy (BSE) scare.

Christopher Graham, the Information Commissioner, referring to a comment by Prime Minister David Cameron that freedom of information was 'furring up the arteries of government', defended the FOIA:

> I am afraid that the Freedom of Information Act will always be troublesome, but it will be troublesome in a good cause. The Freedom of Information Act, properly implemented, and going hand in hand with openness and transparency, is a force for good in 21st century democracy.[3]

The FOIA has undoubtedly been used as a political tool. But it has also been used by millions of requesters, both individual and corporate, to garner a huge range of valuable information. Public sector expenditure, not just that of central government, has attracted unprecedented scrutiny as a result of the Act, with private sector contractors also deeply affected. Grant funding, planning permission applications, development plans, government-compiled statistics, lobbying efforts, public procurement details, departmental meeting minutes, public service contracts – these are all potentially accessible under the Act. Increasingly, this sort of information is also being made proactively available, for example, under the Coalition government's transparency agenda.

Tony Blair's government had made freedom of information a manifesto commitment before coming to power. But it could be argued that a number of different developments had made the Act almost inevitable. Perhaps the most influential of these was the creation and growth of the internet. With such a huge range of information from all sources already easily accessible to anyone using the internet, and with few, if any, effective mechanisms for blocking the dissemination of information via that route, a government seeking to protect information that others want was frequently going to be fighting a losing battle. The *Spycatcher* case (*Attorney General* v. *Guardian Newspapers Ltd (No.2)* [1990] 1 AC 109) had already shown the limits of the government's power to restrain the publication of information, but the internet multiplied this problem to the nth degree with websites accessible from anywhere in the world and publication immediate. Also, with information access regimes becoming increasingly common in other countries, the UK was on the back foot in terms of international legal comparators. Sweden, famously, has had a form of freedom of information legislation in place since 1776. New Zealand has had a freedom of information Act since 1962, the United States since 1966 (strengthened in 1982), Australia since 1982 and Ireland since 1997.

---

[3] Uncorrected transcript of oral evidence (to be published as HC 1849-iii), to the Justice Select Committee's Inquiry on Post-legislative Scrutiny of the Freedom of Information Act 2000, 14 March 2012: **www.publications.parliament.uk/pa/cm201012/cmselect/cmjust/uc1849-iii/uc184901.htm**

1.2 THE CODE OF PRACTICE ON ACCESS TO GOVERNMENT INFORMATION

The Conservative government, resisting calls for legislation, introduced the voluntary Code of Practice on Access to Government Information (the 'Open Government Code') in April 1994 (revised in January 1997), since then often described as one of government's best kept secrets. It fell under the remit of the Parliamentary Commissioner and only applied to organisations under her jurisdiction. This meant that any complaints about how requests were dealt with under the Open Government Code had to be approached in the same way as other complaints about, for example, maladministration by government departments – in other words, via an MP. This cumbersome mechanism, coupled with the lack of real powers on the part of the Parliamentary Commissioner, kept the number of requests under the Open Government Code down, and its influence on public sector culture minimal, save within a few better informed and more progressive central government departments.

Decisions of the Parliamentary Ombudsman, as the Parliamentary Commissioner is also known, were, however, useful, at least in the early days of the FOIA, because the UK Information Commissioner had said he would expect to have regard to decisions of the Ombudsman.

The Open Government Code came into force on 4 April 1994, setting out common standards applicable to all government departments responding to requests for disclosure of information, new procedures enabling those requesting the information to seek internal review of decisions not to disclose, and a new mechanism for external review of such decisions by the Parliamentary Ombudsman.

The opening paragraph of the Open Government Code, under the heading 'Purpose', clearly stated that:

> The approach to release of information should in all cases be based on the assumption that information should be released except where disclosure would not be in the public interest, as specified in Part II of this Code.

A number of MPs later argued for the inclusion of such an assumption – a presumption in favour of disclosure – on the face of the Act. However, amendments to this effect were rejected by the government. The Open Government Code also set out three aims:

- to improve policy-making and the democratic process by extending access to the facts and analyses which provide the basis for the consideration of proposed policy;
- to protect the interests of individuals and companies by ensuring that reasons are given for administrative decisions, except where there is statutory authority or established convention to the contrary; and
- to support and extend the principles of public service established under the Citizen's Charter.

However, the aims were immediately qualified by the need:

- to maintain high standards of care in ensuring the privacy of personal and commercially confidential information; and
- to preserve confidentiality where disclosure would not be in the public interest or would breach personal privacy or the confidences of a third party, in accordance with statutory requirements and Part II of the Code.

The main concerns of the private sector and businesses providing information to government under commercial contracts, grant applications or other submissions were therefore explicitly addressed, to some extent, the focus of the Open Government Code resting squarely on releasing genuinely official information, rather than simply information held by officials.

As part of this voluntary regime, the Chancellor of the Duchy of Lancaster undertook to report annually on the progress of the Open Government Code. In his report (*Open Government: Code of Practice on Access to Government Information, 1995 Report*) on the first full year of the code's operation, he said that 1,353 requests for information had been recorded for 1995 (compared with over 7,000 requests recorded for the first three months of the operation of the FOIA). Code requests were narrowly defined as requests that specifically mentioned the Open Government Code; those for which a charge or standard fee was imposed; or those in respect of which information had been refused under one or more of the exemptions set out in the code.

The Open Government Code only applied to those government departments and bodies which fell within the jurisdiction of the Parliamentary Commissioner (these are set out in Sched.2 to the Parliamentary Commissioner Act 1967). The Open Government Code provided that complaints about the way in which a request had been handled should be made first to the department or body concerned. Only after this should the complaint be referred, via an MP, to the Parliamentary Ombudsman. Guidance on this internal review stage, contained in the Guidance on Interpretation of the Code, 2nd edn, Part I, para.72, recommended that internal reviews should be a 'single stage process'. Further:

> The aim should be to ensure that the applicant has been fairly treated under the provisions of the Code, that any exemptions have been properly applied and that charges are reasonably and consistently applied. It is good practice for such review to be conducted by someone not involved in the original decision.

The Open Government Code, thought by many to give rights of access to information that are superior to those available under the FOIA, nevertheless suffered from a lack of profile, poor enforcement mechanisms and a limited application. It was made obsolete on 1 January 2005 when the FOIA right of access was finally introduced, four years after the Act was passed.

1.2.1   Lessons to be learned from the Open Government Code

Decisions on the application of the Open Government Code made by the Parliamentary Commissioner are unlikely now to have any effect on decisions of the Information Commissioner's Office (ICO). Even when the FOIA first came into effect, such decisions had no binding effect, though the Information Commissioner initially indicated that he expected all public authorities to take decisions of the Parliamentary Commissioner into account when making decisions on disclosure of requests for information:

> In a UK context, it will also be important to consider any decisions made by the Parliamentary Ombudsman when considering complaints under the Open Government Code. Although the Code is not statutory and applies to a much smaller number of public authorities, the public interest test applied by the Ombudsman is identical to that required under the Act. Summaries of cases considered by the Ombudsman under the Code can be found on the Ombudsman's website . . .
> (*Freedom of Information Act Awareness Guidance No.3: The Public Interest Test* (ICO, April 2006))

While public authorities were advised therefore, to establish some familiarity with these decisions, this has been superseded by the body of decision notices promulgated by the ICO, and by superior authorities since the Act came into force; the ICO's current guidance on the public interest test (which replaced *Freedom of Information Act Awareness Guidance No.3*) dated 3 July 2009 makes no mention of Ombudsman decisions.

The Parliamentary Ombudsman published regular reports summarising her investigations into complaints under the Open Government Code. In an informative swansong, the *Parliamentary Ombudsman Monitoring of the Non-statutory Codes of Practice 1994–2005* (HC 59) (the Ombudsman's Report), published in May 2005, Ann Abraham looked at landmark decisions made under the Open Government Code during more than 10 years of its operation.

This 'Greatest Hits' report highlighted many issues which the ICO subsequently found itself having to deal with in the early days of the FOIA. The first of these was delays in resolving complaints. As early as 1998, the then Parliamentary Ombudsman, Sir Michael Buckley, had reported on measures taken to address a backlog in complaints handling, including the setting of new targets (16 weeks for straightforward cases and 23 weeks for more complicated investigations). It was clear from the investigation reports that delays were often caused by a failure on the part of the government department to deal with requests from the Ombudsman promptly.

In his annual report for 2001–02, Sir Michael strongly criticised the Home Office for taking seven months to respond to his draft report, a delay the Home Office said was due to the need to consult other departments and the Prime Minister. The original request for information (from Mr Andrew Robathan MP) had asked how many times Home Office Ministers had made declarations of interest to colleagues or sought the advice of the Permanent Secretary in relation to certain requirements set out in the Ministerial Code of Conduct. The Home Office refused to disclose the information, citing Exemptions 2 and 12 of the Open Government Code. The Ombudsman disagreed, arguing that Exemption 2 was designed to cover advice and opinion rather than factual information and that there could not be an unwarranted invasion of privacy of the kind envisaged by Exemption 12 when the information sought related only to a number, not to identifiable individuals. The Ombudsman recommended that the Home Office disclose the information. However, the Home Office refused to do so, in the first instance of such a refusal in an Open Government Code investigation (leading the Ombudsman to present a Special Report to Parliament, which was published on 13 November 2001).

In a further case in which the Home Office was also involved, the Ombudsman investigated a refusal to provide information relating to the Hinduja brothers' dealings with the Home Office. The Home Office failed to provide the information under dispute to the Ombudsman who, clearly frustrated, issued a draft report to the Home Office saying that the lack of co-operation from the department had effectively made it impossible for him to carry out his work properly. While this finally goaded the department into action, Sir Michael, in his 2001–02 annual report said that a delay of nine months in simply making the relevant papers available was entirely unacceptable. In the report, Sir Michael also said that this sort of response, if it were to continue, would leave his ability to conduct Open Government Code investigations properly in the future open to serious doubt.

Ann Abraham, who took over as Parliamentary Ombudsman in November 2002, started discussions almost immediately with both the Cabinet Office and the Lord Chancellor's Department (as it was then), with a view to preparing a joint Memorandum of Understanding (MoU) to be issued to all bodies subject to the Open Government Code. The MoU set out what departments were required to do in terms of responses to information requests, and, more particularly, what they were required to do in response to the Ombudsman's stipulations once a case was taken on for investigation. The MoU was issued in July 2003, and formed a useful precedent for the agreement subsequently reached between the ICO and the Ministry of Justice on identical issues.

While the MoU helped to produce a more consistent level of response from departments, the Ombudsman reported that it had little impact in those cases involving the politically sensitive areas of ministerial interests and the Ministerial Code of Conduct. The Ombudsman's Report referred to an egregious case involving information requested from nearly 20 departments relating to ministerial gifts. Following a delay of nearly 16 months, during which time departments were waiting for advice from the Cabinet Office (as guardians of the Ministerial Code) as to how to deal with the matter, the Cabinet Office advised departments to refuse to release it on the grounds that the information was covered by Exemption 12 of the Open Government Code (personal privacy). The Ombudsman found that this exemption did not apply, and recommended that the information be released. The Cabinet Office, however, refused to do so, and this became the second case in which there had been a refusal to release information following a recommendation by the Ombudsman in a Open Government Code investigation.

A further issue highlighted by the Ombudsman's Report was that of public interest certificates (Parliamentary Commissioner Act 1967, s.11(3)), i.e. a statement by a Minister that disclosure of a particular document would be 'prejudicial to the safety of the State or otherwise contrary to the public interest'. According to the report, the first time such a certificate was used was in 2003, when there were two instances, both in relation to requests under the Open Government Code.

Finally, the Ombudsman's Report referenced a number of cases demonstrating the way in which the Ombudsman was frequently called on to assess information requests relating to matters of current political controversy. A complainant had requested information relating to a British company's application for export credit support from the Export Credits Guarantee Department (ECGD) in relation to the controversial Ilisu Dam project in Turkey. The ECGD had refused to disclose the information, citing both Exemptions 13 (commercial confidences) and 14 (information provided in confidence), as well as the common law of confidence. The Ombudsman found that Exemption 13 did apply to the information sought but that the public interest test operated in favour of disclosure. However, the ECGD obtained a legal opinion to the effect that, if it were to disclose the information without the consent of the company it could be liable to legal action for breach of confidence. On that basis, the Ombudsman decided not to recommend release of the information. This contrasted with a previous case in which Sir William Reid had ruled, in respect of a similar argument put forward by the Ministry of Agriculture, Fisheries and Food, that it was not appropriate to use grounds not specifically referred to in the Open Government Code in order to justify a refusal to disclose information (the code made no mention of common law issues). However, in that case, he had also accepted an argument for not releasing the information under Exemption 13.

In another highly politically controversial case, the complainant had requested information from the Ministry of Defence and the Foreign and Commonwealth Office relating to a National Audit Office (NAO) report into the al-Yamamah arms contract, including the report itself. The NAO report had been made to Parliament through the Public Accounts Committee and therefore fell under that part of Exemption 15 that covered Parliamentary privilege – the only time that this particular aspect had arisen in an Open Government Code case. The then Chairman of the Public Accounts Committee responded to a query from the Ombudsman, stating that the Committee still wished the report to be kept secret. While recognising the existence of a strong public interest, the Ombudsman took the view that the harm test in this case operated in favour of withholding most of the information sought, although some additional information was released into the public domain. The Ombudsman took into consideration the fact that an MoU had been signed in 1986 between the UK and Saudi Arabian governments (which was still in force), containing an explicit commitment that classified information would not be released.

Interestingly, the Ombudsman was also asked to adjudicate on the Cabinet Office's refusal to supply copies of all documents drawn up by the Attorney General giving advice on the legality of military intervention in Iraq. The Ombudsman found that Exemption 4(d) of the Open Government Code relating to legal professional privilege applied (FOIA, s.42) and that the refusal to disclose the information requested was justified. She noted that the exemption in the code was an absolute exemption and therefore she did not have to consider the public interest in disclosure. This is, of course, in direct contrast with the position under the FOIA, since the s.42 exemption is subject to the public interest test. In its decision notice, *Cabinet Office* (FS50062881, 7 July 2006), the Information Commissioner found that, since the Attorney General's advice dated 7 March 2003 was already in the public domain following a partial leak in April 2005, it was not necessary for him to consider that part of the request.

Finally, demonstrating the huge range of subject matter covered by requests under the Open Government Code, the Ombudsman's Report referred to a request to the Ministry of Defence for information relating to the famous Rendlesham Forest incident, in which numerous sightings of a UFO were reported. Although the Ministry had disclosed considerable information about this incident it had refused to release three documents, citing Exemption 2 (internal advice and discussion) in justification. The Ombudsman noted that the information in the documents (background notes and draft briefings for Ministers in response to a Parliamentary Question) clearly fell within the exemption. The Ministry argued that, as the information contained in the documents was already in the public domain, no public interest would be served by releasing it. Conversely, the Ombudsman took the view that there was no public interest to be served in continuing to withhold information that was mostly already in the public domain and which was, in addition, over 20 years old. The Ministry accepted the recommendation, and released the information not only to the complainant but to others who had previously requested it and been refused. The Ombudsman noted that she had received several congratulatory emails from members of the UFO community following this decision, including one from Alaska.

1.3   HISTORY AND DEVELOPMENT OF THE LEGISLATION

Despite the existence of the Open Government Code, there was still strong pressure to introduce a statutory regime enabling access to public sector information. The Labour Manifesto in 1997, promising such a regime, said:

> Unnecessary secrecy in government leads to arrogance in government and defective policy decisions. The Scott Report on arms to Iraq revealed Conservative abuses of power. We are pledged to a Freedom of Information Act, leading to more open government, and an independent National Statistical Service.
>
> (New Labour, *Because Britain Deserves Better*, Labour Party Manifesto 1997, M/029/97)

Further, in December of the same year, the newly elected Labour government presented a White Paper (*Your Right to Know – The Government's Proposals for a*

Freedom of Information Act (Cm 3818, December 1997)) to Parliament, setting out radical proposals for a new statutory right to obtain information from public authorities.

In introducing the White Paper, the Prime Minister said that, 'The traditional culture of secrecy will only be broken down by giving people in the United Kingdom the legal right to know' (Cm 3818, Preface). (The sound bite would not, of course, be so effective if one were to add 'subject to 23 legal exemptions and over 400 statutory bars'.)

The White Paper was considered by a House of Commons Select Committee on Public Administration, which welcomed the proposals, and a report, Your Right to Know – The Government's Proposals for a Freedom of Information Act, Third Report of Session 1997–98, HC 398-I, published in May 1998, said that a Freedom of Information Act would 'help to begin to change for good the secretive culture of the public service'. The report, in addition to making 44 recommendations and observations, also found the proposals for increased access to information, if implemented in their White Paper form, would have three purposes and effects. They would (para.3):

- Make it easier for members of the public to find out what information government holds about themselves.
- Make it easier for politicians, journalists and members of the public to hold the government to account by making government cover-ups more difficult.
- Make it easier for members of the public to participate in an informed way in the discussion of policy issues, and improve the quality of government decision-making because those drafting policy advice know that they must be able, ultimately, to defend their reasoning before public opinion.

The White Paper was followed by a consultation paper (*Freedom of Information: Consultation on Draft Legislation* (Cm 4355, May 1999)) containing a draft Freedom of Information Bill, which was subject to pre-legislative scrutiny by committees of both Houses of Parliament, as well as to public consultation. The House of Commons Select Committee on Public Administration welcomed the draft Bill, but warned of 'serious deficiencies which, if not remedied, will undermine the potential' (House of Commons Select Committee on Public Administration, Freedom of Information Draft Bill, Third Report of Session 1998–99, HC 570-I, 29 July 1999). Among its specific recommendations for remedying these deficiencies, it called for a purpose clause with a clear presumption in favour of disclosure on the face of the Bill, for the public interest in disclosing information to be balanced against the harm in so doing, for the right of access to apply as broadly as possible and exemptions drawn as narrowly as possible with a more demanding harm test, and for enforceable rights of access to information.

The House of Lords Select Committee looking at it said that the single most important amendment required to the draft Bill was one which would give the Information Commissioner 'a public interest override power in clause 44 to overrule a ministerial decision under clause 14, and to order disclosure' (House of Lords Select Committee, Draft Freedom of Information Bill, First Report, HL 97,

27 July 1999). It also called for the long title of the Bill to be amended from the neutral 'make provision about the disclosure of information' to the purposive 'facilitate the disclosure of information'.

After this very long lead-in period, with examination from no fewer than three parliamentary committees, the Bill was finally introduced into the House of Commons on 18 November 1999, though not to universal acclaim. Critics of the Bill argued that the proposals had been significantly watered down since the draft Bill, and complained that the views of the committees had not been taken on board sufficiently. Once the Act had received Royal Assent on 20 November 2000, there was further criticism of the long delay in implementing it, despite the Lord Chancellor's announcement (Hansard, HL vol.628, col.457, 13 November 2001):

> The Act will be fully implemented by January 2005, 11 months before the timetable set out in the Act itself. The publication scheme provisions will be implemented first, on a rolling programme, starting with central government in November 2002 ... the individual right of access to information held by all public authorities, including government departments, will be implemented in January 2005.

1.4 THE COURTS AND ACCESS TO INFORMATION

As recently as 1989, the Official Secrets Act 1911 prevented government officials or contractors from revealing any information learned in the course of carrying out their duty to any person unless authorised. The comprehensive nature of this prohibition – which applied to any information regardless of whether there was any justification for protection against disclosure or not – was gradually eroded by a series of court cases. In *R* v. *Peter Anthony Galvin* (1988) 86 Cr App R 85 the Court of Appeal was asked to decide whether documents already in the public domain should be excluded from the parameters of the prohibition. Although the court found that the wording of the legislation would not permit this interpretation, it found that no breach of the prohibition had occurred because the document in question had been so widely distributed that there had been implied authorisation for those in possession of it to use it as they saw fit. In 1990, the House of Lords in *Attorney General* v. *Guardian Newspapers Ltd (No.2)* [1990] 1 AC 109 (the *Spycatcher* case) held that an injunction would only be granted where the Crown could show that disclosure of the material in question would be likely to damage the public interest. Since the information (in the form of a book, *Spycatcher*) was already published worldwide and therefore no longer secret, the courts would not grant a continuing injunction against disclosure.

A new Official Secrets Act replaced the 1911 statute in 1989, and restricted the prohibition against disclosure to information about security, defence, international relations and law enforcement.

At the same time, the continually growing power of the courts to look at administrative decision making through judicial review proceedings meant that the relevant decision-making bodies were forced to disclose to the courts background information relevant to the decision-making process. Fairness in the exercise of administrative powers, Lord Mustill said, required that those affected by decisions should be informed of the matters relevant to the decision and be given the opportunity to make representations (*R* v. *Secretary of State for the Home Department, ex p. Doody* [1994] 1 AC 531).

Case law on the tort of breach of confidence, vital to an application of the s.41 exemption in the FOIA for information provided in confidence, also continues to develop significantly from the statement of basic principles set out in the landmark case of *Coco* v. *AN Clark (Engineers) Ltd* [1969] RPC 41. This will be explored further in **Chapter 4** dealing with exemptions, as well as in **Chapter 6**.

1.5 FREEDOM OF INFORMATION IN OTHER JURISDICTIONS

The former Information Commissioner Richard Thomas said he would consider decisions from other jurisdictions that have freedom of information laws and would aim to remain in line with them as far as reasonably possible (without any obligation on him to do so in any particular circumstance). This opened up a huge resource of potential precedents for anyone making decisions on access requests or seeking disclosure. Clearly, the decisions were more likely to be influential if the underlying legislation was similar to the FOIA. Decisions in the United States, Ireland, Canada, Australia and New Zealand were therefore likely to be the most influential in this regard due to the closer similarities in the legislation itself, as well as the common language. While such non-UK decisions may have had some influence in the early days of the FOIA, the body of decisions created under the FOIA is now such as to make references to such jurisprudence much less likely. Freedom of information (FOI) laws in other jurisdictions nevertheless remain useful and interesting comparators for our own regime.

Many other jurisdictions have legislation on access to information. The Foreign and Commonwealth Office published a table[4] in 2004 with an alphabetical list of 53 countries that have such legislation, from Albania to Zimbabwe. Thirty other countries were said to be in the process of introducing access to information legislation. The oldest legislation (in Sweden) dates back over 200 years, whilst many other countries have adopted legislation within the last 15 years. In addition, there are various freedom of information laws and codes which apply to international organisations or political groupings. A variety of factors has led to their introduction, including the creation of the 'Information Society' and the expansion of the internet, pressure from the international community, the transition of countries to democracy, public demand following campaigns by civil society, and political scandals relating to health and the environment.

---

[4]   Appendix C, *Freedom of Information – Getting it Right*, Issue 3, September 2004. It states that the information is taken from David Banisar: *Global Survey: Freedom of Information and Access to Government Record Laws Around the World* (at **www.freedominfo.org**).

While ostensibly sharing a common goal of improving public access to information held by public bodies, the legal regimes vary widely in their content and approach as well as in their effectiveness. There follows a discussion of some of the typical features of access to information regimes and consideration of how they are dealt with in different jurisdictions. This whistle-stop tour of global freedom of information laws does not aim to be comprehensive, but is intended rather to identify a few areas of agreement and of disagreement.

1.5.1 Bodies to which freedom of information applies

Since the drive for freedom of information springs from a desire to improve transparency and accountability in government, it is clear that the legislation must apply to government bodies. Depending on the type of government, this may include local or regional government. The courts, legislative assemblies and the security and intelligence services are normally exempt from application of the legislation.

US legislation only applies to organisations that are controlled by the federal government. State governments, municipal corporations, the courts and Congress are not subject to the regime (though all of the states have their own disclosure legislation). In Canada, the right to information applies to records 'under the control' of a 'government institution'. Irish legislation, like the FOIA, lists bodies to which it applies in a Schedule to the Act; the list includes local authorities, health boards, government departments and other public sector organisations, but does not extend to voluntary hospitals, schools, universities, the police force, a range of government agencies, and commercial state-funded enterprises.

In South African law, the Promotion of Access to Information Act 2000 goes further in providing a right for individuals and government bodies to obtain information from private sector entities where this is necessary to enforce people's rights – a separate Part of the Act is entitled 'Access to Records of Private Bodies'. The UK legislation gives the Secretary of State the power to designate certain private sector entities as public authorities for the purposes of the FOIA (s.5). The Ministry of Justice published a consultation paper *Freedom of Information Act 2000: Designation of Additional Public Authorities* (CP 27/07, October 2007) with a view to such designation, but it was not until late 2011 that an order was made under this power, extending the FOIA to the Association of Chief Police Officers of England, Wales and Northern Ireland, the Financial Ombudsman Service and the Universities and Colleges Admission Service.[5] Further extensions to private sector companies contracting with the public sector, though mooted, have not thus far materialised.

---

[5] The Freedom of Information (Designation as Public Authorities) Order 2011, SI 2011/2598.

1.5.2   The right of access

The right of access is frequently to 'information', but sometimes to 'documents' or 'records'. Where documents are specified, these are sometimes defined to include mechanical or electronic records. The use of the term 'information', as in the FOIA, is thought to be more flexible. Often, requests must be made in writing and a response deadline of 20 or 30 days is common, though there are usually provisions enabling the deadline to be extended in given circumstances.

1.5.3   Proactive publication

Another common feature of freedom of information legislation is a requirement that government agencies publish information or documents proactively. This is reflected in the UK legislation in the duty on public authorities to maintain publication schemes. In the United States, each agency must publish a large amount of agency-specific information, including a description of the organisation of the agency, the internal reports of the agency, its regulations for reviewing information that it holds, statements of the general methods or agency procedures, and other sources of data that could be useful to the public.

The Indian regime includes a requirement that public bodies publish information on their structure and duties, relevant facts concerning important decisions and policies, reasons for their decisions to those affected by such decisions, and background facts prior to initiation of projects.

In Ireland, public bodies are required to publish information relating to their structure, functions, duties, descriptions of records, and the internal rules, proce-dures, practices, guidelines and interpretations of the relevant department or agency.

1.5.4   Exemptions

Not surprisingly, very similar exemptions are found in many of the access to information laws. In some cases certain exemptions are mandatory, i.e. prohibitions on disclosure, in contrast with the FOIA where exemptions, whether they are absolute or qualified, are to be applied at the discretion of the authority to which the request is addressed (with the exception of the exemption for statutory bars where the prohibition stems not from s.44 of the FOIA per se, but from the individual bars themselves).

The most common exemptions concern the protection of national security and international relationships, personal privacy, commercial confidentiality, law enforcement and public order, information received in confidence and internal discussions. Privacy, protecting internal decision making and national security tend to attract the highest level of protection. The United States has an unusual exemp-tion covering geological or geophysical information, including information about wells. In the wake of 9/11, the US government created new exemptions for 'critical infrastructure information' and all information held by the Office of Homeland Security, though the latter was subsequently amended. Similarly, a provision in the Dodd-Frank Act of 2010 preventing public access to certain types of information obtained by the Securities and Exchange Commission was reversed following a public outcry.

It is common for a harm test to be incorporated into the exemptions, i.e. that the information is only exempt if harm, or substantial harm, would result from disclosure. Many laws include a public interest test requiring the public interest in withholding the information to be balanced against the public interest in disclosure.

1.5.5 Charging

The level of fees charged for requests is a critical factor in the effectiveness of any freedom of information regime. Where fees are too high, access to information is placed outside the reach of ordinary people. US charging provisions distinguish between requests for educational or journalistic purposes, and those for commercial purposes. Agencies may charge commercial interests 'reasonable standard charges' in respect of their costs of searching for, reproducing and reviewing the information requested. Requests for educational or journalistic purposes attract only duplication fees. Where requests fall outside these two categories, reasonable standard charges may be made for document search and duplication. Documents are to be provided at no charge, or at a reduced charge:

> if disclosure of the information is in the public interest because it is likely to contribute significantly to public understanding of the operations or activities of the government and is not primarily in the commercial interest of the requester.
>
> (Freedom of Information Act 1966, s.552(a)(4)(A)(iii))

Ireland amended its freedom of information charging regime (Freedom of Information (Amendment) Act 2003) to allow the government to impose fees for requests and appeals. The Irish Information Commissioner, Emily O'Reilly, in a report into the impact of the charges for making freedom of information requests introduced by the Minister for Finance in July 2003, found that overall usage of the Act had fallen by over 50 per cent while requests for non-personal information had declined by 75 per cent (*Review of the Operation of the Freedom of Information (Amendment) Act 2003* (Irish Information Commissioner, June 2004)). The Irish Commissioner's most recent annual report (2010) includes a graph showing that, from a low of around 12,000 in 2004 (a fall from around 20,000 in 2003) the number of requests had steadily increased, with 15,429 requests to public bodies in 2010.

Japanese law provides for a request fee and a disclosure fee which must be within the limit of actual expenses and in accordance with government regulations. These fees may be reduced or waived in cases of economic hardship or for other 'special reasons'.

Some countries also impose charges for appealing refusals. The Irish legislation provides for a payment of €15 to accompany a FOIA request, €75 in respect of a request for an internal review and €150 for an application to the Information Commissioner for a review.

Proposals in the United Kingdom to amend the fees regime were abandoned (in an announcement by Prime Minister Gordon Brown on 25 October 2007) following widespread opposition and allegations that the proposals were politically driven. A 2011 submission to the Justice Select Committee by the Ministry of Justice has once again raised the possibility that fees could be introduced.[6]

1.5.6   Third party rights

There has been considerable criticism of the FOIA for its failure to provide rights for third parties whose interests are affected by the disclosure of information. Many access to information laws require the public body to which the request has been made to notify third parties, and to give them the right to make representations. The United States is the best known example, though in fact no right of action is afforded by the Freedom of Information Act – a more general right, which would permit an affected third party to bring an action to prevent disclosure, is provided by the Administrative Procedure Act 1946 (see *Chrysler Corp* v. *Brown* (1979) 441 US 281, US Supreme Court).

The South African legislation requires the public authority to 'take all reasonable steps to inform a third party to whom or which the record relates of the request' within 21 days. The third party has a statutory right to make written or oral representations as to why the request should be refused, and the public authority is under an obligation to give 'due regard to any representations made by a third party' (Promotion of Access to Information Act 2000).

In Japan, a public body which has received a request for certain types of information (as specified) must notify the third party concerned and give him an opportunity to provide a written opinion, before making a decision to disclose (unless the third person's whereabouts are unknown). If the third party opposes disclosure, the public body, when making a decision to disclose, must immediately notify him in writing of the decision to disclose being made, the reason for it, and the date of implementation of disclosure, which must be at least two weeks later (Law Concerning Access to Information held by Administrative Organs 1999, art.13).

Canada also provides statutory rights for third parties to be notified of an intended decision to disclose specified information, to be given the opportunity to make representations and to be notified of the public body's decision on disclosure following consideration of the representations. The third party may apply to the Federal Court of Canada to seek an order against disclosure.

---

[6]   Memorandum to the Justice Select Committee: Post-Legislative Assessment of the Freedom of Information Act 2000, Ministry of Justice, December 2011.

1.5.7 Appeals and enforcement

In most jurisdictions, where a decision by a public body on disclosure of information is challenged, the first step will be an internal review by the public body concerned. If the results of the review are still unsatisfactory to the applicant, there will usually be a right to appeal the internal review decision to a third party. In the best enforcement regimes this will usually be an independent Information Commissioner or Ombudsman.

The Canadian Information Commissioner receives complaints and can investigate and issue recommendations but does not have the power to issue binding orders. He, or the applicant, can seek review of a refusal to disclose in the Federal Court of Canada. In Ireland, the Office of the Information Commissioner is able to make binding decisions which can be appealed on a point of law. The Ministry of Justice has the power to issue certificates preventing the release of information.

Japan has an Information Disclosure Review Board within the Cabinet Office, consisting of 12 members approved by both Houses. Cases are referred to the Board by the head of the body that has made the decision under dispute. Decisions of the Board may be appealed to the courts. In South Africa, the Human Rights Commission oversees the functioning of the Act, earlier proposals to create an Open Democracy Commission and specialised information courts having failed to make it to the statute book. While this has advantages in placing access to information alongside human rights enforcement, the Commission has reported that its work on information rights is hampered by a lack of funding.

The United States lacks a central regulator of information rights, the district courts having exclusive jurisdiction in relation to decisions under the Freedom of Information Act. The courts will normally consider all the issues of the case and will look at the procedures followed by the agency in trying to locate the requested information, but have no power to order disclosure where an exemption applies. Each of the individual states has legislation on access to government records, and some states also have information commissions which review decisions.

In most countries there is a final level of appeal to the national courts.

1.5.8 Application in the United Kingdom

Within the United Kingdom, the FOIA applies to England, Wales and Northern Ireland. Separate legislation in Scotland applies to public authorities that operate solely in, or with regard to, Scotland, and is enforced by a separate Scottish Information Commissioner (Freedom of Information (Scotland) Act 2002). Likewise, the Scottish Executive has issued its own Code of Practice on Access to Scottish Executive Information. The Scottish legislation is very similar, but not identical, to the FOIA, and is not specifically addressed in this publication. We have also seen some divergence between the two regimes developing as a result of differences in approach by the two Information Commissioners, as well as by the courts.

1.6 OTHER UK LEGISLATION ON ACCESS TO INFORMATION

Probably the most significant pieces of UK legislation in this area, prior to the FOIA, were the Data Protection Acts of 1984 and 1998 (the latter implemented Council Directive (EC) 95/46 on the protection of individuals with regard to the processing of personal data and on the free movement of such data). Although one of the main purposes of data protection legislation is the antithesis of freedom of information – to protect information and keep it confidential – the data protection legislation also introduced an important right for individuals to have access to information held about themselves, initially in the form of electronically processed data, but extended by the Data Protection Act 1998 (DPA) to apply also to non-electronic records that are held in a structured form. **Chapter 8** looks more closely at the data protection legislation and how it interacts with the FOIA, but the basic rule is simple enough to understand (if not to apply): information will be exempt from disclosure under the FOIA if it constitutes 'personal data' of someone other than the requester, and if disclosure would breach any of the data protection principles set out in Sched.1 to the DPA. Anyone receiving a request for information must therefore be able to determine whether the information is personal information and whether disclosure of the information would contravene any of the eight data protection principles governing the use of personal information, as set out in the DPA.

Also of importance are the Environmental Information Regulations. First introduced in 1992, these regulations (originally SI 1992/3240), which also implement an EU Directive (EU Directive 2003/4/EC on public access to environmental information), provide access to information about the environment held by public bodies. Lacking any effective enforcement mechanism and not widely publicised, they did not have a significant impact, but the revised Environmental Information Regulations 2004, SI 2004/3391 (EIR), brought into force on the same date as the FOIA, on 1 January 2005, and also enforced by the Information Commissioner, have enjoyed a higher profile. The definition of 'environmental information' for the purposes of the EIR is very wide, and includes elements of the environment, such as land, water, biological organisms, etc. as well as measures and activities which affect or are likely to affect these, and information on the state of human health and safety. If information falls within the remit of the EIR, then a request for such information must be treated in accordance with the procedures set out in the regulations, and not in the FOIA. Just to make life more difficult, the exemptions in the EIR are similar to, but by no means the same as, the exemptions in the FOIA. The similarities and differences between these two parallel regimes have caused some confusion. The EIR are dealt with in more detail in **Chapter 9**.

In addition to these major pieces of legislation, there is a patchwork of smaller pieces of legislation which has, over the past decade, incrementally improved public access to official records. A number of these were drafted by the Campaign for Freedom of Information, and started life as Private Members' Bills. Where there exists a separate statutory right to information, it is likely that the s.21 exemption in the FOIA (for information reasonably accessible otherwise than by an access request) will apply.

One of these statutory rights was introduced by the Local Government (Access to Information) Act 1985, which amended the Local Government Act 1972 (by inserting Part VA) to provide rights of access to council meetings, reports and papers. (Limited rights existed previously in the form of the Public Bodies (Admission to Meetings) Act 1960.) There are specific exemptions for a number of types of personal information, as well as for contractual terms, and expenditure in relation to contracts for the acquisition of property or the supply of goods and services.

The Access to Personal Files Act 1987 (now repealed) gave the public the right to see manually held social work and housing records about themselves. The Access to Medical Reports Act 1988 provided the right for applicants to see reports produced about them by doctors for an employer or insurance company. The Access to Health Records 1990 provided wider access to information on individuals' medical records, though this was largely superseded by the DPA.

The Environment and Safety Information Act 1988 gives people the right to see enforcement notices issued following breaches of environmental protection legislation.

1.7 THE INFORMATION COMMISSIONER – ENFORCING THE REGIME

Chapter 10 examines closely the legal enforcement mechanisms of the FOIA. This short section does not aim to duplicate that, but attempts rather to look at the policy approach the Information Commissioner tends to take vis-à-vis his dealings with government departments.

The approach was set out, to a large extent, in an agreement in February 2005, when the Department for Constitutional Affairs (DCA) (as it was then) and the Information Commissioner signed an MoU,[7] the stated purpose being 'to promote good standards of co-operation between Departments and the Commissioner'. Following criticism of the content of this MoU in the press, the Information Commissioner, writing in *The Guardian* (Media, Letters, 4 April 2005) denied that it skewed the complaint process in the government's favour, and said that the key commitment in the MoU was that government departments provide all relevant information in relation to a valid complaint swiftly. He confirmed that, in relation to relevant information, the MoU 'sets out a number of corresponding undertakings from my office – such as keeping it secure and not disclosing it improperly to others'.

---

[7]   Memorandum of Understanding (MoU) between the Secretary of State for Constitutional Affairs (on behalf of government Departments) and the Information Commissioner, on co-operation between government Departments and the Information Commissioner in relation to sections 50 and 51 of the Freedom of Information Act 2000 (the 'FOI Act') (including ss.50 and 51 as applied, as amended, by Regulation 18 of the Environmental Information Regulations 2004), signed 24 February 2005.

The signing of the MoU followed in the footsteps of the Parliamentary Ombuds-man. In an attempt to address 'a lack of knowledge within departments about the Code, unacceptable delays in responding to my Office and, in some cases, a lack of co-operation with my investigations', the Ombudsman had initiated discussion with the Cabinet Office and the DCA resulting in an MoU, published by the Cabinet Office on 22 July 2003. This MoU[8] (the 'PCA MoU') sets out what timescales and procedures departments were expected to adhere to in their dealings with the Ombudsman. In particular, departments were required to:

- respond in full within three weeks of receipt of the Ombudsman's statement of complaint;
- reply to the draft investigation report within three weeks;
- contact the Parliamentary Commissioner for Administration (PCA) as soon as possible if these timescales were not going to be met;
- provide all relevant papers as quickly as possible;
- avoid citing new exemptions following receipt of the draft report.

While the majority of commitments specified in the PCA MoU are ones entered into by government departments, the Ombudsman in turn stressed that she would not disclose the information provided to her by the department, and that the decision on whether or not to disclose the information remained that of the department.

The commitments in the MoU entered into by the Information Commissioner with the DCA are far more extensive. There must be a suspicion that, rather than being a tool to increase acceptance by, and co-operation with, public bodies in their duties in relation to access to information, as the PCA MoU undoubtedly was, it was instead driven by a realisation on the part of the DCA that the Information Commissioner himself is subject to the freedom of information regime and could be asked to disclose information he holds. Under the provisions of the FOIA he would have to decide whether any exemptions applied and whether there was a public interest in disclosure. There is a statutory prohibition on disclosure by the Infor-mation Commissioner or his staff of any information obtained by them for the purposes of the Act, and which 'relates to an identified or identifiable individual or business' (Data Protection Act 1998, s.59), unless the disclosure is made with 'lawful authority'. There will be lawful authority for a disclosure which is, among other things, 'necessary in the public interest'. These provisions appear to leave the Information Commissioner a considerable amount of discretion.

The Information Commissioner undertakes in the MoU to:

- contact the relevant department when he receives an application under s.50 of the FOIA, as soon as practicable and in any event within 10 working days;
- provide the department with details of the complainant's application;

---

[8] Memorandum of Understanding on co-operation between government Departments and the Parliamentary Commissioner for Administration of the Code of Practice on Access to Government Information, Cabinet Office, Propriety and Ethics Team, July 2003.

- request all relevant information and invite comment;
- aim to establish a single channel of communication.

He also agrees not (normally) to serve an information notice under s.51 of the FOIA on any government department unless he believes that relevant information is being withheld from him or that there has been undue delay in providing the information requested, and to inform the department in advance where he does intend to serve an information notice.

These are administrative matters designed to make enforcement of the FOIA a co-operative, rather than a confrontational, act. This co-operative approach is further enhanced by the obligations entered into by the Information Commissioner in relation to the disclosure of information provided to him. While the PCA MoU mentions in passing the fact that the Ombudsman will not disclose information provided to her, the MoU contains nine numbered paragraphs (9–17) headed 'Obligations in relation to information provided in accordance with this MoU', which set out a range of procedures designed to protect information provided.

Paragraph 9 states that the Commissioner:

> will not disclose to the Complainant or to any third party any information provided to him by a government Department either under the terms of this MoU, or as a result of serving a notice under section 50 or 51 of the FOI Act unless:

- the Department consents to the disclosure, or
- subject to paragraph 26, all appeal proceedings have been exhausted.

While the Information Commissioner's position is undoubtedly different from that of public authorities holding information provided to them from private sector companies, the MoU does make a strong contrast with the guidance issued to government departments, which are told not to accept such provisions from private sector companies. The statutory Section 45 Code of Practice[9] states, at para.26:

> It is highly recommended that public authorities take appropriate steps to ensure that such third parties, and those who supply public authorities with information, are aware of the public authority's duty to comply with the Freedom of Information Act, and that therefore information will have to be disclosed upon request unless an exemption applies.

Further, at paras.34 and 35:

> Where there is good reason, as recognised by the terms of the exemption provisions of the Act, to include non-disclosure provisions in a contract, public authorities should consider the desirability where possible of making express provision in the contract identifying the information which should not be disclosed and the reasons for confidentiality. Consideration may also be given to including provision in contracts as to when consultation with third parties will be necessary or appropriate before the information is disclosed.

---

[9] Secretary of State for Constitutional Affairs' Code of Practice on the Discharge of Public Authorities' Functions under Part I of the Freedom of Information Act 2000 (issued pursuant to s.45 of the FOIA).

Similar considerations will apply to the offering or acceptance of confidentiality obligations by public authorities in non-contractual circumstances. There will be circumstances in which such obligations will be an appropriate part of the acquisition of information from third parties and will be protected by the terms of the exemption provisions of the Act. But again, it will be important that both the public authority and the third party are aware of the limits placed by the Act on the enforceability of expectations of confidentiality, and for authorities to ensure that such expectations are created only where to do so is consistent with their obligations under the Act.

Clearly (and not unreasonably), government departments want certainty that if they provide information to the Information Commissioner he will not then disclose it in response to a request under the FOIA. In some other jurisdictions, the prohibition on disclosure of information provided as part of an investigation into whether such information should be disclosed or not by the Information Commissioner's counterpart is more stringent – in Japan a sentence of one year's hard labour could be the penalty for such disclosure.

Government departments undertake in the MoU to:

- provide all relevant information as quickly as possible and in any event within 20 working days of being contacted by the Information Commissioner, unless otherwise agreed;
- provide any additional relevant information subsequently requested by the Information Commissioner as quickly as possible and in any event within 10 working days;
- provide all information requested including any redacted information;
- inform the Information Commissioner, giving reasons, where they are not able to provide the information within the time periods.

It is, however, most unlikely that the Information Commissioner would ever be minded to disclose information provided to him in the context of an investigation. There are clearly a number of exemptions which would almost certainly apply to any information held by the Commissioner, including ss.30, 31, 36 and 41. The MoU also contains a get-out clause, stating that 'nothing in this MoU shall operate to restrict or otherwise inhibit the exercise of the Commissioner's or Department's powers and duties under the FOI Act or the EIRs'.

Perhaps then, the significance of this MoU will be as a precedent for agreements between private sector companies and public authorities, given that it has been created by the two authorities with lead responsibility for implementing and enforcing the Act. The Information Commissioner has indeed publicly stated that he hopes public authorities will follow the approach taken in the MoU.

1.8 FREEDOM OF INFORMATION – THE FUTURE

Since the FOIA was brought into force in the United Kingdom, the huge number of requests made annually to public authorities has demonstrated its immediate popular appeal. Perhaps a direct measure of its success has been a number of attempts to limit its scope. A notorious Private Member's Bill (the innocuously named Freedom of Information (Amendment) Bill) introduced in the House of Commons in December 2006, sought to exclude Parliament altogether from the freedom of information (FOI) regime. Although the Bill managed to pass through all stages in the Commons, it failed to find a sponsor in the House of Lords, perhaps as a result of mounting public indignation. There was also widespread opposition to proposals by the Ministry of Justice to amend the FOI fees regime. The effect of these proposals, now abandoned, would have been to make it easier for public authorities to refuse politically sensitive requests and to handicap the media, FOI campaigners and other multiple requesters.

The Coalition government promised to 'extend the scope of the Freedom of Information Act to provide greater transparency'.[10] This promise has been to some extent already fulfilled by the first use of the s.5 power (see **1.5.1**). Greater transparency has also been achieved through the transparency agenda which saw, in June 2010, publication by HM Treasury of data from the Combined Online Information System (COINS), a system used by the Treasury to collect financial data from across the public sector to support fiscal management, the production of Supply Estimates for Parliament, the production of public expenditure statistics, the preparation of Whole of Government Accounts (WGA) and to meet data requirements of the Office for National Statistics. The data were published in raw form with a promise that the government would work towards publication of the same data in future in a simpler, more accessible format.

In the same month, the government published the names of individual civil servants earning more than £150,000. This was extended in October 2010 to the names and salaries of civil servants earning more than £82,900.

In November 2010, the government published all new items of central government expenditure over £25,000. Details of about £80bn of spending on items over £25,000 between May and September were published – in line with a pre-election commitment by the Conservatives.

While the FOIA has remained remarkably unchanged since enacted in 2000, it is not completely untouched. The Constitutional Reform and Governance Act 2010 (CRAGA) made a number of fairly minor changes. Section 63 of the FOIA provides that information contained in a 'historical record' cannot be withheld on the basis of certain specified exemptions. A record was defined as a historical record 30 years after it was created. The CRAGA amended this so that public records must now be transferred to the National Archives 20 years from the date of creation, rather than 30 years. This necessitated a consequential change to the FOIA, with the result that information contained in a record that is 20 years old cannot be withheld under ss.30(1), 32, 33, 35, 36 (for the most part) or s.42 of the FOIA. However, the new rule does not apply across the board, and information to which the remaining parts

---

[10]   *The Coalition: Our Programme for Government* (May 2010).

of ss.36, 28 and 43 apply can continue to be withheld until the 30-year point. This amendment, at the time of writing, has not yet been brought into force.

A further, more controversial change, also introduced by the CRAGA, was an absolute exemption for communications with Her Majesty the Queen (and the heir to, or second in line to, the Throne) and a qualified exemption for communications with other members of the Royal Household.

Further changes to the FOIA are imminent. The Protection of Freedoms Act 2012 (PFA), when brought into force, will amend s.11 of the FOIA to require public authorities to provide information held as a dataset (raw factual material that has not been adapted or altered in any way), or part of a dataset, to a requester in a re-usable format. Public authorities would be able to charge for providing the dataset. This seems to be an attempt to re-invigorate the little-used Re-use of Public Sector Information Regulations 2005,[11] SI 2005/1515 (PSI Regulations), which provide a very weak right of access to public sector information. As, however, the new duty on public authorities will be restricted to 'as far as is reasonably practicable', it remains to be seen whether this will prove more effective than the PSI Regulations or not.

The PFA also seeks to close what was seen as a potential loophole in the FOIA; s.6 of the FOIA makes companies that are wholly owned by a single public authority or by the Crown subject to the FOIA. However, a company partly owned by one public authority and partly by another has not been made subject to the FOIA, despite being wholly publicly owned. The PFA would bring companies wholly owned by more than one public authority within the scope of the FOIA. Finally, the PFA also makes changes to the role of the ICO, including changes to the tenure of the Information Commissioner, increased powers to charge for services and reduced need for approval from the Secretary of State for operational decisions.

Further changes may be in the pipeline. The Ministry of Justice has said that it is consulting with over 200 further entities on bringing them within the scope of the FOIA, and that further designation orders could be made in 2012. The bodies being consulted include: the Advertising Standards Authority; approved regulators under the Legal Services Act 2007, including the Law Society and the Bar Council; awarding bodies (where not already covered); the British Standards Institution; the Carbon Trust; the Energy Saving Trust; harbour authorities (where not already covered); the Independent Schools Inspectorate; the Local Government Association; the NHS Confederation; the Quality Assurance Agency; the Schools Inspection Service; and the Panel on Takeovers and Mergers. The government has said that, in addition, it intends to consult, in 2012, housing associations and the Housing Ombudsman about their possible inclusion in a s.5 order.

Changes may also be recommended by the Justice Select Committee, which launched a 'Post-Legislative Scrutiny of the Freedom of Information Act' in December 2011. The Committee's call for evidence asked witnesses to consider:

- Does the Freedom of Information Act work effectively?

---

[11] These regulations implement Directive 2003/98/EC of the European Parliament and of the Council on the re-use of public sector information.

- What are the strengths and weaknesses of the Freedom of Information Act?
- Is the Freedom of Information Act operating in the way that it was intended to?

As at time of writing the Committee had not reported,[12] but witnesses had called on the Committee to recommend a raft of changes, including the introduction of an application fee for each FOIA request, the lowering of the fees threshold, the extension of the FOIA to all government contractors, and the exclusion of Cabinet minutes from the scope of the FOIA.

Whatever changes are in store, it is essential that the government finds a balance between the rights of the public to have access to public sector information in the interests of accountability and transparency, and the need to protect sensitive information, disclosure of which could be damaging either to the public interest, or to legitimate private sector concerns. The FOIA has already brought about a radical change in the law and practice on access to government information, but there will always be a debate as to whether the correct balance has been achieved, as it is surely impossible that any access to information regime will suit the conflicting needs and wishes of all the many players involved – the information applicants (including the media), public authority decision makers, third party information providers, Ministry of Justice officials responsible for issuing guidance, Ministers with the right to veto release, the ICO, the Information Tribunal and the courts.

1.9 TERMINOLOGY

Throughout this handbook, unless the context indicates otherwise, references to 'the Tribunal' refer to either the Information Tribunal, as it was called until 17 January 2010, or the First-tier Tribunal (Information Rights) as it is now formally known. It is also referred to more informally as the Information Rights Tribunal.

1.10 KEEPING UP TO DATE WITH DEVELOPMENTS

Readers are referred to the practical journal *Freedom of Information*, as an excellent resource for keeping up to date with developments as they happen – **www.foij.com**.

---

[12] April 2012. The first report was due to be published on 3 July 2012.

CHAPTER 2

Publication schemes

Patricia Barratt, Clifford Chance LLP

2.1 BACKGROUND

    (2)   A publication scheme must –

        (a)   specify classes of information which the public authority publishes or intends to publish,

        (b)   specify the manner in which information of each class is, or is intended to be, published, and

        (c)   specify whether the material is, or is intended to be, available to the public free of charge or on payment.

    (3)   In adopting or reviewing a publication scheme, a public authority shall have regard to the public interest –

        (a)   in allowing public access to information held by the authority, and

        (b)   in the publication of reasons for decisions made by the authority.

(Freedom of Information Act 2000, s.19)

Publication Schemes could certainly prove to be a powerful vehicle for greater openness, depending on how much public authorities choose to include in them.
(House of Commons Select Committee on Public Administration in the report on its pre-
legislative scrutiny of the draft Bill: Freedom of Information Draft Bill, Third Report of
Session 1998–99, HC 570-I, 29 July 1999)

Publication schemes – called 'a sort of Cinderella' by Richard Thomas, the then Information Commissioner, in his evidence to a Parliamentary Select Committee[1] – are an often overlooked element of the freedom of information regime. Requesters and practitioners, and certainly the media, focus on the requests for information under s.1 of the Freedom of Information Act 2000 (FOIA), and the nature of the exemptions, rather than on publication schemes.

The current Information Commissioner, Christopher Graham, seems to share this view, one question in the ICO's 2011 consultation on publication schemes[2] being: 'What can be done to improve the public's awareness of publication

---

[1] House of Commons Constitutional Affairs Committee, Freedom of Information Act 2000 – Progress towards implementation, First Report of Session 2004–05, HC 79-II, 7 December 2004.

[2] *Consultation: Revising Publication Schemes Under Sections 19 and 20 of the Freedom of Information Act* (ICO, September 2011): **www.ico.gov.uk/about_us/consultations/ closed_consultations.aspx**.

schemes?' The Scottish Information Commissioner, Kevin Dunnion, has also identified problems with publication schemes, saying, in his introduction to the Scottish ICO's consultation on publication schemes in 2010 that '[i]t is clear, however, that even after six years of operation, the purpose of publication schemes is still not always well understood'.

Yet the purpose of publication schemes is simple enough. It is to impose a legal requirement on all public authorities to publish information proactively. It is certainly the case that a great deal of valuable information is available directly through publication schemes. However, there are a number of reasons why they are outshone by their more forward sister. They were initially brought in in waves (see **2.2**), before the main s.1 access right, and without the publicity surrounding the s.1 right. Also, the FOIA's requirements in relation to publication schemes are stated in very generalised terms. So, while there are specified classes of information which are entirely removed from the ambit of the FOIA by absolute exemption (e.g. all information directly or indirectly supplied by, or relating to, bodies dealing with security matters (s.23), or information contained in court records (s.32)), the FOIA did not specify what classes of information must be included in a publication scheme. (It is doubtful whether the requirement introduced by the PFA that public authorities include information about 'datasets' in their publication schemes should be considered to be an exception to the general rule that classes of information are not generally required, since this relates to the way in which information is held, rather than the nature of the information itself.) Some may say this was a deliberately inclusive approach: everything must go in, apart from that which is exempt. Others, more cynical, have argued that this lack of even basic minimum content requirements means that the schemes are meaningless.

For public authorities subject to the FOIA, and for those seeking information under the FOIA, however, publication schemes are likely to be the starting point. The staged way in which the FOIA was implemented means that public authorities were required to produce and maintain a publication scheme a considerable time (up to two years) before requests under the FOIA could be made. This will therefore have been most authorities' first experience of the new regime. The old Code of Practice on Access to Government Information, 2nd edn (1997) included a voluntary commitment on the part of central government departments and the public bodies which were signatories to make certain types of information available. This information included the facts and analysis of the facts behind major policy proposals and decisions, explanatory material on departments' dealings with the public (including rules, procedures, internal guidance to officials and administrative manuals), reasons for administrative decisions, and information about the operation of public services, though it was subject to the exemptions set out in Part II of the Code. There was no structural framework to the provision of this information and only limited enforcement capability: those seeking information would generally begin by making a request in writing to the relevant authority.

Under the FOIA, however, the first port of call should be the authority's publication scheme, and its public website. Any information accessible through the publication scheme, or the authority's website, is automatically exempt from disclosure by the authority in response to requests (see **2.7.1**). While the authority does not have to supply the information requested by way of a s.1 request, because of the duty to provide advice and assistance (s.16) it should ensure that the requester knows how to, and is able to, access the information. Section C of the ICO's *Guide to Freedom of Information,* 'What should we do when we receive a request?', states that where information requested is included in the publication scheme, 'you should give this out automatically, or provide a link to where the information can be accessed' (p.21).

2.2 IMPLEMENTING THE PUBLICATION SCHEME PROVISIONS

To facilitate processing of submissions by the ICO, the provisions relating to publication schemes were brought into force a considerable time before the main right of access, and implementation of these provisions was staggered according to the type of public authority, with central government departments the first to jump (or to be pushed). The Information Commissioner published a table showing three dates for each type of authority: the date from which he would accept submissions, the final deadline for submission of the publication scheme, and the date by which public authorities were required to have adopted and be operating an approved publication scheme. From this date, public authorities were required to make the information contained in their publication schemes available to the public in accordance with the terms of the schemes.

Publication schemes were initially approved for a period of four years (although the Information Commissioner reserved the right to vary this for particular publication schemes, if appropriate). The ICO subsequently announced that the deadline for re-approval for all sectors would be June to December 2008.

However, the way in which the ICO gave approval to publication schemes was radically changed following a consultation, with the result that approval and re-approval deadlines are no longer relevant (see **2.6.1**).

2.3 WHAT IS A PUBLICATION SCHEME?

Section 19 of the FOIA requires all public authorities to whom the FOIA applies to 'adopt and maintain' a publication scheme, which must be approved by the Information Commissioner. The publication scheme must set out the classes of information that the authority publishes, or that it intends to publish, and the manner in which it publishes each class of information. It must also state whether the information is freely available or whether there is a charge. In adopting a scheme, the public authority must have regard to the public interest in allowing public access to information held by the authority, and the publication of reasons for decisions made by the authority.

Described, more prosaically, by the ICO as 'a guide detailing types of infor-mation which are to be made routinely available' (*Publication Schemes: Approval Documentation* (ICO, April 2003)) the purpose of the schemes 'is to ensure a significant amount of information is easily and routinely available'. They are also intended 'to encourage organisations to publish more information proactively and to develop a greater culture of openness'.

The publication scheme provisions mirror similar requirements set out in the information access laws of a number of other jurisdictions, including the United States, Australia and New Zealand. In the United States, the relevant provisions are known as the 'reading room' requirement (Freedom of Information Act 1966, s.552(a)(2)), and they require public bodies subject to the US 1966 Act to publish information falling within specified categories, including rules of procedure and a description of all forms and papers produced, as well as statements of policy and legal rules of general applicability. Amendments to the US 1966 Act introduced the electronic reading room concept, requiring records created after 1 November 1996 to be made available by electronic means, as well as records released in response to a request which 'the agency determines have become or are likely to become the subject of a subsequent request for substantially the same records'. The Canadian Access to Information Act 1982 requires the designated Minister to publish a bulletin, updated at least once a year, containing 'a description of all classes of records under the control of each government institution in sufficient detail to facilitate the exercise of the right of access under [the] Act'. In New Zealand, under comparable provisions contained in the Official Information Act 1982 (s.20), the Ministry of Justice is required to publish a separate list for each department and organisation subject to the 1982 Act, a general description of the categories of documents held by it, a description of the manuals containing policies by which decisions are made, as well as the name of the officer to whom requests for information should be sent. Specified documents are publicly available as of right. Irish legislation (the Freedom of Information Act 1977) requires each public body to prepare and publish a reference book giving a description of the classes of records held by it, including the rules, procedures, etc. used by the body for the purposes of any enactment or scheme administered by it, as well as any details that might be reasonably necessary in order to exercise the right of access.

2.4 CLASSES

As described above, many access to information laws require public authorities to publish lists consisting of classes or categories of information that are publicly available. It is also usual for such legislation to contain some indication of what that means in practice, by specifying types of documents or records that must be included. The UK legislation provides no such indication, the only requirement being that the authority has regard to the public interest in allowing access to information and in publishing reasons for decisions.

The White Paper, *Your Right to Know*, harbinger of the FOIA, stated that:

> ... Experience overseas consistently shows the importance of changing the culture through requiring "active" disclosure, so that public authorities get used to making information publicly available in the normal course of their activities. This helps to ensure that FOI does not simply become a potentially confrontational arrangement under which nothing is released unless someone specifically asks for it.
>
> We believe it is important that further impetus is given to the pro-active release of information. So, the Act will impose duties upon public authorities to make certain information publicly available, as a matter of course. These requirements will be consistent with the other provisions of the Act – including its harm and public interest tests. They will be broadly along the lines of those in the *Code of Practice*, namely:
>
> - facts and analysis which the Government considers important in framing major policy proposals and decisions;
> - explanatory material on dealings with the public;
> - reasons for administrative decisions to those affected by them;
> - operational information about how public services are run, how much they cost, targets set, expected standards and results, and complaints procedures.
>
> (*Your Right to Know – The Government's Proposals for a Freedom of Information Act* (Cm 3818, December 1997), paras.2.17 and 2.18)

However, this requirement to publish specified types of information was not reflected in the draft Bill. The House of Commons Select Committee on Public Administration in the report on its pre-legislative scrutiny of the draft Bill argued in favour of a clearer definition of classes, and for the inclusion, on the face of the FOIA, of a requirement to publish internal guidance:

> Good schemes might provide, for example, for the publication of departmental manuals, rules and internal guidance ... the routine publication of government contracts (contract price, unit prices, performance standards), and the publication of all information which has been the subject of previous Freedom of Information requests.
>
> We recommend that the obligation to publish information be strengthened in the Bill. It should specify more clearly the type of information that authorities will be required to publish. In particular authorities should be obliged to publish internal manuals and guidance as a matter of statutory duty.
>
> (House of Commons Select Committee on Public Administration, Freedom of Information Draft Bill, Third Report of Session 1998–99, HC 570-I, 29 July 1999, paras.46 and 47)

There was a further attempt[3] to amend the Bill as it went through Parliament so as to require all public authorities to publish (subject to applicable exemptions):

> any manuals, instructions, precedents and guidelines used by the officers or employees of the authority, for the purpose of –
>
> (a)   interpreting any enactment, or
> (b)   administering any scheme for which the authority is responsible, and to make adequate reference to the existence of such information in its publication scheme.
>   (House of Commons Standing Committee B, 6th sitting, 20 January 2000, Part I)

---

[3]   Amendment no.65 tabled by Mr Maclennan MP, Standing Committee B, Part 8, 20 January 2000.

This was intended broadly to replicate wording in the Open Government Code, which required authorities:

> to publish or otherwise make available, as soon as practicable after the Code becomes operational, explanatory material on departments' dealings with the public (including such rules, procedures, internal guidance to officials and similar administrative manuals as will assist better understanding of departmental action in dealing with the public) except where publication could prejudice any matter which should properly be kept confidential under Part II [the Exemptions] of the Code
>
> (Code of Practice on Access to Government Information, 2nd edn (1997), Part I, para.3(ii))

It was also claimed that such a provision was present 'in every English language freedom of information law throughout the world' (House of Commons Standing Committee B, 6th sitting, 20 January 2000, Part I.).

The government resisted the amendment, however, on the basis that, while it might be an appropriate requirement for some public authorities, the reach of the legislation was much broader than that of the Code, and included many very small entities, such as doctors' surgeries and dental practices for whom such a requirement could be overly burdensome and inappropriate. Although a number of ways round this problem were suggested, the government maintained its position that the best way to regulate publication schemes was to require authorities to have their scheme approved by the Information Commissioner, or adopt a model publication scheme.

What is meant by 'classes' was initially left, therefore, to some extent, to the interpretation of the individual authority, subject to the approval of the ICO. When the ICO overhauled the publication scheme system in 2009, all public authorities were required to adopt the ICO's model publication scheme, which contains specified classes (see **2.6**).

2.5 APPROVAL BY THE INFORMATION COMMISSIONER

'The judgment about what is appropriate in an individual publication scheme is a matter not for the Government but for the Information Commissioner', said a Home Office Minister, David Lock, during the passage of the Bill through Parliament.[4]

All publication schemes must be approved by the Information Commissioner. With some 115,000 public authorities affected by the FOIA, according to government pronouncements, the ICO clearly had a mountainous task, even taking into account the staggered introduction of the requirement to adopt publication schemes and the existence of a model publication scheme. In giving evidence before a Select Committee, the Deputy Information Commissioner said that:

> given the size of the task, it was not possible for us to cross check each and every instance of that [whether the scheme put information into the public domain that was not there

---

[4] Standing Committee B, Part 2, col.189, 20 January 2000.

before]. The way we approached the approval of publication schemes was very much getting all public authorities, if you like, on to a first base.

(House of Commons Constitutional Affairs Committee, Freedom of Information Act 2000 – Progress towards implementation, First Report of Session 2004–05, HC 79-II, 7 December 2004)

The Parliamentary Select Committee highlighted this in its report:

However, the sheer number of schemes approved in the time available meant that these schemes were apparently assessed in terms of their form, not their content. That is, the ICO staff did not have time to check what the publication schemes actually contained, but rather how they were structured.

(House of Commons Constitutional Affairs Committee, Freedom of Information Act 2000 – Progress towards implementation, First Report of Session 2004–05, HC 79-I, 7 December 2004)

Approval was normally given for a period of four years, though the Information Commissioner did have the power to approve schemes for a different period or to revoke his approval (see **2.6**).

Since the introduction of the model publication scheme in 2009, the ICO no longer approves individual or sector-specific publication schemes. Rather, every public authority must adopt the Information Commissioner's model publication scheme (as described in **2.6.1**), which remains valid until further notice.

2.6 MODEL PUBLICATION SCHEMES

To cut out duplication and to spare small public authorities the burden of devising a publication scheme from scratch, the FOIA permits the use of model publication schemes. Section 20 provides that the Information Commissioner may approve model publication schemes for public authorities falling within particular classes. The Act also provides that model publication schemes may be drafted by the Information Commissioner or by 'other persons'.

The Information Commissioner initially approved a number of different model publication schemes for use by different sectors. A public authority which fell within that sector and which adopted the sectoral model publication scheme did not need to get the approval of the Information Commissioner for its scheme (unless it had changed the model publication scheme).

If the Information Commissioner refuses to approve a proposed model publica-tion scheme on the application of any person, he must give a statement of reasons for his refusal to the applicant (s.20(5)). Similarly, if the Information Commissioner refuses to approve any modifications that a public authority has made to the model publication scheme, he must give a statement of reasons for his refusal to the public authority (s.20(6)).

The Information Commissioner may provide that his approval of a model publication scheme expires at the end of a specified period (s.20(3)). He also has the power to revoke his approval for a model publication scheme, though he must issue a notice of revocation giving a six-month notice period before the approval is revoked (s.20(4)). The notice must include a statement of the Information Commissioner's reasons for revoking the approval (s.20(7)). Approval for all publication schemes in operation prior to the introduction of the new model publication scheme expired on 1 January 2009.

2.6.1 The revised model publication scheme

Between January and August 2007, the ICO ran a series of consultation seminars for different public sector categories (broadly, central government, non-departmental public bodies, health sector bodies, local government councils, local government services, education bodies and police authorities). Feedback indicated that public authorities would welcome a generic model scheme containing seven higher level classes of information. In April 2008, the ICO published guidance on a model publication scheme prepared and approved by the Information Commissioner which was to be adopted without modification by the public authority. The scheme would not require further approval and would be valid until further notice. This new model publication scheme became fully effective on 1 January 2009. There are two versions of the model publication scheme, one for all public authorities subject to the FOIA, and one for public authorities which are only subject to the FOIA in respect of some of their functions (such as the BBC).

A public authority can adopt the model publication scheme simply by placing a link to it on its website or otherwise making it available. There is no longer any requirement to notify the Information Commissioner. The public authority may not amend the model publication scheme, and should produce a 'Guide to information' to show the actual information it publishes, how it will be published and what charges are to be made.

The scheme represents a commitment to publishing information within certain broad classes (set out below). It does not specify particular pieces of information or charges.

The model publication scheme commits an authority:

- To proactively publish or otherwise make available as a matter of routine, information, including environmental information, which is held by the authority and falls within the [seven] classifications below.
- To specify the information which is held by the authority and falls within the classifications below.
- To proactively publish or otherwise make available as a matter of routine, information in line with the statements contained within this scheme.
- To produce and publish the methods by which the specific information is made routinely available so that it can be easily identified and accessed by members of the public.
- To review and update on a regular basis the information the authority makes available under the scheme [this is also a statutory requirement: see **2.11**].

- To produce a schedule of any fees charged for access to information which is made proactively available.
- To make its publication scheme available to the public.

The seven classes of information referred to are described in broad terms, as follows:

[1] Who we are and what we do.

Organisational information, locations and contacts, constitutional and legal governance.

[2] What we spend and how we spend it.

Financial information relating to projected and actual income and expenditure, tendering, procurement and contracts.

[3] What our priorities are and how we are doing.

Strategy and performance information, plans, assessments, inspections and reviews.

[4] How we make decisions.

Policy proposals and decisions. Decision making processes, internal criteria and procedures, consultations.

[5] Our policies and procedures.

Current written protocols for delivering our functions and responsibilities.

[6] Lists and Registers.

Information held in registers required by law and other lists and registers relating to the functions of the authority.

[7] The Services we Offer.

Advice and guidance, booklets and leaflets, transactions and media releases. A description of the services offered.

The guidance specifies that classes of information will not generally include:

- Information the disclosure of which is prevented by law, or exempt under the Freedom of Information Act, or is otherwise properly considered to be protected from disclosure.
- Information in draft form.
- Information that is no longer readily available as it is contained in files that have been placed in archive storage, or is difficult to access for similar reasons.

The Financial Services Authority publication scheme (**www.fsa.gov.uk/pages/ information/publication_scheme/index.shtml** and set out at **Appendix A**) provides a useful example of what kinds of information might be contained in the seven broad classes of information. Where a charge might be made for information, this is flagged with a pound sign (£). The headings are, or contain, links to the information described.

The authority must indicate clearly to the public what information is covered by the scheme and how it can be obtained. Where possible, information should be provided on a website. Where this is impracticable, public authorities should indicate how information can be obtained by other means.

In exceptional circumstances some information may be available only by viewing in person, in which case contact details are to be provided. If an appointment to view the information is required, it should be arranged within a reasonable timescale. Information must be provided in the language in which it is held or in any other language that is legally required.

The guidance to the model publication scheme also sets out when charges may be made for information under the scheme (see **2.8**). While there is a separate version of the model publication scheme for authorities which are subject to the FOIA only in respect of certain of their functions, the two versions of the model scheme are identical except that this second version includes the words:

> Some bodies are public authorities only for part of their functions. For these bodies, this scheme covers only information about the functions for which the organisation is a public authority.

Although there is now only (essentially) one model publication scheme which all public authorities must adopt, they must do so with reference to the appropriate definition document.

Definition documents

Definition documents set out the types of information the ICO expects particular types of authority to publish and list in their guide to information. Smaller authorities (such as parish councils, nurseries, primary schools or individual NHS practitioners) may have their own template guides to information rather than definition documents.

The following is a list of the definition documents (and template guides to information) available on the ICO website:

Central government

- Government departments
- House of Commons
- House of Lords

Northern Ireland
- The Northern Ireland Assembly
- Northern Ireland Government departments
- Northern Ireland non departmental public bodies
- District Councils, Northern Ireland
- Education and library boards, Northern Ireland

Wales
- The National Assembly for Wales
- Welsh Assembly Government
- Welsh Assembly Government sponsored bodies

Local Government
- Principal local authorities
- Joint authorities and boards, e.g. fire and rescue authorities, passenger transport authorities, waste disposal authorities, port health authorities, where established as a joint or combined authority.
- Local fisheries committees
- National parks and Broads authorities and conservation boards
- Charter Trustees
- Template guide to information for parish councils
- Template guide to information for parish meetings
- Template guide to information for Community Councils in Wales
- Template guide to information for Community Councils in Wales (Welsh language version)

Health
- Health bodies in England
- Health bodies in Wales
- Community Health Councils, Wales
- Health bodies in Northern Ireland
- Health and Social Services Councils, Northern Ireland
- Health regulators
- Template guide to information for dentists
- Template guide to information for dentists (Welsh language version)
- Template guide to information for general practitioners
- Template guide to information for general practitioners (Welsh language version)
- Template guide to information for opticians
- Template guide to information for opticians (Welsh language version)
- Template guide to information for pharmacists
- Template guide to information for pharmacists (Welsh language version)

Education
- Universities
- Colleges of further education
- Schools in England
- Schools in Northern Ireland
- Schools in Wales
- Template guide to information for schools
- Template guide to information for schools (Welsh language version)

35

Police
- Police authorities
- Police forces

Other Bodies
- Armed Forces
- Museums, libraries, art galleries and historical collections
- Non departmental public bodies
- Wholly owned companies

A public authority is expected to publish everything which is listed in the relevant definition document unless:

- it does not hold the information;
- the information is exempt under one of the FOIA exemptions or EIR exceptions, or its release is prohibited under another statute;
- the information is archived, out of date or otherwise inaccessible;
- it would be impractical or resource-intensive to prepare the material for routine release.

2.7   ACCESSING PUBLICATION SCHEMES

In addition to the statutory requirement that all public authorities maintain and adopt a publication scheme, each public authority is also required to 'publish its publication scheme in such manner as it thinks fit' (s.19(4)). There was some debate over this wording as the Bill passed through Parliament, one MP identifying this as a dangerous loophole.[5] Continuing, Mr Maclennan MP pointed out that this wording leaves the manner of publication of an authority's publication scheme entirely up to the authority, with no provision for review by the Information Commissioner:

> An authority could publish its scheme in an obscure form, which could make it extremely difficult to inspect. There could be a single copy, which could be held in the office of a chief executive and made available for perusal only by appointment and at an unacceptably high cost.

The Minister (Mr Mike O'Brien, then Parliamentary Under Secretary of State for the Home Department) responded by saying that a requirement to have the Information Commissioner's approval for the manner of publication would be unnecessary since:

> It is in the authority's interest to publish the scheme and make it widely available, as one of the scheme's effects would be to reduce the number of requests under clause 1 and reduce the burden on the authority.

---

[5]   Mr Maclennan MP, Standing Committee B, Part 7, 6th sitting, 20 January 2000, Part I.

The Minister also thought that making the manner of publication subject to the ICO's approval would be unnecessarily bureaucratic and entail considerably more work for the Information Commissioner.

Although the Information Commissioner does not have statutory authority over the manner of publication, guidance on the ICO's website says that public authorities should ensure that their model scheme and guide to information are available on their website, public notice board, or in any other way the public authority normally communicates with the public.

Many publication schemes are easily accessible online. Public authorities will frequently have a direct link to the publication scheme from their home page.

Good publication schemes should include details of how to access information where the applicant has special requirements, for example, by offering to make the information available, where possible, in a variety of formats such as Braille, audio, or in a language other than English. The Metropolitan Police publication scheme, for example, states it is available in Arabic, Bengali, Chinese, Greek, Gujarati, Hindi, Punjabi, Serbian, Turkish and Urdu.

Information which falls within one of the classes in a publication scheme does not have to be directly accessible from the publication scheme, and does not have to have been published already. For example, an authority may include the minutes of Committee X. It will then be required to publish all minutes of Committee X but may, as a matter of policy, publish such minutes after a specified period, whether that be one day or three months.

2.7.1   Principle of reasonable accessibility

There is no obligation on public authorities to provide information in response to a s.1 request where the information is 'reasonably accessible to the applicant' by other means (FOIA, s.21). The FOIA specifies that information may be reasonably accessible even where the information is not freely available but is subject to a charge. It also specifically provides that this exemption (which is an absolute exemption) does apply where the information is available in accordance with the authority's publication scheme. If a payment is required this must be specified in, or determined in accordance with, the scheme.

In some cases, however, the fact that payment is required may result in the information not being reasonably accessible. Guidance issued by the Information Commissioner suggests, for example, that where a public authority is asked for information contained in its annual report, or other long report, it may not be reasonable to require the applicant to purchase a copy of the report if the request is only for a small amount of the information contained in it (*Freedom of Information Act Awareness Guidance No.6: Information Reasonably Accessible to the Applicant by Other Means*, version 2 (ICO, January 2006)).

2.8   CHARGING FOR INFORMATION IN PUBLICATION SCHEMES

The fact that information falls within a class of information in a public authority's publication scheme means that the public authority is committed to publishing that information, but does not mean that the information must be made available without charge. Indeed, the FOIA requires public authorities to spell out in the publication scheme which information is available free of charge, and which information is subject to charges. There are no provisions regulating how much public authorities may charge for information under the publication scheme – the Freedom of Information and Data Protection (Appropriate Limit and Fees) Regulations 2004, SI 2004/3244 (Fees Regulations) only apply to requests made under the s.1 access right, and not to information provided under a publication scheme.

However, the FOIA does not give public authorities the power to charge for providing information outside the fees regime set up for s.1 access requests. If a public authority were to attempt to charge for information where statutory authority did not exist, that authority could be acting ultra vires. There may be situations in which a public authority has the power to charge but only on a cost recovery basis, whereas in other cases there may be authority to make a specified profit margin.

In *Bedgrove Junior School* (FS50194697, 30 July 2009) the ICO found that charges made under a publication scheme which had not been approved by the ICO (and did not follow the ICO's model publication scheme) were invalid. The public authority in question, Bedgrove Junior School, had asked a requester to pay a charge for a copy of a number of policies which were referred to in the authority's publication scheme. On examining the authority's publication scheme, the ICO determined that it had been modified from the (pre-2009) model scheme. In practice this meant the public authority was operating an unapproved scheme.

Any charges made in accordance with that scheme would be invalid (unless they were permitted under other statutory authority, e.g. FOIA, s.9(3)).

The ICO found the authority was in breach of s.19(1)(a), in failing to obtain approval for the modified publication scheme, and that the charges specified in the publication scheme were invalid.

The ICO model publication scheme allows for fees to be charged where it can be justified and it requires these charges to be published. If a charge is to be made, the basis for the charge must be made clear.

Where a charge applies, it must be clear what the charge is for and the amount. The Information Commissioner recommends that public authorities include a schedule of charges in their guide to information which is regularly updated. Such a schedule should provide details of all the different types of charge that may be made, such as any printing, copying or postage charges and also statutory charges that apply to any specific types of information.

The following example is provided in the ICO's guidance *Can I Charge for Information in a Publication Scheme?*, version 2 (January 2012):

HM Land Registry is able to charge for the supply of various categories of information, such as an official copy of a register or title plan, in accordance with the Land Registration Fee Order 2006.

Within the FOIA regime, the only sanction available in the case of public authorities which attempt to overcharge for information contained in the publication scheme is the 'nuclear' option of revocation of approval by the Information Commissioner, though doubtless there would be a dialogue prior to such a step being taken. In the *Bedgrove* case, the decision notice did not require the authority to take any further action; it noted that the Information Commissioner had no power to order repayment of the money charged, but recommended the public authority return the money as a goodwill gesture. The decision notice included links to guidance on publication schemes. Although not specifically stated, it is to be assumed that the Information Commissioner will have obtained assurance that the authority had adopted or was about to adopt the correct model publication scheme.

The model publication scheme says:

The purpose of this scheme is to make the maximum amount of information readily available at minimum inconvenience and cost to the public. Charges made by the authority for routinely published material will be justified and transparent and kept to a minimum.

Material which is published and accessed on a website will be provided free of charge.

Charges may be made for information subject to a charging regime specified by Parliament.

Charges may be made for actual disbursements incurred such as:

- photocopying
- postage and packaging
- the costs directly incurred as a result of viewing information

Charges may also be made for information provided under this scheme where they are legally authorised, they are in all the circumstances, including the general principles of the right of access to information held by public authorities, justified and are in accordance with a published schedule or schedules of fees which is readily available to the public.

If a charge is to be made, confirmation of the payment due will be given before the information is provided. Payment may be requested prior to provision of the information.

Copyright issues may also arise. Ordnance Survey, which publishes a vast quantity of commercial information, makes clear on its website, **www.ordnancesurvey.co.uk**, that some of the information available through the publication scheme will be subject to Crown copyright:

The material featured on the Ordnance Survey website is subject to Crown copyright. We authorise visitors to the site to make one free copy – by downloading to a printer or to electronic, magnetic or optical storage media – of any items featured on the site for the purposes or private research, study and reference.

Any other copy or use of Crown copyright materials featured on the site, in any form or medium, is subject to our prior approval. If you would like to discuss any copyright issue you should contact us.

More generally, Ordnance Survey describes its policy on charging fees for information as follows:

Freedom of Information Fees Policy

The majority of requests for information under FOI will be free of charge. Nevertheless, regulations made under the Freedom of Information Act 2000 make provision for fees to be levied in some circumstances.

In cases where we expect significant staff time to be involved in locating and retrieving the information required, we shall estimate the time likely to be needed. If this estimate is less than 24 working hours, no fee will be charged. Should the estimate clearly exceed 24 working hours, we shall first endeavour to agree with you a reduction in the scope of the enquiry that will bring the estimate below 24 hours. If this proves not to be possible, we shall use our discretion to either:

- refuse the request on grounds of disproportionate cost; or
- issue a Fees Notice in accordance with the Act.

Fees will be calculated at an hourly rate of £25.00 and will be subject to VAT.

In most cases we shall waive our right to charge for disbursements such as printing, CDs, photocopying and postage costs. If we do decide to charge for disbursements, a Fees Notice will be issued as above.

You have 60 days in which to pay the fee. If payment has not been received at the end of these 60 days, the enquiry will be closed.

Where a fee has been paid, and the actual time spent on locating and retrieving the information is less than the estimate, a refund will be made for each full hour not used. If the actual time spent exceeds the estimate, no further fee will be due.

If you do not agree with our charging decision, you can ask the Information Commissioner to intervene, as detailed on our Appeals page.

The Department for Business, Innovation and Skills includes a section on charging in its publication scheme:

Where a standing charge is applied for a publication, the charge will be as permitted by *Charges for Information: When and How – Guidance for Government Departments and other Crown Bodies* (PDF).

We indicate for each class of information in our publication scheme whether a charge is likely to apply to information within the class. Where a charge is applied, this is indicated in the listing of specific publications in our Publications pages or on request from the appropriate contact for hard copies.

Information is published free of charge on our website (i.e. there is no charge by us, although the user would have to meet any charges by their internet service provider, personal printing costs, etc.). For those without internet access, a single printout as on the website is available by post from the Information Rights Unit (contact details above). However, requests for multiple print-outs may attract a charge for the cost of retrieval, photocopy, postage, etc. We would let you know this at the time of your request. Any charges applied would be payable in advance.

The Department for Business, Innovation and Skills, its Agencies and UK Trade & Investment (UKTI) operate a number of schemes where information is provided by way of a charged-for service. Typically, what is provided under such services is a mix of information already held in a recorded form by the Department, its Agencies or UKTI and of information not already held in recorded form.

The ICO's guidance *Can I Charge for Information in a Publication Scheme?*, version 2 (January 2012) makes it clear that where fees are charged for material available under the publication scheme, the costs of such fees must be calculated separately from charges made under the Fees Regulations, and that the Fees Regulations do not apply to information that is routinely made available.

Where fees are charged they should be justified, clear and transparent. The guidance says that if a public authority does not make it clear in its guide to information that charges will be made for information then it will be unable to charge for it.

The ICO guidance recommends that public authorities include a schedule of charges in their guide to information, and that this should be regularly updated. The schedule, it says, should provide details of all the different types of charge that may be made, such as any printing, copying or postage charges and also statutory charges that apply to any specific types of information. It provides the following:

> As the Environmental Information Regulations 2004 oblige public authorities to publish a schedule of their charges (Regulation 8(8)(a)), this approach should be extended to information which is made available on a routine basis.

Level of charges

> . . .
>
> We strongly recommend that the level of charges should be compatible with the principle of promoting public access to the information held by public authorities. While we cannot be prescriptive about the level of charges, we would expect a public authority to be able to justify them based on a transparent and publicly available charging policy or policies.
>
> In making information available proactively an authority must consider the public interest in allowing access to the information. We will consider high levels of charges for routine information to be contrary to promoting public access to official information. Also information that is subject to high charges may not be considered as being reasonably accessible for the purposes of section 21 of the Act.
>
> It is worth remembering that the public and the Information Commissioner will be easily able to compare different charging regimes across the public sector.
>
> In practice, we expect that for much of the information which is routinely made available there will be either minimal or no cost. This will include information available from websites or supplied in hard copy form with any charges only being for the cost of any printing, copying or postage involved.

Examples of charges that are reasonable:

Printing, copying or postage

- An authority can charge for these in order to recover costs. It is still expected that any charges will be in accordance with the authority's published charging policy and schedule of charges.

Charges under statutory charging regimes

This will be self-explanatory to those authorities who can make such charges, but they should be made on a clear basis.

'Commercial' publications

This can cover a range of circumstances, such as:

- the need to charge in order to guarantee the continued collection and publication of the information;
- where information has been collected and analysed for commercial purposes and where this has required professional time and skill; and
- information which is normally made available on commercial terms as part of the authority's trading activities.

Examples of charges that would not be considered to be reasonable:

- Staff time – we would not expect to find this included in charges for information that an authority makes available to the public as part of its regular activities. (There is an exception where the authority is entitled to recover research fees for retrieving archived material.)
- Where the only justification for charges is that they have traditionally been made.

Environmental information

Environmental information which is regularly made available by electronic means (for example the information can be downloaded from a website) should be included in an authority's guide to routinely release information. This information should not be charged for.

Regulation 8 refers to the ability to charge a 'reasonable amount' for the supply of environmental information. In practice this should not present any conflict with the charging policy connected to the wider proactive release of information. The requirement in Regulation 8 for public authorities to publish and make available a schedule of charges will complement the publishing of a schedule of fees for information which is routinely made available.

2.9 PUBLICATION SCHEMES FOR COMPANIES DESIGNATED UNDER SECTION 5

Any person may be designated as a public authority for FOIA purposes under s.5 if it:

(a) appears to the Secretary of State to exercise functions of a public nature, or
(b) is providing under a contract made with a public authority any service whose provision is a function of that authority.

There is no provision in the FOIA for any derogation from the effect of ss.19 and 20 and therefore designated entities will also have to adopt and maintain the model publication scheme. The designation will only relate to the functions performed by the entity which are public functions and, similarly, the entity's publication scheme will only need to list classes of information relevant to those functions. The first orders were made in 2011, when the Association of Chief Police Officers (ACPO) of England, Wales and Northern Ireland, the Financial Ombudsman Service and the Universities and Colleges Admissions Service were designated. All three have adopted the model publication scheme, with the Financial Ombudsman Service consulting, as part of its preparations for being designated, on whether or not to publish its decisions. Although ACPO's website currently states that its publication scheme is 'under development' it has information set out under the seven classifications, as required by the model publication scheme.

2.10 DATASETS, THE INFORMATION ASSET REGISTER AND THE PUBLIC SECTOR INFORMATION DIRECTIVE

Derived from a consultation exercise into Crown copyright (and announced in the White Paper, *The Future Management of Crown Copyright* (Cm 4300, March 1999)), the idea of an information asset register (IAR) was intended to be a one-stop shop for potential re-users of government-generated or government-held information.

In practical terms, it is supposed to be an online catalogue of unpublished information resources, accessible to anyone with internet access, and containing details of all information held by all government departments and other Crown bodies, focusing on unpublished information. Internet searches suggest, however, that it is easier to access information held by each public authority separately on the IAR it maintains, rather than from the central database. The amount of information, and the extent to which the register is updated, vary considerably between public authorities.

The development of the IAR was supported by Directive 2003/98/EC of the European Parliament and of the Council of 17 November 2003 on the reuse of public sector information (the Public Sector Information Directive), implemented in the UK by the Re-use of Public Sector Information Regulations 2005, SI 2005/1515, which introduced a statutory obligation on public sector bodies to provide access to details about re-usable information held by the public sector. Recital 5 to the Public Sector Information Directive claims:

> Public sector information is an important primary material for digital content products and services and will become an even more important content resource with the development of wireless content services. Broad cross-border geographical coverage will also be essential in this context. Wider possibilities of re-using public sector information should inter alia allow European companies to exploit its potential and contribute to economic growth and job creation.

Article 9 provides for the creation of information asset lists:

Practical arrangements

Member States shall ensure that practical arrangements are in place that facilitate the search for documents available for re-use, such as assets lists, accessible preferably online, of main documents, and portal sites that are linked to decentralized assets lists.

The regulations implement this article by requiring public sector bodies to ensure that a list of significant documents available for re-use is made available to the public, preferably by electronic means and, as far as reasonably practicable, with an electronic search capability.

The main thrust of the Public Sector Information Directive is to ensure that, where public sector information is available for re-use, it is made available on terms that are fair, reasonable and not anti-competitive. It does not require any information actually to be made available for re-use, and even the requirement on the creation of assets lists is sufficiently vague and non-prescriptive to allow considerable room for manoeuvre.

Nevertheless, while the Public Sector Information Directive could be seen as less ambitious than the IAR initiative which predated it, in terms of what it requires of the asset register, it does at least put a voluntary policy initiative on to a statutory footing.

The National Archives guidance note, *Information Asset Register and Freedom of Information – A Co-ordinated Response to Information Access* (revised May 2008), was intended to explain how the IAR, and specifically departmental IARs, 'should contribute usefully to Freedom of Information Publication Schemes and the broader management of information requests under FOI'.

Government departments are required to produce both an FOI publication scheme for the purposes of the FOIA and an IAR for the purposes of the public sector information regime (PSI). The guidance said that information that departments had left out of their publication scheme because, for example, it could not be made widely available without considerable cost, or it was thought to be of limited interest, 'should already be included in departmental IARs, which detail information that may be of interest, yet is not published' (para.15). The guidance also stated that the existence of the IAR would make it simpler for departments to identify where information requested is held and so would facilitate the management of information requests, whether or not covered by the FOIA or the EIR.

The main area of overlap, therefore, between the two regimes, is the respective requirements to produce a list of information held by the public authority, albeit according to differing criteria. It is clear that it would not be possible to combine the two information schemes, although there have been calls to do so, in order to avoid duplication of effort. Publication schemes are intended to be a means of making more information available proactively and, in most cases, free of charge. The IAR is, however, a scheme to facilitate the commercial re-use of public sector information. Despite the cheerleader tones of the guidance note, the divergent aims of these two schemes give rise to a tension and even, potentially, a conflict of interest between them. This tension is perhaps more apparent in the underlying principles than will be the case in practice: requests for access to information under the PSI will typically be in relation to large collections of information as opposed to the much more targeted requests for discrete 'bits' of information which would be appropriate under the FOIA. Further, the PSI entails no obligation to supply the information requested, unlike the statutory obligation under the FOIA to provide information unless subject to an exemption. The other major difference is that information requested under the PSI is intended for re-use, while information accessed under the FOIA, including by way of publication schemes, will generally be subject to restrictions on re-use.

The new provisions in the FOIA, introduced by the Protection of Freedoms Act 2012, seem to be intended to provide a more joined-up approach, with datasets that might be expected to be included in an authority's IAR, or to be subject to the PSI, now required to be included in the authority's publication scheme, and brought within the FOIA enforcement framework.

A joined-up approach was also among the aims of the Coalition government's transparency agenda, whereby it committed to provide a one-stop shop for public sector data, to be published in an open and standardised format, to facilitate re-use (currently at online at **www.data.gov.uk**) (see **3.7**).

2.11 REVIEW OF PUBLICATION SCHEMES

Each public authority is required (under s.19(1)(c)) to review its publication scheme 'from time to time'. This is a requirement to consider whether the nature of the classes and the structure of the scheme are still appropriate, taking into consideration the public interest both in allowing access to information held by the authority, and in the publication of reasons for decisions made by the authority.

Before the introduction of the model publication scheme, a public authority was required to notify the Information Commissioner of any changes made to a publication scheme as a result of a review (or otherwise), and his approval was required where it was proposed to remove classes of information.

A survey carried out by the ICO in relation to the experience of local authorities and FOI found that 'Formal reviews of the Publication Schemes have been reported by the majority of local authorities in England, with most conducting them on a six monthly or annual basis' (*Freedom of Information Act 2000 Survey Findings: Principal Local Authorities* (ICO, February 2004)).

A further finding was that:

> Local authorities have approached the task of developing and reviewing publication schemes in the right spirit, although some may need to think of more regular reviews particularly in the light of patterns of individual requests for information.

The survey also found that local authorities engaging in best practice carried out a review of their publication schemes every six months.

Key messages from the ICO's Development and Maintenance Initiative (DMI) (reported in the Development and Maintenance Initiative Advisory Panel Newsletter, May 2007) on publication schemes were that:

> The maintenance of schemes is haphazard. This is compounded by the current approval process which does not encourage or support systematic maintenance . . .
> Public awareness of schemes is low, and members of the public find some schemes difficult to use.

The duty of public authorities to review their publication scheme has changed as a result of the ICO's requirement that all public authorities must adopt its model publication scheme. The Information Commissioner implicitly recognises that part of the duty to review now falls on the Commissioner; a consultation on publication schemes published in October 2011 said:

> The ICO has decided to launch this consultation due to the following reasons.
> The ICO last updated its model publication scheme and accompanying guidance nearly three years ago. The Act clearly indicates that publication schemes should be regularly reviewed and the public interest in allowing public access to information should be considered.
> Some sectors have now made significant advances with their own transparency initiatives, which have pushed beyond some of the minimum standards in the current publication scheme guidance. The ICO has welcomed these initiatives and the wider government policy initiatives on open data and transparency.
> New web 2.0 technologies are creating new opportunities to analyse and use public information. There are many innovative examples emerging from across the public sector.

While public authorities therefore no longer play a role in reviewing the content of the model publication scheme, they clearly continue to have a duty to review the way in which they implement it. This will include reviewing the content of the information they make available under the seven classes, the appropriateness and transparency of any fees charged, and the way in which information is made accessible, for example, the language or languages in which information is available, and whether provision is made for disabled users.

2.12 ENFORCEMENT

The obligation to adopt, maintain and review publication schemes is a statutory duty on the public authorities who are subject to the FOIA. Failure to do so is a matter, in the first instance, for the Information Commissioner. The Commissioner's policy tends to be to secure compliance by a process of educating and advising public authorities. However, where compliance cannot be achieved by this informal route he may consider exercising his formal enforcement powers set out under ss.50–56 of the FOIA. Where the ICO is satisfied that a public authority has failed to comply with any of the requirements of the FOIA, including the requirements on publication schemes, it may serve an enforcement notice requiring the authority to comply. If the public authority fails to comply with the enforcement notice the ICO may certify that fact in writing to the High Court. The court may then deal with the public authority as if it had committed a contempt of court. The procedures for enforcement are set out in much more detail in **Chapter 10** on enforcement, but it is worth noting that the Information Commissioner's very first foray into enforcement of the FOIA was in relation to publication schemes.

When the initial relevant deadlines for submission of publication schemes had passed, a small minority of public bodies had not established publication schemes. One of these was Allerdale Borough Council, which was required to submit its scheme to the Information Commissioner for approval by 31 December 2002, and to have the scheme active by 28 February 2003. The Information Commissioner therefore served a preliminary enforcement notice (which warns the authority that legal action will be taken if the problem is not resolved). The Information Commissioner has indicated that he would expect this notice to be effective in resolving the problem in a majority of cases, his experience being that most public bodies are keen to co-operate and that delays in setting up a publication scheme were usually due to administrative problems rather than to any reluctance to implement the legislation. However, Allerdale, alone of the bodies on whom preliminary enforcement notices were served, did not respond to the notice.

The Information Commissioner then took enforcement proceedings against the CEO of Allerdale Borough Council for contempt of court, with the aim, the ICO has said, of seeking compliance, rather than of punishing. The Information Commissioner believed that Allerdale would immediately comply once proceedings were served. However, the council failed to respond to the claim form and to a number of letters, and no one from the authority appeared at the directions hearing. Nothing was heard from Allerdale until the day of the actual hearing.

The case was transferred from Macclesfield County Court to Chester Crown Court because of the statutory requirement in the FOIA (s.54) that proceedings must be before a High Court judge. The case is unreported but the ICO has indicated that, on the day of the hearing (in spring 2004), a representative from Allerdale Borough Council explained that it had now implemented a publication scheme. The judge therefore dismissed the case. No explanation was given for the delay, or indeed the earlier failure to respond.

Lessons were learned from the case: the Information Commissioner had issued proceedings against the CEO of Allerdale Council, rather than the council itself. This issue was raised by Allerdale at the last minute at the hearing and it was eventually agreed by all parties that the FOIA required the Information Commissioner to initiate proceedings against the council directly and not against the CEO in person. However, this procedural irregularity had no direct bearing on the result of the case. Moreover, if Allerdale had not established a publication scheme by the day of the hearing then the Information Commissioner would no doubt have requested that the claim form be amended so that proceedings were issued against the council.

There have been very few decision notices by the ICO with direct bearing on publication schemes. The first, *Brockhampton Group Parish Council* (FS50135471, 29 March 2007), involved a request for minutes of a specific Council Management Committee meeting. The public authority in question, Brockhampton Group Parish Council, had adopted the model publication scheme for parish, town and community councils, which had been approved by the Information Commissioner and endorsed by the National Association of Local Councils. This includes under the heading 'Core Classes of Information':

(1) COUNCIL INTERNAL PRACTICE AND PROCEDURE

Minutes of council, committee and sub-committee meetings – limited to the last 2 years.

The council refused to supply the minutes even though, at the time the request was made, they fell within the two-year stipulated period. When pressed by the Commissioner, the council wrote (six months after the initial request) to the requester accusing him of 'pursuing a continual vexatious, repeated and time wasting process to obtain copies of minutes over two years old', and continued to refuse to supply the minutes.

The ICO considered the question of whether the request was vexatious. He found that the fact that the minutes were listed in the model publication scheme demonstrated that there was 'inherent value in the information requested'. The council's contention that the request was vexatious could not therefore be justified on the ground that the request clearly had no serious purpose or value (the ICO considered other grounds also). The Commissioner, unsurprisingly, found that the council was in breach of s.19(1)(b), in that the information in its publication scheme should have been available, and ordered the council to supply the information requested. In a fascinating aside, the council claimed that the requester already had a copy of the requested minutes and that they had a witness prepared to make a statement to that effect. The Commissioner replied that even if such a statement was provided, the ICO would not necessarily find in the council's favour. This is surprising, since evidence that a requester already had in his possession information he was requesting seems like prima facie evidence of vexatiousness, one of the key issues at stake.

In a further case, Argoed Community Council refused to supply a requester with a copy of its standing orders. Not only were the standing orders listed in the council's publication scheme, but there is, moreover, a statutory obligation on all local authorities to supply a copy of their constitution (including their standing orders) to any person who requests a copy, on payment of a reasonable fee (Local Government Act 2000, s.37). Initially, the council seems just to have ignored the request and it was only after the intervention of the Information Commissioner that it issued a refusal notice citing s.21 and referring the requester to the National Association of Local Councils or One Voice Wales for a copy of the orders. The requester had also requested a copy of the council's FOI publication scheme; this was not mentioned in the refusal notice but was eventually provided to the requester. Following further correspondence, the council agreed that the standing orders were not reasonably accessible through the organisations mentioned and agreed to provide a copy to the requester on payment of a small fee, and the issue of a disclaimer. The requester again involved the ICO to complain about the way his request was being handled and to ask the Commissioner to consider whether it was appropriate for the council to insist on a signed disclaimer before supplying the standing orders. The disclaimer required the requester to use the document for the purposes of information only for himself and not to reproduce or transmit in any form or by any means any part of the orders without prior permission from the council.

In its decision notice, *Argoed Community Council* (FS50142974, 29 August 2007), the ICO found that, technically, the information was exempt from disclosure under s.21 because it was reasonably accessible to the applicant via its publication scheme (though not through the bodies to which the council had referred the requester), though it went on to say 'in any case [it] would have been required to provide the information'. It found the council in breach of FOIA, s.1(1)(a) (the duty to inform a requester whether the public authority holds the information requested), as well as s.19(1)(b) (the duty to publish information in accordance with the authority's publication scheme). Though not strictly relevant to publication schemes, the most interesting of the ICO's findings in this case was that 'whilst public authorities can place restrictions on the end use of information, they cannot use these restrictions as a pre-condition of supply'. Exactly how the restrictions are to be placed or enforced in the absence of such a mechanism is not explored. Since there was, in any case, a clear statutory duty on the authority to supply the orders, this was more of a red herring. Perhaps a solution to this problem (for the public authority) would be to specify in the publication scheme that certain classes of information would only be made available on the issue of a disclaimer. In the same way as fees cannot be charged for information disclosed following an FOI request, except in line with the Fees Regulations, but information listed in the publication scheme can be charged for, there would seem to be no legal bar to requiring a disclaimer before releasing information in a publication scheme.

In *Backwell Parish Council* (FS50208722, 2 September 2009), the ICO looked at whether a parish council was required to disclose full bank statements to a requester, on the basis that bank statements were listed as a class of information in the council's publication scheme at the time of the request. The authority in question (Backwell Parish Council) argued that some of the information was exempt under s.40(2) of the FOIA because it was personal data. The ICO agreed, but found that the council was in breach of s.19(1)(b) for not making the information available on request. After the request had been made, the council had tried to remove bank statements from its publication scheme, but the ICO had not approved this change.

The Commissioner took the view is that it was possible for there to be exempt information contained within a class of information listed in an authority's publication scheme. However, by initially refusing to disclose the information in response to a request, even in redacted form, the council failed to fulfil its commitment to publish this information. The Commissioner found that the council was in breach of s.19(1)(b) of the Act.

In a further case, *Traffic Commissioner for the West Midlands Traffic Area* (FS50357622, 5 October 2011), it became clear that the public authority, the Traffic Commissioner for the West Midlands Traffic Area, did not have a publication scheme, although there was a publication scheme for all of the Traffic Commissioners together, available on the Department of Transport website. The Information Commissioner found that this scheme had not been approved by the Commissioner and was not based upon the Commissioner's model publication scheme. The public authority was therefore in breach of s.19(1)(a) of the Act. Moreover, the public authority had failed to provide information requested by the complainant in accordance with its publication scheme (in breach of s.19(1)(b)) and, as it had no control over the scheme it was unable to review it in accordance with the Act, and was therefore also in breach of s.19(1)(c).

However, the Commissioner did not order any remedial steps to be taken because:

1. The complainant had now been invited to view the relevant recorded information for free;
2. The public authority had taken responsibility for its compliance and had demonstrated to the Commissioner that it wanted to improve; and
3. The Commissioner was working with the public authority on an ongoing basis to assist it in improving its compliance with the Act and particular in assisting it with its publication scheme.

The foregoing cases do not involve abstruse legal analysis. They simply confirm what public authorities and others should already know, that a public authority must publish documents included in a publication scheme in accordance with the scheme and that the ICO will enforce the obligations which a public authority enters into when adopting a publication scheme.

The Information Commissioner's role in the shaping of the still-developing FOI regime remains critical. If publication schemes are still the Cinderella of the FOI regime, only the Information Commissioner has the magic wand to make a dazzling transformation.

CHAPTER 3

The right of access

Jackie Gray, Dickinson Dees LLP

3.1 INTRODUCTION

The Freedom of Information Act 2000 (FOIA) sparked an unprecedented level of awareness amongst the media and the public about accessing documentation and information held about them, their community and about local and national issues and causes. Using the FOIA to access information is now common practice for investigative journalists, and is used by individuals and lobbying groups as well as by businesses for commercial use (e.g. regarding business opportunities within the public section).[1]

This chapter aims to provide practical guidance first to members of the public as to how to make an effective request for information under the FOIA, and secondly, to public authorities on how to respond to requests for information under the FOIA. Broadly we will consider the formalities and practicalities of making and responding to requests for information, as well as the type of information that is available by means of the public's right of access under the FOIA.

An individual's right of access to information in fact goes far wider than that prescribed under the FOIA. While interest since 1 January 2005 has naturally focused on rights granted under the FOIA, there are also a number of other statutory rights of access to certain information. These may in fact prove more relevant and useful to an individual in obtaining a required piece of information, particularly as certain of these rights are to information held by private individuals and organisations. In addition, a public authority may need to deal with a request for information asking for mixed types of information.

Accordingly, in addition to considering rights of access under the FOIA, in this chapter we will also consider an individual's right of access to information under the Data Protection Act 1998 (DPA) and we will also refer to the Environmental Information Regulations 2004 (EIR) (which are covered in more detail in **Chapter**

---

[1] For example, see the University College London Department of Political Science Constitution Unit study *FOIA 2000 and Local Government in 2010: The Experience of Authorities in England* (November 2011).

9) and some other statutory rights of access to information (which include rights to access health records, medical reports and certain employment-related information).

The FOIA was intended to enhance, rather than replace, existing information regimes. Indeed, information is exempt from disclosure under the FOIA if it is reasonably accessible to applicants by other means (s.21), which includes obtaining information through other statutory rights of access. Therefore, where it is reasonable to expect them to do so, requesters may still be required to access certain information by means of these other statutory rights rather than under the FOIA.

3.1.1 Initial considerations for an individual wishing to make a request for information

The first consideration in relation to any request for information should be: 'Under what statutory access right should I make my request?' The answer will depend on:

* *the nature and focus of the information desired*: we have identified below the type of information that may be disclosed under some other statutory regimes;
* *the organisation that holds the desired information*: certain information rights only oblige public authorities to disclose information, whereas others apply equally to public and private bodies. We have identified below to whom each statutory right of access applies.

3.1.2 Initial considerations for a public authority responding to a request for information

Equally on receipt of a request for information a public authority's first consideration must be: 'What is the nature of the information requested?' The answer to this question will identify the statutory access regime under which the public authority must respond to that request. We have identified in this chapter the type of information that may be disclosable under some of the other statutory regimes, together with the costs and formality involved in responding to such requests.

If a request for information comprises a mix of environmental information, personal information relating to the individual requesting the information and other information (as is sometimes the case with, for example, requests about planning applications), then a public authority must separate out the requests and deal with each element separately under the EIR, the DPA and the FOIA as appropriate.

The following flowchart at Figure 3.1 provides a useful summary to both applicants and public authorities (or other bodies to whom requests for information may be made under the various statutory access regimes) as to which regime may apply to specific types of requests for information.

The flowchart at Figure 3.2 provides a process for a public authority or others to follow when dealing with a request for personal data (and see **3.3.1** for an explanation of the defined terms used in the flowchart).

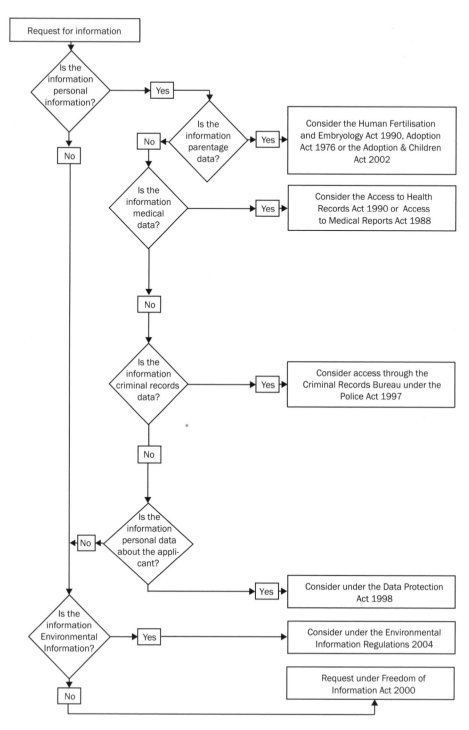

Figure 3.1 Summary of access regimes

3.2 FREEDOM OF INFORMATION ACT 2000

3.2.1 What information can be accessed?

The FOIA provides a right of access to the general public to recorded information held by public authorities. Information is disclosable via publication schemes and in response to requests for information (subject to a number of important exemptions).

When is information 'held'?

Any recorded information in the possession of, or held by a third party on behalf of, a public authority (as defined) is potentially disclosable under the FOIA regime, provided it is held for the purpose and interest of the public authority and is held at the time of the request. The reasons for which a public authority holds information will be relevant, as information which is merely held on behalf of a third party (for example, for preservation or security reasons), where the public authority itself has no interest in the information, will not be disclosable under the FOIA. This is provided for in s.3(2) of the FOIA:

> (2)   For the purposes of this Act, information is held by a public authority if –
>
> (a)   it is held by the authority, otherwise than on behalf of another person, or
> (b)   it is held by another person on behalf of the authority.

For examples of the Information Tribunal considering whether information was held 'on behalf of' the public authority or another person, see *Digby-Cameron* v. *Information Commissioner* (EA/2008/0010, 16 October 2008) and *McBride* v. *Information Commissioner and Ministry of Justice* (EA/2007/0105, 27 May 2008).

Whether information is held on behalf of the public authority or another person will obviously depend on the circumstances in question but, for example, information belonging to a Minister about party political matters, or a purely personal email sent by an employee of a public authority, which is stored on the authority's computer system will not be deemed to be held by the public authority for the purposes of the FOIA. In a new development in 2011, the Information Commissioner issued guidance[2] which indicates that information which is sent via personal email accounts may be held on behalf of a public authority and therefore fall within the scope of the FOIA. The Information Commissioner's approach is that:

> Information held in non-work personal email accounts (e.g. Hotmail, Yahoo and Gmail) may be subject to FOIA if it relates to the official business of the public authority. All such information which is held by someone who has a direct, formal connection with the public authority is potentially subject to FOIA regardless of whether it is held in an official or

---

[2]   See *Official Information Held in Private Email Accounts*, version 1 (ICO, 15 December 2011). This was also the approach followed by the Information Commissioner in its decision notice, *Department for Education* (FS50422276, 1 March 2012). At the time of writing, this decision notice was subject to an appeal to the Information Rights Tribunal.

private email account. If the information held in a private account amounts to public authority business it is very likely to be held on behalf of the public authority in accordance with section 3(2)(b).

(p.2)

Information held by public authorities will comprise information created (solely or partly) by or on behalf of the public authority but also may include information received from third parties, regardless of whether or not that third party was aware that such information may be disclosable under the FOIA. This could include information provided to a public authority by a private sector body, such as correspondence from a private contractor providing services to a public authority, or information about individuals, such as education and benefits records.

Whether or not information licensed to a public authority constitutes information 'held' will depend on the scope of the licence (see *Marlow* v. *Information Commissioner* (EA/2005/0031, 1 June 2006)).

Guidance has been given by the Information Tribunal as to whether electronic records supposedly deleted by public authorities, but which are stored on back-up files or servers, are considered to be 'held' by public authorities (see *Harper* v. *Information Commissioner and Royal Mail Group plc* (EA/2005/0001, 15 November 2005), approved in *Keiller* v. *Information Commissioner and University of East Anglia* (EA/2011/0152, 18 January 2012); [2012] 1 Info LR 128). Electronic records are often still accessible even if deleted from a computer. A public authority must consider the extent to which the information has been deleted, whether it can be recovered, and by what means. If the public authority can simply retrieve the information from a computer's 'recycle bin', hard drive or back-up tapes, then the public authority will normally be expected to do this to comply with an information request. However, if retrieving or restoring the deleted information (e.g. restoring the computer back to its previous state) would involve specialist staff or software or will involve a significant cost exceeding the limit for complying with a FOIA request (see **3.2.3**), then the public authority may be entitled to refuse the request.

Both the First-tier and Upper Tribunals have decided that 'held' can be construed as 'have they got it' in layperson's terms. See in particular *University of Newcastle upon Tyne* v. *Information Commissioner and BUAV* [2011] UKUT 185 (AAC); [2011] 2 Info LR 54 at paras.43–44: 'hold' is 'an ordinary English word to be determined as an issue of fact, reaching a conclusion that was justified by its own matrix of findings of fact'.

The s.12 cost limit 'serves as a guillotine' generally to prevent a search for information becoming too onerous on a public authority (see *Quinn* v. *Information Commissioner and the Home Office* (EA/2005/0010, 15 November 2006), paras.50 and 53). Nevertheless, if previously missing information is subsequently found, a public authority should inform an applicant.

The Information Tribunal has also given useful guidance on the extent to which information is 'held' when the specific information requested is not held by the public authority, but the raw data that form the 'building blocks' from which the requested information could be generated is held (see *Johnson* v. *Information*

Commissioner and the Ministry of Justice (EA/2006/0085, 13 July 2007)). The Tribunal indicated that whether this results in the generation of new information (which is not required by the FOIA) depends on the extent to which something needs to be done to the 'building blocks'; in particular, the degree of skill and judgement applied to the 'building blocks' would have a bearing on whether the information was held. Here, as all that needed to be done amounted to a simple collation of raw data to arrive at the information requested, the Tribunal concluded that the information was held. The question of whether a public authority was generating new information in response to a request has since been the subject of a House of Lords decision in *Common Services Agency* v. *Scottish Information Commissioner (Scotland)* [2008] UKHL 47. This was an appeal from the Court of Session[3] against a decision by the Scottish Information Commissioner in which he ordered the Commons Services Agency (CSA) to disclose particular data in a 'barnardised form' (a method of presenting statistics so as to minimise the risk of individuals being identified from low numbers). The House of Lords considered whether the information in a 'barnardised form' was still held by the CSA for the purposes of the Freedom of Information (Scotland) Act 2002 and concluded that it was, as the CSA held the underlying information at the time of the request and the process of barnardisation was 'a form of disguise, or camouflage' similar to the process of redaction (para.15).

Information is potentially disclosable regardless of the form in which the information is recorded (FOIA, s.84) (for example, whether it is electronically stored, a hard copy, an audio recording[4] or a graph), and includes handwritten notes, opinions and historical data. It is important to bear in mind that, unlike access regimes in other jurisdictions, the FOIA provides a right of access to information rather than to documentation (see *Ingle* v. *Information Commissioner* (EA/2007/ 0023, 29 June 2007), para.7). Therefore, while a specific document, or part thereof, may be exempt from disclosure, some or all of the information contained within that document may be disclosable, perhaps by way of extracting from or redacting the remainder of the document.

The FOIA also only covers information that is recorded (see *Ingle* v. *Information Commissioner*, para.7; and FOIA, s.84). Therefore, information which may be in the knowledge of an employee of a public authority, but which is not, or is no longer (at the time of the request), recorded in a permanent form will not be disclosable.

The FOIA is also not concerned about the quality of the information held by a public authority for the relevant purpose (see *Simmons* v. *Information Commissioner* (EA/2005/0003, 16 December 2005), para.23), nor does it 'give a right to the requester to get the information he or she thinks he should receive' (see *Prior* v. *Information Commissioner* (EA/2005/0017, 27 April 2006), para.21); the concern

---

[3] *Common Services Agency* v. *Scottish Information Commissioner* [2006] CSIH 58.

[4] For example, the Information Tribunal held that a tape recording of court proceedings is a 'document' for the purpose of s.32(1), commenting 'since that term is broadly construed in an age offering so many recording media … Transcripts of tapes are analogous to copy documents' (*Mitchell* v. *Information Commissioner* (EA/2005/0002, 10 January 2005), para.21).

is simply whether or not the requested information is held and potentially disclosable (see *Ingle* v. *Information Commissioner* (EA/2007/0023, 29 June 2007), para.8 – 'no obligation ... to create a record where none exists').

Certain information is excluded or exempt from disclosure under the FOIA:

- personal data about the applicant, disclosure of which is covered by the access regime under the DPA (s.40(1) of the FOIA and see **3.3**);
- environmental information, which is disclosable under the EIR (s.39 of the FOIA and see **3.4** and **Chapter 9**);
- information which is, because of its subject matter or nature, subject to another exemption under Part II of the FOIA. These exemptions are considered in detail in **Chapters 4** and **5**. For example, information is exempt from disclosure under the FOIA if it is available to applicants by other means (FOIA, s.21), as is information which is intended for future publication by the public authority (FOIA, s.22).

There are a number of procedural limitations on disclosure set out in Part I of the FOIA, which are discussed in **3.2.4**.

A number of existing Acts of Parliament have been amended so as to permit disclosure of information under the FOIA that would otherwise have been prohibited or restricted (Freedom of Information (Removal and Relaxation of Statutory Prohibitions on Disclosure of Information) Order 2004, SI 2004/3363). However, decisions of the Information Tribunal have highlighted that there are still some statutory restrictions in other legislation which prohibit disclosure notwithstanding FOIA rights of access and which would render information exempt from disclosure under s.44 of the FOIA (see also **Chapter 4**).[5]

Publication schemes

The first port of call for any potential applicant under the FOIA should be a public authority's publication scheme, which in most cases will be the Information Commissioner's model publication scheme.[6] Any individual, company or other organisation may request a copy of the information made available in accordance with a publication scheme (FOIA, s.19).

---

[5] See *Slann* v. *Information Commissioner and Financial Services Authority* (EA/2005/0019, 11 July 2006), which concerned a prohibition under the Financial Services and Markets Act 2000; *Dey* v. *Information Commissioner and Office of Fair Trading* (EA/2006/0057, 16 April 2007), where provisions of the Enterprise Act 2002 imposed a prohibition on disclosure; and *Meunier* v. *Information Commissioner and National Savings and Investments* (EA/2006/0059, 5 June 2007), where provisions of the Premium Savings Bonds Regulations 1972, SI 1972/765 also meant that the FOIA, s.44 exemption applied.

[6] This was to be adopted by public authorities from 1 January 2009 and replaced the previous sector-specific model publication schemes. However it is anticipated this model publication scheme will be replaced by a new model publication scheme in 2013. See the Information Commissioner's Publication Scheme Action Plan for 2012/13 and **Chapter 2**.

As described in **Chapter 2**, a variety of information, and particularly frequently requested information, is increasingly available via public authorities' publication schemes. The advantages to a potential applicant of making use of this resource are:

- the information will be quickly and easily accessible as publication schemes and a public authority's guide to what it makes available under its publication scheme will often be on the public authority's website;
- the information will often be available via the publication scheme free of charge (under the publication scheme the public authority should set out whether or not it is going to charge to provide a copy of the information). It is clear that the Information Commissioner will assist complainants who are denied information that should be made available in accordance with a publication scheme, even if the costs of providing the requested information potentially exceed the appropriate limit (see **3.2.3**);[7] and
- public authorities are exempt from the obligation to provide information in response to an information request where that information is already available under the authority's publication scheme (FOIA, s.21). Therefore, checking what is made available under the publication scheme first may save the need to go through the process of submitting an information request.

Information requests

The general principle of the FOIA is that any person making a request for information to a public authority is entitled (subject to a number of exceptions and exemptions):

(a)   to be informed in writing by the public authority whether or not it holds information of the description specified in the request; and

(b)   if it does hold the information, to have that information communicated to him (FOIA, s.1(1)).

We have set out in the next section practical guidance to enable a potential applicant to make a request for information under the FOIA, and in **3.2.4** we consider how, and when, the public authority should respond to the information request.

3.2.2   The request – guidance for applicants

Who can make an information request?

A request can be made by any person anywhere in the world. A request can therefore be made by an individual, partnership, unincorporated body or company, whether or not they are UK national or resident, and regardless of the purpose of the request.

---

[7]   See the Information Commissioner's decision notices: *Brockhampton Group Parish Council* (FS50135471, 29 March 2007); and *Argoed Community Council* (FS50142974, 29 August 2007).

To whom can a request be made?

The FOIA grants a right of access to individuals to information held by or on behalf of a public authority, both as defined in the FOIA (s.3(1) and (2)).

The definition of public authorities in the FOIA includes public bodies listed in Sched.1 to the FOIA (as amended by various secondary legislation (ss.3(1)(a)(i) and 4)), certain authorities designated by the Secretary of State for Justice by order under s.5 (ss.3(1)(a)(ii) and 5)[8] and all companies that are 'publicly-owned' (FOIA, s.3(1)(b)); 'publicly-owned' is defined in FOIA, s.6 and covers companies which are wholly owned by a public authority, and when the amendments made in the Protection of Freedoms Act 2012, s.103 come into effect, companies wholly owned by a number of public authorities (see further **3.7**).

For example, public bodies listed in Sched.1 will encompass central government departments, local authorities, the Houses of Parliament, NHS trusts and health authorities, maintained schools and other educational institutions, Academies (under the Academies Act 2010), the police and the armed forces, as well as executive agencies. Some of the bodies listed may only be caught by the FOIA in relation to certain information (for example, the BBC is liable to disclose all information except that held for the purpose of journalism, art or literature).

Section 5 provides the Secretary of State with the power by order to designate as a public authority a person who either appears to exercise functions of a public nature or provides a service under a contract with a public authority which is a function of the public authority's. Following a consultation exercise in 2007, the Freedom of Information (Designation as Public Authorities) Order 2011, SI 2011/2598 was made to designate the Financial Ombudsman Service, the Association of Chief Police Officers and the Universities and Colleges Admissions Service as public authorities from 1 November 2011. This is the first time that the s.5 power has been used. However, following an announcement by the Ministry of Justice in January 2011,[9] the government is currently consulting with a range of other organisations, including the Law Society and Bar Council over extending the FOIA to them via s.5 orders.

Information requests should be addressed to the relevant public authority which the potential applicant believes holds the desired information, either where the public authority has the information in its own possession, or where the information is held on behalf of that public authority by another person (FOIA, s.3(2)).

Formality of the request

(a)   *Legal formality:* The information request must be made in writing, which

---

[8]   FOIA functions of the Lord Chancellor were first transferred to the Secretary of State for Constitutional Affairs (art.4 of the Secretary of State for Constitutional Affairs Order 2003, SI 2003/1887) and then subsequently were transferred to the Secretary of State for Justice with effect from 22 August 2007 (art.7 of the Secretary of State for Justice Order 2007, SI 2007/2128).

[9]   See Ministry of Justice press release 'Opening up bodies to public scrutiny', 7 January 2011: **www.justice.gov.uk/news/press-releases/moj/press-release-070111a**.

includes requests by letter, fax or email, and must include details of the name and address of the applicant (FOIA, s.8(1)(a), (b) and (2)). The Information Commissioner has also suggested that requests can be made via social media such as Facebook or Twitter.[10] The request should also describe in as much detail as possible the required information (FOIA, s.8(1)(c)).

(b) *Practical guidance on how to make a request more effective:*

(i) Provide contact details, or else the public authority cannot respond to, and indeed is not required under the FOIA to deal with, the request. For a request to be valid a first name or initial and surname are required. An email address may be sufficient if it meets this requirement. However the Information Commissioner has issued guidance on the use of pseudonyms and stated that the real name of a requester should be used, therefore known or obvious pseudonyms will render a request invalid.[11]

(ii) Requests may be submitted in English (or in Wales, in Welsh). If requests are made in other foreign languages, the public authority may ask the applicant to resubmit the request in English (or Welsh); otherwise, the public authority is not obliged under the FOIA to respond to a request in other languages.

(iii) A public authority must provide advice and assistance to enable a written request to be submitted if an applicant is unable to do so (see 'Advice and assistance' later in this section). Some public authorities may also provide standard request forms to assist an applicant to make a request (although there is no obligation on an applicant to use such forms).

(iv) Explain the nature and scope of the information desired as clearly as possible. It will be easier for a public authority to respond to a request which focuses on the particular information sought, rather than a general request for information on a wider topic. Therefore, if possible, refer to a specific document containing the information (for example, a report or minutes of a meeting); otherwise, give examples of the type of documentation that may include the information or an indication of when the information may have been originally documented.[12]

(v) The request need not refer expressly to the FOIA, but mentioning this in a request may assist the public authority in identifying and responding appropriately.

(vi) If the information is required urgently, ask the public authority to

---

[10] See the ICO's *Guide to Freedom of Information* at **www.ico.gov.uk/for_organisations/freedom_of_information/guide.aspx**.

[11] See *Valid Request – Name and Address for Correspondence*, version 1 (ICO, January 2009).

[12] The Information Tribunal noted that 'the subject matter of the information must be set out and described as precisely as possible' (see *Lamb* v. *Information Commissioner* (EA/2006/0046, 16 November 2005), para.3). That case highlighted, in the Tribunal's words, 'the danger in not alerting a complainant to the need to specify his request at the earliest possible reasonable opportunity' where a request is unclear (para.19).

respond in a shorter timescale as the public authority is obliged to comply with the request promptly and in any event within 20 working days and therefore may be able to respond quickly (FOIA, s.10(1) and see **3.2.4**).

(vii) An applicant is entitled to request that the information be provided in a particular form, but bear in mind that the public authority may not be obliged to supply the information in a particular form if it is not reasonably practicable to do so (FOIA, s.11 and see **3.2.4**). Note also that requesting a particular form should not be used as a way of avoiding paying for published information.

(viii) An applicant does not have to disclose why he or she wants the information, even if asked by the public authority. This is the principle that the FOIA is 'motive blind' (see *Home Office and Ministry of Justice* v. *Information Commissioner* [2009] EWHC 1611 (Admin); [2011] 1 Info LR 885 at para.23(ii)). It has generally been accepted that there are, however, some circumstances where the motive of the applicant may be relevant, including if the request is a vexatious or repeated request (see **3.2.4** and *Ward* v. *Information Commissioner* (EA/2009/0093, 25 May 2010) at para.22).

(ix) Public authorities may refuse to answer a request altogether on the grounds that it is repetitious (FOIA, s.14(2)) or vexatious (FOIA, s.14(1)); see also **3.2.4** 'Vexatious requests').

(x) Ensure that the information requested is not already available in accordance with the public authority's publication scheme – this will save time and effort. In any event the public authority need not comply with the request in these circumstances (see **3.2.1**, 'Publication schemes'). Information that is requested routinely is likely to have been made available in accordance with the authority's publication scheme. Alternatively it may have been published in a FOIA disclosure log on the public authority's website.

(xi) Try to keep the scope of a request reasonable as if the request would be very time consuming to comply with the public authority may be entitled to refuse to comply with the request on cost grounds (FOIA, s.12 and **3.2.4**).

To whom should the request be sent?

Requests for information under the FOIA can be made to any employee (or agent) of a public authority. However, directing requests to the appropriate person or department within a public authority is likely to bring a quicker and more focused response.

Each public authority (and certainly larger public authorities) should have appointed a nominated officer to deal with, and to advise on, requests for information under the FOIA. A public authority should publish its procedures for dealing with requests for information (or for assistance), including details of an address, email address and telephone number of the person to whom requests for information should be directed (Section 45 Code of Practice,[13] Part II, para.5). If this information is not easily available, it is recommended that a request for information is sent to the relevant public authority's head of legal or to the relevant head of the public authority (e.g. the Minister or head of the executive agency or the chief executive of a local authority), so as to ensure that the request reaches the appropriate person without undue delay.

If an information request is made to an authority that holds the information on behalf of another public authority, the recipient public authority may deal with the request in consultation with the authority that actually holds the information, or may redirect the request as soon as possible to the originating authority, bearing in mind its duty to provide reasonable assistance and advice to applicants (Section 45 Code of Practice, Part III, paras.16–24).

Advice and assistance

A public authority is obliged to provide advice and assistance to applicants, and to those considering making a request for information, so far as it is reasonable to do so (pursuant to its responsibilities under the FOIA, s.16(1)), and in accordance with the Section 45 Code of Practice (see **3.2.4**) (FOIA, s.16(2) and Foreword to the Section 45 Code of Practice, para.13).

The duty to provide assistance is wide-ranging and covers all stages of making and responding to a request, including the type of information that may be accessed under the FOIA, how to formulate a clear and focused request, other sources of the information desired, and the progress of a submitted request. There is 'nothing to prevent an authority volunteering advice and assistance: an applicant does not have to ask for it' (see *Lamb* v. *Information Commissioner* (EA/2006/0046, 16 November 2005), para.2).

Public authorities should be prepared to explain why they are asking for additional information in relation to a request or proposed request (Section 45 Code of Practice, Part II, para.9). The key is for a public authority to be flexible and to provide appropriate advice and assistance in the circumstances having liaised with the applicant (Section 45 Code of Practice, Part II, and the Information Commissioner's guidance: *Good Practice in Providing Advice and Assistance*, version 1 (ICO, December 2008)). See also *Bellamy* v. *Information Commissioner and the Secretary of State for Trade and Industry* (EA/2005/0023, 4 April 2006), para.40, in which the Information Tribunal 'endorses the general desirability that requests for information be treated with as much practical assistance as possible'. The public

---

[13] The Secretary of State for Constitutional Affairs' Code of Practice on the Discharge of Public Authorities' Functions under Part I of the Freedom of Information Act 2000, issued under s.45 of the FOIA, available at **www.justice.gov.uk/information-access-rights/foi-guidance-for-practitioners/ code-of-practice**.

authority should not ask why the applicant or potential applicant is requesting the information, although an applicant is free to disclose this information.

Other than a public authority's right to request further information from an applicant in order to locate and/or identify information requested (where the timescales for responding to the request do not start – see **3.2.4** under 'Timescale for response') (FOIA, ss.1(3) and 10(6)), a public authority will not be entitled to an extension to the standard 20 working day response period to provide all other advice and assistance once a request has been made.

Public authorities should also be aware of their obligations under other Acts of Parliament (such as disability and race discrimination legislation and Welsh language legislation) when providing advice and assistance (Foreword to the Section 45 Code of Practice, para.14). Any employee of a public authority may provide advice and assistance. It is good practice for a record of the advice or assistance to be kept by the public authority, in case it is later queried.

3.2.3   Fees

Publication schemes

A public authority's publication scheme should state whether or not the authority will charge to provide a copy of information made available in accordance with the scheme (FOIA, s.19(2)(c)). If a charge is payable, the amount of the charge should be set out within the public authority's guide to what information it makes available under its publication scheme. The Information Commissioner recommends a schedule of charges (which is updated regularly) should be contained within the public authority's guide to information (see *Can I Charge for Information in a Publication Scheme?*, version 2 (ICO, January 2012)).

Information requests

The fees chargeable by a public authority under the FOIA in respect of information which is not made available under its publication scheme will depend on whether the cost of complying with the request would exceed the 'appropriate limit' (FOIA, s.12).

The appropriate limit has been defined in the Freedom of Information and Data Protection (Appropriate Limit and Fees) Regulations 2004, SI 2004/3244 (Fees Regulations), as £450, or £600 in the case of requests to a public authority listed in Part 1 of Sched.1 to the FOIA which includes central government departments (Fees Regulations, reg.3).

Where a public authority estimates that the cost of complying with the request would not exceed the appropriate limit (see **3.2.4** under 'Appropriate limit'), it can only charge an applicant for the costs which it reasonably expects to incur in informing the applicant that the information is held and communicating the information to the applicant (Fees Regulations, reg.6(2)) (Communication Costs). The

Communication Costs which can therefore be charged include the costs of reproducing the information (e.g. photocopying and printing costs); postage and any
other costs of transmitting the information; and the cost of communicating the
information in the form requested by the applicant under s.11 of the FOIA (Fees
Regulations, reg.6(3)). However Communication Costs do not include the cost of
staff time associated with carrying out these activities (Fees Regulation, reg.6(4)).

If a public authority estimates that the cost of complying with the request would
exceed the appropriate limit (see **3.2.4** under 'Appropriate limit') it need not comply
with the information request (FOIA, s.12(1) and (2)). However, it may offer to do so
and can charge a fee (FOIA, s.13). Unless the public authority has another legal
power to charge, the fee is to be calculated in accordance with reg.7 of the Fees
Regulations. This permits the public authority to charge a maximum fee equivalent
to the costs it reasonably expects to incur in determining if it holds the information,
in locating the information (or a document containing it), retrieving the information
(or a document containing it) and extracting the information from a document
containing it. Communication Costs can also be charged and the costs of staff time
can be calculated at an hourly rate of £25.

Fees notices

If a fee is to be charged, the public authority must, within the timescales for
complying with the request, issue a fees notice to the applicant setting out the
amount of the fee (FOIA, s.9(1)). If an applicant refuses to pay the fee, a public
authority should consider whether it can make available any information that may
be of interest to the applicant free of charge or for a lesser fee (Section 45 Code of
Practice, Part II, para.13).

Where the applicant does not pay the fee within three months of the fees notice,
the public authority is not obliged to comply with the request (FOIA, s.9(2)). If the
applicant pays the fee then the public authority must comply with the request within
the original timescales, disregarding the time period between the issue of the fees
notice and payment of the fee (FOIA, s.10(2)).

For further information on calculating fees under the FOIA, see the Information
Commissioner's guidance: *Fees that May Be Charged when the Cost of Compliance
Does Not Exceed the Appropriate Limit*, version 1 (ICO, March 2012).

3.2.4 The response – guidance for public authorities

A public authority should have in place a system to ensure the efficient processing
of, and advising on, requests for information submitted under the FOIA. While any
employee of a public authority can respond to a request for information, public
authorities may nominate an officer to deal with these requests. Nonetheless, public
authorities should ensure that staff who deal with members of the public, or who
provide information as part of their role, can identify information requests and are

familiar with the requirements of the FOIA and other good practice guidance (Foreword to the Section 45 Code of Practice, para.15).

Two codes of practice have been published under ss.45 and 46 of the FOIA, which provide guidance to public authorities on desirable practice:

- in discharging their functions under Part I of the FOIA (the Secretary of State's Code of Practice on the Discharge of Public Authorities' Functions under Part I of the Freedom of Information Act 2000, issued under s.45) (Section 45 Code of Practice); and
- in relation to records management (the Lord Chancellor's Code of Practice on the Management of Records, issued under s.46).

The codes are available at **www.justice.gov.uk/information-access-rights/foi-guidance-for-practitioners/code-of-practice**. The Information Commissioner (pursuant to his powers under FOIA, ss.47 and 48) has also published a number of guidance notes (available on the ICO website: **www.ico.gov.uk**), to assist public authorities in dealing with various aspects of the FOIA. The Ministry of Justice also publishes a number of useful guidance notes for practitioners, covering procedural matters as well as advice on how to handle specific types of requests, which are available at **www.justice.gov.uk**).

Dealing with a request – initial considerations

It is recommended that a public authority acknowledges receipt of all requests received (or at least those that cannot fully and quickly be responded to), to inform applicants that the request is being dealt with and also as means of keeping track of the progress of compliance with the request. All requests should also as a matter of course be logged by a public authority on receipt for monitoring purposes.

On receipt of a request for information the public authority should:

- *Ensure that the request is a valid request* (see **3.2.2** under 'Formality of request').
- *Consider whether the request is specific enough for the public authority to respond to it:* If a request does not describe the information required in sufficient detail, a public authority may ask for further information or clarification to enable it to respond to the request. If the public authority requests further information from the applicant in order to clarify or identify and locate the information requested, the time limit for compliance (see 'Timescale for response' below) will not commence unless and until the date the further information is received from the applicant (FOIA, ss.1(3) and 10(6)).

    If, once initial assistance has been provided, the applicant is still unable to describe the information requested, or focus the request, in a way that would enable a public authority to identify and locate it, a public authority is not expected to seek further clarification and should just disclose what it can and then explain in a refusal letter why it cannot take the request further.

- *Determine whether or not it holds the information requested*: This is considered in **3.2.1** and **3.2.2**.
- *Assess whether complying with the request could exceed the 'appropriate limit'* (see below, 'Appropriate limit').
- *Consider whether the request is a repeated request for the same or similar information* (see below, 'Repeated requests').
- *Consider whether the request is vexatious* (see below, 'Vexatious requests').
- *Consult with third parties*: As a matter of good practice, a public authority should consult with third parties related to, or with an interest in, the information requested, as to disclosure or whether any exemptions apply, and whether additional explanatory materials should accompany the information to be disclosed (Section 45 Code of Practice, Part IV, paras.25–30). For example, if information is held about a contractor and disclosure could be prejudicial to the commercial interests of the contractor, the public authority will need to consult the contractor for its views on the nature and degree of harm to its commercial interests in order to consider whether the information is exempt under s.43(2) of the FOIA.
- *Consider whether a fee is payable* (see **3.2.3** under 'Fees notices').

Appropriate limit

Under s.12 of FOIA, a public authority is not obliged to comply with a request where it estimates that the cost of complying with the request would exceed the 'appropriate limit' (see **3.2.3** under 'Information requests'). In estimating the cost of complying with the request, a public authority is only entitled to take into account the costs which it reasonably expects to incur in relation to the following permitted activities (Permitted Activities):

- determining whether the information is held (e.g. costs associated with making internal enquiries to establish if the information is held);
- locating the information or a document containing it (e.g. costs associated with searching for the information);
- retrieving the information or a document containing it (e.g. costs associated with recovering documents from off-site storage); and
- extracting the information from a document containing it (e.g. costs associated with writing a report to extract information from a database).

In carrying out the cost estimate, a public authority can use a rate of £25 per hour for staff time incurred in carrying out the Permitted Activities (Fees Regulations, reg.4(3)). This means that if a public authority estimates that it would take more than 18 or (in the case of central government departments and other public authorities listed in Part 1, Sched.1 to the FOIA) 24 hours of staff time to carry out the Permitted Activities, the request need not be complied with.

A public authority cannot therefore take into account the time associated with reviewing the information to identify whether any exemptions apply, considering the exemptions or redacting exempt information from documents before disclosing them as these are not Permitted Activities under reg.4(3) (see the *Chief Constable of South Yorkshire Police* v. *Information Commissioner* [2011] EWHC 44 (Admin)). Nor can a public authority rely on s.12 where it has already undertaken the Permitted Activities (see *All Party Parliamentary Group on Extraordinary Rendition* v. *Information Commissioner and Ministry of Defence* [2011] UKUT 153 (AAC); [2011] 2 Info LR 75), although where it estimates at the outset of a search that it can complete the search within the appropriate limit and subsequently discovers that it cannot, it can take into account the time searching up to the appropriate limit when refusing the request (see *Quinn* v. *the Information Commissioner* (EA/2006/0010, 15 November 2006)).

Where two or more requests 'relate, to any extent, to the same or similar information' and are made by the same person or by people who appear to be acting in concert together, a public authority can aggregate the requests for the purpose of estimating whether the cost of complying with the requests would exceed the appropriate limit. This is provided that the requests have been received within a period of 60 working days (Fees Regulations, reg.5). This therefore prevents an applicant from making a series of related requests separately within a three-month period in order to try to avoid the appropriate limit. For more guidance on how requests can be aggregated and on applying s.12 generally, see the Information Commissioner's guidance: *Requests Where the Cost of Compliance with a Request Exceeds the Appropriate Limit*, version 1 (ICO, March 2012).

Where a public authority does not wish to comply with a request which it estimates would exceed the appropriate limit, it must issue a refusal notice (see below, 'Refusal notices'). Although there is no obligation to provide the applicant with details of the cost estimate, it may assist the applicant to do so. Also, as the public authority has a duty to provide advice and assistance, when issuing a refusal notice it should consider indicating what, if any, information can be provided within the appropriate limit or advising on how the request can be refined or re-focused (see Section 45 Code of Practice, Part II, para.14)

Vexatious requests

Where an applicant makes a vexatious request, a public authority is not obliged to comply with it (FOIA, s.14(1)). Unhelpfully the term 'vexatious' is not defined in the FOIA which has caused public authorities some uncertainty. To assist public authorities, the Information Commissioner has published guidance (*When Can a Request Be Considered Vexatious or Repeated?*, version 5 (ICO, June 2012)) which advises that public authorities should ask themselves the following questions, taking into account the context and history of the request:

- Could the request fairly be seen as obsessive?
- Is the request harassing the authority or causing distress to staff?
- Would complying with the request impose a significant burden in terms of expense and distraction?

- Is the request designed to cause disruption or annoyance?
- Does the request lack any serious purpose or value?

While it is advisable to apply the guiding questions above, public authorities should also ask themselves whether, aside from those questions and looking at matters in the round, the request could be considered vexatious: see *Graham* v. *Information Commissioner* (EA/2011/0133 and EA/2011/0134); [2012] 1 Info LR 121 at para.12, where the Tribunal stated that:

> the word 'vexatious' is an ordinary English word in everyday usage. While the Information Commissioner may have developed his own guidance with respect to this matter; from the perspective of the tribunal the common sense application of the ordinary meaning of the word to the actual circumstances of an individual case must be the correct approach to adopt. The Oxford English Dictionary provides useful guidance as to the meanings of vexatious which may be summarised as 'tending to cause trouble or harassment by unjustified interference'.

There have been a number of Information Tribunal and court decisions relating to the use of s.14 and the principles which apply. These were summarised by the First-tier Tribunal (Information Rights) in the case of *Ward* v. *Information Commissioner* (EA/2009/0093, 25 May 2010) at para.22 (see also *Rigby* v. *Information Commissioner and Blackpool, Fylde and Wyre Hospitals NHS Trust* (EA/2009/0103, 10 June 2010); [2011] 1 Info LR 643):

- Section 14(1) is concerned with whether the request is vexatious in terms of the effect of the request on the public authority, and not whether the applicant is vexatious.
- In the absence of a definition of 'vexatious' in the FOIA, it must be assumed that Parliament intended the term to be given its ordinary meaning. By its ordinary meaning, the term refers to activity that 'is likely to cause distress or irritation, literally to vex a person to whom it is directed'.
- The focus of the question is on the likely effect of the activity or behaviour. Is the request likely to vex?
- For the request to be vexatious, there must be no proper or justified cause for it.
- It is not only the request itself that must be examined, but also its context and history. A request which, when taken in isolation, is quite benign, may show its vexatious quality only when viewed in context. That context may include other requests made by the applicant to that public authority (whether complied with or refused), the number and subject matter of the requests, as well as the history of other dealings between the applicant and the public authority. The effect a request will have may be determined as much, or indeed more, by that context as by the request itself. This is in marked contrast to other types of FOIA appeals where the Tribunal is said to be strictly applicant and motive blind.
- The standard for establishing that a request is vexatious should not be set too high.

In one instance, the Tribunal has also found s.14(1) of the FOIA to apply based on the burdensome cost of complying with the request: see *Independent Police Complaints Commission* v. *Information Commissioner* (EA/2011/0222, 6 September 2011).

Where a public authority determines that a request is vexatious, it must issue a refusal notice advising the applicant of this fact (see below, 'Refusal notices') within 20 working days, unless a previous request from the same applicant was refused on the grounds it was vexatious and it is not reasonable for the public authority to issue another refusal notice (FOIA, s.17(6)).

Repeated requests

A public authority is not obliged to comply with a request for information to the extent that the applicant has previously made the same or a substantially similar request within a reasonable period of time (FOIA, s.14(2)). The Information Commissioner has indicated that what is a reasonable period of time will depend on the circumstances of the case, including how likely it is that the information will change.[14] If a public authority refuses to comply with a repeated request it must issue a refusal notice within 20 working days (see below, 'Refusal notices') unless a previous request from the same applicant was refused on the grounds it was repeated and it is not reasonable for the public authority to issue another refusal notice (FOIA, s.17(6)).

Nature of response

If, having taken into account the initial considerations, a public authority is required to deal with the information request, the general principle of the FOIA is that any person making a request for information to a public authority is entitled:

(a)   to be informed in writing by the public authority whether or not it holds information of the description specified in the request (the duty to 'confirm or deny') (FOIA, s.1(1)(a) and (6)); and

(b)   if that is the case, to have that information communicated to him (FOIA, s.1(1)(b)),

in each case in the timescale set out in 'Timescale for response', and in the format set out in 'The form of the response', both later in this section.

However, each of these rights to information is subject to a number of exemptions set out in Part II of the FOIA (see **Chapters 4** and **5**) (FOIA, s.2). A public authority can therefore be exempt from the duty to confirm or deny it holds the information where to do so may reveal exempt information. For example, if a request is made for particular information about an individual, merely confirming that it is held may

---

[14]   *When Can a Request Be Considered Vexatious or Repeated?*, version 5 (ICO, June 2012).

disclose information which is exempt under s.40 of the FOIA.[15] If a public authority is exempt from the duty to confirm or deny then it need not consider the application of exemptions to the information itself. Where the public authority is exempt from the duty to confirm or deny or from the duty to communicate information, it must however explain this in a refusal notice (as set out in 'Refusal notices' later in this section).

Timescale for response

Public authorities must respond to a request promptly and in any event no later than 20 working days following the date of receipt of the request (or any further clarification or information required in order to identify or locate the information) (FOIA, ss.1(3) and 10(1) and (6)).

Where a fee is payable and a public authority issues a fees notice (see above, 'Fees notices'), then the public authority must still comply with the request within 20 working days, but the time period between the date when the fees notice was issued and the date the fee was paid can be disregarded (FOIA, s.10(2)).The timescales for complying with a request can only be extended in one situation which is when a public authority requires additional time to consider the public interest test in relation to a qualified exemption (FOIA, s.10(3)) (for details of the public interest test, see **Chapter 5**). In these circumstances, the public authority can extend the timescales by a reasonable time. The Information Commissioner has however advised that he considers this to be longer than a further 20 working days[16] (a maximum of 40 working days in total). If the timescales are extended for these reasons, the public authority must still issue a refusal notice identifying the qualified exemption(s) in question and provide an estimate of the timescales for reaching a decision on the public interest test.[17]

The Freedom of Information (Time for Compliance with Request) Regulations 2004, SI 2004/3364 (Time Regulations), made pursuant to s.10(4) and (5) of the FOIA, which came into effect on 1 January 2005, allow certain public authorities a longer maximum period of time than is normally provided to comply with information requests in the following circumstances:

- where the information is held outside the UK a public authority must respond to the request within 60 working days following the date of receipt of the request (Time Regulations, reg.6);
- information requests to a public records office in relation to information wholly or partly contained in a public record (i.e. information transferred to the

---

[15] See, for example, *London Borough of Camden (Council)* (FS50176463, 3 March 2009).
[16] See the ICO's *Guide to Freedom of Information*: **www.ico.gov.uk/for_organisations/ freedom_of_information/guide.aspx**.
[17] See the ICO's *Guide to Freedom of Information*: **www.ico.gov.uk/for_organisations/ freedom_of_information/guide.aspx**.

National Archives by another public authority) must be complied with within 30 working days following the date of receipt of the request (Time Regulations, reg.4);

- where the information must be obtained from a member of the armed forces on active operation, a public authority must apply to the Information Commissioner for an extension of time (which will normally be no more than 60 working days following the date of receipt of the request) and must then respond within the specified time (Time Regulations, reg.5); and
- information requests to the governing body of a maintained school or a maintained nursery school must be complied with within 60 working days following the date of receipt or the 20th working day following the date of receipt, disregarding any working day which is not a school day, whichever is the earlier (Time Regulations, reg.3). The same provisions were extended to Academies from 18 November 2010 by the Freedom of Information (Time for Compliance with Request) Regulations 2010, SI 2010/2768.

However, in each of these circumstances, the extension of time granted to public authorities to comply is subject to the overriding obligation to comply promptly with all information requests.

The period of time within which a public authority must respond to a request for information commences on the day after the date of receipt of the request for information. In effect, this is the date that the request is received by any person within or on behalf of the public authority, and not necessarily the date when the request is received by the authority's nominated FOIA officer or the appropriate person for dealing with the request. Therefore, the public authority should ensure that it has in place an adequate system to ensure that all requests for information are promptly identified and passed to the relevant FOIA officer (or appropriate person) as quickly as possible. It is also good practice to ensure that there is a back-up system to deal with requests in the event that the nominated officer, or any other addressee of a request for information, is absent, including use of 'out of office' email notifications which redirect an applicant to an alternative contact. In this situation the Information Commissioner will not regard a request as received until the applicant has redirected his or her request to the alternative contact (see *Freedom of Information Act Awareness Guidance No.11: Time for Compliance*, version 2 (ICO, September 2008)).

If a request has been transferred from, or referred by, another public authority, the request will be deemed to be received by the public authority on the date that it actually receives the transferred request (i.e. ignoring the period of time in which the transferring public authority received and considered the request) (Section 45 Code of Practice, Part III, para.22).

The form of the response

When providing the requested information to the applicant, a public authority must as far as is reasonably practicable give effect to the applicant's preference as to the form in which he or she would like the information communicated to him or her. This, however, only applies where the applicant expresses a preference for a copy of the information, the opportunity to inspect a record containing the information or the provision of a summary or digest of the information (FOIA, s.11(1)). A decision by the First-tier Tribunal (Information Rights) in *Innes* v. *Information Commissioner* (EA/2011/0095, 26 August 2011) in relation to a public authority's duty under s.11(1) confirms that the duty does not however extend to making the information available in a particular electronic format, e.g. in the form of a Microsoft Excel document.

In considering whether or not it is reasonable to comply with the applicant's preference, the public authority must consider all the relevant circumstances, including the cost (FOIA, s.11(2)). For example, if the amount of work required to provide the information in the form requested would be excessive, or if creating the specified form may damage the original document, or the information is already publicly available and accessible to the applicant in a different form, it may be unreasonable to provide it in the requested form. If it is unreasonable, the public authority must state why, and provide the requested information in a form that is reasonable in the circumstances (FOIA, s.11(3) and (4)).

It may be sensible for public authorities to contact the applicant to determine whether the proposed alternative form is appropriate to him or her, especially if the cost of providing his or her preferred form is likely to be expensive, and also to explain the options available for providing the information.

Refusal notices

If a public authority is not obliged to comply with a request for information because either an exemption under Part II of the FOIA applies or one of the procedural grounds for refusing applies (the cost exceeds the appropriate limit or it is a repeated or vexatious request) then the public authority must explain this in a written refusal notice to the applicant. A refusal notice also needs to be issued where the public authority is exempt from its duty to confirm or deny that the information is held.

The refusal notice must state that the public authority is exempt from complying with all or the relevant part of the request, specify the exemption or procedural limitation relied upon and the reason(s) why it believes the exemption or limitation applies, if it is not otherwise apparent (FOIA, s.17(1)). If a request has been refused on the grounds of a qualified exemption, the refusal notice must also state the public authority's reasons for concluding that the public interest in withholding the information outweighs the public interest in disclosure (FOIA, s.17(3)). The duty to give reasons in these circumstances and the obligation to explain why the relevant exemption applies, however, will not apply if this itself would involve disclosure of exempt information (FOIA, s.17(4)).

Any refusal notice should also give details of the public authority's FOIA complaints policy, and the applicant's right to appeal to the Information Commissioner (FOIA, s.17(7)).

The Information Commissioner has produced guidance to assist public authorities when they are issuing and drafting refusal notices. This sets out in practical terms how each of the requirements of s.17 can be met and what the Information Commissioner will expect public authorities to include in refusal notices. It also includes good practice examples of refusal notices which can be issued in various different situations (see *Writing a Refusal Notice*, version 2.1 (ICO, July 2010) and *Refusing a Request: How to Issue a Refusal Notice*, version 1 (ICO, July 2009)).

The refusal notice must be issued to the applicant within 20 working days of the request. This applies even if a qualified exemption applies and the public authority requires additional time to consider the public interest test, although a further refusal notice will also be required within a maximum further period of 20 working days (see **3.2.4** under 'Timescale for response'). Where the public authority is refusing the request on the grounds that it is repeated or vexatious and has previously refused a request from the applicant on these grounds and it would be unreasonable to do so again, the public authority does not need to issue a further refusal notice (see above, 'Vexatious requests' and 'Repeated requests') (FOIA, s.17(6)).

3.2.5   What if the applicant is not satisfied with a response?

Chapter 10 considers the procedure for making complaints to a public authority under the FOIA, and the appeals process to the Information Commissioner if such complaints are not handled to the applicant's satisfaction.

3.3   PERSONAL INFORMATION

Under the FOIA, access to personal information by an individual who is the subject of the information is subject to an absolute exemption (see **4.5.7**) (FOIA, ss.2 and 40) as the request is instead regarded as a request for access to personal data made under s.7 of the DPA. This section, therefore, summarises how a person may obtain access to information about himself or herself. For more detail about the DPA and its relationship with the FOIA, see also **Chapter 8**.

3.3.1 Data Protection Act 1998

Background

The DPA provides a legal framework for the handling of 'personal data'. Personal data are defined at s.1(1) of the DPA as any data relating to a living individual who can be identified from such data or from such data and other information which is in the possession of, or is likely to come into the possession of, the data controller. The definition includes any expression of opinion about the individual and any indications of the data controller or any other person in respect of the individual.

However, despite being in effect since 24 October 1998, the scope of the definition continues to cause problems and the case law on its interpretation continues to grow. These problems commonly occur when a public authority who is a data controller[18] of personal data has to deal with a request for those personal data either from the subject of the personal data or from another person making a request for the data under the FOIA. More detail about what constitutes 'personal data' and case law on the definition is at **8.3.1**.

What information can be accessed?

Under s.7 of the DPA, an individual has a right of access to personal data about him or her which are 'processed' by a 'data controller' (both as defined in s.1(1) of the DPA) and to be told certain other information relating to the 'processing' of his or her personal data. 'Processing' is given a wide definition in the DPA,[19] including merely holding the relevant personal data. A 'data controller' is the person who determines the purposes for and the manner in which any particular personal data are to be processed (DPA, s.1(1)). Persons (other than employees) who only process data on behalf of a data controller are defined as 'data processors' (DPA, s.1(1)) and have no obligation under the DPA to respond to an access request, but should refer the request to the proper data controller.

The right of access under s.7 is, however, subject to a number of important exemptions listed in Part 4 of the DPA ('non-disclosable data' in the flowchart at Figure 3.2), such as the exemption from s.7 where this is required for the purposes of safeguarding national security (DPA, s.28), or to avoid infringing parliamentary privilege (DPA, s.35A), or where information is available to the public by or under any enactment (DPA, s.34). Some of these other enactments are considered in **3.3.2**.

Some of the exemptions from s.7 are only partial, such as the exemptions to the obligation to disclose certain types of personal data relating to social work, health and education,[20] which in general exempt disclosure of the personal data where the

---

[18] As defined in s.1(1) of the DPA.

[19] DPA, s.1(1)

[20] Section 30 of the DPA, as detailed in the relevant orders (the Data Protection (Subject Access Modification) (Social Work) Order 2000, SI 2000/415 as amended, the Data Protection (Subject Access Modification) (Health) Order 2000, SI 2000/413 and the Data Protection (Subject Access Modification) (Education) Order 2000, SI 2000/414).

disclosure would cause serious harm to the physical or mental health or condition of the applicant or any other person.

Under the DPA, before the FOIA came into force, only limited manual records fell within the scope of personal data and generally personal information held within unstructured manual filing systems fell outside the scope of a request made under s.7.[21] However the introduction of all manual records held by a public authority within the scope of personal data (DPA, s.1(1)(e)), through amendments introduced by s.68 of the FOIA, required some rather specific provisions to reflect the time and cost potentially involved in a public authority dealing with requests for unstructured personal data. As such a new s.9A of the DPA was introduced (FOIA, s.69) providing that a public authority is not obliged to comply with a request made under s.7 in relation to any unstructured personal data where the authority estimates that the cost of complying with the request in relation to the unstructured manual data would exceed the appropriate limit (being 'exempt unstructured manual data' in the flowchart at Figure 3.2).

The estimate for these purposes is calculated in the same way as the estimate carried out under s.12 of the FOIA and in accordance with the Fees Regulations (see **3.2.4** 'Appropriate limit').

The request

A request can be made by any individual or, in the case of a child, a parent or guardian or any other person with parental responsibility for that child on his or her behalf (see Children Act 1989, s.3), whether or not they are UK or EU citizens or resident, and regardless of the purpose of the application. The DPA does not state at what age a child can exercise his or her rights under the DPA, and so the common law on the capacity of the child as ruled by the House of Lords in *Gillick* v. *West Norfolk and Wisbech Area Health Authority* [1986] AC 112 has to be considered (this case concerned capacity of a child to consent to medical treatment, but the subsequent test of maturity and understanding, or 'Gillick competence' test, can be applied to other situations).

Certain other individuals also have a right of access to personal data on behalf of a data subject, including those with authority to conduct the affairs of a data subject, such as guardians or trustees appointed under the Mental Health Act 1983.

The subject access request must be made in writing, which includes requests by letter, fax or email. The request need not be complied with until the appropriate fee is paid to the data controller and the data controller is satisfied as to the identity of the person making the request (see further below). In addition, the data controller can refer back to the data subject if the request is not made in sufficient detail to enable the data controller to identify the personal data that the controller may or may not be processing.

---

[21] See definition of 'data' in s.1(1) of the DPA and *Durant* v. *Financial Services Authority* [2003] EWCA Civ 1746.

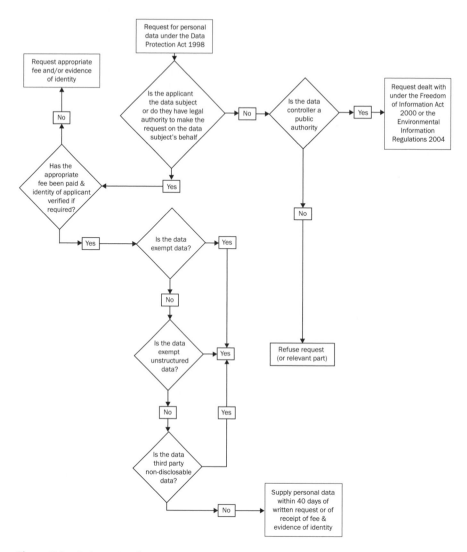

Figure 3.2 Data protection access

As with all requests discussed in this chapter, the applicant for the information, here being personal data, will have a greater chance of succeeding if the request is as specific as possible. In general the courts, in determining whether a holder of information properly exercised its obligations under the relevant statutory regime, are not willing to support the use of the relevant regime for general applications or 'fishing expeditions'. (See *Durant* v. *Financial Services Authority* [2003] EWCA Civ 1746; *Johnson* v. *Medical Defence Union Ltd* [2004] EWHC 2509 (Ch) and *Smith* v. *Lloyds TSB Bank plc* [2005] EWHC 246 (Ch).)

There is no legal requirement for the request to be sent to any particular individual or officer of a data controller. However, if the data controller is notified to the ICO, then the notification details in the public register (accessible online at **www.ico.gov.uk**) will include the contact details for the data controller's data protection contact. Where the data subject has received a fair processing notice, then this may have given the contact details of the data controller's data protection representative, if there is/was one. Otherwise a request could be sent for the attention of the data protection officer at the data controller.

Fees

The DPA provides that a data controller is entitled to charge for responding to a subject access request, subject to certain limits (Data Protection (Subject Access) (Fees and Miscellaneous Provisions) Regulations 2000, SI 2000/191 as amended). Data subjects making standard subject access requests may only be charged a maximum of £10, but this can rise to £50 for access to certain medical and education records (these are defined terms in the DPA, s.1(1) and Sched.6).

The response

The Information Commissioner has published a number of useful guidance notes and practice notes, including a new *Guide to Data Protection*, to assist data controllers in dealing with subject access requests (see **www.ico.gov.uk**).

Under s.7(1) an applicant is entitled to the following (unless an exemption applies):

- to be informed whether any personal data of which that applicant is the data subject are being processed by or on behalf of that data controller;
- if that is the case, to be provided with a description of:

  - the personal data of which that individual is the data subject;
  - the purposes for which they are being or are to be processed;
  - the recipients or classes of recipients to whom they are or may be disclosed;

- to have communicated to him or her in an intelligible form:

  - the information constituting any personal data of which that individual is the data subject; and
  - any information available to the data controller as to the source of those data; and

- to be informed of the logic involved in any decision taking where the process-ing of personal data about the individual is by automatic means for the purpose of evaluating matters relating to him or her such as, for example, performance at work, creditworthiness, reliability or conduct, and this has constituted or is likely to constitute the sole basis for any decision significantly affecting him or her.

Data controllers have up to 40 days in nearly all cases to comply with a subject access request (DPA, s.7(10)). The time limit for compliance will not commence until any fee payable in connection with the information request has been paid (DPA, s.7(2)(b) and the data controller has received such further information as it reasonably requires in order to satisfy itself of the identity of the person making the request (DPA, s.7(3)).

Provided the disclosure by the data controller complies with the requirements of DPA, s.7, then there is no prescribed format for any disclosures under the DPA.

What if the data subject is not satisfied with a response?

The data subject has rights under s.7(9) of the DPA to apply to a court to obtain a court order ordering disclosure by the data controller. Alternatively, the data subject can at any time lodge a complaint with the Information Commissioner, who may then use his powers to commence an investigation under the DPA to request the data controller to give its reasons for not fulfilling the subject access request. Failure to respond or an inadequate response to the Information Commissioner may lead to further enforcement steps being taken by the Information Commissioner under the DPA.

3.3.2   Other access to personal information

Parentage data

For the purposes of the flowchart in Figure 3.1, 'parentage data' means data relating to the parentage of an applicant or other person under the Human Fertilisation and Embryology Act 1990 (HFEA), the Adoption Act 1976 or the Adoption and Children Act 2002.

Access under the HFEA is as follows. The Human Fertilisation and Embryology Authority (the Authority) maintains a register of information relating to:

- the provision of treatment services (as defined in the HFEA) for any identifiable individuals so treated;
- the keeping of gametes of any identifiable individuals or of an embryo taken from any identifiable woman; or
- details of any identifiable individual who was or may have been born as a result of the provision of treatment services (HFEA, s.31).

Any person aged 18 or over may, by notice to the Authority, make a request for any information held by the Authority on him or her, which the Authority must disclose if the person was or may have been born as a result of treatment services (HFEA, s.31(4)). The information must include information as to the true genetic parents of the applicant, where requested. Up until 1 April 2005, the Authority could not be required to give information on the identity of any gametes donor or persons from whom an embryo had been taken. However, such information will be disclosable to any persons born as a result of treatment services provided on or after this date (Human Fertilisation and Embryology Authority (Disclosure of Donor Information) Regulations 2004, SI 2004/1511, reg.2(3)).

In addition, a person under 18 may, by notice to the Authority, inform it of a person the applicant wishes to marry (the 'intended spouse' in the terms of the HFEA) and request that the Authority confirm that the applicant and the intended spouse are not or not likely to be related. Before responding, the Authority must ensure that the minor has had the opportunity to receive proper counselling about the implications of the Authority complying with the request.

Some of the information relating to treatment services will be held by persons licensed under the HFEA to provide the treatment services. Provisions are included in the HFEA to place restrictions on such licensed persons from disclosing this type of registrable information, with the notable exception of information disclosed on an application for access to health records (HFEA, s.33).

Access under the Adoption Act 1976 is as follows. This continues to apply in respect of information concerning persons adopted before 30 December 2005. As soon as an adoption agency has made an adoption order, it must disclose whatever information it considers appropriate about the adopted child to the adopters, charging them to share this information with the child when appropriate, but no later than the child's 18th birthday (Adoption Agencies Regulations 1983, SI 1983/1964, reg.13A).

In addition, the agency must provide access to its records to certain persons, as set out in the appropriate regulations, including a child's guardian or reporting officer for the purposes of the guardian or officer discharging his or her statutory duties (Adoption Agencies Regulations 1983, SI 1983/1964, reg.15).

For persons adopted on or after 30 December 2005, the procedures under the Adoption and Children Act 2002 apply (ss.56–65). The procedures define a special class of adoption-related data, 'protected information' (Adoption and Children Act 2002, s.54) and include regulations on the disclosure of this protected information (Disclosure of Adoption Information (Post-Commencement Adoptions) Regulations 2005, SI 2005/888; and Access to Information (Post-Commencement Adoptions) (Wales) Regulations 2005, SI 2005/2689).

Birth records must be obtained via the relevant adoption agency, which will obtain the official birth record from the Registrar General and forward it to the adoptee, subject to the regulations on the provision of counselling.[22]

---

[22] Adoption and Children Act 2002, s.79(5) and Part 6 of the relevant Disclosure of Adoption Information (Post-Commencement Adoptions) Regulations 2005, SI 2005/588 or Adoption and Children Act 2002, s.79(5) and Part 6 of the relevant Access to Information (Post-Commencement Adoptions) (Wales) Regulations 2005, SI 2005/2689, with counselling provisions at Part 5.

Having obtained information to enable their birth parents or blood relatives to be traced, adopted persons had no method before 1989 of knowing whether those parents or relatives would welcome contact. For this reason, the Registrar General maintains a register, the Adoption Contact Register. However, this register is not open to inspection or access. Each of the adopted persons who want to contact his or her birth parents or relatives or those parents or relatives must apply to be included in the register. If the Registrar General discovers a match between the parties, he must forward the relevant contact details to the adopted person where the parent or relative has indicated that contact will be welcome; no information is forwarded to the parent or relative other than the knowledge that his or her details have been so forwarded (Adopted Children and Adoption Contact Registers Regulations 2005, SI 2005/924, reg.8).

Medical data

For the purposes of the flowchart in Figure 3.1, 'medical data' means information contained in 'medical reports', as that term is defined in the Access to Medical Reports Act 1988, and data making up a 'health record', as defined in the Access to Health Records Act 1990.

Access under the Access to Medical Reports Act 1988 is as follows. Any person may obtain a copy of a medical report on him or her, which is or has been supplied for employment or insurance purposes by a medical practitioner (Access to Medical Reports Act 1988, s.1). A third party can, for purposes connected with employment or insurance, obtain a medical report only with the consent of the data subject, who can insist that a copy of the report be provided to him or her before it is disclosed to the third party (Access to Medical Reports Act 1988, ss.3 and 4). However, the medical practitioner can withhold the report where its disclosure would be likely to cause serious harm to the physical or mental health of the data subject or any others; would indicate the practitioner's intentions in respect of the data subject; or would reveal information about another person or the identity of a third party who has supplied information for the medical report, unless that third party has consented to the disclosure or was a health professional involved in the care of the individual (Access to Medical Reports Act 1988, s.7).

Access under the Access to Health Records Act 1990 is as follows. Certain representatives of a patient may make an application in writing for the patient's health records to the holder of the record (Access to Health Records Act 1990, s.3). A 'health record' is defined as information relating to the physical or mental health of a patient made by or on behalf of the health professional (as defined in the DPA) in connection with the care of the patient, other than information to which the patient is, or could be but for an exemption, entitled to access under the DPA. However, only those parts of the record made on or after 1 November 1991 are subject to the right of access, together with such earlier parts of the record as are necessary to make the parts made on or after 1 November 1991 intelligible (Access to Health Records Act 1990, ss.1(1), 5(1), 11 and 12(2)). Persons who may make application for access to a health record under the Act include:

- where the record is held in Scotland and the patient is incapable within the meaning of the Adults with Incapacity (Scotland) Act 2000 in relation to making or authorising the application, any person entitled to act on behalf of the patient under that Act (Access to Health Records Act 1990, s.3(1)(e)); or
- where the patient has died, the patient's personal representatives or any person who may have a claim arising out of the patient's death (Access to Health Records Act 1990, s.3(1)(f)).

However, the holder of the records can withhold information that in the holder's opinion the patient would not have expected to have been disclosed (Access to Health Records Act 1990, s.5(3)); or where disclosure would be likely to cause serious harm to the physical or mental health of any individual; or is information relating to or provided by a person other than the patient, who can be identified by that information unless that third party has consented to the disclosure or is a health professional who was involved in the care of a patient (Access to Health Records Act 1990, s.5(1) and (2)).

Disclosure of the health records must be made within 21 days of a request, where the records were created within 40 days of the request, or otherwise within 40 days. If any part of the record is unintelligible without an explanation, this must also be given with the disclosure. The cost of making of copies and postage costs can be charged to the applicant (Access to Health Records Act 1990, s.3(4)).

Criminal records data

Applicants are able to apply to the Criminal Records Bureau (CRB) for access to criminal records for employment purposes under the provisions of the Police Act 1997 (PA). The CRB provides applicants with either a criminal record certificate (CRC) or an enhanced criminal record certificate (ECRC), subject to payment of the relevant fee (Police Act 1997 (Criminal Records) Regulations 2002, SI 2002/233 (as amended), reg.4).

In due course the CRB will also issue criminal conviction certificates (CCCs). CCCs will be issued to any individual making an application (PA, s.112(1) – not yet in force in England and Wales) and will set out details of every conviction of the applicant which is recorded in police records or state there is no conviction, as defined in the Rehabilitation of Offenders Act 1974, other than a spent conviction.

CRCs give details of every relevant matter recorded in central police records against the applicant, or state that there is no such matter (PA, s.113A(3)). A 'relevant matter' means a conviction within the meaning of the Rehabilitation of Offenders Act 1974, including a spent conviction, and a police caution (PA, s.113A(6)). An application must be countersigned by a person registered on a list maintained by the Secretary of State (PA, s.120(1), (4) and (5)) and be accompanied by a statement by the registered person that the certificate is required for an 'exempted question' in respect of an applicant seeking paid or voluntary work or training in an occupation which is exempt from the Rehabilitation of Offenders Act 1974 (PA, s.113(2) and (3)). (An exempted question is a question in relation to which the Rehabilitation of Offenders Act 1974, s.4(2)(a) or (b) (effect of rehabilitation) has been excluded by order of the Secretary of State under the Rehabilitation of Offenders Act 1974, s.4(4) (PA, s.113(4)).) A copy of the certificate will be issued directly to the registered person countersigning the application (PA, s.113(4)).

The Secretary of State may issue an ECRC giving details of a CRC, but also providing additional relevant information on an applicant held by chief police officers of local police forces, including relevant non-conviction information (PA, s.113B(1)–(5)) and information on the lists maintained by the Independent Safeguarding Authority.[23] The additional non-conviction information may concern offences which the applicant is suspected of committing, even though his or her responsibility has not been and cannot be proved. The information must, however, be information which the chief constable is of the opinion might be relevant to the specific position applied for. However, careful consideration must be given as to whether such information ought to be disclosed.[24] An application must be countersigned by a registered person and submitted with a statement that the certificate is required for an exempted question asked in the course of considering the applicant for certain positions, including a 'regulated' or 'controlled' activity within the meaning of the Safeguarding of Vulnerable Groups Act 2006. The certificate will be sent to the registered person together with any additional information the chief officer believes ought to be included (PA, s.113B(6)).

An applicant can apply for a new certificate if the information it contains is inaccurate (PA, s.117). It is an offence for a person, with intent to deceive, to make a false certificate, to alter a certificate, to use a certificate which relates to another

---

[23] The Independent Safeguarding Authority was established by s.1 of the Safeguarding of Vulnerable Groups Act 2006 and is responsible for maintaining a list of individuals barred from engaging in regulated activity with children and vulnerable adults (s.2).

[24] In *R (on the application of X)* v. *Chief Constable of West Midlands* [2004] EWCA Civ 1068, a decision by a chief constable under s.115 of the Police Act 1997 (now repealed) to disclose information that a prospective social worker had been charged with an offence of indecent exposure (even though the Crown Prosecution Service offered no evidence on those charges at trial) was not overruled by the Court of Appeal. The Court of Appeal held that there was no presumption against disclosure in a s.115 case. This case was followed more recently in *R (on the application of John Pinnington)* v. *Chief Constable of Thames Valley Police* [2008] EWHC 1870 (Admin). However, in *R (on the application of L)* v. *Commissioner of Police of the Metropolis* [2009] UKSC 3, the Supreme Court ruled that the 'presumption of disclosure unless there is a good reason for not doing so' upheld in previous case law on ECRCs was wrong. It found that the correct approach for the chief police officer under s.115 of the Police Act 1997 was first to ask whether information is relevant and then to consider carefully whether it ought to be included in an ECRC. In exercising this discretion, the chief police officer must give proper consideration to the applicant's right to a private life balanced against the need to protect children and vulnerable adults. Where doubt is cast on the veracity of information, the applicant should have the opportunity to make representations before it is disclosed. In light of this case, chief police officers must now take a more rigorous approach to considering what constitutes 'relevant information', making sure to give appropriate weight to the applicant's privacy. This was followed in *R (on the application of T)* v. *Greater Manchester Police and Another* [2012] EWHC 147 (Admin).

person in a way which suggests that it relates to himself or herself, or allow a certificate which relates to him or her to be used by another person in a way which suggests that it relates to that other person (PA, s.123(1)).

In 2010 the government carried out a review of the vetting and barring (V&B) scheme which was established under the Safeguarding of Vulnerable Groups Act 2006 and commissioned an independent review into the criminal records regime. The outcome of these reviews[25] has resulted in a number of changes to the criminal records regime and the V&B scheme which are made in the Protection of Freedoms Act 2012,[26] the details of which are outside the scope of this book. It is however anticipated that the CRB and the Independent Safeguarding Authority will be merged into one agency in 2012 to provide a barring and criminal records disclosure service, to be known as the 'Disclosure and Barring Service'.[27] This is an area which is therefore expected to change in the near future.

3.4 ENVIRONMENTAL INFORMATION

The EIR (made under powers set out in (i) s.74 of the FOIA; and (ii) the European Communities Act 1972) also came into force on 1 January 2005 (EIR, reg.1), and broadly grant rights of access to environmental information held by or on behalf of public authorities (including some non-public bodies carrying out a public function). 'Environmental information' (which is defined widely by EIR, reg.2(1)) is exempted from disclosure under s.39 of the FOIA. Therefore, requests for such information, and consideration as to whether or not such information must be disclosed or withheld, must be made under the EIR.

Chapter 9 considers the rights of access granted by the EIR, and how to make and respond to a request for environmental information. It is worth noting that, while the right of access to environmental information and the procedures for making and responding to requests for environmental information under the EIR are similar to those provided by the FOIA, there are some key differences, which are highlighted in **Chapter 9**.

3.5 OTHER STATUTORY RIGHTS OF ACCESS TO PUBLIC AUTHORITY INFORMATION

It should not be forgotten that there are numerous other statutory regimes that give the public rights of access to information held by public authorities. Information available under other Acts of Parliament includes, for example:

---

[25] See *Vetting & Barring Scheme Remodelling Review – Report and Recommendations* (Home Office, February 2011) and *Independent Review of the Criminal Records Regime – Government Response* (Home Office, December 2011).

[26] See Part 5 (ss.64–101) of the Protection of Freedoms Act 2012.

[27] See ss.87 and 88 of the Protection of Freedoms Act 2012.

- public records held at the National Archives (under the Public Records Act 1958);
- registration records relating to rights over land held by local authorities and HM Land Registry (under the Commons Registration Act 1965, Land Charges Act 1972, Local Land Charges Act 1975 and Land Registration Act 2002);
- records of registered intellectual property rights (under the Registered Designs Act 1949, Patents Act 1977 and Trade Marks Act 1994);
- records relating to incorporated companies (under the Companies Act 2006); and
- records regarding licensed premises (under the Licensing Act 2003).

Such legislation may prescribe the form for any requests and the form and time-scales for the public authority response, and may include an appeals procedure, all of which vary from those provided by the FOIA. There is also a great deal of information that is available to the public upon inspection of the relevant records, such as the indices kept for the registrations of births, marriages and deaths in England and Wales kept by the Registrar General or superintendent or other registrars.[28] Access to these inspection-only records can be made under the FOIA.

3.6 ACCESS TO INFORMATION HELD BY EUROPEAN UNION INSTITUTIONS

In addition to information held by public authorities, the European Commission has a track record of ensuring that wherever possible, all European Union information is readily available to citizens of the Union.

The key document to prescribe access to European Union information is Regulation (EC) 1049/2001 regarding public access to European Parliament, Council and Commission documents (OJ L 145/43 31.05.2001). Under the Regulation, the European Parliament, Council and Commission are required to provide the widest possible access to documents held by them (including documents received by them) in all areas of activity of the European Union. As with the FOIA, however, there are a number of exceptions that permit the institutions to refuse access (Regulation (EC) 1049/2001, art.4). The Regulation expressly states that it is without prejudice to copyright in any document, so that an applicant's right to reproduce or exploit released documents may be limited (art.16). For political documents the Regulation includes a public interest test in familiar terms. Each of the institutions has also put in place institution-specific procedures detailing its policies and practices for granting public access to its documents.

In parallel with the UK's later introduction of the EIR, Regulation (EC) 1367/2006 addressing access to environmental information (OJ L 264/13 25.09.2006) came into effect on 28 June 2007. As with the EIR, the definition within the

---

[28] The Births and Deaths Registration Act 1953, ss.30–32; and the Marriage Act 1949, ss.64 and 65; and see the range of online information available from National Archives at **www.national-archives.gov.uk**.

Regulation of 'environmental information' is broad (Regulation (EC) 1367/2006, art.2(d) – identical wording to EIR, reg.2(1)). There is also a presumption of disclosure, with Regulation (EC) 1367/2006 stating that there is an overriding public interest in disclosure where the information requested relates to emissions into the environment.

The European Commission published a Green Paper reviewing the Regulation (COM(2007) 185 final 18 April 2007) in 2007. Since then the Commission has put forward two proposals to amend the Regulation. In April 2008 it first put forward proposals to recast the Regulation (Proposal for a Regulation regarding public access to European Parliament, Council and Commission documents, COM(2008) 229 final 30 April 2008) aimed at improving and streamlining the existing Regulation. This was followed subsequently by a new proposal adopted in March 2011 (Proposal for a Regulation amending Regulation (EC) 1049/2001 regarding public access to European Parliament, Council and Commission documents, COM(2011) 137 final). This second Proposal was put forward in the light of the entry into force of the Lisbon Treaty on 1 December 2009 which extended the public right of access to documents of all of the European Union institutions, bodies, offices and agencies to make the Regulation compliant with the Treaty. The European Parliament amended the Proposal significantly in December 2011 and it continues to be the subject of negotiations between the European Parliament, the Council and the Commission.

3.7 RE-USE OF INFORMATION UNDER THE FOIA

It should be noted that there is a distinction between accessing information from public authorities (and other organisations, depending on the relevant statutory regime) and the re-use of that information by the person who receives it. The statutory rights of access to information discussed in this chapter do not automatically grant recipients of information the right to reproduce or re-use documentation supplied under these statutory regimes. Although the FOIA does not provide for the imposition of restrictions on what a recipient can do with that information, normal rules governing re-use of copyright works still apply. This means that permission to re-use information may still be required from the owner of the copyright, who may or may not be the public authority to whom the FOI request has been made. Charges may also be applied for the re-use of the materials provided in addition to any fees paid (or payable) for the supply of the materials under the FOIA.

3.7.1 PSI Regulations

Directive 2003/98/EC of the European Parliament and of the Council on the re-use of public sector information was implemented in the UK on 1 July 2005 by the Re-use of Public Sector Information Regulations 2005, SI 2005/1515 (PSI Regulations). The PSI Regulations introduced a framework within which members of the public and organisations may request a licence to re-use documents held by a 'public sector body' (subject to certain exclusions) but also entitle the affected public authorities (as not all FOIA public authorities are caught by the PSI Regulations) to charge for the re-use of documentation provided to the public. However, the PSI Regulations have not been widely used as a public authority has to identify documents which it makes available for re-use (PSI Regulations, reg.5(2)).

3.7.2 Government transparency agenda

In the 'The Coalition: our programme for government' (May 2010), the Coalition government set out its policy of greater public sector transparency and identified a number of specific transparency-related commitments, including the establishment of a new 'right to data' so that government datasets could be requested and used by the public; and a commitment to ensure data published by public bodies were published in an open and standardised format, to facilitate re-use (currently online at **www.data.gov.uk**). The implementation of these commitments (the transparency agenda) has to date been achieved largely through government policy alone. However, in the case of local government, the Department for Communities and Local Government published a Code of Recommended Practice for Local Authorities on Data Transparency which came into force in September 2011. The code identifies a number of datasets which local authorities are expected to publish and make available for re-use, where possible under the terms of the Open Government Licence.

3.7.3 Protection of Freedoms Act 2012

A number of changes have been made to the FOIA through the Protection of Freedoms Act 2012 (PFA) which will extend some of the requirements of the transparency agenda to a wider range of public bodies and provide members of the public with a legal right to re-use certain data.

The PFA introduces new provisions which will require all public authorities (unless it is not practicable to do so) to supply certain 'datasets' in an electronic form which is capable of re-use, where an applicant asks for information which forms part of a dataset to be provided electronically (PFA, s.102 and FOIA, s.11(1A)). A dataset is defined in a new s.11(5) of the FOIA.[29] Once a dataset has been made available to one applicant for re-use, a public authority will also be required to

---

[29] A dataset is defined as: 'information comprising a collection of information held in electronic form where all or most of the information in the collection: (a) has been obtained or recorded for the purpose of providing a public authority with information in connection with the provision of a service by the authority or the carrying out of any other function of the authority, (b) is factual information which: (i) is not the product of analysis or interpretation other than calculation, and (ii) is not an official statistic (within the meaning given by section 6(1) of the Statistics and Registration Service Act 2007), and (c) remains presented in a way that (except for the purpose of forming part of the collection) has not been organised, adapted or otherwise materially altered since it was obtained or recorded.'

publish the dataset (and up-to-date versions of it) under its publication scheme for other members of the public to re-use it, unless it is inappropriate for the public authority to do so (FOIA, s.19(2A)).

The FOIA as amended by the PFA further provides that where a public authority is the owner of the intellectual property rights in the 'relevant copyright work' forming all or part of a dataset, it will be required to make the dataset available for re-use in accordance with the terms of a 'specified licence' (FOIA, s.11A and 19(2A)). This licence will be specified by the Secretary of State in a code of practice issued under s.45 of the FOIA. It is anticipated that in many cases this will be in the form of the Open Government Licence and will permit free re-use. However, there are also provisions in the FOIA which will permit a public authority to charge a fee in connection with re-use in accordance with regulations to be made by the Secretary of State with the consent of the Treasury (FOIA, s.11B).

The PFA received Royal Assent on 1 May 2012 but at the time of writing is not yet in force.

3.8 CONCLUSION

Together with existing statutory access regimes, the FOIA has significantly widened the scope of public sector information which is now routinely made available to members of the public through both publication schemes and individual access requests. Since the Coalition government came into power there has also been a considerable increase in the amount of public sector information which is now proactively released, for example by central government departments, local authorities and NHS bodies, as a consequence of the transparency agenda[30] (although the Information Commissioner is expected to shortly make changes to publication scheme guidance to reflect the transparency agenda[31] – see **Chapter 2** for more information). The changes to the FOIA made under the PFA mark a significant new development in the evolution of the FOIA which will now provide a framework for enabling members of the public not only to access but to re-use certain public sector information.

---

[30] See *Memorandum to the Justice Select Committee: Post-legislative Assessment of the Freedom of Information Act 2000* (Ministry of Justice, December 2011) at p.45 (Section G, 'Proactive disclosure and publication schemes, key points').

[31] See *Consultation: Revising Publication Schemes under Sections 19 and 20 of the Freedom of Information Act* (ICO, September 2011) and the *Publication Scheme Plan for 2012/13* (ICO, May 2012).

CHAPTER 4

The absolute exemptions

Liz Fitzsimons, Eversheds LLP

4.1 INTRODUCTION

We are now used to the fact that the FOIA established a new statutory right of access to information, affecting records held by or on behalf of more than 100,000 public authorities across England, Wales and Northern Ireland. Although the legislation has been in force for over seven years, new public authorities continue to be added to the regime, guidance is updated and the law and its application continue to evolve. However, the fundamental core of the FOIA remains unchanged: an information request under the FOIA exercises the statutory right to know and this involves two separate obligations on the public authority: first, to confirm or deny whether the information requested is held; and secondly, if held, to communicate the information requested.

The legislation is not technically retrospective. However, the FOIA applies to records no matter when created or obtained compared to when the FOIA came into force or the public authority became subject to it. The practical impact is therefore that it is retrospective in effect. The FOIA obviously affects a public authority's own internal records but it also affects information from third parties contained in records held by the public authority. This may be proposal documentation submitted by a bidder, or notes made by the authority's staff of information provided by a supplier over the telephone. The FOIA applies to all this information no matter what type of record it is in, irrespective of who owns that information or any copyright in it. Moreover, the right to know is freely available to anyone, anywhere in the world, for any reason and without justification, as a result of which the FOIA is said to be 'applicant blind'. This means that a public authority must take no account of who wants the information requested and why they want it when considering an information request and the identity of the applicant and their reasons should not influence the decision on disclosure. However, in very limited cases noted below, a public authority should ignore its normal approach and actively consider the applicant and their individual circumstances. The right of access is covered in detail in **Chapter 3**.

The starting point to the FOIA therefore is that any records held by a public authority may be requested and, if held, must be disclosed. This obligation is not open ended as it has been recognised that there are many situations where, for a variety of reasons, it would not be appropriate for all information held to be disclosed, for example if such sharing would cause harm or distress, breach third party rights or breach other legal obligations. Thus although the FOIA is applicant blind, it is not impact blind. The main counterbalance to the general obligation to disclose is provided by the exemptions in the FOIA of which there are 23 in total. Each covers a situation where it may not be appropriate for all the requested information to be disclosed.

Responsibility for ensuring that the exemptions are properly used rather than abused, whether deliberately or otherwise, lies with the Information Commissioner, whose office investigates and adjudicates on complaints brought by dissatisfied individuals who have made information requests, referred to here as complainants. Although complainants have a right to complain to the public authority concerned if they are not happy about the handling of their original information request, s.56 of the FOIA prevents civil claims against public authorities for damages for any alleged breach of the FOIA. Instead, s.50 of the FOIA entitles any complainant dissatisfied with a public authority's response to their information request to apply to the Commissioner for a decision as to whether the public authority has dealt with the request in accordance with the FOIA. As there are no procedural requirements for doing so and no fee, a significant number of applications are made. The Commissioner must investigate each application, provided he is satisfied that the complainant has already exhausted the authority's internal complaints process, and that the application is made promptly and is not vexatious. Importantly, a complainant is not at risk over costs if the Commissioner's decision about the treatment of the request is not in the complainant's favour, so there is no downside to bringing a complaint to the Commissioner.

There are further rights of appeal, which in the main are without risk of costs for the complainant. This approach has not been affected by the changes to the appeal process due to the reorganisation of the courts and tribunals system since the last edition of this book. Previously, decision notices could be appealed to the Information Tribunal and then to the High Court, Court of Appeal and House of Lords. Now, appeals are normally to the First-tier Tribunal, then the Upper Tribunal (both in relation to Information Rights) and then the Court of Appeal before the Supreme Court (see **Chapter 10** for a detailed explanation of the enforcement and appeal process). For those new to this area, decision notices are indicated by a case reference starting FS50[unique number] for cases under the FOIA and are made by the Commissioner; judgments of the former Information Tribunal and now of the First-tier Tribunal can be distinguished from those of the Upper Tribunal by their case references (indicated for the First-tier by EA/[year]/[case number], or for the Upper by [year] UKUT [case number] (AAC [signifying the relevant Chamber])). For ease, in **Chapters 4** and **5**, decisions by the previous Information Tribunal or current First-tier Tribunal are referred to as a 'Tribunal' decision.

In summary, taken as whole, the FOIA regime is very appeal-friendly and very accessible to individuals. It provides no disincentive to challenging public authorities who refuse to disclose information and it is clear from the number of s.50 applications made that complainants continue to be more than willing and able to exercise this right.

Moreover, a review of Information Commissioner decision notices and Information Tribunal judgments indicates that these bodies will readily order disclosure in the absence of compelling evidence justifying the use of exemptions. Commentary and analysis of all the exemptions is set out below, and in **Chapter 5**, with references to key Information Commissioner decision notices and appeal judgments where relevant.

Readers wishing to keep fully up to date with information on the latest cases on the FOIA are referred to the practical journal *Freedom of Information* (**www.foij.com**).

4.2 THIRD PARTY INFORMATION

As noted above, the FOIA applies to all information which a public authority holds regardless of its provider or ownership. Private sector bodies dealing with public authorities should therefore be aware of the impact of the FOIA in relation to their dealings with the public sector. The aims of the FOIA were and remain to improve transparency and understanding and to drive sound, accountable decision making and expenditure of public monies, being focused on the acts and omissions of public authorities accordingly. However, the evolution of use of the FOIA over time has increasingly shown that there is at the same time a growing interest in understanding more about those private bodies working with the public authorities and the basis on which those private bodies operate and contract.

This development has serious implications for the private sector. Third party owners or providers of information requested from a public authority under the FOIA cannot take action under the FOIA against a public authority in respect of a disclosure decision with which they disagree. Moreover, unless they are a complainant unhappy with treatment of their own information request, they have no right to apply to the Information Commissioner for a decision. Even worse, there is no legal obligation on public authorities under the FOIA to inform such third parties about an information request for data from or about them, whether before disclosing such information or at all. A third party might never know that their information has been requested and disclosed. With the recent changes under the Protection of Freedoms Act 2012 and the government's transparency agenda, the tensions over information access between public and private sector look set to continue.

Assessment of the exemptions, and the decision about whether or not to apply them, is entirely for the public authority. The Code of Practice issued under s.45 of the FOIA on the discharge of public authority functions under Part I of the FOIA (originally issued by the then Lord Chancellor in November 2004 and which is currently being updated) deals with third party consultation in Part IV and makes it clear that consultation is recommended good practice, but normally there is no requirement to consult. Even in cases where the Code suggests it is necessary to do so, it is important to remember that the Code is not legally binding. As we will see below, increasingly the Commissioner is enforcing an approach originally set out in a Tribunal judgment that a public authority cannot assume arguments on behalf of a third party to justify non-disclosure of its information, *Derry City Council* v. *Information Commissioner* (EA/2006/0014, 11 December 2006); [2011] 1 Info LR 1105. Accordingly, not only has an authority no obligation to consult the third party but, if it fails to do so, unless it has grounds of its own to justify non-disclosure, it cannot normally put forward third party arguments for non-disclosure instead. There appears to be some recognition that this may leave such third parties unfairly exposed as a result. In this regard the Upper Tribunal confirmed (when considering arguments about the late reliance on exemptions) that 'As to third parties, the Commissioner must always be alert to their interests if they are not being protected by the complainant or the public authority' (discussed further below): see the joined appeals in *Department for Environment, Food and Rural Affairs* v. *Information Commissioner and Birkett* [2011] UKUT 39 (AAC) and *Information Commissioner* v. *Home Office* [2011] UKUT 17 (AAC); [2011] 1 Info LR 1533. However, this may be cold comfort to the private sector. **Chapter 6** deals with the FOIA implications for the private sector in more detail.

Ideally, third parties providing information to a public authority will have secured a contractual obligation from the authority to consult the third party promptly about any request for their information and to do so prior to any proposed disclosure. However, public authorities are generally nervous of fettering their statutory discretion in relation to compliance with the FOIA and may well have resisted such attempts. In many cases, at best, there may be an obligation on a public authority to use reasonable endeavours to consult in advance of disclosure. Whether consultation results from such a contractual mechanism or otherwise, a common theme will be the very limited time which a third party will normally be given to respond to such consultation, often, at most, five working days to enable the public authority to respond fully within the 20 working day deadline.

The best advice to a third party is two-pronged. First, it must do everything possible to ensure the public authority tells it promptly when a relevant request comes in. Secondly, the third party must be prepared to turn around its response to the consultation quickly and effectively. The key to risk management will be a close working relationship between the third party and public authority involving mutual respect and understanding. This is needed for each to understand the other's position, sensitivities and the limitations on what it can and cannot do. This is essential in order to balance the public authority's need to comply with its statutory duty and the third party's legitimate interest in properly protecting its own information, specifically to allow it to mitigate the risk of its sensitive information finding its way into the public domain. If there is disagreement over a document, then the ultimate sanction for the third party would be an injunction preventing disclosure.

Without some kind of early warning system, public authorities may simply disclose information without the third party knowing. In this case, there are only really two ways to go: either the third party takes it on the chin, or it can sue for damages on the ground that the information was disclosed unlawfully, although there are limited situations in which this will be possible. This approach, of course, is a long way short of satisfactory, not least because litigation carries uncertainty of outcome and further cost. Accordingly, it would be rare for it to arise.

4.3 TYPES OF EXEMPTION

There are two types of exemption to the right of access, described in s.2(1) and (2) of the FOIA. These are:

(a)   absolute exemptions; and
(b)   qualified exemptions.

The exemptions in (b), above, are known as qualified exemptions because they can only apply where the public interest permits (see **Chapter 5** for an analysis of the public interest test).

Of the 23 exemptions in the FOIA, only nine are absolute in whole or part. These are listed in s.2(3). Section 37 was previously wholly qualified but became partially absolute with effect from 19 January 2011 by virtue of amendments made by the Constitutional Reform and Governance Act 2010. The absolute exemptions are:

1.   information accessible to the applicant by other means (s.21);
2.   security matters (s.23);
3.   court records (s.32);
4.   parliamentary privilege (s.34);
5.   prejudice to the effective conduct of public affairs (only where the relevant public authority is either the House of Commons or the House of Lords) (s.36);
6.   communications with Her Majesty and the awarding of honours (except where the exemption is qualified, see **Chapter 5**) (s.37);
7.   personal information (except, to a limited extent, where the exemption is qualified, see **Chapter 5**) (s.40);
8.   confidential information (s.41); and
9.   other legal prohibitions on disclosure (s.44).

The qualified exemptions are examined in **Chapter 5**.

4.4 APPLYING THE EXEMPTIONS

Whenever a public authority refuses to disclose information, it is required to explain why. This means citing the relevant exemptions and justifying their use in the particular context of the request, as to both facts and the date of the request, although there are limited exceptions to this where facts and events following the date of request can properly be considered.

Exemptions may generally be used in two separate situations. First, an exemption may be used in relation to s.1(1)(a) of the FOIA in order to neither confirm nor deny that information is held in response to an information request. The FOIA normally requires public authorities to confirm or deny in writing whether they hold the information requested. The Information Commissioner expects public authorities to disclose whether or not requested information is held unless exceptionally one of the exemptions properly applies and, in the case of qualified exemptions, the public interest test supports the refusal to confirm or deny in the circumstances. The ability to neither confirm nor deny (NCND) whether requested information is held is sometimes referred to in its abbreviated format.

This ability to neither confirm nor deny can be considered in relation to all exemptions, save s.21 (information accessible elsewhere) and s.43(1) (trade secrets) of the FOIA.

This provision should be considered when the mere fact of confirming or denying whether a record is held discloses details which would be exempt from disclosure. In the Information Commissioner's decision notice: *Prison and Probation Ombudsman for England and Wales* (FS50409302, 13 December 2011), it was held to be correct to neither confirm nor deny whether information was held about the number of complaints made against a specific individual in the stated period (FOIA, s.40(2)). This was on the basis that to do so would disclose whether or not any complaints had been made, which would involve disclosure of that individual's personal data in breach of the data protection principles.

If information is exempt from the confirm or deny obligation, it is also exempt from disclosure. If information is not exempt from the confirm or deny obligation, it may still be exempt from disclosure and the public authority should proceed to consider the exemptions in that context in order to fulfil its obligations under s.1(1)(b) of the FOIA.

Where a request is very specific as opposed to being generic and high level, it is more likely that the ability to refuse to confirm or deny will arise. Where the public authority refuses to confirm or deny, it must issue a proper refusal notice to explain its decision and this should explain the applicable exemption and why it applies, as normal. **Chapter 3** deals with mandatory details in refusal notices.

In *Bowbrick* v. *Information Commissioner and Nottingham City Council* (EA/2005/0006, 28 September 2006), the Information Tribunal examined the question of whether exemptions can be claimed for the first time at a late stage in the appeal process, i.e. at the Information Commissioner or (then) Tribunal stage (having not previously been cited by an authority when responding to the request). The Tribunal held that it would be inequitable not to consider exemptions which were relevant, irrespective of when during the proceedings they were brought up. This approach was followed in *Colin P England (1) and London Borough of Bexley (2)* v. *Information Commissioner* (EA/2006/0060 and EA/2006/0066, 10 May 2007), in which the Tribunal confirmed that there was nothing in the FOIA or in the Information Tribunal (Enforcement Appeals) Rules 2005, SI 2005/14, applicable at that time, to prevent the council amending its notice of appeal. Furthermore, 'it would be inconsistent with the Tribunal's own obligations to act in a manner that is compatible with individuals' human rights under the Human Rights Act 1998 for it to, on a technicality, require a disclosure that … would otherwise be protected by [an exemption under the FOIA]'. However, this approach was on the basis that the obligation might arise in exceptional cases and in particular in relation to s.40 of the FOIA.

In *Bowbrick* the Tribunal also explored whether the Information Commissioner has a positive duty to look for exemptions which might apply where not claimed by a public authority. It held that in general terms there is no such duty but the Information Commissioner is not precluded from examining an exemption if he considers that another exemption has been misidentified. Arguments on this approach have moved backwards and forwards subsequently, leading to unhelpful uncertainty at times.

Again, in *Department for Environment, Food and Rural Affairs* v. *Information Commissioner and Birkett* [2011] UKUT 39 (AAC) and *Information Commissioner* v. *Home Office* [2011] UKUT 17 (AAC); [2011] 1 Info LR 1533, the ability of public authorities to claim late exemptions without requiring justification and the ability of the Commissioner to raise new exemptions was confirmed by the Upper Tribunal, which stated: 'it is necessary for the Commissioner to take the initiative in appropriate circumstances and to do so as a matter of duty, not of discretion'. It went so far as to confirm that such changes were even possible in First-tier Tribunal proceedings, subject to the First-tier Tribunal's case management powers. This decision follows the reorganisation of the Tribunal system and so the introduction of new procedural regulations.

Despite this decision but pending its appeal to the Court of Appeal, later in 2011 the Upper Tribunal expressed its doubts about the *Department for Environment, Food and Rural Affairs* v. *Birkett* approach. In the matter of *All Party Parliamentary Group on Extraordinary Rendition* v. *Information Commissioner and Ministry of Defence* [2011] UKUT 153 (AAC); [2011] 2 Info LR 75, the Upper Tribunal expressed 'some general concerns' about 'an indefeasible right' for a public authority to raise whatever exemption it thought fit whenever it wanted. Although this created a great deal of uncertainty for a period, judgments appear to have subsequently supported the *Department for Environment, Food and Rural Affairs* v. *Birkett* approach.

An example of this is the First-tier Tribunal case *Thackeray* v. *Information Commissioner* (EA/2011/0069, 2 December 2011); [2012] 1 Info LR 239, which confirmed that exemptions could be admitted late subject to the Information

Commissioner's discretion being exercised fairly and in the light of the statutory purpose. It was also held to be important that the other side had an opportunity to consider changes and comment before any decision, in other words to ensure fairness and natural justice. However, it too confirmed that there was no need for justification for late reliance.

This was ultimately confirmed by the anticipated Court of Appeal judgment: an appellant or a respondent in an appeal to the Tribunal could raise new exceptions (this was an EIR case) in the Tribunal (*Birkett* v. *Department for Environment, Food and Rural Affairs* [2011] EWCA Civ 1606). The Court of Appeal also declined to refer the matter to the Court of Justice of the European Union.

This approach to late reliance was particularly clear in the decision of the Upper Tribunal in *Information Commissioner* v. *Her Majesty's Revenue and Customs and Gaskell* [2011] UKUT 296 (AAC); [2011] 2 Info LR 11. Here it was decided that the Information Commissioner had been correct to state that information was exempt from disclosure under s.44 (information prohibited from disclosure) in circumstances where the disclosure only became an offence as a result of a public service restructuring which took effect following the public authority's internal review decision (and so was not claimed formally by the public authority) and appeal to the Information Commissioner but before the Commissioner's decision notice. It was confirmed that the Information Commissioner had discretion about his steps for dealing with adjudications under s.50 of the FOIA and that the Commissioner was entitled to consider whether disclosure would have been prohibited at any time when the public authority was required to take steps to disclose the information, even if later than the original request, response or internal review.

It is to be hoped that future decision notices and judgments continue to be consistent in this regard. However, the best approach by any public authority must always be to try to reach the right decision initially in any event but, to the extent that has not been possible, to ensure that all and any flaws in that response are cured and any new exemptions are raised as soon as possible and ideally when carrying out the internal review.

4.5 ABSOLUTE EXEMPTIONS

An absolute exemption applies to all information which falls within the category or class of information it describes. For this reason they are all class exemptions and in assessing whether an absolute exemption applies, the only question is whether the information falls within one of the categories. If it does, then the exemption is engaged and the information is exempt. There is no test of public interest or prejudice.

If an absolute exemption applies, then the public authority does not have to disclose the information and may not even have to say whether it holds it, although it is required to tell the applicant which exemption it thinks applies, and why.

Each of the absolute exemptions is considered below.

4.5.1   Information accessible to the applicant by other means (s.21)

The purpose of this exemption is to ensure that public authorities do not become the natural first choice source for information which the applicant can get elsewhere. The FOIA does not cut across existing legal regimes which provide access to information, nor does it provide alternative means of access to information which is already readily available through commercial publishing operations or existing publicly funded provision. The FOIA is designed to supplement rather than duplicate the ordinary circulation of information to the public through the commercial, electronic and print media and through existing library and archive services.

Provided the information requested is reasonably accessible to an applicant other than in response to his or her information request (s.21(1)) then the exemption will apply. The FOIA confirms that information will be treated as reasonably accessible if:

- it is made available in accordance with the authority's publication scheme (s.21(3)) (in effect, an authority is not obliged to answer individual requests for information if it already makes that information generally available to everyone); or
- it is available by virtue of an obligation under any other legislation (s.21(2)(b)), e.g. information which is accessible under the subject access rules in the Data Protection Act 1998 (DPA) or information about the environment which is available under the Environmental Information Regulations 2004 (EIR).

However, where the information provision is voluntary, or where the information is obliged to be made available only by inspection, special rules apply.

In *Colin P England (1) and London Borough of Bexley (2)* v. *Information Commissioner* (EA/2006/0060 and EA/2006/0066, 10 May 2007), the Tribunal considered the meaning of 'reasonably accessible'. Mr England had sought details of empty residential properties in the Bexley area which the council refused to disclose on the basis that the information was obtainable from the Land Registry website (**www.landreg.gov.uk**). The Tribunal considered whether the fact that only 70 per cent of land in Bexley was registered with the Land Registry was sufficient to engage the exemption in s.21. Bexley Council had argued that the requirement for reasonable accessibility will be satisfied where a requisite amount of information is available from another source. The Tribunal disagreed. The Tribunal held that the word 'reasonably' qualifies the word 'accessible'. Therefore 'reasonably accessible' applies to the mechanisms available to an applicant to obtain information. For s.21 to apply, all the requested information had to be available elsewhere and, in addition, readily available to the applicant from that source.

A further important decision is *Newcastle Upon Tyne Hospital NHS Foundation Trust* v. *Information Commissioner* (EA/2011/0236, 6 January 2012); [2012] 1 Info LR 213, in which the Tribunal held that the fact that information might be accessible through a disclosure application in litigation distinct from the FOIA application did not automatically mean that the information was thereby otherwise 'reasonably accessible' to the applicant within the meaning of s.21 of the FOIA. This was because information obtained through a disclosure application would be subject to limitations as to its use which would not apply to information obtained under the FOIA.

In a similar vein, in the decision notice *Transport for London* (FS50075171, 5 May 2006), the Information Commissioner considered whether it was the accessibility of individual records that needed to be 'reasonable', or whether records as a whole should be considered. The applicant had sought files of prosecutions brought by London Bus Services Ltd (a subsidiary of Transport for London) since the start of 2003. Transport for London believed some of this information to be accessible in court records and therefore refused disclosure in reliance on s.21. The applicant argued that it would be unreasonable to expect him to retrieve court records from a large number of magistrates' courts where the individual records would be held. The Commissioner concluded that it was necessary to consider the accessibility of individual records rather than the effort required to assemble a collection of them all. In other words, reasonable accessibility is not a function of the volume of the information sought.

Note that information may still be 'reasonably' accessible (and therefore exempt under this section) even though it is only available on payment of a fee (s.21(2)(b)), e.g. under the subject access regime in the DPA. Of course, where the cost of obtaining the relevant information requested by other means would be excessive, that might preclude use of the exemption.

Some factors to consider when assessing whether information is readily accessible are as follows:

- Is it is available to purchase through commercial outlets, or is it out of print?
- Is it mass produced in a large print run, or distributed only through scarce or specialist outlets?
- Is it available over the internet or through a public library? Care is needed in this regard in particular since the fact that information is available via a website will not necessarily be sufficient to engage s.21. In *Ames* v. *Information Commissioner and Cabinet Office* (EA/2007/0110, 24 April 2008), the Tribunal considered a case where an applicant who had requested information about the Iraq War dossier on weapons of mass destruction had been referred to another website under s.21. The Tribunal noted that not only were the details not actually available on that website but that simply pointing to a large website, such as for the Hutton Inquiry, would be likely to be insufficient to engage s.21 unless more were done to assist the applicant in accessing the details, such as providing a specific link to the requested details on the website.
- How easily can it be identified? Has it been catalogued or indexed?
- Is it ephemeral or has it been archived?
- Is it subject to onerous conditions of access or subsequent use?

Note, however, that there is a subjective element to the exemption, in the sense that the information must be reasonably accessible to the particular applicant, forcing the public authority to adjust its normal 'applicant blind' approach in some cases. Consider the following points:

- Are any legal access rights available to the particular applicant (e.g. Access to Health Records Act 1990, s.3, which provides that the holder of a health record shall allow access to the health record of a deceased person on application by that person's personal representative, by supplying them with a copy or an extract)?
- Does the applicant have access to otherwise closed or private sources of information, by virtue of some particular quality, entitlement or qualification?
- Does the applicant possess enhanced skills or resources which may bring otherwise inaccessible information within reach (e.g. research, technical or linguistic skills)?
- Is the applicant disadvantaged in some way (e.g. because of disability, educational or economic circumstances) which might render information inaccessible which would otherwise be readily accessible to the general public? The Commissioner's guidance stresses that although there is normally no duty, for example, to make translations or adjustments for applicants, public authorities should consider these needs and it may be reasonable for them to accommodate them. This should also be considered in the light of the duty under s.16 of the FOIA to provide reasonable advice and assistance to any applicant for information.

Section 21(3) of the FOIA imposes additional obligations on public authorities who seek to rely on this exemption where the public authority is not under any legal obligation to provide the information but chooses to make it available, such as on request, or, even if a legal obligation to provide the information applies, it is limited to an obligation to make that information available for inspection. In such cases the information will not be exempt unless it is also available through the public authority's publication scheme. Moreover, where details are only available by inspection, the Commissioner has confirmed that s.21 would only apply after consideration of the individual circumstances of the applicant to ensure that the details were reasonably accessible to him or her.

In the Commissioner's decision notice *Northamptonshire County Council* (FS50368428, 15 November 2011), the applicant requested a copy of the local government pension scheme admission agreement between the council and a third party. The council was obliged to make the agreement available for inspection at the offices of the administering authority, the council, under para.11 of Sched.3 to the Local Government Pension Scheme (Administration) Regulations 2008, SI 2008/239 and invited the applicant to make an appointment to do so. The applicant complained to the Commissioner as he wanted a copy of the document and did not want to inspect it. The Commissioner stated that the council should take into account whether or not the applicant was able to travel to the council's offices to view the information. As the applicant had previously done so several times and not raised any reasons why he could not do so again, it was agreed that the information was properly exempt under s.21(1). On appeal, the Tribunal found that because the appellant lived some distance from the council's offices and would need to take time off work to inspect the information, it was not reasonably accessible. Some legal obligations to make information publicly available are limited to inspection, as above. However, others oblige an authority to permit inspection and to provide the information on request (even if subject to payment of a fee) and in such cases, the conditions in s.21(2)(b) are met.

Technology is raising additional issues in respect of assessing whether or not information is reasonably accessible elsewhere. Where an appellant complained that it was difficult for him to access the details of staff email addresses from a university website due to a medical condition, the Tribunal confirmed that there is a clear difference between accessing information and harvesting it to make use of it once accessed (*Benson* v. *Information Commissioner and Governing Body of the University of Bristol* (EA/2011/0120, 10 November 2011)). The Tribunal also recently considered the issue of whether s.21 required information (as opposed to the documentation containing the information) to be reasonably accessible. The appellant requested details of motorcycle bays in Westminster and the authority provided him with an online link to the Traffic Management Order containing the details in PDF format. The appellant wanted the information in a searchable format but the PDF format was not searchable. In the event, it was accepted that the authority no longer held a searchable digital version of the details concerned (which would have originally been required to create the PDF document) but the authority created and provided the appellant with a spreadsheet containing the required details. Accordingly, the Tribunal dismissed the appeal (*Forster* v. *Information Commissioner and Westminster City Council* (EA/2011/0235, 14 May 2012)). The outcome may have been different had the authority held a digital, searchable version of the PDF document and this type of issue is likely to become more relevant due to the Commissioner's FOI 2.0 agenda, being his objective of making as much non-exempt public authority information as possible available online and more readily accessible and re-usable by the public.

Importantly, this exemption does not apply to the requirement to confirm or deny, so even if the exemption means an authority does not have to make information available, the authority is still required to say whether or not it holds the information.

Public archives and public records

Information held in public archives or by the National Archives (which incorporates what was referred to previously as the Public Records Office) may be exempt under s.21 if the information requested is catalogued and included in the relevant authority's publication scheme (or its parent authority's publication scheme).

The National Council on Archives has been replaced by the Archives and Records Association which operates a Public Services Quality Group. Although this is a professional membership body for archivists, its role is to improve the level of public services offered by the sector, including by providing good practice guides on improving archiving services.

Another point has been considered by the Information Tribunal in the context of s.21. In *Prior* v. *Information Commissioner* (EA/2005/0017, 27 April 2006), the Tribunal noted that whether or not a complainant accepts the substance of the information provided is not a matter for consideration under the FOIA. The only obligation of a public authority is to provide the information it holds that fits the description specified in the request.

4.5.2   Security matters (s.23)

This exemption covers all information originating from or relating to one of the security bodies listed in s.23(3). Section 23 states that information held by a public authority is exempt information if it was directly or indirectly supplied to the public authority by, or relates to, any of the following bodies:

- Security Service (i.e. MI5);
- Secret Intelligence Service (i.e. MI6);
- Government Communications Headquarters (i.e. GCHQ) (and this includes any unit or part of a unit of the armed forces which is required by the Secretary of State to assist GCHQ in carrying out its functions);
- Special forces (such as the SAS);
- Tribunal established under the Regulation of Investigatory Powers Act 2000, s.65;
- Investigatory Powers Tribunal established by the Interception of Communications Act 1985, s.7;
- Tribunal established by the Security Service Act 1989, s.5;
- Tribunal established by the Intelligence Services Act 1994, s.9;
- Security Vetting Appeals Panel;
- Security Commission;
- National Criminal Intelligence Service;
- Service Authority for the National Criminal Intelligence Service; and
- Serious Organised Crime Agency (SOCA).

A certificate signed by a Minister certifying that the information to which it applies was directly or indirectly supplied by, or relates to, any of the above bodies shall, subject to s.60 (which governs appeals against ministerial certificates), be conclusive evidence of that fact.

The exemption also applies to the duty to confirm or deny, to the extent that confirming or denying would involve disclosure of any exempt information (whether or not already recorded). It will therefore be appropriate in many cases for a public authority neither to confirm nor deny the existence of the information requested. It may equally be appropriate to rely on the exemption even where the public authority does not hold the information. To avoid unwanted inferences from the information concerned, the Commissioner's guidance suggests that it may be necessary also to mention other potential exemptions when relying upon s.23. This was considered by the Commissioner in his recent decision notice *Home Office* (FS50407164, 20 February 2012) and confirmed that although ss.23(1) and 24(1) of the FOIA are mutually exclusive, their provisions enabling a public authority to neither confirm nor deny whether requested information is held, under ss.23(5) and 24(2) respectively, are not mutually exclusive. Despite that, the decision noted 'that consistent citing of s.23(5) is usually sufficient to obscure the possibility of the involvement of security bodies and that citing this section in conjunction with s.24(2) is often not necessary to achieve this result'. The public authority's reluctance to confirm which of the exemptions in this regard were engaged led the Commissioner to find that it sought to rely on both of them.

The approach to s.23(1) and the NCND provisions under s.23(5) (including their relationship with the NCND provision under s.24(2)) has now been clarified by the Tribunal in *All Party Parliamentary Group on Extraordinary Rendition* v. *Information Commissioner and the Foreign and Commonwealth Office* (EA/2011/0049, EA/2011/0050, EA/2011/0051, 3 May 2012). This is at present the leading case on these provisions. The Tribunal held that:

- A broad but purposive approach is to be taken to s.23(1).
- The term 'supplied by' refers to how the public authority came to hold that information; the term 'relates to' refers to the contents of the information. Both are questions of fact, to be determined on the balance of probabilities, taking a broad approach.
- The NCND provisions under s.23(5) and s.24(2) are not mutually exclusive. They can and will often need to be relied upon together.

Application of the exemption in practice

The principles summarised above can be applied as follows. The first part of the exemption refers to information directly or indirectly supplied by one of the security bodies, so the question of whether or not this applies will turn on the source rather than the content of the information requested. For this part of the exemption, the content of the information is irrelevant (e.g. it need not relate to national security). The exemption in this case also applies regardless of the impact from its disclosure and even if no harm would result.

In so far as the application of the exemption turns on the second part of it (i.e. whether information relates to any of the security bodies), it will be capable of covering a wide range of subject matter, whether of a policy, operational or administrative nature.

In relation to any particular item of information, it will be a question of fact whether it falls within s.23 or not. Where the origin of information is unclear, the exemption should be applied with care, and if possible after consultation with the author.

The FOIA does not specify how remote from the original source information needs to be before it ceases to be indirectly supplied by or related to one of the security bodies. As such, if it is possible to trace a discrete piece of information back through each transmission to its original source, then this would seem to be sufficient, however many hands it has passed through and even if the wording has changed along the way.

The s.23 exemption applies to all records, regardless of their age, including historical records, except for historical records held by the National Archives or the Public Record Office of Northern Ireland. The s.23 exemption ceases to be an absolute exemption after 30 years and the exemption will become subject to the public interest test at that point. The current 30-year rule (in terms of records being transferred to the National Archives and also becoming historic records accessible under the FOIA) is due to change to the 20-year rule once ss.45 and 46 respectively of the Constitutional Reform and Governance Act 2010 (which amend Part 6 of the FOIA on historic records) come into force, although the legislation does provide for exceptions and different approaches for different records to be made possible. Section 37 (communications with Her Majesty) is an example of where a different approach will be taken (see below).

Ministerial certificates

Ministerial certificates require the signature of a Cabinet Minister, the Attorney General or the Advocate General. It is not necessary to have a certificate to rely on s.23 but a certificate will normally reinforce a public authority's position in any legal proceedings and determine the forum for hearing an appeal (the First-tier Tribunal (Information Rights) rather than the Information Commissioner). As such, certificates are primarily relevant to enforcement proceedings and need not be served until such proceedings commence. Serving a certificate when answering a request will normally be premature and might involve unnecessary work, although public authorities should consider the need for a certificate at a reasonably early stage to take account of the time needed to prepare one.

Although s.23(2) provides that it is conclusive evidence that information falls within this exemption where it is certified as such by a Minister, this can still be challenged under s.60. Further, s.23 also only permits Ministers to certify specific information – which precludes the preparation of certificates in expectation of future requests. By contrast, certificates issued under s.24 (national security) can be general and prospective. If the authority elects neither to confirm nor deny (and so will not need to disclose) pending such a certificate, it would normally be obliged to explain the non-disclosure in accordance with s.17 of the FOIA. However, to the extent such statement would disclose the exempt information, the authority is not obliged to do so (s.17(4)).

Interaction with other exemptions

The security matters exemption may overlap with a number of other exemptions: namely, national security (s.24), defence (s.26), international relations (s.27) and the economy (s.29). There is nothing to prevent a public authority claiming exemption under several, or indeed all these heads, if appropriate.

It is worth remembering, however, that except for national security, the other exemptions do not provide for ministerial certificates. Further, all of them are qualified exemptions and therefore subject to the public interest test. This could give rise to procedural difficulties if an applicant challenges their efficacy. If, for example, a public authority claimed exemption under both the s.23 (security matters) and s.26 (defence) exemptions, then the route for appeal would be:

- an appeal to the First-tier Tribunal (Information Rights) under s.60 against the s.23 certificate, by either the applicant or the Commissioner;
- a challenge by the applicant to the Commissioner on the balance of the public interest (although this may be adjourned pending the outcome of any s.60 appeal); and
- a challenge by the applicant to the Commissioner on the s.26 exemption, although again it may be appropriate for the Commissioner to adjourn this pending hearing of the s.60 appeal.

In addition, to the extent that the s.23 exemption was claimed but a ministerial certificate was not issued, the Commissioner would be entitled to deal with any complaint to him and did so in his recent decision notice, *Foreign and Commonwealth Office* (FS50366315, 16 January 2012).

4.5.3 Court records (s.32)

Information contained in court records and other similar documents is absolutely exempt from disclosure under the FOIA. In essence, the exemption covers:

- any document served on or by a public authority; and
- documents held or created by a court, or a person conducting an inquiry or arbitration,

in each case, for the purposes of proceedings.

Documents served on or by a public authority

This covers documents created by the parties to litigation and will include information contained in normal litigation documentation relevant to the court, including:

- claim forms and statements of defence;
- witness statements, medical and other experts' reports and exhibits;
- skeleton arguments;

- standard disclosure lists;
- allocation questionnaires or pre-trial checklists (listing questionnaires);
- application notices; and
- trial bundles.

Where an authority is party to litigation, documents provided to it by the other parties under their disclosure obligations will normally be exempt. However, the exemption will not extend to information contained in exempt documents if the information is also held by the public authority in another form. So, for example, if an authority is litigating over a contract, the contract will not be exempt (assuming the authority holds a copy in its files) just because that contract is included in the authority's statement of case. This is because the opening line in s.32 reads 'Information held by a public authority is exempt information if it is held *only* by virtue of being held in [court documents etc.]' (s.32(1)) (author's italics).

In practical terms, this means that information will usually only be susceptible to the s.32 exemption where it is known to the public authority solely because it is contained in documents served on the authority by another party in litigation, or where it is held by the authority solely because it was recorded in connection with litigation. Unlike legal litigation privileged information protected under s.42 of the FOIA, to engage s.32 the proceedings must have commenced, not just be contemplated. Prior to proceedings being issued, a public authority may need to rely on s.42 instead in respect of the preparation of the documents to be used in the proceedings.

Documents held or created by a court

For the purposes of s.32, a 'court' includes a tribunal or other body exercising the judicial power of the State. As well as the civil and criminal courts (comprising magistrates' courts, county courts, the Crown Court, the High Court and Court of Appeal), this includes the Supreme Court (which replaced the Appellate Committee of the House of Lords in 2009) and the Judicial Committee of the Privy Council, and the judicial functions of coroners. It would probably exclude the Court of Justice of the European Union and the European Court of Human Rights, which are not UK domestic courts. 'Proceedings' includes any inquest or post mortem.

This part of the exemption would cover information contained in documents such as:

- judgments and orders of the court which have not been published;
- notebooks of judges, tribunal members, coroners and other judicial officers;
- notices of hearings;
- summaries prepared by judicial assistants; and
- court or tribunal internal memoranda and correspondence which relate to particular proceedings.

The point about the s.32 exemption is that there are separate and specific regimes for access to information held by courts and tribunals and/or as between the parties to the legal proceedings, designed to give those bodies and the public authority party to such legal proceedings control over the information they hold. Special rules set out a comprehensive code governing the disclosure of court records and documents served in the course of proceedings. For example, rule 5.4 of the Civil Procedure Rules 1998 (CPR) deals with access to court documents in certain civil proceedings. For certain types of proceedings (such as in the family court, where children need to be protected), only limited classes of persons may access court documents. The FOIA does not exist to provide indirect access to these records. The greater public interest is considered to lie in preserving the courts' own procedures for disclosure, and the s.32 exemption therefore functions to ensure that the courts can continue to control this.

There is a distinction, of course, between the courts themselves – which are not public authorities under the FOIA – and the government departments responsible for organising the court and tribunal systems, which are. Thus Her Majesty's Courts and Tribunals Service is an agency of the Ministry of Justice and the Northern Ireland Courts and Tribunals Service is a separate authority. Information held by the latter is accessible under the FOIA in the normal way, as is information held by the police, the Legal Services Commission and the Legal Ombudsman.

The phrase 'created by … a court' in s.32(1)(c) was considered by the Information Tribunal in *Alistair Mitchell* v. *Information Commissioner* (EA/2005/0002, 10 January 2005). The Tribunal at that time concluded that in the context of s.32(1)(c) (as opposed to s.32(1)(a)), the phrase must be interpreted as referring to judicially created documents. On this basis it held that a court transcript was not an exempt document because it was not created by the judge. Subsequently, guidance from the Commissioner issued in 2009 specifically confirmed that court transcripts created for the purposes of court proceedings (even if not by a judge but by the court's administrative staff, whether employed, contracted or otherwise engaged for that purpose) are exempt under s.32. This followed the Tribunal judgment in *Ministry of Justice* v. *Information Commissioner* (EA/2007/0120 and EA/2007/0121, 29 July 2008).

It was the Information Commissioner's view in the decision of *Doncaster Metropolitan Borough Council* (FS50080312, 7 August 2007) that s.32(2) should not be interpreted as requiring that the primary reason for holding information should be its status as a court record. The Commissioner did not accept the council's argument that the FOIA requires him to consider what the primary purpose for holding the information is, since the section refers to the information being held 'only' because it was obtained or created in the course of the relevant proceedings and for those purposes.

Documents held or created by a person conducting an inquiry

Inquiries will be subject to the FOIA unless they are legally independent of the sponsoring authority. A public authority may therefore hold information which falls within s.32 either because it conducted an inquiry itself or because it was the inquiry's sponsoring authority. However, there is a very important limitation on the application of the exemption to inquiries. The exemption can only apply where an inquiry has a statutory constitution or is set up under royal prerogative (even if a judge heads the proceedings). This might include:

- inquiries which are required to be held by specific statutory provision;
- a discretionary inquiry or hearing designated by an order under s.16(2) of the Tribunals and Inquiries Act 1992; or
- an inquiry set up by the exercise of a statutory power (e.g. under Local Government Act 1972, s.250).

There are numerous examples of specific inquiries set up under an enactment (such as the Marchioness Inquiry under the Merchant Shipping Act 1995) but many inquiries are not. Examples of inquiries which would normally fall outside the scope of s.32 are:

- departmental 'leak' inquiries;
- Lord Butler's review of the intelligence published prior to the invasion of Iraq on weapons of mass destruction; and
- Lord Penrose's inquiry into the collapse of the mutual life assurer Equitable Life.

Documents held or created by a person conducting arbitration

'Arbitration' is defined by reference to Part 1 of the Arbitration Act 1996, which applies only where there is a written arbitration agreement. Arbitration involves an impartial, independent third party hearing both sides (usually in private) and issuing a final and legally binding decision to resolve the dispute.

The exemption would normally apply to information contained in, for example:

- notes taken by an arbitrator;
- written decisions or reports of the arbitration;
- a written arbitration agreement that is created by a person conducting an arbitration;
- internal correspondence between persons involved in the conduct of an arbitration; and
- a letter from a person conducting an arbitration requesting further evidence.

The interpretation of s.32 (and to a degree, the FOIA regime as a whole) is being challenged in the *Kennedy* litigation on the basis that its provisions should be read down to be consistent with human rights legislation, specifically art.10 of the European Convention on Human Rights, namely the right to freedom of expression, including freedom to receive information without interference by public authority. The appellant also claims his rights are enhanced because he is a journalist and therefore is acting as a social watchdog. The Court of Appeal initially considered the art.10 point to be arguable (as it considered the wording of s.32(2) to be ambiguous on the question of whether the exemption continued to apply long after the relevant inquiry has ended) and remitted the interpretation to the Tribunal. However, once the Tribunal's 'report' made its way back to the Court of Appeal, the Supreme Court had apparently decided in *Sugar* v. *British Broadcasting Corporation* [2012] UKSC 4, that art.10 had no application to the FOIA. Therefore, the Court of Appeal in *Kennedy* v. *Charity Commission* [2012] EWCA Civ 317 dismissed the appellant's appeal. It did, however, grant permission to appeal to the Supreme Court. The exact scope of s.32(2) therefore remains unclear.

4.5.4 Parliamentary privilege (s.34)

Information is exempt where necessary to prevent infringement of parliamentary privilege. Similarly, the duty to confirm or deny does not apply if or to the extent that exemption is required, for the same reason.

It is outside the scope of this book to discuss at length the nature of parliamentary privilege. It is sufficient for our purposes to note that while parliamentary privilege is not intrinsically regarded as a reason for secrecy, it is deemed a form of immunity applying to the House of Commons and House of Lords which is necessary for them to function independently, without external interference. The most significant privilege is the right of freedom of speech and proceedings in Parliament, which effectively means that MPs and peers cannot be sued or prosecuted for anything they say in debates or proceedings, nor can any court or tribunal call into question what has been said in Parliament (see Bill of Rights 1688, art.9). As it applies to the FOIA, it means that no external authority can adjudicate on Parliament's right to withhold information where that right is exercised on grounds of parliamentary privilege. It should be noted that the same protection under s.34 is not available to all the UK administrations, such as the National Assembly for Wales.

Both the House of Commons and the House of Lords are public authorities for the purposes of the FOIA (individual MPs and peers are not) and both have publication schemes. Information included in these publication schemes will normally be exempt under s.21.

For the most part, the s.34 exemption will apply to information generated and held by the Commons or Lords which are unpublished, such as:

- committee reports and report drafts;
- memoranda submitted to committees, and draft memoranda;
- internal papers prepared by the Officers of either House directly related to the proceedings of the House or committees (including advice of all kinds to the Speaker or Lord Chancellor or other occupants of the Chair in either House, briefs for the chairmen and other members of committees, and informal notes of deliberative meetings of committees);
- papers prepared by the Libraries of either House, or by other House agencies such as the Parliamentary Office of Science and Technology, either for general dissemination to Members or to assist individual Members, which relate to, or

anticipate, debates and other proceedings of the relevant House or its committees, and are intended to assist Members in preparation for such proceedings;

- correspondence between Members, Officers, Ministers and government officials directly related to House proceedings;
- papers relating to investigations by the Parliamentary Commissioner for Standards;
- papers relating to the Registers of Members' Interests; and
- Bills, amendments and motions, including those in draft, where they originate from Parliament or a Member rather than from Parliamentary Counsel or another government department.

As well as information generated and held by the Commons or Lords themselves, s.34 could extend to information held elsewhere (for example, by central government departments) if related to parliamentary proceedings. If so, then the department concerned must consult with the appropriate House authorities before disclosing. Importantly, although it is open to a department to refuse disclosure on s.34 grounds, only the House authorities can conclusively certify the exemption (as permitted by s.34(3)). Since any person breaching privilege may be punished by Parliament, failure to engage the exemption where it applies may result in serious sanctions. Departments should normally therefore seek advice from the relevant officials to ensure that privilege is asserted (and duly certified) where it is proper to do so. For the House of Commons, the relevant official is the Speaker of the House; for the House of Lords, it is the Clerk of the Parliaments. Each House asserts privilege over its own material. Particular care should be taken with requests for information contained in:

- any of the unpublished working papers of a select committee of either House, including factual briefs or briefs of suggested questions prepared by the committee staff for the use of committee chairmen and/or other members, and draft reports (most likely to be held by a department where a Minister is or has been a member of such a committee);
- any legal advice submitted in confidence by the Law Officers or by the legal branch of any other department, to the Speaker, a committee chairman or a committee, or any official of either House;
- drafts of motions, Bills or amendments which have not otherwise been published or laid on the Table of either House;
- any unpublished correspondence between Ministers or department officials on the one hand, and any member or official of either House on the other, relating specifically to proceedings on any Question, draft Bill, motion or amendment, either in the relevant House or in a committee; and
- any correspondence with or relating to the proceedings of the Parliamentary Commissioner for Standards.

Much information which is privileged is now routinely published by Parliament itself anyway, and this goes well beyond the record of proceedings. It includes internal administrative documents and even individual Members' expenditure against parliamentary allowances. Information published in this way does not cease to be privileged (it remains Parliament's decision whether or not to continue publication) but disclosure of published information cannot be taken as infringing parliamentary privilege in a way which would engage the s.34 exemption (although the information may be eligible for exemption under s.21, being reasonably accessible to the applicant other than under the FOIA).

Note that s.34 is not intended to enable the withholding of information which would be disclosable but for its being contained in parliamentary papers. So, while the draft of a memorandum responding to a select committee report may itself be privileged, factual information included in it may not be. The factual information would normally have to be disclosed unless it cannot be extracted without revealing what else is in the draft report.

There will also be a range of information which is not published by Parliament but which is also not related to parliamentary proceedings and therefore not protected by parliamentary privilege. The best examples of this are:

- papers prepared by the Libraries of either House or other House agencies, intended to provide general or specific background information on matters not currently under examination or expected or planned to be considered in formal proceedings of either House or their committees;
- Members' correspondence and other communications not specifically related to proceedings of either House or of one of its formally constituted committees (correspondence between a Member and a Minister about a constituency issue that is not the subject of proceedings is not privileged, but correspondence about a draft motion, amendment or Question is privileged);
- the deliberations of parliamentary bodies established by statute (although if they are discussing matters relating to the preparation of formal proceedings in Parliament, those deliberations may well be privileged); and
- meetings of political parties and other committees.

4.5.5 Prejudice to the effective conduct of public affairs (s.36)

This is actually a qualified exemption (see **Chapter 5**), except in relation to information held by the House of Commons or House of Lords, where it is absolute, presumably for reasons of parliamentary privilege. A detailed analysis of s.36 is set out in **Chapter 5**.

4.5.6 Communications with Her Majesty and the awarding of honours (s.37)

Originally, this exemption was wholly qualified, but with effect from 19 January 2011 it has become, in part, an absolute exemption. Section 37(1)(a), (aa) and (ab) are now absolute with the balance of the provisions remaining qualified by the public interest test. Accordingly, if information falls within the scope of (a) communications with the Sovereign; or (aa) communications with the heir to, or the person who is for the time being second in line of succession to, the Throne; or (ab) communications with a person who has subsequently acceded to the Throne or become heir to, or second in line to, the Throne, then the exemption is engaged and no disclosure is necessary. Care is needed to ensure that the requisite parties are involved and in the right capacity, e.g. the Prince of Wales as heir, rather than in the context of the Duchy of Cornwall (see the decision notice in *Department for Business, Innovation and Skills* (FS50387051, 8 February 2012)). It should be noted that requests received prior to the effective amendment to s.37, which is not retrospective, must still involve the public interest test.

The right to neither confirm nor deny is available with this exemption and in respect of information covered by s.37(1)(a), (aa) or (ab) would also be an absolute exemption.

There are special rules on historic records in relation to s.37 (see **Chapter 5**) but the information falling within the absolute exemption will not be affected by the anticipated changes to the normal 30-year rule on historic records (which, once enabled, will in most cases reduce to 20 years as provided for by the Constitutional Reform and Governance Act 2010, ss.45 and 46). Instead, once s.63(2)(E) and (F) of the FOIA are enabled, information within the s.37 absolute exemption will become a historic record on the later of the date five years after the death of the relevant person, or 20 years after the creation of the relevant record.

The balance of the exemption will be considered as a qualified exemption in **Chapter 5**.

4.5.7 Personal information (s.40)

The interface between freedom of information and data protection is extraordinarily complex and has not simplified over time since the FOIA came into force. The key to understanding it is to recognise that neither regime is absolute. On the one hand, the FOIA promotes openness and transparency by requiring public authorities to disclose information proactively (through publication schemes) and on request. On the other, the DPA protects personal information by restricting the way our personal data can be used and shared with third parties. Importantly, however, the basic principles in both cases are subject to exemptions. In the case of the FOIA, the exemptions permit public bodies to refuse to disclose information, and in the case of the DPA, they permit the use and disclosure of information with more freedom than would otherwise be allowed.

The exemption in s.40 of the FOIA relating to personal data acknowledges the tension between freedom of information and data protection and attempts to reconcile the two. It does so with some difficulty and a great deal of legislative contortion. As a result, s.40 is one of the most difficult exemptions to apply in practice.

To understand s.40 it is necessary to have a degree of understanding about the DPA. The DPA regulates the use of personal data, being information which relates to a living individual who can be identified from that information, or from that information and other information in the possession of or likely to come into the possession of the public authority. This includes opinions expressed about that person.

The details will be personal data if they are: automatically processed, i.e. in any IT system; or, if a hard copy, are in a 'relevant filing system', i.e. readily accessible by reference to the individual, such as by a temporary staff member looking through a filing cabinet of files; or are an accessible record, i.e. as defined in s.68 of the DPA, such as a medical record, and, following the introduction of the FOIA, for public authorities only, such a record includes any other recorded information whether or not inside a relevant filing system.

If personal data relate to race/ethnic origin, political opinions, religious/similar beliefs, trade union membership, physical/mental health or condition, sexual life, criminal proceedings and outcomes, this is 'sensitive personal data' as defined under s.2 of the DPA. Examples would be criminal allegations or convictions, or sickness records. The DPA sets more stringent conditions for the permissible disclosure of sensitive personal data than for ordinary personal data.

The individual to whom the personal data relate is the 'data subject' (DPA, s.1). The body which decides the purposes and manner of use of the personal data, e.g. an employer in relation to an employee's details, is a 'data controller' (DPA, s.1). Bodies which simply use personal data on behalf of a data controller to provide an agreed service but not for their own account act, in that regard, as a 'data processor', not a data controller.

Data controllers are subject to the DPA and must comply with its terms for any use – known as 'processing' – of personal data, including the disclosure of such data. This means that where a public authority acts as a data controller, it must comply with the data protection principles set out in Sched.1 to the DPA.

The data subject can obtain a copy of his or her own personal data by making a subject access request to the data controller under s.7(1)(c) of the DPA, to which there are limited exceptions (exceptions include the protection of third party personal data). However, this is subject to the DPA recommending that such third parties be consulted to obtain their consent to disclosure. This is replicated by the 'best practice' obligation to consult third parties in the Section 45 Code of Practice (FOIA, s.45). A data subject may also give the data controller notice of objection under s.10 of the DPA (the right to prevent processing likely to cause damage or distress) which the data controller must then consider and implement if appropriate.

The rules for dealing with requests for personal data depend on who is making the information request and whether the requestor is the data subject himself or herself (or his or her authorised agent), or a third party.

Where the personal data are requested by the data subject (or by his or her authorised agent on his or her behalf), this falls under s.40(1) of the FOIA and the response should make it clear that such personal data are exempt from disclosure to the data subject under the FOIA accordingly but will be dealt with instead under s.7 of the DPA as it must be treated as a subject access request. The purpose of s.40(1) of the FOIA is to ensure that the freedom of information regime does not duplicate or cut across the subject access regime under the DPA. This part of s.40 is absolute and does not require consideration of the public interest test.

By contrast, if the information request is for the personal data of a third party, the public authority should consider s.40, commencing with s.40(2). This provides that personal data requested by someone other than the data subject is exempt where either of two conditions apply, set out in s.40(3) and (4). The duty to confirm or deny is also excluded if either of these conditions apply. Within s.40(3) and (4) there are actually three exemptions.

In this regard s.40 is not completely applicant blind, since it requires the authority to know whether the applicant is the relevant data subject or not and to treat him or her differently accordingly.

The first condition is met if disclosure of the personal data falls under s.40(3)(a)(i) and (3)(b). This combination provides an absolute exemption where disclosure of personal data to a third party would contravene any of the eight data protection principles (as set out in the DPA) governing the use of personal information.

However, the first condition can also be met if disclosure of the personal data falls under s.40(3)(a)(ii) and (3)(b). By contrast, this provides a qualified exemption where disclosure of personal data to a third party would contravene s.10 of the DPA (that is, the right of the data subject to prevent processing likely to cause damage or distress). Its qualified nature means that the public interest test must be considered in addition.

Finally, the second condition is met if disclosure of the personal data falls within s.40(4). This provides a qualified exemption where personal data are exempt from the data subject's own right of access by virtue of any of the provisions of Part IV of the DPA (that is, the exemptions in ss.27–39 which apply to issues like national security, crime and taxation, and regulatory activity). Strangely, a data subject may be prevented from accessing his or her own personal data as a result of DPA exemptions but a third party may have a greater opportunity of accessing those details under the FOIA as a result of the application of the public interest test in addition.

The cumulative effect of s.40(3) and (4) is that information which is protected from disclosure under the DPA cannot normally be obtained using the FOIA. This sounds straightforward enough, but it is far from easy to apply in practice. A detailed exposition of s.40(3) and (4), including the approach taken by the Information Commissioner and the Tribunal, is set out in **Chapter 8**.

4.5.8   Confidential information (s.41)

Information which a public authority obtained from outside the organisation (including from another public authority) is exempt from disclosure under s.41(1) if disclosure would be an actionable breach of confidence. Public authorities are also not obliged to confirm or deny possession of confidential information to the extent that this would in itself be an actionable breach of confidence (s.41(2)).

Importantly, the exemption cannot apply to an authority's own confidential information (although it can still apply to information which is confidential to an authority's individual officers and staff) because s.41 refers to information 'obtained by the public authority from another person'. Further, although government departments are treated as separate entities for the purposes of the FOIA (s.81(1)), a government department cannot claim s.41 exemption on the grounds that disclosure of information would be actionable by another government department (because the government cannot sue itself). The same applies between Northern Ireland departments, but not between a Northern Ireland department and a UK department.

What is confidential information?

The legal rules which define confidentiality are continually developing. It is outside the scope of this book to explore the law of confidence in detail. The issue is, however, analysed in some detail in **Chapter 6**. Salient points include the following.

The leading Tribunal case on s.41 is *Derry City Council* v. *Information Commissioner* (EA/2006/0014, 11 December 2006); [2011] 1 Info LR 1105. In that case, the Tribunal set out the common law test for confidentiality, as follows:

- Does the information have the necessary quality of confidence to justify the imposition of a contractual or equitable obligation of confidence?
- Was the information communicated in circumstances that created such an obligation?
- Would disclosure be a breach of that obligation? and
- If this first part of the test is satisfied, would the public authority nevertheless have a defence to a claim for breach of confidence based on the public interest in disclosure of the information?

This test has been subsequently applied in numerous cases, but has been refined over time in respect of cases relating to the FOIA.

It should also be noted that 'actionable breach' of confidence is not the same as an arguable breach of confidence case. Although to claim this exemption it is not necessary for legal proceedings to be threatened or commenced against an authority, it is necessary to show that if action were brought, the information provider would be likely to win. In *Higher Education Funding Council for England* v. *Information Commissioner and Guardian News and Media Ltd* (EA/2009/0036, 13

January 2010); [2011] 1 Info LR 1034, the Tribunal decided that this element of the exemption requires action 'which, on a balance of probabilities, would succeed', including following consideration of any public interest defence to such legal action (see below).

It is important for practitioners to note that, even if the common law conditions for confidentiality are met, an action for breach of confidence will fail (and therefore the exemption will not apply) if disclosure is in the public interest. This is known as the public interest defence and derives from common law, not the FOIA. So, although the FOIA exemption for confidential information is absolute (i.e. not subject to a public interest test), if a public authority judges that a breach of confidence will not be actionable because the authority has a public interest defence to a claim, then the authority would normally have to disclose that information, notwithstanding its confidentiality.

In practice, information with some commercial value which is not easily available from other sources is likely to be confidential and information about an individual which he or she would consider private, especially if personal (which traditionally may have been seen as too trivial to be protected in this way) is now being treated as confidential (e.g. a staff appraisal, salary details for junior employees, etc.). Three important factors must be assessed whenever a public authority is applying s.41:

- whether or not information is protected by confidentiality will depend largely on its nature and the circumstances in which it was obtained, particularly whether, at the time, the authority expressly agreed to keep it confidential (there are guidelines in the Section 45 Code of Practice (see below) on when an authority should agree to confidentiality restrictions);
- special considerations apply if the information in question is personal data; and
- if information is disclosed in breach of a duty of confidence, then the authority may be liable to a claim for damages; if, on the other hand, information is withheld when it should be disclosed, sanctions under the FOIA may apply. The application of s.41 must therefore be approached with care, and legal advice sought where appropriate.

The Tribunal examined the first limb of the common law test of confidence (whether information has the necessary 'quality of confidence' to make it worthy of protection) in *S* v. *Information Commissioner and General Register Office* (EA/ 2006/0030, 9 May 2007). The case arose from a request from an individual whose brother had died unexpectedly. The deceased's partner, who had been present at the death, had registered it with the General Register Office (GRO) but the appellant had asked the GRO to amend the death certificate to reflect the fact that the deceased's mother had also been present. The GRO refused. The appellant subsequently asked for all documentation underlying the GRO's decision. The GRO did provide some information but refused to disclose a letter from the deceased's partner, on the basis that it was exempt under s.41. The letter had been sent in response to a request from the GRO, seeking clarification of her whereabouts at the time of her partner's death. She did not want the information in the letter disclosed to the applicant and further argued that there was nothing in the letter that the appellant was not already aware of. The Tribunal considered whether information loses its quality of confidence if it is already known to an applicant under the FOIA independently of an information request. It held that it does not, on the basis that dissemination to a limited number of people (including the applicant) does not prevent information being considered confidential. Underlying the Tribunal's decision was the principle that every person will have a different perception of an event and each individual's recollection will vary, so that information known to an applicant may not in fact correspond exactly to information which an authority holds. So while the facts underlying the content of the disputed letter may have been known to the applicant, the way in which those facts had been recalled by the letter's author imputed a personal element to the information which meant that it should retain its confidentiality. Indeed, the Tribunal was satisfied that even where a synopsis of the information had been provided, the personal element would remain and with it the necessary quality of confidence.

The Tribunal was asked to consider some interesting questions regarding confidentiality and the application of s.41 in *Bluck* v. *Information Commissioner and Epsom and St Helier University NHS Trust* (EA/2006/0090, 17 September 2007); [2011] 1 Info LR 1017. The case arose from a request for the medical records of a deceased person. The deceased's mother sought hospital records for a period leading up to her daughter's death at Epsom and St Helier NHS Trust. The Trust refused disclosure on the basis that the information was confidential and could only be released with the consent of the deceased's next of kin (which had been refused). Citing the Court of Appeal decisions in *Coco* v. *AN Clark (Engineers) Ltd* [1968] FSR 415 (the leading authority on the law of confidence), *Ash* v. *McKennitt* [2006] EWCA Civ 1714 and the House of Lords decision in *Attorney General* v. *Guardian Newspapers Ltd (No.2)* [1990] 1 AC 109, counsel for the appellant argued that:

1.   there is a clear public interest in the disclosure of information in cases where a hospital has been negligent in the treatment of a patient, leading to that patient's death, the public interest lying in the fact that negligence is exposed and can be avoided in the future;
2.   a claim of breach of confidence was not sustainable in the absence of any detriment likely to be suffered by either the deceased or her estate;
3.   so much of the information contained in the deceased's medical records had already passed into the public domain that it no longer had the required quality of confidence; and
4.   a claim of breach of confidence could not survive the death of the person whose private information was at issue and the personal representative of that person could not enforce, post mortem, any such claim which might have existed while they were alive.

Consequently, it was argued that any breach of confidence was not actionable as required by s.41(1)(b).

In relation to the appellant's first submission (public interest), the Tribunal held that the public interest in maintaining the s.41 exemption was not outweighed by the arguments for disclosure. If a patient was aware that his or her medical records may at some stage be disclosed to the public, the patient may not give full disclosure to hospital staff, therefore risking an incorrect diagnosis and further harm. The Tribunal rejected the argument that the passage of time since death, the admission of negligence by the hospital and the extent to which information had already been released, was sufficient to outweigh the public interest in maintaining confidence.

In response to the appellant's second submission (the requirement for detriment in order to sustain a claim of breach of confidence), the Tribunal interpreted the Court of Appeal's decision in *Ash* v. *McKennitt* to mean that, 'if disclosure would be contrary to an individual's reasonable expectation of maintaining confidentiality in respect of his or her private information, then the absence of detriment in the sense apparently contemplated ... [by the appellant] is not a necessary ingredient of the cause of action'.

In relation to the appellant's third submission (public domain), the Tribunal decided that the information had not lost the necessary quality of confidence because there was a significant amount of information contained in the medical records which had not been disclosed in earlier correspondence. This was obviously not known by the appellant (because she was not able to inspect the information) and therefore the challenge on this point failed.

In addressing the appellant's final point (claim for breach of confidence), the Tribunal took into account counsel's contention that the absence of definitive authority on whether a duty of confidence survives death created a substantial doubt as to whether a claim for breach of confidence would succeed. In the absence of any compelling authority, all parties reverted to general principles. The appellant's case was that once a person has died, there is no one capable of enforcing a duty of confidence. The Information Commissioner and the hospital Trust argued that the basis of the equitable obligation of confidence stemmed from the purpose of a doctor's obligation of confidence and was therefore a legal, not just a moral and ethical, obligation (supported by the terms of the Hippocratic Oath). They argued that a doctor having accepted the obligation of confidence was an essential part of the doctor/patient relationship and it would be unconscionable for him or her to disclose information to the public either before death or afterwards. Consistent with the decision of Megarry J in *Coco* v. *Clark*, the Tribunal concluded that a duty of confidence is capable of surviving death. After a lengthy discussion of relevant case law and commentary, the Tribunal also decided that any breach of confidence would indeed be actionable by the deceased's personal representatives and therefore the requested information did constitute exempt information for the purposes of s.41. Although once an individual dies their personal information can no longer be protected as personal data under the DPA (which only covers living individuals), confidentiality issues should always be considered in such cases.

Accordingly, although traditionally detriment from disclosure has been a necessary element for a breach of confidence action, the *Bluck* case confirmed that this was not always necessary. Even if still required, what amounts to a 'detriment' is wider than might have previously been thought and in *Bluck* included the invasion of privacy. This approach was followed in *Higher Education Funding Council for England* v. *Information Commissioner and Guardian News and Media Ltd* (EA/2009/0036, 13 January 2010); [2011] 1 Info LR 1034, where it was noted that detriment could include reputational damage but that detriment was not required in cases involving disclosure of private information (sometimes referred to as the tort of misuse of private information as opposed to a breach of confidence) rather than commercial information. This follows a line of cases flowing from the House of Lords judgment in *Douglas* v. *Hello!* [2007] UKHL 21.

Confidential information and the Section 45 Code of Practice on the Discharge of Public Authorities' Functions under Part 1 of the FOIA

The overriding purpose of freedom of information is to ensure openness and transparency in the public sector. It will therefore be apparent to readers that sweeping confidentiality restrictions on information held by public authorities are necessarily incompatible with the FOIA. The code of practice issued in 2004 under s.45 of the FOIA by the Lord Chancellor of the Department for Constitutional Affairs (now the Ministry of Justice), referred to here as the 'Section 45 Code of Practice' and sometimes known as the 'Access Code', sets out guidance on when public authorities should accept information in confidence, and also on when to consult third parties where an authority plans to disclose its confidential information.

In relation to information provided to a public authority by a third party:

- the public authority should only accept that information is in confidence where possession of the information is necessary in connection with the authority's functions and where it would not otherwise be provided;
- the public authority should not agree to hold information in confidence unless the information is genuinely confidential; and
- the public authority should only agree to express confidentiality provisions where these are capable of justification to the Information Commissioner.

Although the Section 45 Code of Practice does not have the legal force of the FOIA itself, it nevertheless has considerable clout. The Information Commissioner has a duty to promote its observance and a legitimate expectation that authorities will comply with it. The courts will also normally refer to the Code when determining any question of compliance. The Code is currently being updated but has not yet been re-issued.

When considering whether to agree to hold information in confidence, here are some useful pointers:

- consider the nature of the interest to be protected and whether it is really necessary to hold information in confidence to protect that interest;

- consider whether it is possible to agree a limited duty of confidentiality, for example by clearly stating the circumstances in which the authority would disclose information;
- if the information will only be provided on condition that it is kept confidential, how important is the information in relation to the authority's functions?
- consider the nature of the person from whom the information is to be obtained and whether that person is also a public authority to whom the FOIA and the Section 45 Code of Practice apply (authorities must be particularly cautious about agreeing to keep information confidential where the supplier of the information is also a public authority).

It should be remembered that whether a public authority is subject to an obligation of confidence will not necessarily be limited to those cases where it has deliberately agreed to do so. An obligation of confidence may be implied in any event depending upon the nature of the information provided and/or the type of provider of the information or the authority's relationship with them. In *S* v. *Information Commissioner and General Register Office* (above) a key factor was that the interview which preceded the clarifying correspondence was expressly confidential and although, on the face of the subsequent correspondence between the parties to the interview and its content, there was nothing to expressly indicate confidence, it was held that the expectation of confidence from the interview extended to protect the subsequent correspondence.

The Section 45 Code of Practice also deals with consultation with third parties where an authority cannot disclose third party material without risking a breach of confidence. The Code says that:

- where disclosure cannot be made without consent (e.g. because this would in itself be a breach of confidence) the authority should consult the third party with a view to getting its consent to disclose, unless this is not practicable (for example because the third party cannot be located or because the costs of consulting would be disproportionate); and
- if the authority believes the cost of consulting to be disproportionate, then it should consider what is the reasonable course of action in the light of the requirements of the FOIA and the circumstances of the request.

This approach can be seen in practice in the recent decision notice, *Medicines and Healthcare Products Regulatory Agency* (FS50366396, 4 January 2012), although this revolved around the use of s.43, commercially prejudicial information: see **Chapter 5**.

In essence, if the authority has consent to disclose, there would be no actionable breach of confidence so it will not be able to rely on s.41. If the authority notifies a third party of its intention to disclose and the third party objects, the authority may still disclose if it chooses, and the third party can only prevent disclosure by injunction (there is no mechanism under the FOIA for the third party to prevent disclosure). If the authority discloses without consulting at all, then the third party will have no redress under the FOIA. Its only remedy would be a claim against the authority for damages, perhaps with an injunction to prevent further disclosure.

The public interest defence to breach of confidence

As noted above, when considering the application of s.41, an authority must assess whether a public interest defence to a claim exists. If it does, then the exemption cannot apply. The following principles should be applied when assessing the likelihood and force of a public interest defence:

- where a duty of confidence exists, there is a general public interest in favour of keeping that confidence;
- there is no general public interest in the disclosure of confidential information in breach of a duty of confidence – in other words, for a public interest defence to arise, there must be a specific factor in favour of disclosure;
- there is a public interest in ensuring public scrutiny of the activities of public authorities, so, if disclosure would enhance this scrutiny, this will weigh in favour of disclosure; examples might be:

    - information revealing misconduct or mismanagement of public funds;
    - information demonstrating that a public contract is not providing value for money;
    - information which would correct untrue statements or misleading acts by an authority;

- on the other hand, where the interests of a private person (whether an individual or an organisation) are protected by a duty of confidence, the public interest in scrutiny of public authority information is unlikely to override that duty;
- the FOIA itself has no influence on the nature of any public interest which attaches to the disclosure of information – so the fact that the FOIA might require disclosure were it not for s.41 is irrelevant;
- public authorities must have regard to the interests of the person to whom the duty of confidence is owed but the authority's own interests are not relevant; and
- the identity of the person requesting the information and the reason for the request are both irrelevant – the question is not whether disclosure to the applicant would be a breach of confidence, but whether disclosure to the public would be a breach (a request from a journalist or pressure group must be treated in the same way as a request from a person who is conducting historical research).

There is unlikely to be a public interest defence in cases where:

- the duty of confidence arises from a professional relationship;
- disclosure would affect the continued supply of important information (e.g. information from whistle-blowers); or

- disclosure would involve some risk to public administration or public or personal safety.

In *Derry City Council* v. *Information Commissioner* (EA/2006/0014, 11 December 2006); [2011] 1 Info LR 1105, the Tribunal considered whether a concluded agreement between two parties (where one is a public authority) could constitute information provided by one of them to the other as required by s.41. In this case Ryanair sent a fax (marked 'private and confidential') to the council (owner of Derry City Airport) setting out a number of terms for the operation of scheduled flights from London to Derry. No formal agreement was ever drawn up and so the parties were deemed to have conducted their business on the basis of the terms set out in the fax. Nearly six years after the fax was originally sent, the *Belfast Telegraph* wrote to the council and made an information request for information relating to its terms of business with Ryanair. The council refused to disclose on the basis that the fax contained exempt information pursuant to s.41.

The Tribunal considered whether the information contained in the fax could constitute information provided by one party to the other, as required by the words 'from any other person' in s.41(1)(a). It reasoned that to characterise an agreement as a process by which a public authority obtained information from another party imposed too great a strain on the wording of s.41. On application to the facts, a formal agreement, irrespective of the form it took, could not be said to have been provided by one party to the other and the fax therefore fell outside the scope of the exemption. It should be noted that there may be a difference where a business has existing terms and conditions (developed without any input from the authority), which it supplies to actual and potential customers such as the authority in confidence, where its terms are genuinely protected. However, decisions also show the reluctance of the Commissioner to accept that normal contract provisions are confidential, unlike, for example, schedules of specific technical details provided by the supplier for insertion in the contract. The key to s.41 is whether or not the information is truly confidential and not simply labelled as such (whether by contractual definition or stamp) and in reality provided by an external source to the authority.

In the context of the public interest defence to a claim to confidentiality, the Tribunal in the *Derry City Council* case was asked by counsel for the respondent to consider the Court of Appeal decision in *London Regional Transport* v. *Mayor of London* [2001] EWCA Civ 1491. The respondent argued that the public interest defence to a breach of confidence claim was applicable not just where there was some specific harm involved, but also where it was necessary to inform public debate. The Tribunal agreed with this submission to a certain extent but stressed that it is important to distinguish between (1) an issue on which the public interest is justifiably exercised at the time and (2) an issue of public interest which extends only as far as a half-hearted wish to be more fully informed on a matter of relatively low significance.

In addition, the Tribunal confirmed that in relation to the question of whether there is a public interest defence, 'there is no requirement to show exceptional circumstances' and 'the defence is not confined to specific and confined categories of case' (this approach was endorsed in *McTeggart* v. *Information Commissioner and Department of Culture, Arts and Leisure* (EA/2006/0084, 4 June 2007)). That said, it is still rare for a public interest defence to override an obligation of confidence to enable disclosure of confidential information under the FOIA because if the arguments are evenly balanced, the obligation of confidence should remain and not be overridden.

4.5.9   Other legal prohibitions (s.44)

Disclosures which are prohibited by other legal rules are also exempt from the FOIA. The FOIA does not cut across existing legal regimes which restrict access to information, nor does it provide alternative means of access to information which is expressly protected. The introduction of the FOIA triggered a review of existing legislation by the then Department for Constitutional Affairs (DCA) to determine whether various statutory restrictions on disclosure of information were consistent with the FOIA. Where the DCA determined that restrictions were not consistent, the relevant statutes were to be amended, using powers conferred by s.75 of the FOIA. As the impact of the FOIA has spread, it is clear that the statutory prohibitions which remained are continually being re-assessed and tested in the light of the FOIA, so it is likely that this process of change will continue. Practitioners should therefore ensure they check up-to-date versions of any statutory provision where a restriction on disclosure may have existed in the past and check up-to-date decision notices and judgments as to whether it continues to be accepted that the provision does prohibit disclosure.

There are three types of existing legal provisions which will apply in this context:

- disclosures prohibited by statute;
- disclosures which would be incompatible with EU law; or
- disclosures which would be a contempt of court.

It will be immediately apparent that the exemption applies to any disclosure which is a criminal offence, or subject to regulatory, public or civil law restriction. It does not, however, extend to disclosures which are unlawful at common law (except by reason of contempt of court), so the FOIA is no basis for avoiding a disclosure which might be a tort or breach of contract. Breaches of common law are dealt with, where appropriate, by specific exemptions, such as those covering breach of confidence (s.41) and defamation (s.79).

There will be many bars to disclosure falling within this category, far too numerous to list here. The fundamental principle underlying the exemption is that the FOIA does not cut across other legal restrictions on disclosure. So, where disclosure is prohibited by the Official Secrets Act, the DPA or the Human Rights Act 1998, for example, the FOIA will not compel a public authority to make information available. There are similarly many restrictions relating to tax and social security, and various prohibitions on disclosure of information obtained in the course of investigations by bodies such as the Equality and Human Rights Commission and the Parliamentary Commissioner for Administration, better known as the Parliamentary Ombudsman. Certain information obtained by regulators such as the Financial Services Authority, together with utilities watchdogs like Ofgem, Ofwat and Ofcom, will also be exempt under the FOIA (note that depending upon the nature of the information, the EIR may be more relevant to the utilities regulators), although the application of the exemption will depend on the circumstances in which the information was obtained by the watchdog and the precise scope of its statutory powers.

Care is needed when considering what amounts to a 'Community obligation' as this will not include all types of legal direction or obligation emanating from the European Union bodies. The critical issue is whether or not the obligation is directly binding on the public authority concerned. Accordingly, it does include EU Regulations, EU Treaties and their protocols with such direct effect, Directives (where they have such direct effect), a Decision (to its addressees only) but not recommendations or opinions.

Regardless of the circumstances and even if there are weighty factors in favour of disclosure of the requested details in the public interest, as the exemption is absolute, the public interest will not override a valid prohibition on disclosure protected by s.44. Thus in *Thomas* v. *Information Commissioner and the Auditor General for Wales* (EA/2010/0145, 16 March 2011), an audit report confirmed there were serious issues to be addressed by a council, including lack of accountability, ineffective scrutiny and weak self-regulation. However, the information supporting the report had been collected under the Public Audit (Wales) Act 2004 and since its s.54 prohibited disclosure of those details, the Auditor General was not able to disclose details of any councillors involved and the use of s.44 of the FOIA was upheld.

The Upper Tribunal considered when the prohibition must be in place for s.44 to be claimed, compared to the timing of the request, response and internal review in *Information Commissioner* v. *Her Majesty's Revenue and Customs* v. *Gaskell* [2011] UKUT 296 (AAC); [2011] 2 Info LR 11. There was an information request to the Rent Service (part of the Department for Work and Pensions) for certain details of letting agents providing rental information to it for the South Devon area and for details of the particular agent who provided it with certain specific rental information on two Dawlish properties. An anonymised copy of the list was provided but the specific details requested were withheld for reasons of personal information, confidential information and commercial prejudice, ss.40(2), 41 and 43(2) of the FOIA respectively. On internal review, the information was still withheld but also on the basis of s.36 (prejudice to the effective conduct of public affairs). A complaint was made to the Commissioner and between that date and the

Commissioner issuing his decision notice, the Rent Service was reorganised and became part of the Valuation Office Agency, or VOA within HM Revenue and Customs (HMRC).

The VOA raised a new exemption with the Commissioner when responding to his investigation, s.44. This was on the basis that the information was now held by VOA and if it were to disclose it pursuant to any decision notice (or otherwise under the FOIA), it would breach s.18 of the Commissioners for Revenue and Customs Act 2005 which prohibits disclosure by HMRC officials of information held by HMRC in connection with a function of the Revenue and Customs. This provision had not applied at the time of the complainant's request, did not apply (and so was not raised in responses) at the time of the initial refusal notice, nor at the time of the internal review refusal notice. The Commissioner's decision notice, which held that the details were exempt under s.44 and should not be disclosed, was appealed. The First-tier Tribunal disagreed with the Commissioner and held that he had no discretion in relation to specifying steps to be taken under s.50(4) in relation to enforcement of compliance with the FOIA, meaning he had no power to consider a new exemption not previously claimed by the public authority in its refusal notices, even in these circumstances. An appeal against that finding led to the matter being considered by the Upper Tribunal where it assessed the impact of this type of case, described as one of 'retrospective difficulty'. The issue of the date at which relevant facts can be considered in relation to a decision on disclosure (i.e. at the date of the information request, or later – and if so how late) are central to this judgment.

The Upper Tribunal found that the Commissioner had a discretion (not a fixed duty) in respect of the exercise of his powers under s.50(4) (deciding on the steps which must be taken by the authority to comply with the FOIA), which enabled him to decide on late exemptions. More importantly in this case, the Tribunal found that the Commissioner 'was entitled to consider whether disclosure would have been prohibited at the point in time when HMRC officials would have been required to take steps to disclose the information'. In other words, facts and the applicable law in force at the actual time of the disclosure could be considered, even though later than the request and refusal notices.

Section 44 is considered further in the context of procurement and s.43(2) in **Chapter 5**.

CHAPTER 5

The qualified exemptions

Liz Fitzsimons, Eversheds LLP

5.1 INTRODUCTION

Chapter 4 looked at the absolute exemptions, which protect whole classes of information falling within the various categories set out in the Freedom of Information Act 2000 (FOIA). The qualified exemptions are very different. The qualified exemptions apply:

- only where the public interest permits – that is to say, only if the public interest in maintaining that exemption outweighs the public interest in disclosing the information; and
- in some cases, only if disclosure would prejudice the interests described in the exemption (such as, for example, the effective conduct of public affairs), and so for these exemptions the question arises not only of what interests they protect, but also the prior question of what prejudice means. In these cases, the prejudice test must be met for the exemption to be engaged; the public interest test must then be met if the exemption is to be effective as a basis for refusing to disclose the requested information.

As noted, the public interest test applies to all the qualified exemptions. The prejudice test applies only to some. The prejudice-based exemptions are clear from their language as they refer specifically to 'prejudice' or similar terms, such as 'inhibit' or 'endanger'. If an exemption is not prejudice based, it is class based. The prejudice exemptions are:

- national security (s.24);
- defence (s.26);
- international relations (s.27(1));
- relations within the UK (s.28);
- the economy (s.29);
- law enforcement (s.31);
- audit functions (s.33);
- the effective conduct of public affairs (s.36);
- health and safety (s.38); and
- commercial interests (s.43(2)).

The remaining qualified class-based exemptions – for which only the public interest is relevant – relate to:

- information intended for future publication (s.22);
- international relations (s.27(2), which relates to information obtained from another state);
- investigations and proceedings conducted by public authorities (s.30);
- formulation of government policy (s.35);
- communications with Her Majesty, etc. (s.37) (to the extent not absolute);
- environmental information (s.39);
- personal information (s.40) (to the extent not absolute);
- legal professional privilege (s.42); and
- commercial interests (s.43(1), which applies only to trade secrets).

The exemptions to which the prejudice test does not apply are listed at **5.3**. The exemptions to which it does are listed at **5.4**.

Readers wishing to keep fully up to date with developments on the application of the exemptions are referred to the practical journal *Freedom of Information* (**www.foij.com**).

5.2 APPLYING THE PUBLIC INTEREST TEST

There is no definition in the FOIA of 'public interest'. Indeed, the legislation says nothing at all on the subject, beyond the fact that in the case of two-thirds of the Act's exemptions, the public interest is a fundamental consideration. Section 2 says that if a public authority receives a request for information which may be subject to a qualified exemption, then the authority must apply the public interest test in considering whether or not to disclose that information. To be precise, the test in s.2(1)(b) (in respect of the obligation to confirm or deny) and s.2(2)(b) (in respect of the obligation to disclose information held) is whether:

> in all the circumstances of the case, the public interest in maintaining the [exemption] outweighs the public interest in disclosing [whether the public authority holds] the information.

Given that so many of the FOIA exemptions are qualified, a good grasp of what we mean when we talk about the public interest is essential for the correct handling of information requests under the FOIA.

There are other areas of English law to which public interest considerations apply, and all of them predate the FOIA. There is the public interest defence to claims for breach of confidence (see **Chapter 4**) and for infringement of copyright. The Public Interest Disclosure Act 1998 protects whistle-blowers in the workplace on public interest grounds, intended to promote the detection and exposure of misconduct and malpractice likely to endanger employees. Even in these contexts, however, there is nothing which usefully serves as a working definition. As noted by

Lord Hailsham, 'the categories of public interest are not closed' (*D* v. *National Society for the Prevention of Cruelty to Children* [1978] AC 171 at 230). However, although the 'public interest' is a flexible concept and dependent upon the facts of each case, the Commissioner's guidance makes clear that it will always be 'something which serves the interests of the public'. There is accordingly a distinction between 'things in the public interest' and 'things which merely interest the public'.

There is a large volume of guidance about the public interest through decision notices and, more importantly, judgments of the Tribunals and courts. There is also official guidance from the Information Commissioner both generally and in respect of individual exemptions.

5.2.1 The concept of the public interest

One very helpful judicial summary of the public interest comes from an Australian case, *Commonwealth of Australia* v. *John Fairfax Ltd* (1981) 32 ALR 485 (endorsed by the House of Lords in the *Spycatcher* case: *Attorney General* v. *Guardian Newspapers Ltd (No.2)* [1990] 1 AC 109) in which the court said:

> It is unacceptable in our democratic society that there should be a restraint on the publication of information relating to government when the only vice of that information is that it enables the public to discuss, review and criticize government action.
>
> Accordingly, the court will determine the government's claim to confidentiality by reference to the public interest. Unless disclosure is likely to injure the public interest, it will not be protected.
>
> The court will not prevent the publication of information which merely throws light on the past workings of the government, even if it be not public property, so long as it does not prejudice the community in other respects. Then disclosure will itself serve the public interest in keeping the community informed and in promoting discussion of public affairs. If, however, it appears that disclosure will be inimical to the public interest because national security, relations with foreign countries or the ordinary business of government will be prejudiced, disclosure will be restrained. (pp.51–2)

In the early days of its passage through Parliament, the Freedom of Information Bill gave public authorities discretion to consider whether information should be disclosed on public interest grounds. This changed at the report stage, when consideration of the public interest was made a duty. Parliament recognised that for freedom of information to work there would have to be a fundamental shift from the historic Westminster culture of need-to-know to a new 'open' era of right-to-know. As a result, the legislation was redrafted to reflect the principle, stated by Lord Falconer, that 'information must be disclosed except where there is an overriding public interest in keeping specific information confidential'.

5.2.2 The balancing exercise

The public interest test described in s.2 of the FOIA stipulates that a qualified exemption can only apply where the public interest in maintaining an exemption outweighs the public interest in either confirming or denying information is held, or disclosing information. For ease, references which follow discuss the obligation to disclose. However, the same points are relevant to the obligation to confirm or deny. It should be noted that public authorities are encouraged normally to confirm they hold information even if its disclosure is exempt. It is only if the actual confirmation that such information is or is not held would trigger the relevant exemption that the authority should consider whether it is exempt from the duty to confirm or deny.

The wording of s.2 has several significant implications. First, it requires public authorities to consider the public interest both for and against disclosure (or, more precisely, the public interest 'in maintaining the exemption' versus the public interest in disclosure). Only where the scales favour exemption can the duty to disclose be disapplied. Secondly, it sets the default at 'disclose'. If the arguments are evenly balanced then the outcome must be to disclose. Accordingly, the burden of proof in justifying an exemption rests with the public authority. To do so, it must effectively be able to demonstrate two things: that there is a pressing need for non-disclosure, and that to override the right of access is a necessary and proportionate way of meeting that need.

The balancing exercise must therefore start from this general standpoint of competing interests determining an outcome. It does not, however, mean simply considering any public interest arguments which might be available. As the Tribunal has stated in *Bellamy* v. *Information Commissioner and the Secretary of State for Trade and Industry* (EA/2005/0023, 4 April 2006):

> not all public interest considerations which might otherwise appear to be relevant to the subject matter of the disclosure should be taken into account. What has to be concentrated upon is the particular public interest necessarily inherent in the exemption or exemptions relied upon.

The particular circumstances of each case are therefore absolutely vital in balancing public interest arguments. To underline this, in *Hogan and Oxford City Council* v. *Information Commissioner* (EA/2005/0026 and EA/2005/0030, 17 October 2006); [2011] 1 Info LR 588, the Tribunal has stated that public authorities must not maintain blanket policies for refusing information of a certain type:

> the public authority is not permitted to maintain a blanket refusal to disclose all information of a particular type or nature. The question to be asked is not: is the balance of public interest in favour of maintaining the exemption in relation to the type of information? The question to be asked is: is the balance of public interest in favour of maintaining the exemption in relation to *this* information, and in the circumstances of *this* case? The public authority may well have a general policy that the public interest is likely to be in favour of maintaining the exemption in respect of a specific type of information. However such a policy must not be inflexibly applied and the authority must always be willing to consider whether the circumstances of the case justify a departure from the policy.

The judgment further confirmed that factors in favour of disclosure could be generalised across exemptions and should be construed broadly. By contrast, the factors against disclosure could not, and not only should 'the public interests [be] expressed explicitly or impliedly in the particular exemption provision at issue' but they should also be construed narrowly.

From a purely operational perspective, given the nature of the public interest test and the fact that the burden of proof for justifying its application lies with the authority, whenever a decision maker comes to a view about where the balance lies, having assessed the relevant competing interests in the particular circumstances, he or she should clearly document:

- all the circumstances that have been considered;
- the specific public interests in favour of withholding information in the particular case, and the weight given to each;
- the specific public interests in favour of disclosure of information in the particular case, and the weight given to each;
- the considerations given to timescales; and
- the considerations given to partial disclosure (e.g. by redacting information which qualifies for exemption but disclosing everything else).

Aside from helping authorities to make assessments in the future, this will also provide the basis for a defence to any complaint or appeal. Proper decision making on the public interest test is driven objectively by the facts of the case and the application of the law under the FOIA, rather than by the discretion of the public authority making the decision.

5.2.3   Practical guidance from the Information Commissioner

In *The Public Interest Test*, FOIA guidance issued by the Information Commissioner in May 2012 (20120504, version 1.0), the Commissioner has provided some examples of factors which might apply in favour of disclosure when considering the public interest, and factors which are irrelevant.

Factors in favour of disclosure

The guidance confirms that the public interest in disclosure reflects 'a wide range of values and principles relating to the public good or what is in the best interests of society' and reinforces that 'there will always be a general public interest in transparency'. Examples of specific factors include the following:

1.   *To promote public understanding and provide a full picture.*
2.   *To promote transparency and accountability and safeguard democratic processes.*
3.   *To ensure good decision making by public authorities, including to ensure standards of integrity are upheld and that there is justice and fair treatment*

for all. This is because it will improve the quality of decisions and administration if authorities and officials have to provide reasoned explanations for their actions.

4.   *To ensure the best use of resources and fair competition in a mixed economy.* For example, where public services are outsourced to the private sector there is a public interest in genuine competition and value for money – disclosure of information about gifts and expenses will also reassure the public of the probity of elected officials.

5.   *To remove plausible suspicion of wrongdoing.*

The Information Tribunal in *Pugh* v. *Information Commissioner and Ministry of Defence* (EA/2007/0055, 7 December 2007) confirmed previous decisions on the public interest test.

> There is an assumption built into the FOIA that disclosure of information by public authorities on request is in the public interest in order to promote transparency and accountability in relation to the activities of public authorities. The strength of that interest and the strength of competing interests must be assessed on a case-by-case basis.

That followed the Tribunal decision in *Secretary of State for Work and Pensions* v. *Information Commissioner* (EA/2006/0040, 5 March 2007); [2011] 1 Info LR 716. This confirmed:

> There is no provision in FOIA comparable to regulation 12(2) of the Environmental Information Regulations 2004 which expressly requires public authorities to apply a presumption in favour of disclosure when considering exceptions to the general duty to disclose under those regulations. It can be said, however, that there is an assumption built into FOIA, that the disclosure of information by public authorities on request is in itself of value in the public interest in order to promote transparency and accountability in relation to the activities of public authorities. What this means is that there is always likely to be some public interest in favour of the disclosure of information under the Act. The strength of that interest and the strength of the competing interest in maintaining any relevant exemption must be assessed on a case by case basis: s.2(2)(b) requires the balance to be considered 'in all the circumstances of the case'.

Judgments still oscillate between whether there is a presumption in favour of disclosure in the public interest, or whether a public authority should instead consider as one of the pro-disclosure factors the assumption that disclosure will be in the public interest. Either way, there is no burden of proof on a public authority to establish that disclosure is in the public interest but rather a need to establish countervailing arguments as to why maintaining the exemption is in the greater public interest in the particular case.

Factors which are irrelevant

1.   *A risk of information being misunderstood, either because it is technical or incomplete.* The Queensland Information Commissioner memorably rejected the use of this factor on the ground that it is 'based on rather elitist and

paternalistic assumptions that government officials and external review authorities can judge what information should be withheld from the public for fear of confusing it, and can judge what is necessary or unnecessary in democratic society' (*Re Eccleston and Department of Family Services and Aboriginal and Islander Affairs* (1993) 1 QAR 60).

2. *A risk of embarrassment.*

3. *The 'class' or 'type' of information is not of itself normally an argument against disclosure.* This is particularly the case for non-prejudice exemptions where simply because information falls within a class-based exemption there is no inherent harm from disclosure, as confirmed by the Tribunal in *Alcock* v. *Information Commissioner and Chief Constable of Staffordshire Police* (EA/ 2006/0022, 12 December 2006).

4. *The suggestion that poor record keeping would be likely to result from disclosure is given little or no weight if argued as a factor against disclosure* (see further analysis of ss.35 and 36 below).

5. *Interests which are private in nature*, whether of the requestor in obtaining the information or a public authority in withholding embarrassing information.

6. *The identity or motives of the requestor.*

In addition to these factors, Parliament has made it clear that the motives of the person making the request for information will not be relevant in application of the public interest test (Hansard, HL vol.617, col.921, 17 October 2000, Lord Falconer):

> As far as public interest between disclosure on the one hand and the maintenance of exemption on the other is concerned, it has to be looked at objectively. One looks at the impact of disclosure, that is, making it public. What is the impact of the exemption being maintained? That should be looked at objectively rather than in terms of whatever the motive may be of the person applying. That does not mean that the motive of the person applying may not coincide with factors that could be relevant to what damage may be done and what assistance could be served by making the matter public. But individual motives will not be relevant to that.

This re-enforces the 'applicant blind' approach which public authorities normally need to take to comply with the FOIA.

5.2.4 Decisions of the Information Commissioner and Tribunal judgments

The Information Commissioner and also the First-tier Tribunal and the predecessor Information Tribunal (both for ease referred to as 'the Tribunal' in **Chapters 4** and **5**) and the Upper Tribunal have considered the public interest when adjudicating on appeals brought before them, and there is now a considerable body of guidance to be obtained from an analysis of these cases. Those of most relevance are considered below in the context of the exemptions to which they relate.

Traditionally, cases involving a number of exemptions – or exceptions under the Environmental Information Regulations 2004 (EIR) – have had the public interest test applied to each exemption or exception separately (detailed consideration of the EIR can be found in **Chapter 9**). This approach was challenged by Ofcom in relation to a request to release details of the locations of all UK mobile phone base stations (a case considered under the EIR). The authority argued that the public interest test factors should be aggregated and applied to all the relevant exceptions together rather than individually and appealed its case to the European Court of Justice who ruled in its favour (*Office of Communications* v. *Information Commissioner* [2011] EUECJ C-71/10; [2011] 2 Info LR 1). The Information Commissioner has accepted that in EIR cases, due to its European Directive foundations, aggregation is permitted.

In 2012 the Information Commissioner issued updated guidance on the public interest test, in respect of both the FOIA (as noted above) and the EIR. In the latter (*How Exceptions and the Public Interest Test Work in the Environmental Information Regulations*, 20120504, version 1.0) the aggregation of public interest factors is dealt with expressly:

> If more than one exception is engaged in relation to the same piece of information, and the balance of the public interest test for each of them is in favour of disclosure, the authortiy may then weigh the public interest in disclosure against the aggregated weight of the public interest arguments for maintaining all the exceptions.

Although the equivalent FOIA guidance does not refer to aggregation, the EIR note continues: 'The Commissioner's view is that [the ability to aggregate public interest arguments] does not apply to FOIA.'

Despite this, there continues to be pressure to adopt the EIR approach on aggregation in cases under the FOIA. This was most recently confirmed in the Upper Tribunal in the case of *Chief Constable of Devon and Cornwall* v. *(1) Information Commissioner and (2) SM* [2012] UKUT 34 (AAC) (1 February 2012). This involved a request for the locations of fixed number plate recognition cameras operated by or for the police force. Citing the *Ofcom* decision, the Upper Tribunal commented: 'it now appears to be established that the public interest in maintaining two or more exemptions must be aggregated when weighing it against the public interest in disclosure.' Similarly, in *Summers* v. *Information Commissioner and Commissioner of Police for the Metropolis* (EA/2011/0186, 24 February 2012), the Tribunal observed (obiter) that the principle from the *Ofcom* case applied also to the FOIA.

As it is a superior tribunal, a decision of the Upper Tribunal sets a precedent. However, the Commissioner's approach to cases under the FOIA remains that his guidance on the public interest test as referenced above still stands as drafted although he keeps relevant developments and judgments under review. The Commissioner's position may accordingly evolve in the near future so as to accept that aggregation applies to the FOIA as well as the EIR.

5.3 CATEGORIES TO WHICH THE PUBLIC INTEREST TEST (BUT NOT THE PREJUDICE TEST) APPLIES – CLASS-BASED QUALIFIED EXEMPTIONS

Information falling within these categories will be exempt only if the information concerned falls within the class of information described by the exemption *and* if the public interest in withholding information outweighs the public interest in disclosing it.

5.3.1 Information intended for future publication (s.22)

Most public authorities are now proactive about releasing information independently of their obligations under the FOIA and, in any event, under s.19 of the FOIA authorities have obligations to proactively publish information through a publication scheme (see **Chapter 2** for more details). The s.22 exemption is intended to facilitate this process by ensuring that individual requests do not dictate publication timetables or force publication prematurely (unless, of course, the public interest requires this). In effect, the exemption allows authorities to manage proactive publication according to the particular exigencies of preparation, administration and other circumstances. So, for example, where an authority has commissioned a report for which a publication date has been set, s.22 may allow it to withhold the content of the report until the 'official' publication date, provided it is reasonable to do so.

To qualify for the exemption, information must meet three conditions:

- it must be held by the authority with a view to its publication by the authority or by someone else at some future date (although the precise date need not have been determined);
- the intention to publish must exist at the time the FOIA request is made; and
- it must be reasonable in all the circumstances for the authority to withhold the information until the future date of planned release.

'Publication' means any information which is addressed to the public at large or any section of it. For most public authorities this will therefore include the scheduled publication of announcements, press releases, speeches, interviews and articles, email bulletins, information available online and information retrievable electronically, including books, journals, periodicals and newspapers. For central government it will also include consultation papers, White Papers and Green Papers, reports and responses to select committee reports. Publication of research and statistics may also be covered.

What does 'with a view to publication' mean?

Section 22 can apply whether or not the actual date of publication has been determined, and whether or not publication will be by the authority itself or by someone else. The requirement that information must already have been held with a view to publication at the time the request is made means only that an authority cannot avoid disclosing something (for example, because it might be embarrassing) by deciding after it receives a request that the information will be published at some future date.

Information which an authority intends to pass on to another organisation for publication by it would normally also engage the exemption, as, perhaps, would information held by an authority which it has no intention of publishing itself, but which it knows will be published by someone else. Naturally, it is not enough in these circumstances that a decision whether or not to publish is pending.

It is important that the information to be published can be sufficiently identified. In the decision notice, *Ministry of Justice* (FS50121803, 14 April 2009), the Commissioner refused to allow the Ministry of Justice to rely on s.22 in respect of a request for prison-related information about a number of notorious murderers, even though it intended to transfer the details to the National Archives (TNA) at some point in 2005. Although it was agreed that 'publication' included transfer to TNA for it to make the information available to the public by inspection, the authority was not able at the time of the request 'to clearly point out the information it intended to publish'. In effect it was 'working out what to transfer to TNA' as part of the same exercise of 'working out what in fact s.22 applied to' and in those circumstances the exemption was not engaged.

A view to publication must be current and continuing, and in this sense will cover drafts of information intended to be published, e.g. notes for a speech. Once a draft has been superseded, however, information which is removed from the subsequent draft will not normally be s.22 exempt unless there remains a justifiable ground on which it can still be said to be held with a view to publication (although, of course, other exemptions may apply instead). Thus the material finally agreed to be included in the speech would be protected but the information removed from the final speech would probably cease to be protected under s.22.

Applying the public interest test

In relation to s.22, disclosure is planned at some future date anyway, therefore the public interest in this context turns not on whether to disclose but on *when* – that is, on whether it is reasonable to withhold disclosure until the intended future date.

The public interest in allowing public authorities to release information in a manner and form, and at a time, of their own choosing is important. In the general run of public affairs, publication is planned and managed according to prevailing circumstances and authorities should rightfully be able to make their own arrangements. Considerations relevant to assessing the public interest might therefore include:

- the nature of the proposed publication timetable itself (the more distant, contingent or indeterminate the prospective publication date, the less heavily it might weigh in favour of exemption and the less reasonable delay might be);

- possible detrimental effects of early/delayed publication – for example, if disclosure might damage a third party's private interests or give rise unnecessarily to public concern, then this might favour withholding;
- whether simultaneous disclosure is a consideration in itself – accelerated disclosure to a freedom of information applicant may be unfair to others;
- pre-publication procedures – whether immediate disclosure would undermine consultation with, or pre-publication disclosure to, a particular person (it is normally good practice, for example, to disclose information about a complaint to the complainant or the subject of the complaint before publication);
- publication procedures – for example, the reports of public inquiries are often published under the protection of the Parliamentary Papers Act 1840 to avoid defamation or other civil action;
- previous undertakings – for example, where Ministers have promised to inform Parliament first about certain information, or where family members should be informed first about matters relating to a relative.

In the decision notice *Department of Education for Northern Ireland* (FS50123357, 21 September 2006), the Information Commissioner examined a request for disclosure of financial information relating to the South Eastern Education and Library Board (SEELB). The case focused on a report commissioned from KPMG following a statutory inquiry in 2004 and financial difficulties within SEELB resulting from the overspending of £6 million in 2003/4 and 2004/5. The KPMG report was due for publication in October 2006, six months after the information request had been made, and the department cited s.22, arguing that premature disclosure of the report would not be in the public interest because it would lead to considerable adverse press which would be highly damaging to the conduct of public affairs and the delivery of public services. The Commissioner noted that SEELB's financial difficulties had attracted considerable media coverage and that there is a public interest in transparency about issues of financial management and accountability in public authorities. At the same time, he acknowledged that what interests the public is not necessarily the same as what is in the public interest. In deciding that the public interest in disclosure was not outweighed by the public interest in maintaining the exemption, the Commissioner commented that the potential impact of media interest in an issue is not in itself a valid reason to withhold information which would inform the public about a matter of such importance as the financial health of an education board.

However, the Information Commissioner's decision notice in *Governing Body of the University of Liverpool* (FS50349323, 13 June 2011) illustrates when the public interest may support maintaining the exemption. An information request was received for a PhD thesis in circumstances when all PhD projects required such a thesis to be published to the academic community. In this case its publication was delayed because it was deliberately embargoed for five years on the basis that its disclosure would inhibit commercial publication of the thesis. The embargo would be lifted once the book on the subject of the thesis was published (and the thesis would then be available in the university library), or, if there were no publishing deal, the thesis would be made available in the library as normal. The privately funded PhD contained research thought to be of real commercial value to the researcher. The researcher had a proposed publishing contract in June, submitted the thesis in July and it was requested in August before the researcher signed a publishing contract in September 2010 with a view to publication around August 2011. The contract contained a provision prohibiting publication of the thesis before then.

The Commissioner agreed that the exemption was engaged and that the public interest in maintaining the exemption outweighed the public interest in disclosure because it was reasonable to delay publication as proposed. This was due in particular to the likely damage to the author and to the university's reputation from premature disclosure, as well as because of potential damage to the author's and the publisher's commercial interests (there was a need to protect the market for such future publications). It was emphasised that disclosure was only delayed for a specific amount of time which enhanced the public interest in waiting for publication and that where the information contained third party comments, use of which was key to the author's ongoing relationships and academic career, it was not in the public interest to undermine those sources by premature disclosure.

5.3.2   International relations (s.27(2))

Section 27 is a prejudice-based exemption (see **5.4**) except in so far as it relates to confidential information which is obtained from a foreign state or an international organisation or international court. Information from these bodies is exempt irrespective of any question of prejudice (but still subject to the public interest test) (s.27(2)). The focus of s.27(2) is on the source of the information and the circumstances under which it was obtained.

An 'international court' is one established by a resolution of an international organisation of which the UK is a member, or by an international agreement to which the UK is a party. The International Court of Justice, European Court of Justice, International Criminal Court and European Court of Human Rights all qualify as international courts for the purposes of the FOIA.

An 'international organisation' is one whose members include two or more states. For these purposes, a 'state' includes the government of any state, and any organ of government, such as a state's legislature and executive, and also territories outside the UK including Crown dependencies like Jersey and Guernsey, British Overseas Territories like Gibraltar, and territorial entities not necessarily recognised otherwise as states.

The UK itself need not be a member state of an organisation for it to qualify as an international organisation, so, as well as the United Nations and the European Union, OPEC is covered, as is the Organisation of American States. The definition also extends to any organ of such an organisation, which would include, for example, the European Commission and European Parliament.

For the purposes of s.27(2) 'confidential information' is defined in s.27(3) as:

> information obtained … at any time while the terms on which it was obtained require it to be held in confidence or while the circumstances in which it was obtained make it reasonable for the state, organisation or court to expect that it will be so held.

This allows for the possibility that a duty of confidence may arise by reasonable expectation or by express agreement. It is therefore wider than the s.41 exemption for confidential information generally, which reflects the common law position rather than the conventionally wider restrictions which parties agree by written contract. Also in contrast with s.41, s.27(2) and (3) are not conditional on a breach being actionable.

Applying the public interest test

Some examples of factors to consider when assessing the public interest as it relates to confidential information falling within s.27 are whether:

- disclosure would be contrary to international law (e.g. a breach of a treaty obligation);
- disclosure would undermine the UK's reputation for honouring its international commitments and obligations;
- disclosure is likely to undermine the willingness of the state, international organisation or court that supplied the information to supply other confidential information in future (or would be likely to have such an effect on the willingness of states, international organisations or courts in general);
- disclosure is likely to provoke a negative reaction from the state, international organisation or court that supplied the information, which would damage the UK's relations with it and/or its ability to protect and promote UK interests;
- disclosure is likely to result in another state, international organisation or court disclosing – contrary to the UK's interests – confidential information supplied to the UK; or
- the state, international organisation or court that supplied the confidential information has objected to its disclosure, and whether good relations with it are likely to suffer if the objection were ignored.

Authorities should also consider consulting the Foreign and Commonwealth Office when considering disclosing information which may affect the UK's international relations.

5.3.3 Investigations and proceedings (s.30)

In essence, s.30 serves to ensure that the FOIA cannot be used to circumvent the rules of disclosure governing criminal investigations and proceedings. There are two very separate exemptions within s.30 and each applies in distinct circumstances. The first, s.30(1), applies to information which has been held at any time for the relevant purposes – even if those purposes have since ceased to apply. The second, s.30(2), focuses on the confidential source of the information and only applies if it was obtained or recorded for specific purposes.

Section 30(1)

The s.30(1) exemption itself has three separate parts. The first (s.30(1)(a)) relates to information held relating to *particular* criminal investigations or proceedings and applies to information which an authority has held at any time for an investigation which it has a *duty to conduct* in order to ascertain:

- whether a person should be charged with an offence; or
- whether a person charged with an offence is guilty of it.

The s.30(1)(a) exemption is primarily intended to cover information obtained by the police, National Criminal Intelligence Service or the Serious Fraud Office during the course of an investigation, and also information and evidence which leads to the bringing of charges, but it could also apply to criminal investigations conducted by organisations like:

- HM Revenue and Customs;
- Department for Business, Innovation and Skills;
- Department for Environment, Food and Rural Affairs;
- Food Standards Agency;
- Environment Agency;
- Health and Safety Executive;
- Financial Services Authority; and
- Office of Fair Trading.

The s.30(1)(b) exemption applies to investigations which may lead to criminal proceedings which the authority has the *power* (but not necessarily the duty) to conduct. It is therefore relevant primarily to authorities with regulatory or investiga-tory functions which may conduct investigations with a view to deciding whether to charge and take proceedings against a person for a criminal offence.

Following on from s.30(1)(b), s.30(1)(c) applies to *actual* criminal proceedings which the authority has the *power* to conduct itself. The exemption will therefore apply to authorities such as the Crown Prosecution Service and any other public authority with prosecution functions.

Section 30(1) will not exempt information which is unrelated to particular investigations or proceedings – such as statistics on conviction rates – since the information must relate to one or more *specific cases*. However, the exemption is not limited by time, so it will continue to apply to relevant information even after investigations and proceedings are finished (although, of course, the conclusion of proceedings may affect the application of the public interest test). Thus in the Information Commissioner's decision notice, *Commissioner of the Metropolitan*

Police (FS50363995, 20 December 2011), the investigation file into a 1948 massacre in Malaysia was requested but properly refused under s.30(1)(a)(i). (For an example of even older information being successfully withheld, see *Marriott* v. *Information Commissioner and Metropolitan Police* (EA/2010/0183, 6 October 2011), concerning late-19th century information related to the 'Jack the Ripper' investigation.) Likewise, even if the data were created before the s.30(1)(a)–(c) investigation or proceedings and so were not created or obtained for them or during them but were later used for those purposes, the data will be protected.

Section 30(2)

The s.30(2) exemption is not restricted to particular investigations or proceedings but is nevertheless quite narrow, being limited by two quite specific requirements.

First, it can only apply if the information in question was obtained or recorded for the purposes of the authority's functions in relation to one of four categories listed in s.30(2)(a)(i)–(iv). Secondly, the information must have come from confidential sources.

THE AUTHORITY'S FUNCTIONS

Section 30(2) can only apply to information held by a public authority where:

(a)   it was obtained or recorded by the authority for the purposes of its functions relating to:

    (i)   investigations falling within subsection (1)(a) or (b),

    (ii)   criminal proceedings which the authority has power to conduct,

    (iii) investigations (other than investigations falling within subsection (1)(a) or (b)) which are conducted by the authority for any of the purposes specified in section 31(2) and either by virtue of Her Majesty's prerogative or by virtue of powers conferred by or under any enactment, or

    (iv)   civil proceedings which are brought by or on behalf of the authority and arise out of such investigations, and

(b)   it relates to the obtaining of information from confidential sources.

In relation to s.30(2)(a)(iii), the specified purposes are for:

(a)   ascertaining whether any person has failed to comply with the law;

(b)   ascertaining whether any person is responsible for any conduct which is improper;

(c)   ascertaining whether circumstances exist or may arise which would justify regulatory action in pursuance of any enactment;

(d)   ascertaining a person's fitness or competence in relation to the management of bodies corporate or in relation to any profession or other activity which he or she is, or seeks to become, authorised to carry on;

(e)   ascertaining the cause of an accident;

(f)   protecting charities against misconduct or mismanagement (whether by trustees or other persons) in their administration;

(g)   protecting the property of charities from loss or misapplication;
(h)   recovering the property of charities;
(i)   securing the health, safety and welfare of persons at work; and
(j)   protecting persons other than persons at work against risk to health or safety arising out of or in connection with the actions of persons at work.

One effect of the wording of s.30(2) appears to be that, if an authority sets up an inquiry which may reveal illegality, but which the authority does not have express statutory or prerogative power to conduct, then the information obtained or recorded for that inquiry will not be exempt, even if obtained from confidential sources.

CONFIDENTIAL SOURCES

Confidential sources will usually be informants or whistle-blowers whose identity an authority would want to protect. Such sources will not normally extend, however, to personnel working covertly to gather information, nor to information gathered using covert technology.

Unlike under s.41 on confidential information, in order to engage s.30(2), the information itself need not be confidential; it is the relationship with the source which must be confidential. In practice, depending upon the nature of the information involved, the personal information and/or confidential information exemptions may also apply to information obtained from confidential sources in which case ss.40 and/or 41 respectively should be considered before looking at s.30(2).

In *Alcock* v. *Information Commissioner and Chief Constable of Staffordshire Police* (EA/2006/0022, 12 December 2006), the Tribunal confirmed that s.30(2) is a class-based exemption and therefore there is no need for prejudice to be shown for it to be engaged. In assessing the public interest in favour of disclosure it is relevant that the applicant already knows a substantial amount of the information sought.

Applying the public interest test

At the heart of s.30 lies the importance to law enforcement of public confidence in the investigations and proceedings to which the exemption refers. Public confidence can obviously be fostered by transparency, but it also requires the processes themselves to deliver justice effectively. As the White Paper *Open Government* (Cm 2290, July 1993) stated in Chapter 3, para.3.12:

> There should be no commitment to disclose information which would help potential lawbreakers and criminals, put life, safety or the environment in danger ... Investigation of suspected crime ... must normally be kept secret from the suspect and others. Witness statements, names and addresses of witnesses and reports from the police and others to prosecutors could, if disclosed other than as required by the courts, jeopardise law enforcement or the prevention or prosecution of crime, or be extremely unfair to a temporary suspect against whom (in the event) no real evidence existed. It is in the interests of both the individuals concerned and the integrity of the prosecution process

that material relating to both live and completed prosecutions and to prosecutions which do not go ahead can be kept confidential.

In balancing public interest considerations, public authorities will need to consider the potential effects of a disclosure and the nature and seriousness of the matter being pursued.

The ability of the police, HM Revenue and Customs and other public authorities to obtain information in pursuance of their investigative processes is critical to the prevention and detection of crime and to the integrity and effectiveness of the criminal justice system. Certain disclosures, particularly in relation to confidential sources, could have extremely serious consequences, lead to serious risk of injury or loss of life and be damaging to the willingness of other individuals to supply information.

When considering the balance of the public interest, a weighty consideration will be the extent to which disclosing or withholding information would:

- promote or diminish the chances of a successful prosecution, bringing future charges or making arrests;
- promote or diminish the chances of a fair trial;
- be fair to those who have not been prosecuted, in cases where a decision has been taken not to proceed;
- assist or hamper the gathering of intelligence information from confidential sources such as informants, whistle-blowers or calls to Crimestoppers;
- further the interests of justice through the participation of victims, witnesses, informants, suspects or offenders in investigations and proceedings – and either protect or endanger them as they do so;
- assist or impede other ongoing or future proceedings;
- prevent or facilitate the commission of crime.

It was confirmed by the Information Tribunal in *Digby-Cameron* v. *Information Commissioner and (1) Bedfordshire Police and (2) Hertfordshire Police* (EA/2008/0023 and EA/2008/0025, 26 January 2009) that the starting focus point was the purpose of the exemption: to protect and encourage witnesses and informants so that they were not deterred; to maintain an independent criminal process and to ensure that the criminal system was the sole forum for deciding criminal guilt. This was confirmed by the Tribunal in *Breeze* v. *Information Commissioner and the Chief Constable of Norfolk Constabulary and the Crown Prosecution Service* (EA/2011/0057, 2 March 2012). In *Toms* v. *Information Commissioner* (EA/2005/0027, 19 June 2006), the Information Tribunal considered the application of the public interest test in the context of s.30(1). It noted that the question of how competing public interests should be balanced does not constitute an exercise of discretion. The relevant question is whether the FOIA has been properly applied to the facts and requires an analysis of both fact and law. In addition, the Tribunal noted that in assessing the balance of the public interest, regard should be had, inter alia, to such matters as the stage or stages reached in any particular investigation or criminal proceedings, whether and to what extent the information has already been released into the public domain and the significance or sensitivity of the information requested.

Factors supporting disclosure include cases where there may be a need to put the record straight, or justifiable concern about an investigation or prosecution. For instance, in the case of *Guardian Newspapers Ltd* v. *Information Commissioner and Chief Constable of Avon and Somerset Police* (EA/2006/0017, 5 March 2007) it was noted that justifiable concerns about the lack of any proper vigour in the investigation would be a decisive factor. The overriding concern though will always be to ensure that the outcome of any investigation or proceedings is not put at risk.

Section 30 is often considered hand in hand with s.31 (law enforcement) but the two exemptions are mutually exclusive and can only be used in the alternative, even if the public authority is one of those few authorities potentially able to apply s.30. In those cases s.30 should be considered before s.31 (which is considered further in relation to prejudice-based exemptions below).

5.3.4   Formulation of government policy (s.35)

Section 35 is another exemption which is limited to a narrow group of public authorities, government departments (defined in s.84 of the FOIA) and the Welsh Assembly but not the devolved Scottish administration. It too is often considered hand in hand with a prejudice exemption, in this case s.36 (prejudice to the effective conduct of public affairs) and the exemptions are mutually exclusive. Accordingly, where potentially available to a public authority, s.35 should be considered before s.36 (which is considered in more detail below, in relation to prejudice-based exemptions).

The application of s.35 turns on the content of the information in question and, in the case of s.35(1), in particular whether it relates to the formulation or development of government policy.

The purpose of the exemption is to protect the internal deliberative process as it relates to policy making – in other words, according to the Tribunal, to allow the government a 'safe space to protect information in the early stages of policy formulation and development' where the threat of public exposure might otherwise compromise candid and robust discussions about policy (*Office of Government Commerce* v. *Information Commissioner* (EA/2006/0068 and EA/2006/0080, 2 May 2007)).

The exemption is intended to ensure that the FOIA does not deter policy makers from full and proper deliberation, where, for example, the prospect of disclosure might discourage the exploration of extreme options, the keeping of detailed records and the taking of hard choices, or where disclosure might prejudice good working relationships, the neutrality of civil servants and ultimately the quality of government.

However, the Information Commissioner's view is that the exemption can only apply where there is clear, specific and credible evidence that the formulation or development of government policy would be materially undermined by the threat of disclosure under the FOIA.

In *Secretary of State for Work and Pensions* v. *Information Commissioner* (EA/2006/0040, 5 March 2007); [2011] 1 Info LR 716, the Tribunal examined s.35 and found that as it is a class exemption there should not be an automatic assumption that disclosure of the information will be harmful. Accordingly, the Tribunal insisted that each case be considered in the light of its particular circumstances.

Government policy

'Policy' is not defined. According to the Information Commissioner, it will usually cover the development of options and priorities for Ministers who determine which options should be translated into political action, and when.

The *Modernising Government* White Paper (Cm 4310, March 1999) refers to policy as the process by which governments translate their political vision into programmes and actions, to deliver outcomes or desired changes in the real world.

Policy can be sourced and generated in various ways. For example, it may come from Ministers' ideas and suggestions, manifesto commitments, significant incidents (such as a major outbreak of foot and mouth disease), EU policies or public concern expressed through letters, petitions and the like. Proposals and evidence for policies may come from external legal advisers, stakeholder consultation, or external researchers, as well as civil servants.

Importantly, policy is unlikely to include purely operational or administrative matters but must normally be of general application, i.e. at governmental level across departments. For instance, decisions about applications for licences or grants are likely to involve not the formulation of policy, but rather its application.

Government policy is seen as distinct from departmental or other types of policy. This implies policy which has had Cabinet input or represents the collective view of Ministers or which applies across government. It also implies some political process. Departmental policy will frequently be derived from and be identical to government policy, but where departmental policy applies only to the internal workings of the department it would not be caught (e.g. departmental policy about working hours or estate management). Likewise, policy on specific, individual cases is unlikely to be protected by s.35.

'Formulation' and 'development' of policy

These terms do not have precise meanings.

'Formulation' suggests the output from the early stages of the policy process, where options are generated and sorted, risks are identified, consultation occurs and recommendations and submissions are put to a Minister.

'Development' is sometimes used interchangeably with formulation, but also goes beyond it. It may refer to the processes involved in improving on or altering existing policy, for example through piloting, monitoring, reviewing, analysing or recording the effects of existing policy. At the very least, formulation and development suggests something dynamic – in the sense that something must be happening to the policy. The exemption cannot apply to a finished product, or a policy which has been agreed, is in operation or has already been implemented.

In *Secretary of State for Work and Pensions* v. *Information Commissioner* (EA/2006/0040, 5 March 2007); [2011] 1 Info LR 716 the Information Tribunal recognised that 'formulation' cannot and should not always be envisaged as a 'continuing process of evolution'. Where appropriate, the formulation process can be considered separately at each stage rather than as a continuum. The formulation in question in this appeal related to the national identity cards scheme and the Tribunal considered that it would be beneficial to treat the formulation as a two-stage process rather than an ongoing one. The first stage was made at a macro level: the decision to introduce a scheme. The second stage was planned on a micro level and related to the detailed implementation of the scheme at departmental level and secondary legislation. It therefore followed that information compiled for the purpose of formulating policy in the first 'macro' stage was not necessarily exempt simply because the micro stage was still ongoing at the time of the request.

The High Court upheld the decision of the Tribunal which re-affirmed this approach in *Office of Government Commerce* v. *Information Commissioner* [2008] EWHC 737 (Admin). This appeal also related to documentation generated in the course of the government's identity cards project. In this instance, the material requested comprised two Gateway Review reports. The Gateway process was introduced by the Office of Government Commerce in 2000 as the centrepiece of its initiative to promote best value for money in government procurements. Under the Gateway process a government programme or project should be examined at critical stages in its life cycle with the aim of ensuring that it can progress successfully from stage to stage.

The Tribunal examined the definition of 'formulation'. Whilst accepting that the s.35 exemption was engaged, the Tribunal ultimately ordered disclosure. Its reasoning was that the requests were made 18 months after the reports had been produced, by which time the decision had already been taken to proceed with the introduction of identity cards and a Bill had been presented to Parliament for public debate. In other words, the 'formulation' value of the information was no longer current and could not compete with the considerable public interest in disclosing information about a controversial government project.

Another leading case on the interpretation of s.35(1) is *Department of Health* v. *Information Commissioner, Healey and Cecil* (EA/2011/0286 and EA/2011/0287, 5 April 2012), which concerned two 'risk registers' documenting the risks associated with implementing what the Tribunal called the 'far-reaching and highly controversial' NHS reforms under what was then the Health and Social Care Bill. In ordering the disclosure of one of the registers, the Tribunal observed that policy making is often a curve rather than a straight line, with the process 'dipping in and out' of the need for a 'safe space' for the formulation and development of policy. A 'safe space' may, for example, be much needed when the policy is unformulated; however, this need might dissipate once a policy decision is taken, then later become more acute again if aspects of the policy need to be reconsidered.

Factors to consider when applying the exemption

The following questions may be relevant to the application of the exemption:

- Would release of the information in this particular case make civil servants less likely to provide full and frank advice or opinions on policy proposals? Would it, for example, prejudice working relationships by exposing dissenting views?
- Would the prospect of future release inhibit consideration and debate of the full range of policy options (for example, if on reflection some of them seem extreme)?
- Would the prospect of release lead to civil servants defending everything that is or has been raised during deliberation (in anticipation, for example, of certain things later being discounted)?
- Would the possibility of future release deter the giving of advice which is ill-considered, vague, poorly prepared or written in unnecessarily brusque or defamatory language? Would the prospect of release in fact enhance the quality of future advice? If so, then this would weigh in favour of release.
- Is the main reason for applying the exemption to spare a civil servant or Minister embarrassment? If so, then the exemption is not appropriate, although decisions have noted a clear distinction between protecting civil servants, especially those who are more junior, compared to politicians.

Applying the public interest test

Arguments against disclosure might include:

- the need to maintain the quality of government policy making by facilitating free and frank exchanges between civil servants ('the chilling effect') and the thorough consideration of all policy options, however extreme, without inducing the need to defend them ('safe space');
- the need to maintain the quality of records, working relationships and a neutral civil service (although arguments that disclosure may lead to poor record-keeping will be disregarded);
- the fact that the particular circumstances of the case indicate that public participation in the policy is inappropriate.

Arguments in favour of disclosure might include that:

- public participation in the policy is appropriate (in the sense of permitting people to contribute to policy prior to a final decision). Note:

- participation cannot be meaningful without access to relevant recorded information about how policy decisions are reached, what options are being considered and why some are excluded and others preferred;
- without public participation in key policy decisions, certain individuals or groups will enjoy undue influence in the policy-making process;
- a key driver for freedom of information is to provide access to information which will facilitate informed participation in the development of government proposals or decisions which are of concern to them;
- information disclosed prior to a decision being taken will facilitate more informed public debate;

- accountability for government decisions (i.e. the need for government to explain why something has happened, or to demonstrate sufficient rigour in taking account of all relevant considerations, including addressing legitimate objections, or that it is keeping its word and delivering what it has promised). Note:

  - disclosure of information is desirable where it may expose wrongdoing, the fact that wrongdoing has been dealt with or dispels suspicions of wrongdoing or of 'spin';
  - access to information under the FOIA may facilitate objective assessment, particularly where information obtained direct from the civil service (as opposed to government press offices) has not been spun;
  - there will usually be a strong public interest in favour of disclosure where a policy decision is going to lead to large-scale public expenditure;
  - similarly, there will usually be a strong public interest in favour of disclosure where a policy decision involves departure from routine procedures or standard practice. This was certainly the case with material relating to the identity cards scheme in *Secretary of State for Work and Pensions* v. *Information Commissioner* (see above), in which the public interest in disclosure outweighed the arguments for exemption. However, it is worth noting that in this case, the Tribunal ordered that the information be provided in redacted form in order to protect the identity of junior civil servants involved in the policy process.

A good example of the application of the public interest test can be found in *Department for Education and Skills* v. *Information Commissioner and Evening Standard* (EA/2006/0006, 19 February 2007); [2011] 1 Info LR 689. A journalist asked the Department for Education and Skills (DfES) to disclose the minutes of all senior management meetings at the department from June 2002 to June 2003 in relation to the setting of school budgets. The DfES initially refused the request, citing s.35(1)(a). The journalist's complaint to the Information Commissioner focused on the DfES's alleged failure to distinguish policy making (exempt under s.35) from operational decisions (not exempt under s.35). He also emphasised the considerable public interest in the information.

When weighing the arguments for and against disclosure, the Tribunal examined the following concerns in relation to the disclosure of minutes:

- loss of frankness and candour;
- danger of government by cabal;
- impact on record keeping; and
- potential damage to relations between civil servants and Ministers and to the accountability and role of civil servants in policy formulation.

The DfES's position hinged on 'grave adverse affects' which it was thought 'would inexorably result from the disclosure requested'. First, it was argued that the threat of future disclosure would discourage candour and boldness in the giving of advice, the consideration of options and the exchange of views. Secondly, the authority referred to a series of 'secondary signals' which disclosure would send out. The loss of confidentiality in policy discussion, particularly in relation to the minutes of senior committees in close proximity to Ministers, could threaten the role and integrity of the whole of the civil service. Such a relationship was an important constitutional safeguard which had served all governments well over the years. Public identification of a particular official with specific policy advice could also undermine the political neutrality of the civil service and exacerbate the suspicion sometimes exhibited by Ministers of an incoming administration towards an official apparently identified with a policy no longer in favour. The corollary to a politicised civil service was 'sofa government' or government by cabal, which is to say government influenced by special political advisers working independently of senior civil servants and therefore free of public scrutiny. There was also a concern that risk of disclosure would discourage the proper keeping of minutes.

The Tribunal was not convinced by these arguments and felt that the 'chilling effect' outlined by the DfES was not sufficiently compelling to tip the public interest in favour of maintaining the exemption. On the risk to confidentiality it indicated that 'confidentiality is not always, we think, treated by Ministers as sacrosanct'. On government by cabal, its view was that:

> the use of political advisors rather than career civil servants goes back at least to Churchill and represents a growing trend, lamented by oppositions of whichever political complexion. Whether it is likely to accelerate if there is a greater risk of disclosure of the dealings of civil servants with each other and with ministers, we do not feel confident to predict. It will certainly not be curbed by any decision of ours.

On the likely negative effect on record keeping, it stated simply that: 'Good practice should prevail over any traditional sensitivity as we move into an era of greater transparency'.

The Tribunal's analysis of the public interest provides useful guidance for decision makers. Broadly, the salient points are as follows:

- While the seniority of officials participating in recorded discussions may in some cases increase the sensitivity of the matters minuted, no information within s.35(1) is exempt simply on account of its status, its classification or the seniority of those whose actions are recorded.

- The timing of the request is fundamental – disclosure of discussion of policy options while the policy is still in the process of formulation is highly unlikely to be in the public interest, unless for example it would expose wrongdoing within government; at the same time, factors of great relevance at the time of the recorded discussions or advice may carry little, if any, weight two years later – in this case a policy announcement had been made in July 2003 and implemented in July 2004; the request was made in January 2005; it was therefore clear that 'the time and space needed had been available and put to good effect'.
- The words 'in all the circumstances of the case' indicate that, where appropriate, weighing the public interest may involve a consideration of any wider impact on the conduct of government (in this case, the 'secondary signals' referred to above).
- That said, in judging the likely consequences of disclosure on officials' future conduct, we are entitled to expect of them 'the courage and independence' of highly educated and politically sophisticated public servants who understand the importance of their impartial role as counsellors to Ministers of conflicting convictions.
- There may be good reason in some cases for withholding the names of more junior civil servants who would never expect their roles to be exposed to the public gaze.
- We are entitled to expect of our politicians when they assume power in a department a substantial measure of political sophistication and fair-mindedness – to remove or reject a senior official because he or she is identified with a policy which has lost favour would betray a serious misunderstanding of the way the executive should work and would be unjust – it must be assumed that Ministers will behave reasonably and fairly towards officials who promoted policies which the new incumbent rejects.
- The central question in every case is the content of the particular information in question – every decision must be specific to the particular facts and circumstances under consideration.

Accordingly, the Tribunal held that there was an overwhelming general public interest in transparent policy making on a funding matter of enormous public concern and so it ordered the information to be disclosed.

This case also confirmed that the wording 'relates to' should be broadly construed, not least because its breadth is balanced by the application of the public interest test, and would include information forming background to the formulation or development of government policy. That said, s.35(4) imposes special public interest considerations in relation to such factual background information and under s.35(2) such details should be disclosed where possible once the policy-making decision concerned has been taken.

A recent development has added an interesting twist to this area. The Commissioner issued two decision notices, *Cabinet Office* (FS50347714, 12 September 2011) and (FS50362603, 13 September 2011). The authority was ordered to disclose requested minutes of meetings of a Cabinet Sub Committee on Devolution to Scotland and Wales and the English Regions, from 1997 and 1998. The Cabinet Office claimed that the details were exempt under ss.28, 35(1)(a) and 35(1)(b). It added s.42 in the course of the Commissioner's investigations. The Commissioner agreed that s.35(1)(a) and (b) were engaged but disagreed with the authority on the application of the public interest test. The Commissioner found that save for two specific categories of information, the public interest in disclosure outweighed the public interest in maintaining the exemption since the disclosure was unlikely to result in harm to the convention of collective ministerial responsibility, particularly given the passage of time. There was a specific public interest in informing current and future debate about devolution and a general public interest in transparency and openness in decision making. It was held that s.28 was not engaged and that only limited details were exempt under s.42. In respect of the two types of information the Commissioner excepted from disclosure under s.35, the Commissioner agreed that there was a public interest in preventing the convention from being undermined, which carried significant weight and supported maintenance of this exemption.

The Cabinet Office appealed and the Tribunal proceedings progressed to the point of a date being listed for the first hearing on 13 and 14 March 2012. However, in the meantime, there had been internal consultation within government which led to the Attorney General issuing a certificate on 8 February 2012 under s.53(2) of the FOIA, exercising the ministerial veto over disclosure under the FOIA and therefore overruling the Commissioner's decision notices. This was only the third time the veto power had been relied upon (the other two instances also relating to Cabinet minutes, one relating to the decision to commence war against Iraq, the other to another request for minutes of meetings discussing Scottish devolution). The Commissioner and the government have disagreed about whether this case was an appropriate one for use of the veto, which the Commissioner and Cabinet Secretary had previously agreed should only be used in exceptional cases and in accordance with the government's published policy statement on use of the veto: Statement of HMG Policy: Use of the executive override under the Freedom of Information Act 2000 as it relates to information falling within the scope of section 35(1) (Ministry of Justice). The Attorney General's statement exercising the veto confirmed the Minister's view that disclosure would not be in the public interest as it would be 'damaging to the doctrine of collective Cabinet responsibility and detrimental to the effective operation of Cabinet government'. The Commissioner thought that instead the Cabinet Office should have completed the Tribunal appeal process, using closed evidence if necessary and considered challenging the use of the veto by judicial review proceedings but (as in previous cases) disregarded that option. The Commissioner did, however, report to Parliament under s.49(2) of the FOIA on the matter, confirming that use of the power of veto would be kept under close review and that one outcome of its use might be to amend the FOIA as a consequence of considering 'whether the disclosure of Cabinet and Cabinet Committee minutes is an unintended consequence of the [FOIA]', para.7.9, the Information Commissioner's Report to Parliament (on the Attorney General's veto on disclosure of the minutes of the Cabinet Sub-Committee on devolution for Scotland, Wales and the Regions), 24 February 2012.

Department of Health v. *Information Commissioner, Healey and Cecil* (EA/ 2011/0286 and EA/2011/0287, 5 April 2012) – the risk registers case referred to above – also saw the Tribunal concluding that the evidence did not support the government's 'chilling effect' argument. On 8 May 2012, the government used the ministerial veto under s.53(4) for the fourth time, this time to block the disclosure of the register which the Tribunal had ordered to be disclosed. The Commissioner is keen to ensure the veto is only used if a case is genuinely 'exceptional'. The Commissioner's report to Parliament on this use of the veto notes concerns that the use of the veto has spread to a new area of the policy process and is outside the approach set out in the Statement of Policy on use of the veto. The veto has been exercised in another FOIA case subsequently, triggering a fifth Information Commissioner's Report to Parliament (September 2012) on this subject.

Section 35 also has provisions dealing with Ministerial communications (s.35(1)(b)), advice from the Law Officers (s.35(1)(c)) and information relating to the operation of a ministerial private office (s.35(1)(d)). The Commissioner has issued guidance on each of these although they are used far less frequently than the exemption for policy formulation.

5.3.5 Communications with Her Majesty, etc. (s.37)

Section 37 relates to royal communications and honours. Where royal communications involve the Sovereign, the heir to the Throne, the second in line to the Throne, and/or a person who has subsequently become heir to/second in line to the Throne, the information is absolutely exempt without consideration of the public interest test (see **4.5.6**). This applies to information requests with effect from 19 January 2011.

However, the balance of information described in the exemption, namely:

• communications with other members of the Royal Family or with the Royal Household; or
• the conferring by the Crown of any honour or dignity

is subject to the public interest test.

Care is needed to ensure a party falls within the 'Royal Family' or 'Royal Household' as these terms are not defined in the FOIA, although the Commissioner has issued helpful updated guidance on this exemption.

Information within this section of the FOIA is not always subject to the same provisions on historical records as other affected exemptions. This situation is due to change further once amendments to the FOIA made by the Constitutional Reform and Governance Act 2010 are enabled.

The exemption may apply both to the duty to confirm or deny information is held and/or to the duty to disclose information if held.

5.3.6 Environmental information (s.39)

Section 39 exempts information which an authority is obliged to make available in accordance with the Environmental Information Regulations 2004 (EIR), or would be obliged to make available but for an exception in those regulations. As decision notices and judgments on matters under the FOIA and the EIR have developed, a much clearer picture has emerged about the scope of such 'environmental information', which is much broader than originally thought by practitioners.

The exemption may apply both to the duty to confirm or deny information is held and/or to the duty to disclose information if held.

In essence, information which falls within the EIR must be processed in accordance with the EIR. The public interest test is applied differently under the EIR compared with the way it is applied under the FOIA. The EIR are dealt with in full in **Chapter 9**.

5.3.7 Personal information (s.40)

The s.40 exemption is for the most part an absolute exemption (s.40(1), (2) and (3)(a)(i)) but there are limited circumstances in which it is only qualified (s.40(2) and either (3)(a)(ii) or (4)). See **Chapter 8** for a full analysis of the interaction between the FOIA and the DPA.

The exemption may apply both to the duty to confirm or deny information is held and/or to the duty to disclose information if held.

5.3.8 Legal professional privilege (s.42)

Information which attracts legal privilege is exempt under the FOIA – subject to the public interest test – from both the duty to disclose and the duty to confirm or deny (where this would in itself disclose information which is privileged).

Legal professional privilege (LPP) protects material from disclosure on the ground that a client must be sure that what he or she and his or her lawyer discuss in confidence will not be disclosed to third parties without his or her consent. Unfortunately, having been largely settled since the 16th century, the application of LPP has been significantly undermined following the case of *Three Rivers District Council* v. *Governor and Company of the Bank of England* (the *Three Rivers* litigation). Widely criticised, the litigation has had a substantial impact on the traditional approach to LLP. This has been exacerbated by the imposition of a public interest test by the FOIA in relation to LPP, which is another significant shift in the application of previously settled legal principles.

As a result of these changes to LPP, there are likely to be documents to which authorities would expect LPP to apply but to which, in fact, LPP may not apply. Further, there may be documents to which LPP did apply at the time the document was produced but to which privilege has later ceased to apply. In both cases, information which an authority would wish and expect to be exempt will not be exempt (at least under s.42).

LPP is divided into two categories: legal advice privilege and litigation privilege. This section provides an overview only of this complex area; a complete discussion of all detail relevant to LPP is outside the scope of this book. The Scottish legal system also recognises the principle of privilege attaching to documents and communications to prevent their disclosure in a manner similar to that in England and Wales which is explained below, including legal professional privilege and litigation privilege; however, the exact manner in which it is applied in practice can differ between the jurisdictions.

Legal advice privilege

A communication is protected by legal advice privilege if it is made:

- confidentially; and
- between a client and his or her lawyer; and
- for the purpose of seeking or giving legal advice or assistance; and
- within a relevant legal context explaining why the client needs that advice.

Relevant legal context and legal advice

This last requirement is new and comes from one of the *Three Rivers* cases on LPP, the 2004 House of Lords decision in *Three Rivers District Council* v. *Bank of England (No.6)* [2005] 1 AC 610. The effect of this judgment is that to be privileged, the advice should be given as to what should prudently and sensibly be done in relation to rights, liabilities, obligations or remedies of the client whether under public or private law. This gives the advice its relevant legal context. The decision widened the more restrictive view of what amounted to 'legal advice' which had been taken previously by the Court of Appeal in *Three Rivers District Council* v. *Bank of England (No.6)* [2004] QB 916. The House of Lords accepted that advice on presentational and other matters, provided it was given in a relevant legal context was also protected legal advice.

The *Three Rivers* litigation arose out of the collapse of BCCI following fraud on a vast scale perpetrated by its senior staff. The creditors and the liquidators of BCCI sued the Bank of England for misfeasance in public office in respect of its supervision of BCCI. The Bingham Inquiry was set up to consider whether the action taken by the UK authorities, including the bank, had properly discharged their public law duties. Shortly after the inquiry was established, three bank officials were appointed by the Governor to deal with all communications between the bank

151

and the inquiry and with the bank's solicitors in relation to the inquiry. They became known as the Bank's Inquiry Unit (BIU). The bank received legal advice from its lawyers on every aspect of the presentation of its evidence and submissions to the inquiry. Preparatory work was carried out by the BIU including discussions with present and former bank staff involved in the licensing or supervising of BCCI. The flow of factual information from the bank to its lawyers was usually channelled through the BIU. Specific requests for factual matters to be investigated and reported to its lawyers were often made by its lawyers to the BIU who then delegated those fact-finding tasks to others within the bank.

The House of Lords agreed that this provided the relevant legal context and privilege covered obtaining advice from the lawyers on how to reduce criticism by the inquiry because it concerned what 'should prudently and sensibly be done' in the context of the legal inquiry. The case emphasises that not all communications between client and lawyer will be protected and that care is needed in this regard. It is not all advice from a lawyer which is protected but advice in relation to the law.

What is 'legal advice' for the purposes of LPP?

In *United States of America* v. *Philip Morris Inc and Others* [2004] EWCA Civ 330, the Court of Appeal said that the leading modern authority on the practical application of the principles governing privilege is still *Balabel* v. *Air India* [1988] Ch 317. In that case Taylor LJ said (at 330–1):

> The test is whether the communication or other document was made confidentially for the purposes of legal advice. Those purposes have to be construed broadly. Privilege obviously attaches to a document conveying legal advice from a solicitor to client and to a specific request from the client for such advice. But it does not follow that all other communications between them lack privilege. In most solicitor and client relationships, especially where a transaction involves protracted dealings, advice may be required or appropriate on matters great or small at various stages. There will be a continuum of communication and meetings between the solicitor and client. Where information is passed by the solicitor or client to the other as part of the continuum aimed at keeping both informed so that advice may be sought and given as required, privilege will attach. A letter from the client containing information may end with such words as 'please advise me what I should do'. But, even if it does not, there will usually be implied in the relationship an overall expectation that the solicitor will at each stage, whether asked specifically or not, tender appropriate advice. Moreover legal advice is not confined to telling the client the law; it must include advice as to what should prudently and sensibly be done in the relevant legal context.

A little later (at 331–2) Taylor LJ said that the scope of the privilege had to be kept within justifiable bounds. He stated in relation to documents recording information or transactions or recording meetings that:

> Whether such documents are privileged or not must depend on whether they are part of that necessary exchange of information of which the object is the giving of legal advice as and when appropriate.

The House of Lords *Three Rivers* decision unanimously endorsed the approach of the Court of Appeal in *Balabel* v. *Air India* [1988] Ch 317, and in particular Taylor LJ's comments.

There will always be borderline cases in which it is difficult to decide whether or not the advice is given in a legal context. Much will depend upon whether it is reasonable for the client to consult the special professional knowledge and skills of a lawyer. However, there will normally be a relevant legal context when a client seeks advice from a lawyer.

The client

Another change to the traditional LLP approach introduced by the *Three Rivers* litigation was that the Court of Appeal introduced a new and much narrower concept of 'the client', which would no longer be every person at the client organisation.

The Court of Appeal held that only the members of the BIU should be regarded as the client for the purpose of LPP, not any employee – even though it accepted that a company can only act through its employees. Nevertheless, the Court of Appeal gave no guidance about how to determine who the client is. The House of Lords agreed that defining the client was a significant issue but gave no further judicial guidance. The definition of 'client' has therefore become critical to determining whether a document is protected by legal advice privilege.

The client would seem to include in-house lawyers, senior officers whose duties include instructing the client's lawyers and those specifically appointed to communicate with the client's lawyers on particular matters. However, this is a particular issue with large and complex public authorities. Assessment should be made as to who has a genuine need to be involved and to seek and obtain legal advice. It should be noted that privilege will not automatically protect legal advice shared between parent and subsidiaries or other connected parties. Likewise, care is needed about how in-house lawyers channel legal advice from external lawyers to their internal client.

Communications between an employer and his or her in-house lawyer where the lawyer is providing legal advice in his or her capacity as legal adviser will qualify for LPP, but where the lawyer acts in an administrative or executive capacity the communications will not be privileged. For example, the Tribunal confirmed that a report prepared by a solicitor acting in her capacity as a monitoring officer was not privileged (*Surrey Heath BC and McCullen* v. *Information Commissioner* (EA/2010/0034, 11 August 2010)). In-house lawyers are treated in the same way as external lawyers in the vast majority of, but not all, cases involving LPP.

Litigation privilege

A communication is protected by litigation privilege if it is made:

* confidentially; and

153

- for the sole or dominant purpose of obtaining evidence or to provide advice in relation to litigation by or against the client; and
- where such litigation is actual, pending or contemplated.

Unlike litigation privilege, legal advice privilege can only apply to communications passing directly between a lawyer and his or her client. Legal advice privilege cannot apply to correspondence between a lawyer and a third party, or between a client and a third party, even if the communication is for the purpose of obtaining information to be submitted to the client's lawyer. Litigation privilege is therefore wider than legal advice privilege and the definition of client is not as restricted, although care should still be taken.

'Litigation' for this purpose covers adversarial proceedings. Adversarial proceedings are not defined, but include court proceedings and arbitration. Non-adversarial proceedings, such as inquiries or investigations, are excluded.

The test for determining whether litigation privilege can be invoked in relation to any communication where litigation has not commenced is whether there was a real likelihood that litigation was reasonably in prospect at the time when the communication was made. There must be a real prospect of litigation as distinct from a mere possibility, but the prospect does not have to be more likely than not. The requirement that litigation be reasonably in prospect is satisfied if the party seeking to claim privilege can show that he or she was aware of circumstances which rendered litigation between himself or herself and a particular person a real likelihood.

Some information may be protected by both legal advice privilege and litigation privilege.

Can privilege be lost?

Privilege can be lost where the underlying confidentiality in a document is lost or where the client waives the right to LPP in a document. The Tribunal held that where a summary of legal advice was provided to a full council meeting, it was not protected by LLP (*Kirkcaldie* v. *Information Commissioner and Thanet District Council* (EA/2006/001, 4 July 2006)).

Waiver of LPP for one document in a series of documents may, depending on the facts, also waive privilege in other related documents. The court will ensure fairness and prevent a party from cherry-picking and waiving privilege only in those documents which assist it. Waiver of privilege in respect of part of a document will extend to the entire document, unless the subject matter of the remaining part is completely different. Partial waiver should be distinguished from redaction of a document whereby privileged material is edited out: disclosure of the unprivileged part of the document will not waive privilege in the privileged part.

Applying the public interest test

The public interest in maintaining the legal privilege exemption will normally be substantial because legal privilege itself derives from the public interest in maintaining confidentiality between lawyer and client.

In *Bellamy* v. *Information Commissioner and Secretary of State for Trade and Industry* (EA/2005/0023, 4 April 2006), the Tribunal stressed the importance of legal professional privilege: 'under English law the privilege is equated with, if not elevated to, a fundamental right at least insofar as the administration of justice is concerned'. The Tribunal took the view that Mr Bellamy had failed to adduce sufficient considerations which would demonstrate that the public interest in justifying disclosure was outweighed by the public interest in maintaining the exemption. It commented that, 'there is a strong element of public interest inbuilt into the privilege itself. At least equally strongly countervailing considerations would need to be adduced to override that inbuilt public interest'. There is a line of case law referred to in *Bellamy* which reinforces the intrinsic nature of LPP, culminating with *R (Morgan Grenfell & Co Ltd)* v. *Special Commissioner and Another* [2003] 1 AC 563. Here Lord Hoffmann remarked that: 'Legal profession privilege is a fundamental human right long established in the common law. It is a necessary corollary of the right of any person to obtain skilled advice about the law.' Several other cases echo this approach.

In *Kitchener* v. *Information Commissioner and Derby City Council* (EA/2006/0044, 20 November 2006), when considering the public interest test, the Tribunal again reinforced the fundamental nature of LPP. It recognised that an inherent part of a fair trial is access to legal advice and representation. If either the lawyer or his or her client could be forced to disclose what either had said to the other, this would undermine the very part of the process that our legal system seeks to protect. A client and his or her lawyer could not speak frankly if there was a possibility that disclosure might be ordered later.

The Tribunal in this case also noted the fact that the exemption covered by s.42 is not absolute in nature and since Parliament did not make it an absolute exemption, decision makers should take care not to make it one by default. However, it too recognised the very weighty public interest in maintaining LPP.

There are a number of factors which, as a matter of principle, will weigh in favour of maintaining LPP in the face of an information request for privileged information:

- decisions by public authorities must be taken in a fully informed legal context;
- authorities require legal advice for the effective performance of their operations and that advice must be given by lawyers who are fully apprised of the factual background;
- legal advisers must be able to present the full picture, which will include arguments in support of their final conclusions and arguments that may be made against these (it is in the nature of legal advice that it will set out the arguments both for and against a particular view, weighing up their relative merits, and highlighting perceived weaknesses in any position);

- without such comprehensive advice, authority decision making may be compromised because it would not be fully informed;
- disclosure of legal advice could materially prejudice an authority's ability to protect and defend its legal interests;
- disclosure might unfairly expose a legal position to challenge and diminish the reliance which may be placed on the advice; and
- even where litigation is not in prospect, disclosure of legal advice may carry a risk of prejudicing an authority in future litigation, and legal advice connected with one department could have wider implications for other departments.

Public interest factors weighing in favour of disclosing privileged information might include that:

- circumstances are such that the government would waive privilege as a tactic to discourage anticipated litigation;
- departments should be accountable for the quality of their decision making and this may require transparency in the decision-making process and access to the information on which decisions were made; and
- in some cases there may be a public interest in knowing whether or not legal advice was followed.

A significant LPP case which did not reach the Tribunal but which resulted in the Information Commissioner issuing an enforcement notice concerned the government's refusal to disclose advice from the Attorney General on the legality of military intervention in Iraq (enforcement notice of 22 May 2006). The Legal Secretariat to the Law Officers (LSLO) at the Attorney General's office had refused to disclose on the basis that the information at issue was covered by LPP and was therefore exempt under s.42. The Commissioner's decision is particularly interesting because he was obliged to weigh the fundamental nature of LPP against the need for the public to challenge and debate government decisions on a matter of such enormous importance and sensitivity.

During 2005 a multitude of requests were made seeking information relating to the advice given by the Attorney General to the Prime Minister on the legality of military action in Iraq in 2003. In forming his opinion, the Commissioner considered two documents written by the Attorney General: one on 7 March and the other on 17 March 2003. A 17 March statement addressed to the House of Lords (in the form of a written answer) was already on the public record and therefore not part of the requested information. However, the Commissioner referred to it in his deliberations as to whether the public interest lay in favour of disclosing other contemporaneous information.

The 7 March advice was published by the government following a partial leak in April 2005. It was nevertheless part of the requested information at the time when the requests had been made and therefore the Commissioner deemed it necessary to consider whether or not it was exempt from disclosure under s.42.

In his enforcement notice the Commissioner's reasoning largely followed that of the Tribunal in *Kitchener* (above), namely that 'there must be a reasonable expectation that [legal advice] will remain confidential to ensure that the legal opinion is full and frank'. The Commissioner also acknowledged the long-standing convention that neither the advice of the Law Officers nor the fact that their advice has been sought is disclosed outside the government, a convention specifically recognised in para.24 of the Ministerial Code. The Commissioner also noted that the subject matter of the request required the reasons favouring non-disclosure to be applied with 'especial force in the context of a decision of such gravity, sensitivity and difficulty in policy terms, legal complexity and diplomatic sensitivity ... and in the context of advice given personally by the Attorney General at the highest levels of government'.

The arguments in favour of disclosure centred around the ability of the public to 'understand, debate and challenge decisions taken by the government'. Here, 'there is a public interest in the government being able to demonstrate that the decision has been fully debated and that the appropriate advice has been sought from professional advisors'. There was also a public interest in understanding the legal basis for the decision to join the invasion of Iraq and to know that the government had acted in accordance with the rule of law. In particular, the Commissioner noted that it was important that the public understood the process which led from the 7 March advice to the 17 March statement since the latter came to an unequivocal conclusion and it was on this advice that the House of Commons relied when deciding to support military action by vote on 18 March 2003.

The Commissioner felt that there was a further public interest in disclosure arising from the uncertainty about the status and nature of the 17 March statement:

> It would have been reasonable for Parliament and the public to assume that the 17 March statement had been based on a thorough analysis of all relevant legal considerations and that its unequivocal conclusion reflected a similar conclusion ... in an Opinion or Advice prepared by the Attorney General ... it was a legitimate assumption that there was at least full consistency and continuity between the 7 March advice and the 17 March statement.

Following a series of government leaks which had preceded the Commissioner's consideration of the case, it had become public knowledge that the 7 March advice did not reach a firm conclusion. To this extent the 7 March advice and the 17 March statement were inconsistent and therefore the balance of public interest was tipped in favour of disclosure because the public might otherwise have been falsely led to believe that the decision to engage in military action was based on a 'firm and confident analysis'. In order to be satisfied that the decision in relation to Iraq was based as far as possible on a sound legal foundation, there was a public interest in understanding the chain of events between the 7 March advice and the 17 March statement.

In making his decision, the Commissioner was particularly conscious of the necessity of the government receiving legal advice in confidence. He acknowledged that LPP is a fundamental principle under English law but the fact that it had not been made an absolute exemption meant that there must be circumstances in which the public interest in disclosure was so strong that it could be overridden. The premise behind the implementation of the FOIA was that it enables the public to access information about the way the government has reached decisions and thereby seeks to improve trust and confidence.

The balance of the public interest did not require the disclosure of those parts of the requested information which were uncirculated drafts or documents of a preliminary, provisional or tentative nature or which might reveal legal risks, reservations or possible counter-arguments as expressed by any of those involved in the provision of advice, or information informing that advice. However, the balance of the public interest did require the disclosure of those parts of the requested information which led to or supported the concluded views that were made public by the Attorney General in the 17 March statement.

By the enforcement notice dated 22 May 2006, the LSLO was required to publish a disclosure statement setting out the substance of all the recorded material within the requested information which led to or supported the views made public by the Attorney General in the 17 March statement.

Subsequently, Tribunal judgments have clarified cases in which the public interest may favour disclosure and that such factors need not be exceptional. In *Mersey Tunnel Users Association* v. *Information Commissioner and Merseytravel* (EA/2007/0052, 15 February 2008); [2011] 1 Info LR 1066, the Tribunal confirmed that relevant factors included where a significant number of individuals were affected by the legal advice, where a significant amount of money was involved and where there was a lack of public authority transparency. Other factors might be where an authority had misrepresented the legal advice (*Heimark* v. *Information Commissioner and LB Hackney* (EA/2011/0162, 29 November 2011)), or where the authority ignored the legal advice (*Thornton* v. *Information Commissioner and Department of Health* (EA/2009/0071, 10 February 2010)).

The court's approach to s.42 is summarised in its decision in *Department for Business, Enterprise and Regulatory Reform* v. *O'Brien and Information Commissioner* [2009] EWHC 164 (QB), where it concluded that for disclosure, it is necessary to show clear, compelling and specific justification that at least equals the public interest in protecting the information in dispute. The court referred to the strong 'in-built' public interest in maintaining LPP.

The exemption may apply both to the duty to confirm or deny information is held and/or to the duty to disclose information if held.

5.3.9 Commercial interests (s.43(1))

There are two separate qualified exemptions under s.43 which serve to protect the legitimate interests of business. Section 43(1) applies to trade secrets, for which there is no requirement to assess the prejudice which disclosure might cause, because this is inherent in the meaning of a trade secret. If information is a trade secret, then it will be exempt, subject to the public interest test.

There is no definition of a trade secret, either in the FOIA or in English law generally. However, the essence of a trade secret is generally taken to comprise three elements (*Lansing Linde Ltd* v. *Kerr* [1991] 1 WLR 251):

- it must be specific information used in a trade or business;
- it must not generally be known – which usually means that the owner must have limited, or at least not permitted, its widespread publication; and
- it must be information which, if disclosed to a competitor, would be liable to cause real or significant harm to the owner.

In 1997, the Law Commission, seeking views on the criminalisation of trade secrets as part of a consultation paper, identified four categories:

- formulae for highly specific products;
- technological secrets;
- strategic business information; and
- collations of publicly available information, such as databases.

These categories have not, however, been formally drafted into protected categories. There appear to be no decision notices to date upholding the use of s.43(1) alone but a number of cases confirming when information does not amount to a trade secret, such as the guide charts to Hay job evaluation scheme methodology (*London Borough of Southwark* (FS50078603, 5 June 2007)). However, there is an approach which suggests that the tests for s.43(1) are very similar to those for s.43(2), and in some cases both exemptions are held to apply without having to consider the trade secret issues in more detail (*Department of Health* v. *Information Commissioner* (EA/2008/0018, 18 November 2008); [2011] 1 Info LR 1135).

An analysis of s.43(2), and the application of the public interest test to s.43 generally, follows later in this chapter.

This exemption cannot be used to avoid the duty to confirm or deny whether or not the requested information is held.

5.4 PREJUDICE-BASED EXEMPTIONS

The public interest test applies to each of the exemptions set out below in the usual way. However, unlike the exemptions referred to already, for the following group of exemptions to apply, disclosure of information must, or must be likely to, give rise to the prejudice referred to in each category. The prejudice test was not intended by Parliament to be weak, but rather Lord Falconer wanted public authorities to establish that prejudice was 'real, actual or of substance'. Decisions subsequently indicate that although the degree of prejudice need not be substantial, it must be more than trivial, a test which can be underestimated.

The likelihood of such prejudice arising is also key. *Hogan and Oxford City Council* v. *Information Commissioner* (EA/2005/0026 and EA/2005/0030, 17 October 2006); [2011] 1 Info LR 588 confirmed that the prejudice test involves three steps: the need to identify the relevant interests which are impacted; the need to explain the nature of the prejudice; and the need to substantiate the likelihood of such prejudice arising. The Tribunal in the *Hogan* case also confirmed that where the higher threshold of 'would prejudice' was claimed, the likelihood of prejudice must be more likely than not, although this did not mean the prejudice had to be certain to result.

The lower threshold is 'would be likely to prejudice' which is a lower standard than 'more probable than not' but more than hypothetical and remote so as to present 'a real and significant risk' (*John Connor Press Associates Ltd* v. *Information Commissioner* (EA/2005/0005, 25 January 2006)).

An analysis of each of the prejudice-based exemptions follows.

5.4.1 National security (s.24)

Information which is not covered by the absolute exemption for security matters under s.23 will still be exempt if exemption is required to safeguard national security. The exemption applies also to the duty to confirm or deny.

Like s.23, s.24 also provides that certification by a Minister is conclusive evidence of exemption.

National security

The term 'national security' has never been defined in UK legislation, and both domestic and European courts have considered that the assessment of the threat to national security is essentially a matter for the executive. The House of Lords judgment in the appeal of Shafiq Ur Rehman against deportation made clear that a precautionary approach to national security was proper: it is necessary not only to consider circumstances where actual harm has occurred or will occur to national security, but also to consider preventing harm, or the risk of harm, occurring (*Secretary of State for the Home Department* v. *Rehman* [2001] UKHL 47). Their Lordships also found that, in order to constitute a threat to national security, a risk need not be 'direct or immediate'. The approach taken in *Rehman* has become a touchstone of the Tribunal's approach to national security (see the speech of Lord Slynn at paras.15–18). For example, it was relied upon by the Tribunal to withhold information about interception of MP's telephone calls (*Norman Baker MP* v. *Information Commissioner and Cabinet Office* (EA/2006/0045, 4 April 2007)).

Despite the absence of a definition, it is possible to infer certain statements about the meaning of national security from case law and statute. For example:

- the security of the nation includes its well-being and the protection of its defence and foreign policy interests, as well as its survival;
- the nation does not refer only to the territory of the UK, but includes its citizens, wherever they may be, or its assets wherever they may be, as well as the UK's system of government; and

- there are a number of matters which UK law expressly recognises as constituting potential threats to, or otherwise being relevant to, the safety or well-being of the nation, including terrorism, espionage, subversion, the pursuit of the government's defence and foreign policies, and the economic well-being of the UK. However, these matters are not exhaustive. Government would regard a wide range of other matters as being capable of constituting a threat to the safety or well-being of the nation. Examples include the proliferation of weapons of mass destruction and the protection of the critical national infrastructure, such as the water supply or national grid, from actions intended to cause catastrophic damage.

As common sense would suggest, national security has to be a sufficiently flexible concept to meet genuine need. However, national security is not the same as protecting the interests of the government of the day. Official information that would be embarrassing or inconvenient to the government if made public is not of itself a matter of national security.

A risk to national security is capable of arising where information is anodyne when taken in isolation, but where it can be pieced together with other publicly available information to form a 'mosaic' of information which can threaten national security (see *Summers* v. *Information Commissioner and Commissioner of Police for the Metropolis* (EA/2011/0186, 24 February 2012), where the Tribunal found that the total annual cost of police protection for the Royal Family and Royal sites should be withheld on national security grounds).

As a qualified exemption, s.24 is contingent on two things. First, the test for reliance on the exemption is that non-disclosure should be required for the purpose of safeguarding national security. It is vital to consider the impact of disclosure rather than the content or source of the information concerned. An authority must be prepared to demonstrate the need to withhold the information requested, and if steps could be taken to allow information to be disclosed while safeguarding national security in some other way, those steps will need to be considered. As to the meaning of 'required', it is not sufficient that the information sought simply relates to national security. Rather, the exemption must be 'reasonably necessary' for the safeguarding of national security (*Kalman* v. *Information Commissioner and Department for Transport* (EA/2009/0111, 8 July 2010); [2011] 1 Info LR 664). Secondly, even if exemption is required for this purpose, the exemption is also subject to the public interest test.

Applying the public interest test

In reality, of course, the public interest and the maintenance of national security are very closely allied. True safeguarding of national security is a very weighty factor for non-disclosure. A recent example is the Commissioner's decision about a request for independent assessment reports into airport security scanners, *Department of Transport* (FS50413571, 12 January 2012). However, the public interest does sometimes require disclosure of details in these cases, such as of the police informant records which were approximately 100 years or more old and had to be disclosed once names had been removed (*Metropolitan Police* v. *Information Commissioner* (EA/2008/0078, 30 March 2009)).

The exemption may apply both to the duty to confirm or deny information is held and/or to the duty to disclose information if held. This is an exemption when 'neither confirm nor deny' is likely to be used more often than with many other exemptions and the Commissioner has issued practical guidance on this point.

5.4.2   Defence (s.26)

Section 26 makes information exempt if its disclosure would, or would be likely to, prejudice:

(a)   the defence of the British Islands (which is wider than the UK and includes, e.g. the Isle of Man) or any colony; or

(b)   the capability, effectiveness or security of any relevant forces (meaning the armed forces – which is not defined – and any forces co-operating with those forces).

The exemption may need to be considered alongside s.23 (security bodies) and s.24 (national security) but its use is not limited to the Ministry of Defence or the armed forces. This is a qualified exemption which turns not on the description of particular information but on the effects of disclosure. In every case, therefore, it is a question of assessing the risk of prejudice that disclosure may cause to the matters in (a) or (b), regardless of the content of the information, the kind of document in which the information is contained, or its source.

Relevant examples falling within this exemption might be:

• defence policy and strategy, military planning and defence intelligence;
• the size, shape, organisation, logistics, order of battle, state of readiness and training of the armed forces;
• the actual or prospective deployment of those forces in the UK or overseas, including their operational orders, tactics and rules of engagement;
• the weapons, stores, transport or other equipment of those forces and the invention, development, production, technical specification and performance of such equipment and research relating to it;
• plans and measures for the maintenance of essential supplies and services that are or would be needed in time of conflict;
• plans for future military capabilities;
• plans or options for the defence or reinforcement of a colony or another country;
• analysis of the capability, state of readiness, performance of individual or combined units, their equipment or support structures; and

- arrangements for co-operation, collaboration, consultation or integration with the armed forces of other countries, whether on a bilateral basis or as part of a defence alliance or other international force.

Applying the public interest test

The public interest in avoiding prejudice to defence matters will be strong in most cases, so will outweigh the public interest in disclosure unless the harm or prejudice likely to result from disclosure would be trivial or minor.

There is at the same time widespread public interest in defence policy and the activities of the armed forces, so it is appropriate that the public should be able to understand how and why key decisions are taken to promote accountability. Where disclosure will inform debate, the public interest in disclosure will carry more weight. Examples might include disclosure of information relating to:

- the safety of military personnel or loss of life;
- risks to the safety of civilians;
- the use of land or the environmental impact of military activity (for which s.39 may also be relevant);
- the factual and analytical bases used to develop defence policies; and
- the use of public funds.

Clearly the public interest will weigh against disclosure where this might undermine the conduct of a specific military operation or have an adverse impact on security or safety. Further, the disclosure of information in the face of an objection from an allied country, or in breach of a clear undertaking to preserve confidentiality, may well prejudice the UK's defence relations by restricting exchanges of information or by jeopardising military co-operation.

Even in a case where the relevant information was on the use of unmanned aerial vehicles in Afghanistan, which is an issue of public disquiet, with a very significant and legitimate public interest in the activities of the armed forces in Afghanistan (which is also controversial and in the media, increasing the weight of public interest), and which uses large amounts of public funds, it was not enough to outweigh the public interest in maintaining this exemption in the circumstances (*Ministry of Defence* (FS50325462, 23 February 2011)).

Related issues

Authorities which deal routinely with defence information will usually have their own specific clearance procedures for dealing with requests. Officials should always comply with such procedures because they will have been written to reflect the legal restrictions which apply to the organisation. The FOIA preserves all existing statutory prohibitions on disclosure, the breach of some of which is a criminal offence.

In many cases, it will also be appropriate for an authority to consult the Ministry of Defence before disclosing potentially exempt defence information.

The exemption may apply both to the duty to confirm or deny information is held and/or to the duty to disclose information if held.

5.4.3 International relations (s.27(1))

Section 27(1) exempts from disclosure information which would, or would be likely to, prejudice:

- relations between the UK and any other state;
- relations between the UK and any international organisation or international court;
- the interests of the UK abroad; or
- the promotion or protection by the UK of its interests abroad.

Information, the disclosure of which is potentially covered by this exemption, spans a broad spectrum and could include, for example:

- reports on, or exchanges with foreign governments or international organisations such as the EU, Nato, United Nations, Commonwealth, World Bank or International Monetary Fund;
- information about the UK's activities relating to UK citizens or companies abroad, particularly their consular and commercial interests;
- information about other states' views or intentions provided in the course of diplomatic and political exchanges of views;
- details of inward and outward state visits and visits by Ministers and officials;
- information supplied by other states on diplomatic or other channels;
- discussion within the UK government on approaches to particular states or issues;
- information relevant to actual or potential cases before an international court; and
- details of the UK's position in multilateral or bilateral negotiations.

Applying the public interest test

The fundamental question when applying the public interest test under s.27 is whether the public interest in disclosure is outweighed by the damage or likely damage that would be caused to the UK's international relations, its interests abroad or its ability to protect and promote those interests.

For prejudice which is likely to be trivial – for example, where disclosure about the content of a discussion with a foreign official would be unlikely to provoke any significant negative reaction or have any significant detrimental effect on other states' willingness to have similar discussions with the UK in the future – the public interest in disclosure is likely to prevail.

Correspondingly, for prejudice likely to be more serious – such as disclosure about the UK's attitude to an international issue of concern to a particular state which would provoke a strong negative reaction and could, for example, make it less likely that British companies would be awarded government contracts in future with that state – the public interest in disclosing would have to be more specific and compelling to justify disclosure. The same would be true of a disclosure which would be likely to weaken significantly the UK's bargaining position in international negotiations, inhibit other governments' willingness to share sensitive information, or inhibit frankness and candour in diplomatic reporting.

The Tribunal has consistently held that 'prejudice can be real and of substance if it makes relations more difficult or calls for particular diplomatic response to contain or limit damage which would not otherwise have been necessary' and that prejudice does not 'necessarily require demonstration of actual harm to the relevant interests in terms of quantifiable loss or damage' (*Campaign Against the Arms Trade* v. *Information Commissioner and Ministry of Defence* (EA/2007/0040, 26 August 2008); [2012] 1 Info LR 78).

For a good example of where the use of s.27(1) was upheld, see the Commissioner's decision regarding documentation relating to Cyprus Sovereign Base Areas, *Cabinet Office* (FS50300590, 21 March 2011). Although there was a 'clear and valid' public interest in its disclosure, especially to improve understanding and inform debate, 'there is a powerful public interest' in maintaining international relations and protecting the UK's interests abroad, especially where prejudice would (not just would be likely to) result.

The exemption may apply both to the duty to confirm or deny information is held and/or to the duty to disclose information if held.

5.4.4   Relations within the UK (s.28)

Section 28 will apply where disclosure would, or would be likely to, prejudice relations between any administration in the UK and any other such administration.

For s.28 purposes, 'administration in the UK' means the UK government itself, and the various devolved administrations within the UK. These are:

- the Scottish administration;
- the Executive Committee of the Northern Ireland Assembly; and
- the National Assembly for Wales.

Local authorities and the Greater London Assembly are excluded, as are the Scotland, Northern Ireland and Wales Offices which are part of the UK government. In relation to references to the UK, this does not include the wider British Islands, such as the Channel Islands.

Section 28 applies – regardless of the nature or content of the information in question – where the effects of disclosure would, or would be likely to, prejudice relations between any of the administrations covered – that is, between the UK government and any of the devolved administrations, and also between any of the devolved administrations themselves.

In essence, there are now three devolved administrations within the UK, and the UK government represents UK interests in matters which are not devolved to Scotland, Wales or Northern Ireland. Policy responsibility for non-devolved matters lies with UK government Ministers and departments, and in these areas the Secretaries of State for Scotland, Wales and Northern Ireland are responsible for ensuring that the interests of those parts of the UK are properly represented and considered.

Accordingly, there are two distinct circumstances in which s.28 might apply: where information requested under the FOIA has been obtained from or shared between administrations; and where information held by one administration could prejudice relations because that administration does not want other administrations to see it, or because other administrations would not want the information to be disclosed.

There is a Memorandum of Understanding (MoU) between the UK administrations (Command Paper 5240) to facilitate good communication with one another. The MoU also includes safeguards to ensure that information shared with other administrations is appropriately protected. In certain circumstances, this means that confidentiality is expected although the terms of the MoU are not legally binding and the law of confidence and s.41 (confidential information) may be relevant in such cases. An expectation of confidentiality will not be a conclusive demonstration of prejudice likely to result from disclosure, but it will be a relevant consideration. Likewise, sensitivity and protective markings will not be conclusive but merely indicative. However, it will always be sensible to consult with the originating administration prior to disclosure.

More specific concordats sit beneath the MoU, such as for dealing with EU policy issues.

There will be many circumstances in which information shared between administrations might be prejudicial to relations if disclosed. Some examples might be:

- sensitive information about devolved matters which predate devolution, held by UK government departments but concerning devolved administrations (see the earlier reference at **5.3.4** in relation to s.35 to use of ministerial veto after the Commissioner ordered disclosure of Cabinet Committee minutes claimed to be exempt, including under s.28 (*Cabinet Office* (FS50362603, 13 September 2011));
- information held by devolved administrations relating to reserved or excepted matters;
- briefing or comments on another administration's plans or policies;
- an options analysis in an area of reserved policy which also includes an assessment of the operation of policy in a devolved area; and
- information about another administration which has come direct from a third party.

Note that, as with the other qualified exemptions, potential embarrassment is not enough to justify its use.

Applying the public interest test

The exigencies of open government have to be balanced with the political imperatives underlying the devolution settlement, namely trust, co-operation, information sharing and respect between the four administrations. The prospect of harming the effective functioning of the devolved relationships will be a significant factor in assessing whether to disclose information.

In weighing the public interest, it is important to consider the following:

- the wider public interest in freedom of information and any particular commitments given by administrations;
- the commitment to sharing information between the four administrations;
- the commitment to respecting confidential information shared between bodies and any genuine need for and expectation of confidentiality;
- the nature and extent of prejudice to the relationships between administrations that might be caused by the disclosure of a particular piece of information;
- the importance of ensuring appropriate frankness and candour of discussion between administrations;
- the extent to which other exemptions may be relevant;
- the impact on future working relationships and the need for prompt and frank exchanges of information;
- how recent or historic the details are; and
- how the information may help improve public understanding or debate.

In *Cabinet Office* (FS50295029, 23 February 2011), the use of s.28 by the Cabinet Office was upheld by the Commissioner in relation to information about the negotiation with Libya of the Prison Transfer Agreement for Mr Al Megrahi from the Scottish prison where he was imprisoned for murder following the Lockerbie bombing. The exemption was engaged taking account of the expectations under the MoU and the significance of the agreement's negotiation for relations between Westminster and the Scottish Executive and its content. The public interest in disclosure mirrored those factors considered in respect of ss.27 and 35 and in addition there was public interest in disclosure of information about how the two administrations in Scotland and England 'are (or are not) co-operating in practice'. The Commissioner gave notable weight to the need for disclosure as a result. Despite that and the passage of time, the Commissioner recognised 'the very strong public interest in preserving strong relations' between the administrations and the fact that prejudice would not be limited to the current matter but also might affect 'a range of future policies and issues'.

The exemption may apply both to the duty to confirm or deny information is held and/or to the duty to disclose information if held.

5.4.5 The economy (s.29)

Information is exempt if disclosure would, or would be likely to, prejudice:

- the economic interests of the UK or any part of the UK;
- the financial interests of any administration in the UK (being an administration as defined for s.28 purposes).

The duty to confirm or deny does not arise to the extent that doing so would defeat the object of the exemption.

Economic interests

'Economic interests' include the central aim of government to provide economic and financial management which supports the maintenance of a stable macroeconomic framework, maintains sound public finances and promotes UK economic prospects and productivity, i.e. for communal UK benefit. Associated with these issues is the maintenance of a competitive financial services market, and efficient tax and benefits systems. The exemption exists in recognition of the instability and economic damage to the wider economy that could be caused by the disclosure of some information.

This is different from the management of the economy and from the commercial impact of an individual business (even when a major economic force) on the UK.

Financial interests

'Financial interests' are more focused and concentrate on the financial interests of any of the administrations. The phrase means the efficient conduct of the financial aspects of government administration to minimise the cost to the taxpayer. Public accountability necessitates that sufficient information is available to assess the probity and cost-effective nature of such dealings. This must be balanced against the damage to an administration's financial interests which might result if too much information is disclosed about its financial dealings, or if information is disclosed too soon after a particular event. This component of the exemption exists in recognition of the long-term cost to the taxpayer which could result from disclosure (premature or otherwise) of certain information.

Information which may fall within s.29 includes:

- information contained in Standing Committee and financial stability papers (e.g., HM Treasury, the Bank of England, the Financial Services Authority);
- vulnerability assessments, for example, of emerging market economies;
- gilt auctions – the size of offering at a gilt auction has a short-term but nevertheless significant sensitivity which could influence price and therefore the cost of borrowing for the government;
- budget information – release of budget information ahead of formal announcement, particularly in relation to tax and national insurance, might lead to

pre-emptive action by companies and individuals, leading to a reduction in tax payable to the government;

- government cash flows and borrowing requirements – premature disclosure is likely to be market sensitive; and
- terrorism reinsurance – disclosure of information about claims could potentially prejudice the economic interests of a part of the UK.

Applying the public interest test

There is a legitimate public interest in the UK's economic policy, taxation and financial management, and release of some information will promote public understanding and informed debate (and, indeed, government has been seeking to increase transparency in this area).

Some specific factors will weigh in favour of disclosure:

- the need to hold public authorities to account for their stewardship of public resources; and
- the objective of building public trust and establishing transparency in the operation of the economy so as to increase the credibility of economic policy decision makers and enhance the UK's reputation as a fair and honest business environment.

Factors weighing in favour of withholding information might include:

- where disclosure could result in financial instability within institutions or countries, either in the UK or abroad;
- where disclosure could pre-empt announcements on taxation, national insurance or benefits;
- where selective disclosure of the information could affect financial markets – financial regulation and government policy require the transparent release of market-sensitive data simultaneously to the whole market because this reinforces confidence in market integrity, thereby reducing the cost of capital in financial markets; selective or premature release of information undermines confidence in dealing in UK markets;
- where information has been obtained from confidential sources (e.g. overseas governments or regulators) and these relationships would be damaged by disclosure and reduce the likelihood of information being made available in the future; and
- where the information consists of assessments of an institution's or economy's viability.

Authorities should consider consulting HM Treasury and/or other relevant government departments before releasing information which might fall within s.29.

In *Derry City Council* v. *Information Commissioner* (EA/2006/0014, 11 December 2006); [2011] 1 Info LR 1105, the Tribunal considered the relationship between economic interests and commercial interests. On the facts of the case, it concluded that the economic interests of the region depended on the commercial interests of the council's airport. Consequently, if commercial interests were likely to be prejudiced then this would have a detrimental impact on the economic interests of the region and the exemption in s.29 would be engaged.

In the Commissioner's decision notice *HM Revenue and Customs* (FS50095271, 13 June 2007), the complainant had requested details of EC Treaty challenges to UK tax legislation. These contained details of estimates of the actual or potential cost to the exchequer of aspects of UK tax law being found to be in breach of the EC Treaty. HMRC withheld this information on the basis of s.29. It explained that the estimates were worst case scenarios which were extremely uncertain. Because of the level of uncertainty the Information Commissioner considered that the potential impact on investors from the release of the information gave rise to potential prejudice to UK economic interests. The Commissioner considered that the economy is sensitive to even small changes in investor confidence and disclosure of the information could lead to more than just a small change in investor confidence. Release of the EC Treaty challenges information could therefore pose a real or significant risk to the UK economy and s.29 was therefore engaged.

The exemption can also be used by public authorities outside the Treasury and Cabinet Office. An example is set out in the decision notice *Land Registry* (FS50208350, 4 May 2010). A request was received for various source codes used in particular IT systems of the authority. This was refused on the basis of s.29 and s.43(2). The Land Registry is a government department but also a trading fund, i.e. it must generate its own income to pay its expenses and raises funds from its trading for the government amounting to hundreds of millions of pounds each year, which income is of serious importance to the UK's financial interests. The Land Registry's IT systems are central to this trading and so important that they are part of the UK's National Critical Infrastructure. Disclosure of the requested details, combined with other public knowledge and bearing in mind attempts to hack into the authority's systems, evidenced that prejudice would be likely to result from disclosure. Very strong weight was given to the public interest in maintaining the exemption because of the substantial prejudice which could be caused to the UK's financial interests by disclosure.

The exemption may apply both to the duty to confirm or deny information is held and/or to the duty to disclose information if held.

5.4.6   Law enforcement (s.31)

The application of s.31 turns on the likely *effects* of disclosure rather than the source of the information or the purpose for which it is held – which are covered under s.30. As such, s.31 will only be relevant (and can only be used) in cases where s.30 is not relevant (and cannot be used). The two exemptions can be claimed in the alternative but s.30 should be considered before s.31. However, s.31 is available to a much wider range of public authorities than s.30 since it is not limited to those which have a duty or power to conduct criminal investigations or prosecutions. Section 31 is also a considerably broader exemption than s.30 because it is relevant to information which authorities hold for the law enforcement purposes of other bodies, not only for their own purposes.

The exemption operates by reference to a list of law enforcement interests which might be prejudiced by disclosure of information. Some are very wide, others very specific. Information is exempt if its disclosure would, or would be likely to, prejudice:

(a)   the prevention or detection of crime;
(b)   the apprehension or prosecution of offenders;
(c)   the administration of justice;
(d)   the assessment or collection of any tax or duty or of any imposition of a similar nature;
(e)   the operation of immigration controls;
(f)   the maintenance of security and good order in prisons or in other institutions where persons are lawfully detained;
(g)   the exercise by any public authority of its functions for any of certain specified purposes (see below);
(h)   any civil proceedings which are brought by or on behalf of a public authority and arise out of an investigation conducted for certain specified purposes (see below) by or on behalf of the authority exercising either prerogative powers or powers conferred by or under any enactment; or
(i)   any inquiry held under the Fatal Accidents and Sudden Deaths Inquiries (Scotland) Act 1976, to the extent that the inquiry arises out of an investigation of the type referred to in paragraph (h) above, for certain specified purposes (see below).

As will be clear, paragraphs (a)–(f) stand by themselves and refer to a series of law enforcement interests which could be prejudiced by disclosure.

Paragraphs (g)–(i) can only apply in relation to the specified purposes set out below (s.31(2)):

(a)   to ascertain whether any person has failed to comply with the law;
(b)   to ascertain whether any person is responsible for any conduct which is improper;
(c)   to ascertain whether circumstances exist or may arise which would justify regulatory action in pursuance of any enactment;
(d)   to ascertain a person's fitness or competence in relation to the management of bodies corporate or in relation to any profession or other activity which he or she is, or seeks to become, authorised to carry on;
(e)   to ascertain the cause of an accident;
(f)   to protect charities against misconduct or mismanagement in their administration (whether by trustees or other persons);
(g)   to protect the property of charities from loss or misapplication;
(h)   to recover the property of charities;

(i)   to secure the health, safety and welfare of persons at work; and
(j)   to protect persons other than persons at work against risk to health or safety arising out of or in connection with the actions of persons at work.

The prevention or detection of crime and the apprehension or prosecution of offenders

The above terms appear throughout English law and have no special meaning within the context of the FOIA. They may apply specifically or in general terms. Examples of circumstances in which potential prejudice (i.e. resulting from disclosure) may make the exemption bite are:

- intelligence about anticipated criminal activities (disclosure here has a high potential to prejudice the prevention or detection of the crime in question, and the apprehension of the alleged offenders);
- information relating to planned police operations, including specific planned operations, and policies and procedures relating to operational activity;
- information relating to the identity and role of police informers (to which a number of other exemptions are also likely to be relevant, including those under ss.30, 38, 40 and 41);
- information relating to police strategies and tactics in seeking to prevent crime (the disclosure of such information has a high potential to undermine legitimate police objectives carried out in the public interest);
- information disclosure of which would facilitate the commission of any offence;
- information disclosure of which would prejudice the fair trial of any person against whom proceedings have been or may be instituted (to which, again, a number of other exemptions may also be relevant, particularly, with reference to s.44, in relation to disclosures which would breach art.6 of the European Convention on Human Rights); and
- the effect of small separate disclosures building up a mosaic of information which as a whole would be of assistance to criminals and as a result prejudicial.

APPLYING THE PUBLIC INTEREST TEST

Maintaining confidence in law enforcement and the criminal justice system is obviously crucial to the public interest, but it is a consideration which can weigh both for and against disclosure. Much is done through police and community consultation (and the media) to keep citizens informed about the ways in which the police carry out their responsibilities. On occasions, however, there will be some tension between this emphasis on openness and the need to maintain the confidentiality of specific operations or policies. Similar considerations will apply to other law enforcement bodies.

It is also important to be aware that prejudice may arise incrementally, as well as from a single disclosure. Clearly, disclosure of information on a single specific police operation designed to apprehend alleged offenders could be prejudicial. What, though, about disclosures of more general information relating to police strategies and tactics? Such disclosure may undermine legitimate police objectives and hamper future operational activity by limiting the value of those strategies and tactics once disclosed (or by providing valuable intelligence to perpetrators of crime).

Examples of specific considerations which might be relevant to this section include:

- the effects of crime on individuals, e.g. it would not be in the public interest to disclose details of a surveillance operation and thus potentially compromise that operation, where the target was a person suspected of a series of violent assaults;
- the effects of crime on society, e.g. it may not serve the public interest to disclose in advance the arrangements for an operation to combat graffiti and other criminal damage in a specific area; and
- the effects of crime on the economy, e.g. it may be against the public interest to disclose specific police strategies for action against those failing to pay fines or other penalties.

In *Colin P England (1) and London Borough of Bexley (2)* v. *Information Commissioner* (EA/2006/0060 and EA/2006/0066, 10 May 2007), counsel for the respondent argued that the exemption in s.31(1)(a) did not apply to information relating to empty properties in Bexley, as it was not specifically collated for crime prevention purposes. The Tribunal rejected this submission on the basis that the exemption does not contain any express link to the purpose for which information has been obtained, or the function of the public authority. Previous decisions had all concerned information collected for specific crime prevention purposes (e.g. *Hogan and Oxford County Council* v. *Information Commissioner* (EA/2005/0026 and EA/2005/0030, 17 October 2006); [2011] 1 Info LR 588). However, the Tribunal felt that this was only coincidental and there is no explicit reference to support the proposition that s.31(1)(a) does not apply to information obtained otherwise than for specific crime prevention purposes.

The administration of justice

There is no definition of the administration of justice, but it should be interpreted broadly. In particular:

- the exemption does not only concern the operation of the courts – justice is administered through courts and tribunals, through arbitrators, and through alternatives to litigation;

- all categories of justice are included (criminal, civil, family or administrative), as are matters which may not fit into that classification or which are general in nature;
- justice may be administered by professional judges and adjudicators, or by lay magistrates or panel members, or by jurors;
- administration of justice need not imply an adversarial context – it includes non-contentious or uncontested business, and inquisitorial processes (such as inquiries and coroners' courts);
- ensuring public access to justice is part of the administration of justice; and
- the administration of justice may be prejudiced in an individual case, or by something happening to the general process by which justice is delivered.

In the normal course, the administration of justice could be prejudiced by disclosures relating to:

- the operation of the judicial appointments system;
- the ability of a judge to deliver justice effectively, fairly and fearlessly in a particular case;
- the ability of a judge, or of the judiciary, to deliver justice effectively in more general terms;
- the business of the running of the courts and tribunals (though other exemptions might also be relevant);
- the enforcement of sentences and the execution of judgments;
- the ability of litigants to bring their cases, or a particular case, to court;
- the prospects of a fair trial taking place;
- the effectiveness of relationships between different agencies involved in the administration of justice (e.g. premature disclosure of plans to redistribute functions between different agencies could lead to a breakdown of co-operation);
- a range of other matters and systems that support the administration of justice (e.g. the operation of the legal aid system, or IT systems – disclosure of the security measures on computer systems would facilitate unauthorised access and thereby make them vulnerable to interference); and
- the maintenance of an independent and effective legal profession.

APPLYING THE PUBLIC INTEREST TEST

Clearly, the public interest in the administration of justice is very high, as indicated by the overlapping exemptions for ss.30 (investigations) and 32 (court records). However, in addition to this, there is a public interest in the separation of powers between courts and the executive. This effectively means that there is a public interest in the government acknowledging that the administration of justice is within the courts' particular domain, and in recognising that the courts are, constitutionally, the ultimate arbiters of the law.

As such, although the nature, degree and likelihood of prejudice to the adminis-tration of justice will be an essential part of weighing the balance of public interest, government recognition of the courts' position means that authorities should take particular care whenever concluding that the public interest in avoiding prejudice is outweighed. Circumstances where prejudice in a particular case is outweighed by the prevention of prejudice more generally might be one example of where the balance may lie in favour of disclosure. There may be other circumstances, particularly at the administrative margins of the administration of justice (as opposed to the judicial centre of the system), where the operational impact of a prejudicial disclosure is more diffuse, and considerations of administrative trans-parency weigh more strongly. Precisely because prejudice to the administration of justice encompasses such a wide range of circumstances, the specific factors relevant to individual cases may be particularly important to the operation of this exemption.

Tax

Taxes, duties and impositions of a similar nature include:

- income tax;
- corporation tax;
- VAT;
- insurance premium tax;
- petroleum revenue tax;
- national insurance contributions;
- climate change levy;
- excise duties (e.g. on tobacco, oil, beer, spirits and wine);
- motor vehicle duties;
- air passenger duty; and
- stamp duty.

Disclosures likely to be prejudicial to the assessment or collection of these levies include:

- details of plans to close tax loopholes;
- information held in relation to the tax affairs of companies or individuals;
- information which informs plans for future investigations;
- third party information which aids the collection of tax or duties; and
- details of strategies, investigative practices or even negotiating tactics used to assist in the collection of taxes or duties.

APPLYING THE PUBLIC INTEREST TEST

There is a strong public interest in having stable and secure public finances. These are crucial to the stability and sustainable growth of the UK economy and to the delivery of resources to fund public services. An efficient and well administered tax system also improves the competitiveness of business and supports the government's social and welfare objectives. A central requirement of a modern and fair tax system is that everyone pays the proper amount of tax and receives the benefits to which they are entitled. Tax avoidance and evasion reduce the revenue available for delivering public services, and distort the incentives that the tax system aims to offer, unfairly shifting a greater tax burden on to honest and compliant taxpayers.

Of course, disclosure of information promotes public awareness of how taxes work, which helps make it simpler for individuals and business to pay taxes. Authorities should take into account the public interest in the proper administration of taxation both in general and in particular cases, and in the avoidance of disruption or distortion of markets, or in the successful delivery of tax policy objectives.

Operation of immigration controls

'Immigration controls' is not defined in the FOIA but it will obviously cover the physical immigration controls at points of entry to the UK, as well as the arrangements made (whether in or under legislation, or as a matter of policy or procedure) in connection with entry to and settlement in the UK, including the investigation of offences relating to immigration.

Clearly, the disclosure of information would be prejudicial under this head if its release into the public domain would help people to evade immigration controls (although, as long as that is likely to be the consequence of release, the information itself need not be about immigration controls).

Examples of circumstances where disclosure might prejudice the operation of immigration controls include disclosure of:

- *information about the extensive counterfeiting of travel documents of a particular country*, on the basis of which travel documents issued by that country should be subjected to particular scrutiny. In this case, the disclosure of the information or the identity of the targeted country might be prejudicial because it could alert counterfeiters (and persons making use of their services) to use another country's travel documentation;
- *information which would reveal an incidence of suspected illegal working which is to be investigated by the immigration service*. In this case, the disclosure of the information about the proposed investigation might be prejudicial because it could alert employers of the illegal workers in advance and allow them to escape investigation; and
- *information on proposed changes to visa regimes*. The imposition or amendment of visa regimes usually takes place with little or no notice to the public. This is because visa regimes are generally introduced to prevent evasion or abuse of immigration controls by nationalities which, over time, have been shown to pose a higher risk of evasion or abuse than other nationalities when seeking to enter the UK. Therefore, the disclosure of information relating to

visa regimes could, in some cases, prejudice the operation of immigration controls because it would encourage persons from the countries which are due to be affected to seek to enter the UK before the changes are introduced, thus avoiding the more stringent regime which has necessarily been developed.

APPLYING THE PUBLIC INTEREST TEST

Immigration controls are important in order to regulate entry to and settlement in the UK, in which there is a clear public interest.

In the immigration context, there are a number of public interest considerations which may favour disclosure in the context of a particular request. There is a public interest in ensuring that there is public confidence in the operation of our immigration controls, and one way to ensure this is to keep the public informed of policies, developments and proposals for the future, and the reasons underlying them. Linked with this is the public interest in ensuring that the public have access to correct information. Immigration is an emotive issue and inaccurate information should not be allowed to circulate uncorrected in the public domain.

It is in the public interest to provide information which confirms the performance of immigration control – for example, by providing statistics on the number of passengers and applications that are handled by the UK Border Agency. There is also a public interest in establishing that the implementation of immigration control is carried out in accordance with the published statements and policies by providing, wherever possible, details of implementation of immigration control.

There is also a public interest in ensuring that those who are subject to immigration controls are aware of those controls and how they operate, as this may discourage such persons from seeking to enter the UK illegally.

Equally, there are a number of public interest considerations which may, in the context of a particular request, favour non-disclosure. For example, there is a public interest in ensuring that:

- people are not able to evade or abuse the UK's immigration controls in order to enter the UK illegally;
- the efficiency and integrity of the UK's immigration controls are not undermined; and
- investigations into suspected immigration offences can be conducted effectively.

Maintenance of security and good order in prisons

'Security' and 'good order' are not defined in the FOIA but common sense suggests that 'security' will include everything related to the secure custody of detainees, the safety of the prison population, and the detection and prevention of activity (criminal or otherwise) prohibited under prison rules. It is likely that 'good order' refers to measures intended to counter individuals' disobedience or concerted indiscipline, and which promote a safe and orderly prison regime. Note, however, that this exemption is intended to preserve security and good order not only in prisons but also in 'other institutions where persons are lawfully detained'. This includes young offenders' institutions, secure hospitals, secure training centres, local authority secure accommodation and immigration detention and removal centres.

Since the exemption focuses on the effects of disclosure, information would presumably cause harm if its release would compromise security, lead to the breakdown of good order or impair an institution's ability to restore either.

A key aspect of this, therefore, is the need to ensure that changes to prison routine are introduced in a carefully managed way, with prisoner reaction being assessed and expectations managed so that when the change is introduced there is not an immediate adverse reaction that may put staff and prisoners at risk. Premature release of information about a potentially unpopular policy change could therefore be prejudicial. Hypothetical examples of information relevant to good order might be information about proposed changes in the home detention curfew (or tagging) policy or incentives and earned privileges scheme, or information about changes in meal times or arrangements for visits.

An example of security-related information might be information detailing the times and routes of prisoner escorts, and information relating to good order may include, for example, the strategy for dealing with concerted prisoner indiscipline or the contingency plans for responding to other types of incident.

Conversely, information on physical security at a prison which is assessed as having little or no impact on the risk of prisoner escape if disclosed, might not be considered to prejudice security and should therefore be disclosed.

APPLYING THE PUBLIC INTEREST TEST

There is a public interest in ensuring public confidence in the operation of the prison system, which may be achieved by informing the public of policies, developments and proposals for the future. The public interest is clearly not served, however, by releasing information which may aid prisoners to escape, may cause unrest, or may put anybody within an institution at risk.

Section 31(1)(g), (h) and (i)

As noted above, these exemptions operate only where:

- disclosure would prejudice one of the processes in s.31(1)(g), (h) or (i); and
- that process is for one of the purposes listed in s.31(2); and
- the public interest allows.

The following paragraphs assess the application of each paragraph of s.31(1) in turn.

SECTION 31(1)(G) – FUNCTIONS OF A PUBLIC AUTHORITY

'Functions' refers to an authority's powers and duties. These derive either from statute or from the royal prerogative, and the connected purposes in s.31(2) indicate that the provision is chiefly concerned with those systems operated by authorities to ensure that proper standards of conduct and safety are met. 'Function' should be construed widely to include all the duties and powers of an authority, according to the House of Lords in *Hazell* v. *Hammersmith and Fulham LBC* [1991] 2 WLR 372. Notwithstanding this, s.31 does not limit the application of the exemption to particular central functions, since in reality many authorities and departments exercise functions for the purpose of ascertaining whether any person has complied with the law (s.31(2)(a)), ascertaining whether any person is responsible for any conduct which is improper (s.31(2)(b)), ascertaining the cause of an accident (s.31(2)(e)), or securing the health, safety and welfare of persons at work (s.31(2)(i)).

SECTION 31(1)(H) – CIVIL PROCEEDINGS ARISING OUT OF STATUTORY OR PREROGATIVE INVESTIGATIONS

'Civil proceedings' certainly comprises non-criminal legal action before a court or tribunal, but it could stretch to include other proceedings such as, for example, some forms of regulatory enforcement proceedings. Much will depend on the terms of any regulatory regime, and on the particular circumstances involved.

The prejudice in question must be to the civil proceedings themselves, but there is no need to give that an artificially narrow interpretation. It is capable, for example, of applying to prejudice to the authority's position in such proceedings.

The proceedings must arise, directly or indirectly, out of an investigation. The investigation, in turn, must have been conducted for one of the specified purposes in s.31(2), though the same is not true for the proceedings themselves (even if, in practice, this will be likely). For example, having ascertained that someone has improperly disclosed sensitive information to journalists, a public authority may attempt to prevent publication of that material by a breach of confidence action.

The investigation must have been conducted either:

- by virtue of the royal prerogative (many investigations undertaken by government departments are undertaken under prerogative powers, because the residual source of their legal powers – where not expressly conferred by statute, for example – resides in the Crown; this is particularly the case regarding investigations in the context of the internal management of government departments); or
- by or under an enactment – that is to say, by virtue of provisions in an Act of Parliament or in an instrument made under powers contained in an Act (this will include, in particular, statutory regulations).

Both the civil proceedings and the investigation may be undertaken either by the authority itself, or by another body on the authority's behalf.

This provision has potential to overlap with s.31(1)(c) (the administration of justice) and with s.32 (court records) and s.42 (legal professional privilege). The general public interest considerations likely to be engaged are therefore those relating to the administration of justice and the proper conduct of legal proceedings.

SECTION 31(1)(I) – INQUIRIES UNDER THE FATAL ACCIDENTS AND SUDDEN DEATHS INQUIRY (SCOTLAND) ACT 1976

The 1976 Act provides for public inquiries to be held in respect of fatal accidents, deaths of persons in legal custody, sudden, suspicious or unexplained deaths, or deaths which occur in circumstances giving rise to serious public concern. As the Lord Advocate's powers to investigate deaths in Scotland under this legislation are wide-ranging, this provision will have relevance to UK government departments operating in Scotland in a wide variety of circumstances where a death occurs, even where the death does not occur in legal custody. For Whitehall departments, these will of course be in areas of reserved policy/operations, such as, for example, defence (deaths of Ministry of Defence service personnel based in Scotland) or immigration (deaths of asylum seekers in Home Office detention in Scotland), and in such cases the relevant exemptions (s.26, s.31, etc.) may also apply.

Like s.31(1)(h), this provision is limited by the following factors:

- the prejudice must be to the inquiry;
- the exemption applies only to the extent that the inquiry arises out of an investigation;
- the investigation must have been conducted for one of the purposes specified in s.31(2); and
- the investigation must have been conducted under statutory or prerogative powers (although not necessarily under the 1976 Act itself).

Some statutes, which have their own provisions about inquiries into deaths, expressly allow for the disapplication of the 1976 Act to prevent a death triggering two parallel statutory inquiries (e.g. Health and Safety at Work etc. Act 1974, s.14(7)). Such provisions will limit the application of this exemption.

The s.31(2) purposes most likely to be relevant to the investigations referred to in connection with the 1976 Act are:

- ascertaining whether any person has failed to comply with the law;
- ascertaining whether any person is responsible for any conduct which is improper;
- ascertaining whether circumstances which would justify statutory regulatory action exist; and
- ascertaining the cause of an accident.

HEALTH AND SAFETY

A good example of where s.31 may be relevant to a public authority is provided by the Tribunal's judgment in *Stevenson* v. *Information Commissioner and North Lancashire Primary Care Trust* (EA/2011/0119, 30 December 2011). The primary care trust (PCT) received a letter from the chief executive of its Morecambe Bay trust dealing with concerns about 'service issues'. The letter was frank and written in the expectation of confidence. There was a very prompt information request for the letter. The PCT has a legal obligation to monitor and improve healthcare provision to the PCT by its local trusts. This was found to be a s.31 function. The PCT was concerned that disclosure of the letter would have a negative impact on its ability to obtain the ongoing and candid provision of information from trusts needed to meet this requirement, especially since it had no power to compel the provision of such information. It was agreed that s.31(1)(g) and s.31(2)(j) applied and because of the public interest in avoiding setting precedent value in such cases and the chilling effect of disclosure, the information was exempt.

The exemption may apply both to the duty to confirm or deny information is held and/or to the duty to disclose information if held.

5.4.7 Audit functions (s.33)

This exemption is intended to protect the effectiveness of the audit functions of certain public authorities. It applies where the disclosure of information would, or would be likely to, prejudice an authority's functions relating to (a) the audit of the accounts of other public authorities; or (b) the examination of the economy, efficiency and effectiveness with which other public authorities use their resources in discharging their functions (s.33(1)).

In many cases, certain types of auditors or audits have specific statutory obligations not to disclose information obtained for the purposes of/in the course of such audits, in which case s.44 (prohibited disclosures) should be considered.

While much of the information that an auditor holds could be disclosed and may indeed be prepared with a view to publication, there may be cases where disclosure would prejudice the audit function. Information which may be relevant to this exemption includes audit methodologies, communications between the bodies auditing and being audited, disclosures to auditors and draft reports. This exemption is not available to the public authority being audited which holds information relevant to the audit, although other exemptions may apply in that case.

Disclosure might prejudice audit functions in the following ways:

- *Relations with audited bodies and audit third parties may be compromised* – there may be information that originates from an audited body which, if disclosed, could harm relations between the auditors and that body, and so affect the ability of the auditors to carry out their functions effectively.
- *Disclosure may interfere with audit methods* – in the interests of an audit's effectiveness, it may be important that details of the audit method, including,

for example, the specific files that the auditor intends to examine, are kept from the audited body before the audit takes place. Disclosure of audit methods after an audit may also prejudice subsequent audits where, for example, an auditor intends to use the same method. Similarly, releasing information about how the auditing body derives its conclusions could also prejudice the audit function.

- *Public reporting and scrutiny* – before publication, many public sector auditors discuss their emerging findings and draft report with the audited bodies and other affected parties to ensure accuracy and completeness of the evidence on which they base their conclusions and recommendations. In the case of the National Audit Office (NAO), it may also be under a duty to inform Parliament first of the findings of its reports. If information from an audit were disclosed before official publication, this may pre-empt the proper reporting process and could lead to preliminary findings (which had not been fully tested) being given the same currency as fully tested conclusions. This may undermine the fairness of the audit process and create a misleading impression of both the auditor and the body being audited, possibly causing unwarranted damage to the reputation of either. In these circumstances the audit function would clearly be prejudiced.

Applying the public interest test

There is a strong public interest in ensuring that auditors can effectively carry out audits of public authorities. Much of the information that auditors produce is made available for the same general public interest reasons that support the principles of the FOIA. These include:

- making the reasons for a public body's decisions evident;
- enhancing the scrutiny and improving the accountability of public bodies;
- contributing to public debate; and
- increasing public participation in decision making.

The audit process facilitates the accountability and transparency of public authorities for decisions taken by them, which in turn facilitates accountability and transparency in the spending of public money. In general, most value for money audits lead to a public report with these express aims. There is therefore a clear public interest in protecting the effectiveness of the audit process. However, there is also a counterbalancing public interest in making available information which would lead to greater public confidence in the integrity of the audit process by allowing scrutiny, not only of the audited body, but also of the auditor's performance. In many cases the balance of the public interest will change over time, with the key issue likely to be whether the final report has been published.

The Commissioner upheld the use of s.33(1)(b) and s.33(2) by the NAO in respect of an audit of the Olympic Delivery Authority (ODA) in *National Audit Office* (FS50352197, 26 May 2011). This involved a request for further details of certain late running London Olympic Games 2012 projects referred to in an interim NAO report, details of which had been obtained during the audit exercise. Although the report was published prior to the request, due to the ongoing nature of the Olympic Games project as a whole, the exemption was engaged because disclosure would be likely to prejudice future ODA audits. The fact that generally the Olympic Games project was on track and references to the delays had been published and not hidden reduced the weight of the public interest in disclosure. Balanced against that, there was a strong public interest in the NAO being able to conduct future audits effectively and efficiently, especially with the ODA, because of the ongoing nature of the relationship and project. As a result the public interest in maintaining the exemption outweighed the public interest in disclosure.

Auditing departments and agencies must be aware of the confidentiality requirements of legislation that governs the particular bodies they audit. For example, the external auditor of HM Revenue and Customs, the NAO, is bound by the Finance Act 1989, which makes it a criminal offence to disclose taxpayers' information.

The exemption may apply both to the duty to confirm or deny information is held and/or to the duty to disclose information if held.

5.4.8 The effective conduct of public affairs (s.36)

The s.36 exemption recognises the critical role in effective government of free and frank discussion. However, s.36 can only apply in cases where the information in question is not exempt under s.35 (although the two may be claimed in the alternative). Accordingly s.35 should be considered before s.36. It is likely that s.36 will tend to apply to areas which do not relate to policy – such as management, delivery and operational functions. Further, s.36 exempt information need not relate to government Ministers. It can include any advice and discussion taking place at official level and is not limited to the narrow group of public authorities which can claim s.35.

The fundamental difference between ss.35 and 36 is that the latter turns on the effects of disclosure rather than the nature of the information itself. In other words, s.36 can apply irrespective of what the information is, if disclosure:

(b)   would, or would be likely to, inhibit:

    (i)   the free and frank provision of advice, or

    (ii)   the free and frank exchange of views for the purposes of deliberation, or

(c)   would otherwise prejudice, or would be likely to prejudice, the effective conduct of public affairs.

What do 'advice' and 'exchange of views' cover?

There is very little guidance on what is meant by these terms. 'Advice' can be internal (e.g. from officials to Ministers) or external (e.g. from third parties). It includes any advice whether made by an authority, or to it. Any 'exchange of views' is limited only by having to be for the purposes of deliberation. This will include processes of decision making, opinion forming or evaluation, but is likely to exclude casual or trivial exchanges.

The term 'inhibit' does not feature elsewhere in the FOIA. It suggests a suppressive effect, i.e. a situation where communications would be less likely to be made, or would be made in a more reticent or circumscribed fashion, or would be less inclusive.

In considering its effects, it may be relevant to consider whether disclosure may:

- make it more likely that the person offering advice will be unwilling to do so in future;
- inhibit that person from offering unwelcome advice;
- make it more likely that the person being advised will not ask for advice in future;
- have a similar inhibiting effect on other people in future;
- make it more likely that advice will be given that is materially different because of the possibility of disclosure;
- make people less likely to engage in discussion (whether oral or written) as part of the deliberative process;
- distort or restrain that discussion; or
- result in pressure being brought to bear on officials to provide particular advice.

What does the 'effective conduct of public affairs' cover?

This provision deals with situations which fall outside the other specific circumstances covered by s.36. In debates on the Bill, Lord Falconer explained that it is intended to cover residual cases which cannot be foreseen, but where it is necessary to withhold information in the interests of good government. As a result, when the FOIA was originally introduced, because it is a broadly expressed exemption, it was thought that not only would clear justification have to be provided when seeking to rely on it but that it could not be used if other exemptions were available, i.e. it was the last option to be used in isolation for the information concerned. Subsequently, guidance and practice have changed and the exemption is now frequently relied upon, including in combination with other exemptions.

In *Guardian Newspapers Ltd (1) and Heather Brooke (2)* v. *Information Commissioner and British Broadcasting Commission* (EA/2006/0011 and EA/2006/0013, 8 January 2007); [2011] 1 Info LR 854, the Tribunal discussed two questions of law which are relevant to decision makers seeking to rely on s.36. First, the Tribunal considered the application of s.36(2)(b), and specifically the question of whether disclosure of information might be 'inhibiting'; the meaning of 'would be likely to'; and the meaning of 'reasonable opinion', in the context of the requirement for the exemption to apply 'in the reasonable opinion of a qualified person'. Secondly, it examined the application of the public interest test to the information in the minutes themselves. The case concerned the disclosure of the minutes of the BBC governors' meeting which took place on the day the Hutton Report was released. The BBC had refused to disclose, claiming exemption under s.36 on the grounds that publication would inhibit the free and frank exchange of views for the purposes of deliberation in governors' meetings.

In interpreting the phrase 'would or would be likely to', the Tribunal followed the decision of Munby J in *R* v. *Secretary of State for the Home Office* [2003] EWHC 2073. 'Would' requires that the mischief in question (the 'inhibition' of free and frank deliberations) would 'probably' occur (i.e. with a greater than 50 per cent chance, on the balance of probabilities); 'would be likely to' requires that there would be a 'very significant and weighty chance' that it would occur, even if the risk fell short of being more probable than not.

In consideration of the interpretation and application of 'reasonable opinion' the Tribunal concluded that 'the substance of the opinion must be objectively reasonable'. The Tribunal also considered whether the process by which the opinion was arrived at was relevant. It concluded that in order to satisfy the statutory wording 'the opinion must be both reasonable in substance and reasonably arrived at'. It would certainly undermine the purpose of the FOIA (to provide a general right of access to information) if the qualified person was not required to give proper consideration to all relevant matters, or if he or she was able to take account of irrelevant matters.

The Tribunal concluded by allowing the appeal because in its opinion, at the time the information request was made, the public interest in maintaining the s.36 exemption did not outweigh the public interest in disclosing the information contained in the minutes of the BBC governors' meeting on 28 January 2004.

To summarise, the Tribunal determined that both the reasonableness of the opinion and the reasonableness of the process by which the opinion is reached are relevant considerations. Public authorities should therefore expect to have to adduce specific relevant evidence in respect of the submissions to the qualified person and his or her response in order to provide an audit trail to establish the opinion was reasonably arrived at and was objectively reasonable, based on good faith and the proper exercise of judgment.

Even if the process is flawed, cases have confirmed that provided that the opinion is still overridingly reasonable, this will not be fatal. In any event, flaws in the process can be cured within a reasonable time which can be taken to be no later than when any internal review of the matter has been completed (see *McIntyre* v. *Information Commissioner and Ministry of Defence* (EA/2007/0068, 11 February 2008) and *Thackeray* v. *Information Commissioner* (EA/2011/0069, 2 December 2011); [2012] 1 Info LR 239).

The Commissioner must either accept the opinion of the reasonable person, or reject it as being unreasonably arrived at and/or unreasonable in substance. The *Wednesbury* standard of reasonableness as used in public law applies to the latter, being the standard of unreasonableness of decision making which risks being overturned on judicial review (*Associated Provincial Picturehouses Ltd* v. *Wednesbury Corporation* [1947] 1 KB 223). This was summed up by Lord Diplock as being a decision 'so outrageous in its defiance of logic or accepted moral standards that no sensible person who had applied his mind to the question to be decided could have arrived at it' (*Council of Civil Service Unions* v. *Minister for the Civil Service* [1983] UKHL 6, at [410]). Accordingly 'in practice this means that the Commissioner must consider whether the opinion should be overturned or otherwise readdressed on the basis that it represents a view or an opinion that no reasonably qualified person would have taken' (see *Thackeray* v. *Information Commissioner*, above, at 53). If the Commissioner accepts that the exemption is engaged, that automatically means that it is accepted that the prejudice is not trivial and would or would be likely to occur.

The qualified person

Importantly, use of s.36 (save in relation to statistical information, s.36(4)) is contingent on the reasonable opinion of a qualified person, which means that it can only apply with the authority of one of the officials listed in s.36(5). This indicates that s.36 must be used with great deliberation. However, it is important to note that s.36 cannot be claimed if no such qualified person has yet been authorised under s.36(5). Public authorities can liaise with the Ministry of Justice if they are unsure. Although the power can be exercised by the authorised role holder, or the acting role holder, it cannot be delegated further. In addition, the Tribunal in *Guardian Newspapers Ltd (1) and Heather Brooke (2)* v. *Information Commissioner and British Broadcasting Commission* (above) commented on the meaning of 'qualified person' in s.36(5)(o)(ii). It was surprised by the BBC's view that authorisation entitled it to delegate the decision to any individual governor. If an authorisation given to a public authority itself under s.36(5)(o)(ii) entitled it to delegate the task of the qualified person to an individual of its choice, then the subsection would be unnecessary. It was the Tribunal's view that the opinion must be the opinion of the authority's primary decision-making organ, in this case the Board of Governors. In *Thackeray* (see above), the Tribunal held that the qualified person needed to be someone suitably senior, and that his or her power to issue that opinion could not be delegated.

The public interest test

This applies to all s.36 cases, unless the public authority concerned is either the House of Commons or the House of Lords in which case the exemption becomes absolute. For all other authorities, the public interest test must still be considered.

Public interest factors have much in common with those for s.35. The passage of time is often a key factor as where a matter is live, details are raw minutes only, or information will be made available in the future, there is far less public interest in accelerating disclosure. Paradoxically, a sensitive and complex decision may create a greater public interest in disclosure than simple decisions. This is because such cases tend to be more important and full disclosure may dispel suspicions of spin and improve understanding (*Lord Baker of Dorking* v. *Information Commissioner and Department for Communities and Local Government* (EA/2006/0043, 1 June 2007); [2011] 1 Info LR 1390). Another factor which may be relevant is the impact of disclosure on core authority functions: if disclosure may leave the authority unprepared or unable to cope with a reaction, which might affect performance of core functions, disclosure would not be in the public interest.

The exemption may apply both to the duty to confirm or deny information is held and/or to the duty to disclose information if held.

5.4.9 Health and safety (s.38)

Section 38 exempts information if its disclosure would, or would be likely to: (a) endanger the physical or mental health of any individual; or (b) endanger the safety of any individual (s.38(1)). 'Endanger' connotes risk of harm rather than harm itself and some Tribunal decisions have confirmed that 'endanger' means the same as 'prejudice', albeit in an individual context (see *People for the Ethical Treatment of Animals Europe* v. *Information Commissioner and University of Oxford* (EA/2009/0076, 13 April 2010); [2011] 1 Info LR 906). However, this point is not settled (see *British Union for the Abolition of Vivisection* v. *Information Commissioner and Newcastle University* (EA/2010/0064, 11 November 2011) [2012] 1 Info LR 52, where the Tribunal was not satisfied that 'endanger' meant the same as 'prejudice', with a mere risk insufficient to engage the exemption). Despite that, a later Tribunal case reaffirmed the *People for the Ethical Treatment of Animals Europe* decision approach to 'endanger', leaving the line to take unclear (see *Summers* v. *Information Commissioner and Commissioner of the Police for the Metropolis* (EA/2011/0186, 24 February 2012).

The following are some examples of disclosures with an evident potential for the kind of endangerment to which this exemption applies:

- those which would allow individuals, groups or firms to be identified or located and consequently targeted and attacked for their beliefs or practices, including work in controversial scientific areas;
- information about the location and use of speed cameras which may affect driving behaviour and so increase the numbers of road-related deaths or personal injuries; and
- disclosure of sensitive or graphic information about deceased individuals which could cause serious distress to particular individuals such as family members, particularly if they were not previously aware of the details.

Of course, information relating to health and safety may often be environmental information within the meaning of the EIR. If such information is environmental information, exemption from the FOIA under s.39 must be claimed and the disclosure of that information should be considered under the EIR.

Applying the public interest test

It is never in the public interest to endanger the health and safety of any individual. This means that 'there would need to be very weighty countervailing considerations to outweigh a risk to health or safety which was of sufficient severity to engage [s.38]' (see *British Union for the Abolition of Vivisection* v. *Information Commissioner and Newcastle University*, above, at 53). More generally, details to be considered will include:

- the size of the risk involved, the likelihood of the outcome in question, and the extent to which steps might be taken to reduce or manage that risk;
- the nature and seriousness of the resulting outcome were that risk to materialise;
- the possibility that disclosure would help to protect the health or safety of other individuals; and
- the possibility that the anticipated danger could be prevented or managed by other, reasonable, precautions.

There is a public interest in disclosing information in order to reduce the potential danger to people and to increase their personal freedom by making them aware of various risks and enabling them to take appropriate action. A certain level of trust is necessary if the recommendations and information supplied by departments with specific responsibilities to inform the public of health and safety issues are to be acted upon. This trust may be enhanced by a high level of disclosure.

The Commissioner's decision in *NHS Direct* (FS50010888, 30 July 2007) gives an indication of when the public interest in disclosing information is outweighed by the public interest in maintaining the s.38 exemption.

NHS Direct provides health advice and information via a confidential telephone service. In this case the Commissioner was asked to consider whether disclosure of the equivalent geographic numbers of NHS Direct's 0845 numbers would, or would be likely to, endanger the health and safety of individuals. As the service's geographic numbers were not networked through a central computerised system and were not always located within a call centre, a member of the public ringing such a number would likely experience a delay in answer, routing to an inappropriate adviser, or no answer at all. Furthermore, a proportion of NHS Direct's calls are immediately referred to 999 emergency services, accident and emergency wards, or for the urgent attention of GPs. NHS Direct deemed that a delay in response to such a call, or no answer at all, could endanger the health and welfare of individuals. NHS Direct also argued that releasing geographic numbers would inevitably require staff to be allocated to these numbers resulting in prioritisation of these calls over those coming through on 0845 numbers. This might also have the effect of relatively minor issues being dealt with first. As a consequence, there would be longer waiting times on 0845 calls and further risks to the health and safety of callers on this number also. NHS Direct therefore refused to disclose, citing s.38.

In assessing the balance of public interest in his decision, the Commissioner recognised that there is a public interest in the public being able to access information about the cost effectiveness of public services. However, there is also a competing public interest in maintaining confidence in the effective operation of the NHS Direct service and the health and safety of the public should not be put at risk by disclosing geographic numbers unless it is safe to do so. An increased likelihood of risk to the health and safety of individuals using the NHS Direct service was in itself a powerful public interest argument against disclosure. In considering the systems operating at the time that the request for information was made, the Commissioner was satisfied that there was a real risk that disclosure of geographic numbers could damage the efficient and effective service that NHS Direct was already providing and therefore could endanger the health and safety of individuals using the service. In this case, because the endangering of public health and safety was such a strong argument, the public interest in maintaining the exemption outweighed the public interest in disclosure and therefore NHS Direct was not required to disclose its geographic numbers to the applicant.

By contrast, in *Ministry of Defence* v. *Information Commissioner and Rob Evans* (EA/2006/0027, 20 July 2007), it was held that where endangerment risks were slight, or balanced by appropriate measures, disclosure should be made.

Other statutes and policies

There may be legal prohibitions in disclosing information which would endanger an individual's health or safety (and such provisions may vary in Scotland). The most relevant examples include the Rehabilitation of Offenders Act 1974 and s.28 of the Health and Safety at Work etc. Act 1974. It is important to be alert to the possibility of such information being environmental information within the meaning of the EIR, in which case, exemption from the FOIA under s.39 is the necessary route.

The exemption may apply both to the duty to confirm or deny information is held and/or to the duty to disclose information if held.

5.4.10 Commercial interests (s.43(2))

The s.43 exemption has already been addressed as it applies to trade secrets (s.43(1)). As a separate point, s.43(2) provides a more general category of exemption for commercially sensitive information if the disclosure of information would, or would be likely to, prejudice someone's commercial interests (including the authority's own).

Commercial interests are wider than trade secrets and apply to a person's ability to participate competitively in a commercial activity, i.e. the purchase or sale of goods or services, even if only indirectly related. Naturally, financial interests are often ultimately involved but this is not an essential requirement since the exemption is to protect commercial rather than simply financial interests. An organisation's commercial interests might, for example, be prejudiced where a disclosure would be likely to:

- damage its business reputation or the confidence that customers, suppliers or investors may have in it;
- have a detrimental impact on its commercial revenue or threaten its ability to obtain supplies or secure finance; or
- weaken its position in a competitive environment by revealing market-sensitive information or information of potential usefulness to its competitors.

Examples of information the disclosure of which may have particular potential to damage commercial interests include:

- research and plans relating to a potential new product;
- product manufacturing cost information;
- product sales forecast information;
- strategic business plans, including, for example, plans to enter, develop or withdraw from a product or geographical market sector;
- marketing plans to promote a new or existing product;
- information relating to the preparation of a competitive bid;
- information about the financial and business viability of a company; and
- information provided to a public authority in respect of an application for a licence or as a requirement of a licence condition or under a regulatory regime.

Commercial interests of a public authority

Importantly, s.43(2) can apply to an authority's own commercially sensitive information as well as to such information held by the authority relating to outside organisations. It is much used by authorities to protect information which is truly confidential but for which s.41 is not available because it is the authority's internal information. However, s.43(2) will not always be available to authorities as, because they are rarely trading entities, their interests do not always amount to 'commercial interests' according to the Commissioner.

The Tribunal explored this issue in *John Connor Press Associates Ltd* v. *Information Commissioner* (EA/2005/0005, 25 January 2006) which considered whether an authority is required to disclose financial information which might prejudice its own bargaining position during contemporaneous contractual negotiations and a third party's bargaining power for future commercial transactions.

In the winter of 2004–5, the National Maritime Museum (NMM) held an exhibition of artwork by Conrad Shawcross. This exhibition was one of a series of contemporary art events staged under the NMM's 'New Visions' programme. In January 2005, John Connor Press Associates Limited (JCPA) asked the NMM to disclose all documentation and correspondence relating to any payments made to the artist for the exhibition. The NMM duly disclosed the contract together with three invoices and some miscellaneous correspondence which revealed substantial details about the transaction. Crucially though, all financial information had been redacted. The NMM relied upon s.43(2), stating that disclosure would be likely to prejudice the commercial interests of both NMM and Conrad Shawcross.

The Information Commissioner held that, in the light of the 'active and contemporaneous negotiations for a project of a similar nature', the public interest in maintaining the s.43(2) exemption outweighed the public interest in disclosure (*National Maritime Museum* (FS50063478, 20 June 2005)). The Tribunal overruled this decision. The key element to note was the Tribunal's interpretation of the phrase 'likely to prejudice' in s.43(2). The Tribunal insisted that this expression must mean that 'the chance of prejudice being suffered should be more than a hypothetical or remote possibility; there must be a real and significant risk'.

The following reasons were given: (1) the information already disclosed would have provided any prospective exhibitor with a significant amount of valuable information; (2) it had already been disclosed that the NMM had, very unusually, agreed to contribute to the cost of the artist's materials (a piece of information which significantly decreased the bargaining value of the financial information withheld); and (3) the nature of the works made by Conrad Shawcross and the subsequent artist with whom NMM was negotiating were sufficiently different that they could not be valuably compared.

Prejudice to a third party's commercial interests

Public authorities will hold a great deal of information which falls within s.43(2) because disclosure would cause commercial damage to third parties. Third party commercially sensitive information will come into the possession of public authorities in a number of ways, for example:

- as a result of legal, regulatory or licensing requirements;
- in the course of policy development, e.g. information obtained, usually voluntarily, to inform and influence the development of policy, or changes to law or regulation;
- through providing support for business, e.g. information provided by a company or trade association to a public authority to obtain advice, help with a specific project, and/or financial assistance; and
- through procurement of and letting of contracts, e.g. for products, services or research.

Where a third party's commercial interests are to be used to support the application of s.43(2), an authority cannot assume prejudice on behalf of a third party but must instead consult it and obtain its arguments about disclosure. If there is insufficient time to obtain full arguments, the authority can provide them for the third party provided it can prove that the arguments made genuinely reflect those third party

191

concerns (see *Derry City Council* v. *Information Commissioner* (EA/2006/0014, 11 December 2006); [2011] 1 Info LR 1105).

Where a third party cannot be contacted or does not fully co-operate, it is unlikely that its information will be protected against disclosure; see Commissioner's decision notice *Medicines and Healthcare Products Regulatory Agency* (FS50366396, 4 January 2012). There was a drug trial to test a drug called TGN1412 (the drug) in 2006 and sadly six of the eight volunteers suffered multiple organ failure. The Medicines and Healthcare Products Regulatory Agency (MHRA), part of the Department of Health, is the UK regulator for drugs and medical devices and published an interim report with various redacted documents on this incident. A request by lawyers for one of those injured in the drug trial made a request for the documents in unredacted form (being details about the structure of the drug, its manufacturing process, safety trial and evaluation details and information about medical conditions it could be used to treat). The MHRA withheld them initially and following internal review, on the basis of s.43 together with ss.40 and 38. A complaint was made to the Commissioner (focusing only on information withheld under s.43) who investigated accordingly.

It became clear that since the drug trial, ownership of the drug had changed and, in respect of this request, the MHRA had struggled to identify the new owners of the drug. Even once they were identified and consulted via their representatives, the new owners failed to respond directly or through their representatives. The MHRA provided the arguments against disclosure made by the previous owners of the drug and argued that the concerns were likely to be the same for the new owners, which the Commissioner accepted. The MHRA put forward its own reasonable assumptions around those claims to support them. However, the Commissioner took account of the facts that the original concerns dated from 2006 and that the MHRA had been unable to provide evidence about likely prejudice to the new owners who, thus far, had not objected to disclosure and so the MHRA's arguments on prejudice to their interests were speculative. As a result the Commissioner found that 'the MHRA has not demonstrated that disclosure would or would be likely to prejudice the new owner's [sic] commercial interests' and accordingly found that s.43(2) was not engaged and ordered disclosure of the information. This order has now been appealed to the First-tier Tribunal.

This ties in with the recommendations in the Section 45 Code of Practice to consult third parties about requests for their information (see **4.2**). The current outcome of all of these points is that an authority has no legal obligation to consult a third party but, unless it does so, it cannot claim arguments on behalf of such third party; the third party might never know about the request for its information and cannot put forward its arguments for non-disclosure (or have them relied upon) unless consulted by the authority. Despite this, in most cases the third party has no readily available rights either to take action against the authority, or to obtain support or redress from or though the Commissioner. The few judgments which suggest the Commissioner should proactively try to properly safeguard such third party interests when reaching a decision are welcome but may be too little, too late.

With the increasing focus of requests under the FOIA being more about third parties who work with the public sector than about the public sector itself, it is to be hoped that this state of affairs will be fairly addressed by the current post-legislative scrutiny of the FOIA being undertaken.

Areas of particular sensitivity

Certain areas of activity in which all authorities are involved are likely to carry particular risks in relation to commercially sensitive information. One such area is procurement. All public authorities buy goods and services, and a great deal of information which changes hands during the procurement process will be commercially sensitive. Some examples of information to which s.43 is most likely to apply include:

- information relating to general/preliminary procurement activities, e.g. market sounding information; information relating to programme, project and procurement strategies; and contextual information about the authority, its business objectives and plans;
- information relating to supplier selection, e.g. qualification information for potential bidders; information about requirements including specifications; details of the qualification process; and details of qualified bidders;
- information relating to contract negotiation and award, e.g. bids; papers about capabilities of bidders, evaluations of bids, negotiating briefs and recommendations; the contract; information about successful bid and bidder; and information about other bids and bidders; and
- information relating to contract performance and post-contract activities, e.g. information about implementation; information about performance; information about contract amendments with supporting papers; and information which may be provided and reviewed by third parties (e.g. consultants/ auditors).

The requirements of the public procurement regime should also be taken into account in relation to the possible disclosure of information. The Consolidated Public Procurement Directive 2004/18/EC is implemented by the Public Contracts Regulations 2006, SI 2006/5. Their provisions (and those of their Scottish equivalent) prohibit the disclosure of information which suppliers have reasonably designated as confidential in a procurement. If this legislation genuinely prevents the disclosure, the information would be exempt under s.44 but this applies less often than might be thought.

The challenge of balancing the need to comply with procurement law, the law of confidence and the FOIA has been identified and the Office of Government Commerce (OGC) has issued documentation to assist authorities to deal with this (see *FOI (Civil Procurement) Policy and Guidance*, version 2.0 (OGC, November 2008), with related notes and working assumptions). The guidance steps through the stages commonly involved in a procurement exercise and its associated documentation and provides high level suggestions on what documentation it may be safe to disclose, or not, and why at each stage. This has been referred to in a number of decision notices and judgments, including the Tribunal case involving the Department of Health below. However, the guidance should be seen as indicative only and not conclusive as there will still be a need to deal fully with any relevant prejudice test and public interest test on the relevant facts of the case, which might lead to a different outcome. The Cabinet Office has reorganised the OGC into the Efficiency and Reform Group (ERG) and has published the guidance notes *Transparency – Publication of Tender Documents* and *Transparency – Publication of New Central Government Contracts*, both of which were updated in September 2011 and which provide further guidance. Although the guidance notes refer to 'central government', that is construed more widely than might be thought and they are likely to set expectations for the approach to be taken by other public authorities.

In effect, the stage which the procurement process has reached at the time of the request is critical. Generally, the public interest in the disclosure of procurement-related information is not sufficiently strong to override the harm that may be done to commercial interests before the award of the contract. However, the public interest in making information available after the award of the contract – such as the total tender price and evaluation details of the successful tenderer, along with information about the fee rates and other details necessary to understand the nature of the services contracted – is much stronger.

This was clear from the Commissioner's decision notice *Guildford Borough Council* (FS50070214, 18 July 2007), which involved a request for bidder tender information and other details relating to the development of council-owned land. It was noted that during the procurement process the public interest was in maintaining confidence to allow successful completion of the process and selection of the winning bidder. However, once the bidder was selected and the contract awarded, the public interest in confidentiality decreased compared to the increased public interest in knowing the award was to the right company and ensuring value for money.

This approach was endorsed by the Tribunal in *Department of Health* v. *Information Commissioner* (EA/2008/0018, 18 November 2008); [2011] 1 Info LR 1135, where the contract awarded to the provider of an electronic recruitment service was requested. The Department of Health withheld the information under s.44 on the basis that it was bound to maintain the confidential treatment and so non-disclosure of the contract as reasonably requested by the provider under reg.30 of the Public Services Contracts Regulations 1993, SI 1993/3228 (the predecessor to reg.43 of the 2006 Regulations). However, on investigation, the contract had not been obtained from the contractor and so the regulation did not apply and s.44 was not engaged. Section 41 had also been claimed but since the contract had not been obtained from a third party, that exemption could not be relied upon. The department had in addition relied on s.43(1) and (2). The Tribunal was:

satisfied that any of the material in dispute in this case which could constitute a trade secret would also fall more comfortably within the definition in section 43(2) FOIA. Both sections are subject to the same public interest test and on the facts of this case no different arguments are advanced in relation to the public interest test relevant to each section. For this reason ... the Tribunal does not consider it necessary to decide the applicability of section 43(1) FOIA separately as this is subsumed by the decisions made under section 43(2) FOIA.

Whether it is reasonable for a bidder to designate information as confidential will depend upon the nature of the information and the timing of the procurement exercise but it is clear that any such obligation would reduce over time.

The s.43 exemption is considered in further detail in **Chapter 6**.

Copyright

Another issue is a public authority's commercial interests in the disclosure or publication of information. The FOIA obligations to disclose information apply to copyright information as well as to other information. However, the commercial effects of disclosure on the copyright holder (including the authority itself if it is the copyright holder) should be considered, where relevant, in relation to s.43. Of course, copyright protection in a work will continue to subsist even if information is disclosed under the FOIA. A copyright holder may therefore enforce its copyright against any successful applicant under the FOIA who then sought to exploit that information in breach of the copyright.

Thus in *University of Central Lancashire* v. *Information Commissioner and Colquhoun* (EA/2009/0034, 8 December 2009); [2011] 1 Info LR 1170, BSc Homeopathy course materials had to be disclosed on request despite the university's concern that this would be likely to lead to breach of copyright in its materials.

Applying the public interest test

There is a public interest in protecting the commercial interests of both the private sector (which plays an important role in the general health of the economy) and the public sector (whose commercially related functions need in any event to be exercised in the wider context of the public interest).

Conversely, there is a general public interest in the disclosure of commercial information in order to ensure that:

- there is transparency in the accountability of public funds;
- there is proper scrutiny of government actions in carrying out licensing functions in accordance with published policy;
- public money is being used effectively, and that departments are getting value for money when purchasing goods and services;
- authorities' commercial activities, including the procurement process, are conducted in an open and honest way; and
- business can respond better to public sector opportunities.

The exemption may apply both to the duty to confirm or deny information is held and/or to the duty to disclose information if held.

CHAPTER 6

Implications for the private sector

*Robin Hopkins, 11KBW Chambers**

[*This chapter revises and updates the chapter from the previous edition of this book by Hugh Tomlinson QC.]

6.1 INTRODUCTION

It has been widely recognised that freedom of information legislation can have a substantial impact on the private sector. Although the Freedom of Information Act 2000 (FOIA) only places duties of disclosure on public authorities, it potentially allows any applicant to have access to any information held by the public sector. Any information which has been provided[1] to public authorities[2] by businesses is potentially disclosable to any applicant.[3] This includes a huge range of information about the activities of the private sector. The information will have come into the hands of public authorities for a wide variety of reasons, such as through the process of taxation, or as a result of regulation or direct commercial relationships between the public and private sectors.

As many commentators have pointed out, the FOIA represents both a threat and an opportunity for the private sector. The threat is that commercially sensitive material will be made available to competitors or the media with potentially adverse consequences. The opportunity is for the private sector to obtain a huge range of commercially valuable information at extremely modest cost.[4]

---

[1] The duty to disclose applies to information held at the time when the request was received – it does not matter when the information was provided. In that sense, the FOIA has retrospective effect, covering information supplied to or obtained by public authorities at any time in the past.
[2] That is, bodies listed in Sched.1 to the FOIA, to which a number of bodies have been added since enactment, the most recent being the Association of Chief Police Officers of England, Wales and Northern Ireland, the Financial Ombudsman Service and the Universities and Colleges Admissions Service and 'publicly owned companies' as defined by s.6.
[3] Applications can be made by any person and the reason for the application is, in general, irrelevant. Applications can be made anonymously through surrogate data agencies, i.e. agencies which make requests in their own names so that the public authority does not know the identity of the ultimate client.
[4] Public authorities can charge for photocopying and postage but will not charge for the costs of locating the information if this is less than £450 (on the basis of £25 per person-hour), or £600 in the case of central government.

The threat of public disclosure of private sector confidential commercial material is the most immediate issue. Private bodies provide a wide range of sensitive information to public authorities. The threats arising out of disclosure include matters such as the following:

- when a business wins a public sector contract, that competitors will learn the price and contractual levels of performance and might be able to find out the results of performance reviews;
- when a business loses a bid, that competitors may be able to discover details of the bid;
- when a private body has been the subject of a regulatory investigation or inquiry, that competitors or the media might be able to discover details.

If private bodies wish to protect confidential commercial information from disclosure they must take steps do so. It is clear that marking a document as confidential will no longer be a guarantee that the public (including business competitors and the media) will be prevented from gaining access to it. It is necessary to consider a wide range of carefully targeted measures to provide as much protection as possible for information which has been or will be given to public authorities.

There has to date been less focus on the opportunities for the private sector arising from the FOIA. The UK's Coalition government, formed in May 2010, launched the website **www.data.gov.uk**, aimed at the proactive dissemination of information held by public authorities. At the time of writing, this website offered 8,300 datasets. The FOIA, however, remains an invaluable and often under-utilised tool for obtaining specific information relevant to a private sector organisation's individual objectives. Using the FOIA in this way involves detailed analysis of the kinds of commercially useful information which might be held by public authorities and the making of focused requests aimed at obtaining disclosure of information which can be put to commercial use.

In an examination of the impact of the FOIA on the private sector, this chapter will address the four main areas detailed below:

- *FOIA exemptions and the private sector.* This section deals with the operation of the exemptions in the FOIA which are likely to be relevant when commercially important information is held by public authorities, focusing, in particular, on the confidentiality and commercial interests exemptions in the FOIA, ss.41 and 43.
- *FOIA requests and the supplier of information.* The position of private bodies in relation to FOIA requests for information which they have supplied to public authorities is considered, in relation to both consultation and express contractual provision.
- *Practical steps for protecting information.* The risks faced by private bodies are examined together with practical steps which might be taken to protect information from disclosure under the FOIA.

- *Making use of the FOIA.* This section covers the opportunities available for private bodies to obtain information under the FOIA.

In order to keep up to date with developments, readers are referred to the practical journal *Freedom of Information* (**www.foij.com**).

6.2 FOIA EXEMPTIONS AND THE PRIVATE SECTOR

6.2.1 Introduction

Section 1 of the FOIA creates a general right of access to information held by public authorities. This means 'information recorded in any form' (FOIA, s.84) and includes information held by another person on behalf of the authority (FOIA, s.3(2)(b)). It does not, however, include information held by a public authority on behalf of another person (s.3(2)(a)). By virtue of s.1(1), any person who requests information (s.84) from a public authority is entitled (a) to be informed in writing by the public authority whether it holds information of the description specified in the request; and (b) if it does, to have that information communicated to him or her.

This general right of access is, of course, subject to a series of exemptions. Some of these are absolute: if information falls into one of the categories of information which is absolutely exempt from disclosure, then the public authority has no duty to disclose under the FOIA. (It may, however, be entitled to disclose the information voluntarily.) The absolute exemptions are:

- s.21: information accessible by other means;
- s.23: information supplied by or relating to bodies dealing with security matters;
- s.32: information contained in court records;
- s.34: where exemption from the duty of disclosure is required to avoid an infringement of parliamentary privilege;
- s.36: provisions relating to information held by the House of Commons or the House of Lords;
- s.37: provisions relating to communications with the Sovereign and heir to the Throne;
- s.40: where the information constitutes personal data of which the applicant is the data subject;[5]
- s.41: where disclosure of the information would constitute an actionable breach of confidence;[6]
- s.44: where disclosure is prohibited by statute.

---

[5] This is a complex exemption which has some qualified elements and is therefore sometimes described as a hybrid exemption (see **Chapter 8** for a full discussion).

[6] Although this is an absolute exemption, it only takes effect where an action for breach of confidence would be likely to succeed against a defence based on the public interest. In that sense, this can also be thought of as a hybrid exemption.

Other exemptions are qualified – they are subject to the public interest balancing test under s.2(2). This provides that a balancing exercise must be undertaken to determine whether, in all the circumstances of the case, the public interest in maintaining the exemption outweighs the public interest in disclosing the information (with the corresponding test for the public authority's duty to confirm or deny whether it holds the requested information). The qualified exemptions are as follows:

- s.22: information intended for future publication;
- s.24: information required for the purpose of safeguarding national security;
- s.26: information the disclosure of which would be likely to prejudice defence;
- s.27: information the disclosure of which would be likely to prejudice international relations;
- s.28: information the disclosure of which would be likely to prejudice relations between administrations within the UK;
- s.29: information the disclosure of which would be likely to prejudice the economic interests of the UK or the financial interests of any administration within the UK;
- s.30: information held for the purpose of criminal investigations and proceedings and investigations conducted by public authorities;
- s.31: information the disclosure of which would be likely to prejudice law enforcement;
- s.33: information the disclosure of which would be likely to prejudice the exercise of audit functions;
- s.35: information relating to the formulation of government policy;
- s.36: information the disclosure of which would be likely to prejudice the effective conduct of public affairs (this is sometimes described as a hybrid exemption, parts of which are absolute);
- s.37: information relating to communications with Her Majesty and in relation to honours (another hybrid exemption);
- s.38: information the disclosure of which would be likely to prejudice health and safety;
- s.39: information which is subject to disclosure under the EIR;
- s.42: information in relation to which a claim to legal professional privilege could be maintained;
- s.43: information which constitutes a trade secret or the disclosure of which would be likely to prejudice commercial interests.

It should be noted that a request is for information and not documents. This means that one document may contain some pieces of information which are non-exempt, some which are subject to an absolute exemption and some which require the application of a public interest test. Tribunals increasingly insist on the disclosure of as much information as possible within the scope of the request, often ordering the disclosure of a document with only the exempt sections or sentences redacted. The Tribunal has confirmed that, for FOIA purposes, contracts are to be treated as severable, with only the exempt parts being withheld (see *Channel Four* v. *Information Commissioner and British Sky Broadcasting Ltd* (EA/2010/0134, 23 March 2011); [2011] 2 Info LR 241).

While all these exemptions are potentially relevant, those which arise most commonly in the context of private sector information held by public authorities are s.41 (information provided in confidence) and s.43 (information which constitutes a trade secret or whose disclosure is likely to prejudice commercial interests). These will be considered in the next three sections. Private sector organisations should also consider whether their information could be protected under s.44 (disclosure prohibited by statute), particularly where this information is held by a regulator governed by a bespoke statutory scheme, or where EU procurement legislation provides for the non-disclosure of bidders' information. Such scenarios turn very much on their own particulars, whereas ss.41 and 43 are of more general application.

6.2.2   The absolute exemption for information provided in confidence[7]

Introduction

The FOIA is designed to protect confidential information which private bodies have supplied to public authorities from disclosure to applicants. Section 41 provides:

(1)   Information is exempt information if –

    (a)   it was obtained by the public authority from any other person (including another public authority), and

    (b)   the disclosure of the information to the public (otherwise than under this Act) by the public authority holding it would constitute a breach of confidence actionable by that or any other person.

(2)   The duty to confirm or deny does not arise if, or to the extent that, the confirmation or denial that would have to be given to comply with section 1(1)(a) would (apart from this Act) constitute an actionable breach of confidence.

The term 'actionable breach of confidence' is not defined but it appears to mean a claim which would be upheld by the courts (not merely a claim that is arguable). For example, in *Higher Education Funding Council for England* v. *Information Commissioner* (EA/2009/0036, 13 January 2010); [2011] 1 Info LR 1034, the Tribunal concluded at para.30 that the public authority:

must establish that disclosure would expose it to the risk of a breach of confidence claim which, on a balance of probabilities, would succeed. This includes considering whether the public authority would have a defence to the claim. Establishing that such a claim would be arguable is not sufficient to bring the exemption into play.[8]

---

[7]   See generally *Freedom of Information Act Awareness Guidance No.2: Information Provided in Confidence*, version 4 (ICO, September 2008).
[8]   The Tribunal sought assistance from the speech of Lord Falconer in the House of Lords: see Hansard, HL, vol.617, col.2, 17 October 2000.

The corresponding exception under the EIR (reg.12(5)(e)) is worded differently. In effect, it combines the elements of ss.41(2) and 43(2) of the FOIA. Regulation 12(5)(e) provides an exception as follows:

> a public authority may refuse to disclose information to the extent that its disclosure would adversely affect . . . the confidentiality of commercial or industrial information where such confidentiality is provided by law to protect a legitimate economic interest

In one case, however, the Tribunal has held that, when analysing confidentiality, the same approach applies to both reg.12(5)(e) and s.41(2) (see *Jones (on behalf of Swansea Friends of the Earth)* v. *Information Commissioner, The Environment Agency and SI Green (UK) Ltd* (EA/2011/0156, 27 April 2012)).

The information covered

In order to be exempt information under s.41, the information must be obtained 'from any other person', i.e. the exemption does not cover the public authority's own internally generated information. The Information Tribunal has held that a concluded contract between a public authority and a third party does not fall within s.41(1)(a) (see *Derry City Council* v. *Information Commissioner* (EA/2006/0014, 11 December 2006); [2011] 1 Info LR 1105 at para.32(c)). Similarly, in *Department of Health* v. *Information Commissioner* (EA/2008/0018, 18 November 2008); [2011] 1 Info LR 1135, the Tribunal found that information provided by a public authority and then incorporated into a document compiled by a third party consultancy was not 'obtained from' that third party. Whether information regarding the pre-contractual negotiating position of the parties falls within s.41 will depend on the circumstances (*Derry City Council*, above, para.32(d)). This means that the whole of any contract with a public authority is potentially disclosable, 'no matter how confidential the content or how clearly expressed the confidentiality provisions' (*Derry City Council*, above, para.32(e)). However, s.41 may still apply to confidential technical information set out in a contract (*Derry City Council*, above). Furthermore, contracts potentially fall under the exemption in s.43 of the FOIA, which is discussed below.

Requirements for breach of confidence

The importing of the common law concept of breach of confidence into the FOIA makes the assessment of the applicability of the s.41 exemption an extremely difficult exercise. The law continues to evolve as to the precise limits of breach of confidence and public authorities will, inevitably, approach the issue in different ways. As a result, it may be very difficult to predict whether, in a given case, the exemption will protect a particular piece of information.

An essential first step is the analysis of the requirements for establishing an actionable breach of confidence[9] as explained in the case law. The clearest and most often cited statement of the necessary elements is that of Megarry J in *Coco* v. *AN Clark (Engineers) Ltd* [1969] RPC 41 at para.47:

> First, the information itself ... must 'have the necessary quality of confidence about it'. Secondly, that information must have been communicated in circumstances importing an obligation of confidence. Thirdly, there must have been an unauthorised use of the information to the detriment of the party communicating it.[10]

In relation to the first question (necessary quality of confidence), two points should be noted. One is that confidentiality does not attach to trivial or useless information (see *Moorgate Tobacco Co Ltd* v. *Philip Morris Ltd (No. 2)* (1984) 156 CLR 414, 438). This is not a high threshold and will seldom be in issue where a private sector organisation seeks to protect information potentially disclosable under the FOIA.

The second and more important point is that the basic attribute of confidentiality is inaccessibility. The expression 'the necessary quality of confidence' has been defined by antithesis as follows: 'it must not be something which is public property and public knowledge' (Lord Greene MR in *Saltman Engineering Co Ltd* v. *Campbell Engineering Co Ltd* (1948) 65 RPC 203 at para.215; see more recently Arnold J in *Force India Formula One Team Ltd* v. *Malaysia Racing Team and Others* [2012] EWHC 616 (Ch) at [217]). Similarly, in a well-known passage in the *Spycatcher* case in the House of Lords, Lord Goff said:

> the principle of confidentiality only applies to information to the extent that it is confidential. In particular, once it has entered what is usually called the public domain (which means no more than that the information in question is so generally accessible that, in all the circumstances, it cannot be regarded as confidential) then, as a general rule, the principle of confidentiality can have no application to it.
>
> (*Attorney General* v. *Guardian Newspapers Ltd (No.2)* [1990] 1 AC 109, 282)

Confidentiality does not depend on the establishment of absolute secrecy; relative confidentiality is sufficient (see *Franchi* v. *Franchi* [1967] RPC 149 153). The concept of relative secrecy has not been exhaustively analysed in the authorities but a number of points are clear, as follows:

- The fact that information is known to a small number of people does not mean that it is no longer confidential (see *Franchi* v. *Franchi* [1967] RPC 149, 152).
- Information which is only accessible by carrying out specialist research which requires background knowledge and the expenditure of time may still be

---

[9] It should be noted that the position is now slightly different in relation to private information – misuse of private information is developing as a separate tort (see *Campbell* v. *MGN Ltd* [2004] 2 AC 457 and *Douglas* v. *Hello! (No.3)* [2007] UKHL 21). In the present context we are concerned with commercially confidential information and breach of confidence is the relevant form of the tort.

[10] This statement of the law has repeatedly been approved at the highest level: see *Attorney General* v. *Guardian Newspapers Ltd (No 2)* [1990] 1 AC 109 (the '*Spycatcher*' case) per Lord Griffiths at para.268; *Campbell* v. *MGN Ltd* [2004] UKHL 22 per Lord Nicholls at [13] and *Douglas* v. *Hello! Ltd (No 3)* [2007] UKHL 21 per Lord Hoffmann at [111].

confidential.[11] So, in *Attorney General* v. *Greater Manchester Newspapers*, (2001) *The Times*, 7 December, it was held that information which was accessible in a specialist part of a public library to a person with specialist knowledge was not in the public domain. (See also *R* v. *Solicitors Complaints Bureau, ex p. Wylde* [1996] EWHC Admin 98, 'information available to the public can nonetheless remain confidential where in practice it is difficult or impractical to obtain information from the public source'.)

- The fact that the public can only obtain a particular item of information on the payment of a fee or subject to some other restriction does not mean that the information is confidential. (See *Melton Medes Ltd* v. *Securities and Investments Board* [1995] Ch 137 (information not confidential if disclosed in court because the transcript can be obtained for a fee).)
- Information is not confidential if it is generally available to the public, for example, in the press or from public records.

In relation to the second question from *Coco* v. *AN Clark (Engineers) Ltd* (information communicated in circumstances importing an obligation of confidence), both contract and equity should be considered. In broad terms, the law imposes a duty of confidence whenever a person receives information he or she knows or ought to know is fairly and reasonably to be regarded as confidential.[12] Although in the vast majority of cases, this duty will arise out of some transaction or relationship between the parties, this is not necessary to establish the duty.

In relation to the third question, there must be an actual or threatened use of the information for a purpose other than that for which it was imparted to the confidant. There is no need for the claimant to show detriment where personal information is involved (see *Bluck* v. *Information Commissioner and Epsom and St Helier University NHS Trust* (EA/2006/0090, 17 September 2007); [2011] 1 Info LR 1017 at paras.14–15). However, where the 'confider's' interest is purely a commercial one, it may be necessary to show that disclosure will cause damage. In the FOIA context, private sector organisations should be prepared to demonstrate that disclosure of their information is likely to cause them damage, and to make good that case with cogent evidence focused on the particular information in dispute and the circumstances at the time of the request under FOIA.

If the three criteria from *Coco* v. *AN Clark (Engineers) Ltd* are met, it will still be necessary to consider a fourth issue, namely whether a defence to an action for breach of confidence based on the public interest in disclosure would be likely to succeed. The issues arising have been expressed in a number of ways in case law. In the *Spycatcher* case Lord Goff said:

---

[11] See *Collins (Engineers) Ltd* v. *Roberts & Co Ltd* [1965] RPC 429 at 431–2 and, more recently, *Forensic Telecommunications Services Ltd* v. *Chief Constable of West Yorkshire Police* [2011] EWHC 2892 (Ch) at [132].

[12] Per Lord Nicholls, *Campbell* v. *MGN* [2004] UKHL 22 at [14]: in relation to information about an individual's private life the tort is now better described as 'misuse of private information', see note 10.

although the basis of the law's protection of confidence is that there is a public interest that confidences should be preserved and protected by the law, nevertheless that public interest may be outweighed by some other countervailing public interest which favours disclosure. This limitation may apply, as the learned judge pointed out, to all types of confidential information. It is this limiting principle which may require a court to carry out a balancing operation, weighing the public interest in maintaining confidence against a countervailing public interest favouring disclosure.

> *(Attorney General* v. *Guardian Newspapers Ltd (No.2)* [1990] 1 AC 109, 282)

The weighing or balancing exercise referred to by Lord Goff takes on different forms in different kinds of cases, considered below:

- In some cases the public interest in disclosure will simply outweigh the public interest in preserving confidentiality. This was once known as the iniquity defence but is now recognised as being more general.
- This principle has been held to justify disclosure of suspected criminal conduct (*Malone* v. *Metropolitan Police Commissioner* [1979] Ch 344), disclosure of fraudulent business practices (*Gartside* v. *Outram* (1857) 26 Ch 113), alleged corruption by a local authority (*Preston Borough Council* v. *McGrath* (2000) *The Times*, 19 May), dangerous medical practices which endanger the public (*Schering Chemicals Ltd* v. *Falkman Ltd* [1982] 1 QB 1), dangerous medical hazards (*W* v. *Egdell* [1990] 1 Ch 359), information about cults (*Hubbard* v. *Vosper* [1972] 2 QB 84 (in relation to a book about Scientology)) and information concerning the functioning of the Intoximeter device (*Lion Laboratories* v. *Evans* [1985] QB 526 (this case established that the justification of the disclosure of confidential information did not depend on establishing an iniquity)).
- In the rare case where commercial confidential information is also private, then, if there is a disclosure to the media, it is necessary to carry out a balancing exercise between privacy and freedom of expression (*Campbell* v. *MGN Ltd* [2004] AC 457).
- In the case of the disclosure of information concerning the expenditure of public money, there are strong freedom of expression arguments in favour of disclosure, although the public interest must be assessed on the basis of proportionality considerations arising under art.10(2) of the European Convention on Human Rights. (See the discussion in *London Regional Transport* v. *Mayor of London* [2001] EWCA Civ 1491, especially at [57]–[58] (Sedley LJ); see also *Mersey Care NHS Trust* v. *Ackroyd (No.2)* [2006] EWHC 107 (QB).)
- In the case of commercial information, it appears that the public interest in the free flow of commercial information (i.e. the same public interest which renders contracts in restraint of trade void) means that commercial and industrial confidentiality only attaches to 'specific information which an enterprise needs to keep confidential in order to protect its competitive position, not general knowledge of business organisation or methods.' (*R* v. *Secretary of State for Transport, ex p. Alliance against the Birmingham Northern Relief Road* [1999] Env LR 447, 475).

The potential for a public interest defence means that although s.41 contains an absolute exemption, there is substantial opportunity for the person making the request to raise, and the public authority to consider, public interest arguments in favour of disclosure, particularly where there is any suggestion that the information relates to actual or potential wrongdoing. However, in contrast to the approach to 'qualified exemptions' under the FOIA, the presumption is that confidentiality should be preserved unless outweighed by countervailing factors (see *Derry City Council* v. *Information Commissioner* (above) at para.34(m)). (With qualified exemptions, those arguing in favour of disclosure have a 'slight advantage' in that if the factors in favour of disclosure equal those in favour of maintaining the exemption, disclosure must be ordered (see *Cabinet Office* v. *Information Commissioner and Lamb* (EA/2008/0024 and EA/2008/0029, 27 January 2009); [2011] 1 Info LR 782 at para.34).)

The person making the request for disclosure can raise public interest arguments based on government openness, but these can only be general arguments and cannot be based on the FOIA itself. This is because the test as to whether information falls within the s.41 exemption is whether a disclosure otherwise than under the FOIA would constitute an actionable breach of confidence. In other words, what must be considered is whether, but for the FOIA, the disclosure of the information would have been a breach of confidence. This appears to have the result that the public interest in open access to information underlying the FOIA is not a relevant consideration and the definition of confidentiality cannot be influenced by the terms of the FOIA itself.

The s.41 exemption in practice

In practice, reliance on s.41 requires clear explanations and supporting evidence, in relation to the particular information in dispute (as opposed to the type of information, or as opposed to the entirety of a large document) of (i) it being obtained from outside the public authority; (ii) the circumstances in which it was obtained; (iii) why those circumstances import an obligation of confidence; and (iv) details of why and how disclosure of this particular information at the time of the request under the FOIA would have caused damage to the person or organisation which had imparted that information.

It should also be noted that confidential commercial information is capable of constituting a possession within the meaning of art.1 of the First Protocol to the European Convention on Human Rights (ECHR) and can also fall within the scope of the right to respect for private life in art.8 of the ECHR (see *R (Veolia ES Nottinghamshire Ltd)* v. *Nottinghamshire County Council and Others* [2010] EWCA Civ 1214, a case involving access to information under the Audit Commission Act 1998 rather than under the FOIA). If those rights are engaged, then access to such information will only be compatible with ECHR rights if such access pursues a legitimate aim and is proportionate to that aim. This point has been accepted by the First-tier Tribunal as applicable to access under the EIR (see

Staffordshire County Council and Sibelco (UK) Ltd v. *Information Commissioner* (EA/2010/0015, 22 November 2010) at para.151). In other cases, however, the Tribunal has taken the view that ECHR points add little to the analysis required under the FOIA, and by parity of reasoning, the EIR (see *Nottinghamshire County Council* v. *Information Commissioner and Veolia ES Nottinghamshire Ltd and UK Coal Mining Ltd* (EA/2010/0142, 29 December 2010) at para.74).

The s.41 exemption has been relied on in a number of cases considered by the First-tier Tribunal. Examples include:

- Information in connection with licences issued for the exporting to Iran of 'controlled goods', including those allegedly used for military and interrogation purposes (*Department for Business, Innovation and Skills* v. *Information Commissioner and Browning* (EA/2011/0044, 22 September 2011)).
- Information relating to the state of the buildings at higher education institutions (*Higher Education Funding Council for England* v. *Information Commissioner* (EA/2009/0036, 13 January 2010); [2011] 1 Info LR 1034).
- A report prepared by IBM and provided to the Home Office in relation to a tender for biometric software for the proposed identity cards scheme (*Moss* v. *Information Commissioner and Home Office* (EA/2011/0081, 24 April 2012)).
- A copy of the contract between the Department of Health and an external consultancy for the recruitment of NHS staff (*Department of Health* v. *Information Commissioner* (EA/2008/0018, 18 November 2008); [2011] 1 Info LR 1135).
- Notes of an interview between a registrar of deaths and parents of the deceased (*S* v. *Information Commissioner and General Register Office* (EA/2006/0030, 9 May 2007)).
- Agreements between Ryanair and Derry City Council concerning the use of Derry City Airport (*Derry City Council* v. *Information Commissioner* (EA/2006/0014, 11 December 2006); [2011] 1 Info LR 1105).

6.2.3   The trade secrets exemption

Trade secrets are protected by a qualified exemption. By s.43(1), information is exempt information if it constitutes a trade secret. The FOIA does not define 'trade secret' and the English courts have not sought to provide any comprehensive definition of the term (see the discussion of the English law in *Ansell Rubber Co Pty Ltd* v. *Allied Rubber Industries Pty Ltd* [1972] RPC 811) nor to define the precise difference between this and confidential business information. The definition usually cited is that set out in *Lansing Linde Ltd* v. *Kerr* [1991] 1 WLR 251:

> information which, if disclosed to a competitor, would be liable to cause real (or significant) harm to the owner of the secret. I would add first, that it must be information used in a trade or business, and secondly that the owner must limit the dissemination of it or at least not encourage or permit widespread publication.

For illuminating recent discussions of the concept, see *Caterpillar Logistics Services (UK) Ltd* v. *Paula Huesca de Crean* [2011] EWHC 3154 (QB) and *Force India Formula One Team Ltd* v. *Malaysia Racing Team and Others* [2012] EWHC 616 (Ch) at [226–238].

The Information Commissioner has suggested that when attempting to decide whether information is in fact a trade secret, it is helpful to ask:

- Is the information used for the purpose of a trade?
- Is it obvious from the nature of the information or, if not, has the owner made it clear that he or she considers releasing the information would cause him or her harm or be advantageous to his or her rivals?
- Is the information already known?
- How easy would it be for competitors to discover or reproduce the information for themselves?[13]

This appears to be wide enough to cover anything which a private body does which is unique to it, which gives it a competitive edge and which is not generally known. It potentially covers not just product-related information but also working practices and approaches.

The notion of a trade secret includes not only secret formulae for the manufacture of products but also innumerable other pieces of information, such as technical knowledge and experience associated with manufacture of particular goods, and information relating to sales, prices and customers which would be of advantage to competitors.

If a public authority is of the view that information does constitute a trade secret, then the duty to disclose does not apply if the public interest in maintaining the exemption outweighs the public interest in disclosing the information (FOIA, s.2(2)(b)). The public interest in maintaining this exemption involves consideration of matters such as the maintenance of intellectual property rights and the need to protect the flow of commercial secrets to public authorities.

It is of the essence of a trade secret that it is confidential: if it is in the public domain it loses its quality of secrecy. It is difficult to see how the conditional exemption in s.43(1) adds anything to the absolute exemption in s.41. Perhaps for this reason, the trade secrets exemption has only very rarely been discussed in Tribunal case law. For example, in *Department of Health* v. *Information Commissioner* (EA/2008/0018, 18 November 2008); [2011] 1 Info LR 1135, the exemption was pleaded, but the Tribunal ultimately did not need to consider it.

---

[13] *Freedom of Information Act Awareness Guidance No.5: Commercial Interests*, version 3 (ICO, March 2008), pp.3–4; see also *Searle Australia* v. *Public Interest Advocacy Centre* (1992) 108 ALR 163.

6.2.4 The prejudice to commercial interests exemption[14]

If the disclosure of information is prejudicial to commercial interests then it is covered by a qualified exemption. By s.43(2), information is exempt information if its disclosure 'would, or would be likely to, prejudice the commercial interests of any person (including the public authority holding it)'.

The term 'commercial interests' can be interpreted broadly (see *University of Central Lancashire* v. *Information Commissioner and Colquhoun* (EA/2009/0034, 8 December 2009); [2011] 1 Info LR 1170 at para.31).

When considering whether disclosure 'would, or would be likely to, prejudice' commercial interests, the Information Tribunal has held (*Hogan and Oxford City Council* v. *Information Commissioner* (EA/2005/0026 and EA/2005/0030, 17 October 2006); [2011] 1 Info LR 588 at paras.30–34; see also *Derry City Council* v. *Information Commissioner* (EA/2006/0014, 11 December 2006); [2011] 1 Info LR 1105 at paras.17–28) that the proper approach is as follows:

- The nature of the 'prejudice' being claimed must be considered. The decision maker must show that there is some causal relationship between the potential disclosure and the prejudice and that the prejudice is 'real, actual or of substance'.
- The likelihood of the occurrence of the prejudice must be considered. 'Likely to prejudice' has been interpreted as meaning that the chance of prejudice being suffered should be more than a hypothetical or remote possibility: there must be a real or significant risk (see *John Connor Press Associates Ltd* v. *Information Commissioner* (EA/2005/0005, 25 January 2006) at para.15). The alternative limb of disclosure 'would prejudice' places a stronger evidential burden on the public authority than showing that disclosure is 'likely to prejudice'.

If a public authority is of the view that disclosure of the information would be likely to prejudice commercial interests, then the duty to disclose and the duty to confirm or deny do not apply if the public interest in maintaining the exemption outweighs the public interest in disclosing the information (FOIA, s.2(2)(b)).

The essence of successful reliance on this exemption is that the information must, at the date of the request, be current and commercially important, and not widely known (see *Department of Health* v. *Information Commissioner* (EA/2008/0018, 18 November 2008); [2011] 1 Info LR 1135 at paras.63–69).

Cases under s.43 invariably turn on the quality of the evidence, both as to the prejudice relied upon by the public authority and the public interest: compare for example *Cranfield University* v. *Information Commissioner and Peck* (EA/2011/ 0146, 5 March 2012) (where the Tribunal was not persuaded by the public authority's evidence) with *Visser* v. *Information Commissioner and London Borough of Southwark* (EA/2011/0188, 1 March 2012) (where the Tribunal was persuaded).

---

[14] See generally *Freedom of Information Act Awareness Guidance No.5: Commercial Interests*, version 3 (ICO, March 2008).

The s.43 exemption has been considered by the First-tier Tribunal in a number of cases. In some cases the public authority has failed to demonstrate that disclosure 'would or would be likely to prejudice' commercial interests and/or that the public interest favoured the maintenance of the exemption. Notable cases involved the following types of information:

- Information concerning the payments made to an artist by the National Maritime Museum (*John Connor Press Associates Ltd* v. *Information Commissioner* (EA/2005/0005, 25 January 2006)).
- A copy of the contract between the Department of Health and an external consultancy for the recruitment of NHS staff (*Department of Health* v. *Information Commissioner* (EA/2008/0018, 18 November 2008); [2011] 1 Info LR 1135).
- Agreements between Ryanair and Derry City Council concerning the use of Derry City Airport (*Derry City Council* v. *Information Commissioner* (EA/2006/0014, 11 December 2006); [2011] 1 Info LR 1105).
- The contents of agreements between Channel Four and British Sky Broadcasting Limited about the E4 channel (*Channel Four* v. *Information Commissioner and British Sky Broadcasting Ltd* (EA/2010/0134, 23 March 2011); [2011] 2 Info LR 241).
- Course material given to undergraduates (*University of Central Lancashire* v. *Information Commissioner and Colquhoun* (EA/2009/0034, 8 December 2009); [2011] 1 Info LR 1170).
- A training manual used by staff who deal with defaulting borrowers (*Student Loans Company Ltd* v. *Information Commissioner* (EA/2008/0092, 17 July 2009)).
- Pricing information contained in a contract (*Cranfield University* v. *Information Commissioner and Peck* (EA/2011/0146, 5 March 2012)).
- A business plan agreed between a local authority and a provider of leisure centre management services (*Visser* v. *Information Commissioner and London Borough of Southwark* (EA/2011/0188, 1 March 2012)).

6.2.5 Summary

In summary, the effect of these exemptions is that a public authority should not disclose information which has been supplied to it by a private body if:

- such disclosure would constitute a breach of confidence (s.41);
- the information is a trade secret (s.43(1)); or
- disclosure of the information would be likely to prejudice the private body's commercial interests (s.43(2)).

In practice, there is a high degree of overlap between the three exemptions. However, because the first is an absolute exemption it is likely to be the most important in practice, and the first to be considered by the Information Commissioner and/or the Tribunal. For example, any detailed financial information supplied by a private body in a procurement context is likely to fall within both s.41 and s.43(2). But information contained in contracts will usually only be protected under s.43.

Whether or not a particular piece of information falls within one of these exemptions is a fact-sensitive question which will depend on matters such as:

- *the precise nature of the information*: to what extent is it in the public domain, and how commercially sensitive is it?
- *the circumstances in which the information was supplied to the public authority*: whether, for example, it was made clear at the time that the private body regarded the information as confidential;
- *when the information was supplied*: other things being equal it is likely that commercial sensitivity will diminish over time and information supplied, say, five or 10 years ago is much less likely to be exempt than information supplied in relation to a current contract;[15]
- *whether there are any public interest considerations*: for example, in general there is a public interest in knowing how public money is spent – this may mean that public authorities will disclose global figures for sums paid under supply contracts, but not the detailed breakdown of these figures. Arguments for disclosure of the latter sort of detailed information should focus on the particular information in dispute and the particular circumstances surrounding the contract in question, rather than focusing solely on this type of information.

6.3 FOIA REQUESTS AND THE SUPPLIER OF INFORMATION

6.3.1 Introduction

The private body which has supplied confidential information or trade secrets to a public authority has no statutory right to be consulted when an applicant asks for disclosure of this information. In other words, in contrast to the position in some other jurisdictions, there are no formal reverse freedom of information procedures: the supplier of information has no formal status under the FOIA. Under the statute, it is the public authority alone which must deal with the complex analysis required to determine whether the s.41 or s.43 exemptions apply.

There are, however, two potential ways in which a private body can protect its position in relation to FOIA requests for information which it has supplied to a public authority. These are:

---

[15] See, however, *Visser* v. *Information Commissioner and London Borough of Southwark* (EA/2011/0188, 1 March 2012) at para.19, where the Tribunal found that in the circumstances of that case, 'the age of the information was largely irrelevant'.

- by making representations to the public authority in a process of consultation with the public authority;
- by reliance on express provision in its contracts with the public authority.

6.3.2 Consultation

Although there is no statutory right for the supplier of information to be consulted before information is disclosed, the Section 45 Code of Practice makes it clear that consultation should take place where the views of the third party may assist the public authority to determine whether an exemption applies or where the public interest lies (para.35).

Paragraph 27 of the Section 45 Code of Practice provides that:

> In some cases it will be necessary to consult, directly and individually, with [those who supply public authorities with information] in order to determine whether or not an exemption applies to the information requested, or in order to reach a view on whether the obligations in section 1 of the Act arise in relation to that information. But in a range of other circumstances it will be good practice to do so; for example where a public authority proposes to disclose information relating to third parties, or information which is likely to affect their interests, reasonable steps should, where appropriate, be taken to give them advance notice, or failing that, to draw it to their attention afterwards.

This provision places public authorities under a public law obligation to consult with the suppliers of information. This obligation is enforceable in judicial review proceedings in the Administrative Court.

Where information appears to be confidential, public authorities will consult the suppliers of information. If a request for information is refused by the public authority the applicant has four levels of appeal: internal, Information Commissioner, Information Tribunal and High Court. The supplier of information needs to be kept aware of the progress of any appeal against a decision to refuse information with a view to intervening if its interests are adversely affected. (Although there is nothing in the FOIA or the Code requiring the public authority to keep a consulted information supplier informed of the result of an appeal, it is suggested that there would be a public law duty to do so, in order to make consultation rights effective.)

If the request for information is accepted by the public authority, then the third party whose information is released has no right of appeal under the FOIA. It would, however, have two possible remedies:

- an application for judicial review of the public authority's decision to release the information;
- a High Court action for breach of confidence against the public authority.

There are no reported cases in which such applications have been made and it appears that disclosure disputes which have arisen have, to date, been dealt with by agreement.

6.3.3　Contractual provisions

Public authorities cannot contract out of the FOIA. They may be obliged to disclose information in response to requests even if they have agreed not to do so (see later in this section). Nevertheless, the terms of contracts with private bodies may be highly relevant to the disclosure decisions which public authorities will have to make.

Many private bodies seek to impose contractual confidentiality obligations on public authorities. The Section 45 Code of Practice makes it clear that public authorities must consider these clauses with care before agreeing to them. Paragraph 32 states that:

> When entering into contracts with non-public authority contractors, public authorities may be asked to accept confidentiality clauses, for example to the effect that information relating to the terms of the contract, its value and performance will not be disclosed. Public authorities should carefully consider the compatibility of such terms with their obligations under the Act. It is important that both the public authority and the contractor are aware of the limits placed by the Act on the enforceability of such confidentiality clauses.

The Commissioner draws attention to this clause in his *Freedom of Information Awareness Act Guidance No.2* (see p.5). However, it should be noted that the Section 45 Code of Practice makes it clear that there are circumstances in which the preservation of confidentiality between public authority and contractor is appropriate, and must be maintained, in the public interest (para.33). It suggests that where there is good reason to include non-disclosure provisions in a contract, public authorities should consider the desirability, where possible, of making express provision in the contract identifying the information which should not be disclosed and the reasons for confidentiality. The Scottish Information Commissioner has summarised the position in this way:

> information should only be accepted in confidence if it is necessary for the authority to obtain that information in order to carry out its functions and it would not otherwise be provided or could not otherwise be obtained. Authorities should not agree to hold information in confidence if it is clearly not confidential in nature.
>
> (*Foote* v. *Aberdeenshire Council* (Decision 27/2007, 12 February 2007), para.27)

Confidentiality clauses

Confidentiality clauses obviously have an important role to play in the FOI context. They are particularly helpful if they clearly identify the information that may be exempt. It should, however, be borne in mind that the terms of the contract itself often do not constitute 'information provided' for the purposes of s.41: in order to provide protection the clause should relate to information supplied whether as part of the tender process or in accordance with the terms of the contract itself (see **6.2.2**).

213

Although information covered by a confidentiality clause will not automatically attract the protection of s.41, a well-drawn confidentiality clause will be of considerable assistance to the public authority when it is considering a FOIA request.[16]

Clearly, a confidentiality clause will not be compatible with the FOIA if it relates to information which is not, in fact, confidential. In such circumstances, the public authority will be obliged to disclose the information to an applicant (unless, of course, some other exemption applies).

Public authorities will take particular exception to confidentiality clauses which purport to give private bodies a veto over the disclosure of any information, whatever its precise status.

In order to provide maximum protection in the context of FOIA applications, a confidentiality clause should:

- carefully identify (if necessary by reference to a schedule) the information which is said to be confidential. It is important that the clause is not too widely drawn. The more widely drawn the clause the greater the risk that the public authority will disclose in any event;
- give the reasons why the information is confidential (again, this could be in a schedule) (Section 45 Code of Practice, para.34). A provision to this effect is likely to be useful both to the public authority when responding to a FOIA request and to the private body when it is being consulted by the public authority.

It should be noted that the FOIA does not affect the contractual position as between the public authority and a private body. If a public authority agrees that it will not disclose information in a particular category, then a disclosure of such information will constitute a breach of contract even if the public authority had an obligation to disclose. In other words, because no FOIA exemption applied, e.g. even if information is not, in fact, confidential within the meaning of s.41, this will not prevent its disclosure from being a breach of a provision which deems it to be confidential. The Information Commissioner has pointed out that public authorities risk putting themselves in a dilemma: where they cannot avoid breaching either their statutory or their contractual obligations (see *Freedom of Information Act Awareness Guidance No.5: Commercial Interests – Annexe: Public Sector Contracts*, version 3 (ICO, 6 March 2008), p.4). This point may be of particular importance in relation to pre-FOIA contracts with very widely drawn confidentiality clauses.

Consultation provisions

The Section 45 Code of Practice suggests that express consultation provisions might be included in public authority contracts (para.34). Although there is no English case law on the topic, such a clause would plainly be enforceable. (This was

---

[16] See generally, *Freedom of Information Act Awareness Guidance No.5: Commercial Interests, version 3 – Annexe: Public Sector Contracts* (Information Commissioner, 6 March 2008).

accepted by the New Zealand Court of Appeal in *Astra Pharmaceuticals* v. *Pharmaceutical Management Agency Ltd* [2000] NZCA 345, para.37.) The point could be dealt with simply by making it a contractual requirement that the public authority consults with the private body according to an agreed timescale. Bearing in mind the fact that a public authority, in general, has only 20 days to respond to a FOIA request (FOIA, s.10(1)), the timescale must necessarily be a tight one. The following is suggested:

- notification by the public authority of requests within five working days;
- a response by the private body within five days;
- notification by the public authority of its disclosure decision within three days.

It may also be useful to include a contractual mechanism for resolving disputes. This could involve, for example, the appointment of an agreed person as adjudicator to decide whether or not a particular exemption applies. However, it is again important to bear in mind the tight timescales laid down by the FOIA, and any adjudication mechanism must be capable of dealing with disputes within a matter of a few days.

If a dispute cannot be resolved by consultation or a dispute resolution mechanism, then, in the last resort, it will be necessary to seek an interim injunction to restrain disclosure. This could be sought in the Administrative Court (in the course of an action to challenge the decision to disclose). However, in a s.41 case the most straightforward course will be to seek an injunction in the Chancery Division to restrain a breach of confidence. It should, however, be noted that if the FOIA applicant is a media organisation (or is a person intending to publish the information sought), the test for granting an injunction will not be the balance of convenience but the higher test of whether the applicant would be likely to succeed at trial.[17]

6.4 PRACTICAL STEPS FOR PROTECTING INFORMATION

6.4.1 Introduction

Against this statutory and contractual background, it is now possible to consider the practical steps which private bodies can take to protect their information from disclosure. It has been suggested that:

> The logical framework for the steps which need to be taken to protect confidential information is based on answers to the following questions:
>
> - who in the company provides what information to which public authorities?
> - is it clearly recognised which parts of this information are confidential, why and for how long?
> - is confidentiality claimed effectively when or before the information is submitted?
> - has the system been tested to give assurance that the company's information is

---

[17] As laid down by s.12(3) of the Human Rights Act 1998, see *Cream Holdings* v. *Banerjee* [2005] 1 AC 253.

being treated appropriately by the public authority, and does the public authority have up to date details of who to contact if requests are made for access to it?
(Amos and Innes, *A Guide for Business to the Freedom of Information Act 2000* (2001, UCL Constitution Unit))

These questions can usefully be addressed under two general headings:

- *information audit and other steps*: covering the identification of the commercially sensitive information which has been and is being provided to public authorities, and review of the effectiveness of confidentiality arrangements;
- *co-operation with public authorities*: ranging from informal approaches to ascertain the approach being taken to disclosure, to agreed contractual mechanisms for dealing with FOIA issues.

These measures are considered further below.

It should be borne in mind that an essential first step for any private body is to raise awareness amongst its own staff. Staff involved in the provision of information to public authorities, in particular those in sales, marketing and management positions, should be familiar with the way in which the FOIA operates and of the detail of the exemptions. They should also be apprised of the way in which information is likely to be handled by public authorities.

6.4.2   Information audit and other steps

There are a number of possible steps to be taken in order to protect commercially valuable information from disclosure under the FOIA:

- a review should be conducted of the information given to public authorities in the past;
- clear policies and procedures should be established for the management of information and for claiming confidentiality;
- care should be taken, in particular, to segregate information into that which is confidential and that which is non-confidential, and the basis on which confidentiality is being claimed should be clearly set out.

Past information

Private bodies should begin by reviewing the commercially sensitive material which has been submitted to public authorities in the past. Particular areas of concern include:

- tender documentation;
- supply contracts;
- service performance reports;
- collaborative private/public research results;
- information supplied to regulators, e.g. in the context of an investigation or inquiry.

Different public authorities are likely to take different approaches to the disclosure of these types of information. When material has been identified, an assessment of its continuing sensitivity should be carried out. As a general rule, the older the material the less sensitive it is likely to be. When the sensitive material has been identified then one or more of the following steps can be taken:

- Some material may no longer be needed by the public authority, e.g. detailed tender documentation where the bid was not successful. In these circumstances, the public authority could be asked to return the material and to confirm that it no longer holds copies.
- Where it is clear that the public authority continues to require the material, it could be asked to provide express confirmation that it recognises that it is confidential (or is a trade secret) and that it would apply the s.41 or s.43(1) exemptions if a FOIA request is made for this information.
- If the material is such that disclosure would cause prejudice to the private body, then a written explanation of the prejudice could be given to the public authority and its confirmation could be sought that it would apply the s.43(2) exemption if a FOIA request is made for this information.

In relation to material which is already held, the public authority could be asked to agree a consultation procedure of the type which private sector bodies would wish to include in future contracts (see **6.3.3**). Such a procedure would, potentially, be of advantage to both the public authority and the supplier of the information as it would provide informed input into the disclosure decision, and a degree of protection for the public authority against breach of confidence claims.

Future disclosure

In relation to future contracts, an audit can be conducted at the pre-tender stage in order to ascertain what information is likely to be sensitive in the future and how long it is likely to remain sensitive. When this has been done the information could be listed in an appendix to the contract (this approach is suggested by the Information Commissioner; see *Freedom of Information Act Awareness Guidance No.5: Commercial Interests – Annexe: Public Sector Contracts*, version 3 (ICO, March 2008), p.3). The Office of Government Commerce (OGC) has suggested that this approach should be taken and that discussions on this point should be included within general contract negotiations (see *FOI (Civil Procurement) Policy and Guidance*, version 2 (OGC, November 2008)).

A number of practical measures might be taken when preparing and submitting documents to public authorities.

- Sensitive material could be clearly marked and segregated to avoid the risk of inadvertent disclosure. Confidential documents could be watermarked or supplied in a different form or on paper of a different colour from non-confidential ones.

- In some circumstances, documents could be submitted in two versions: one disclosable and one confidential.
- Consideration should be given to whether it is necessary to hand over information to public authorities. In some circumstances, documents could be made available for inspection only.
- Private bodies should avoid providing additional voluntary information to public authorities.
- A record should be kept of all sensitive information supplied, the claims for confidentiality which have been made and the grounds for such claims given to the public authority.

Monitoring

If a private sector body has concerns that a public authority is likely to make inappropriate disclosures of its information, then it will be simple to cross-check the public authority's disclosure procedures using a third party or surrogate data agency[18] – what has been called the 'mystery shopper' procedure. A FOIA request can be made for the information from the public authority to see whether it will, in fact, be disclosed.

6.4.3   Co-operation with public authorities

It is obviously of central importance for private bodies to establish effective communication with public authorities in relation to FOIA disclosure issues. The aim of such communication is to:

- identify the kinds of information which should be kept from disclosure;
- establish a mechanism for consultation in relation to FOIA requests;
- agree confidentiality provisions and procedures for identifying sensitive material; and
- agree policies for document retention and return.

As already discussed, private bodies should take the provisions of the FOIA into account when entering into new contracts with public authorities (see **6.3.3**). This should be discussed at the tendering stage and properly drawn contracts should contain clear express provision in relation to confidentiality and consultation. Useful general guidance on both is provided by the Office of Government Commerce (*FOI (Civil Procurement) Policy and Guidance*, version 2 (November 2008)), currently available at **www.cabinetoffice.gov.uk/sites/default/files/ resources/ogc-foi-civil-procurement-guidance.pdf**.

---

[18]   For this term see the footnote to **6.1**.

6.5 MAKING USE OF THE FOIA

The FOIA can be an important business tool. A substantial proportion of freedom of information requests in the United States are made by businesses seeking information concerning their competitors and the activities of government. There have been a number of requests by UK businesses aimed at obtaining such information under the FOIA. For example, in one case the Information Commissioner ordered disclosure of information about private equity investments made by a local authority requested by an employee of a company which collated and sold statistical reports on investment funds and investment opportunities (*Hertfordshire County Council* (FS50086121, 1 February 2007)). Lobbying groups have also made active use of the FOIA (see *British Union for the Abolition of Vivisection* v. *Home Office and Information Commissioner* [2008] EWCA Civ 870; [2011] 1 Info LR 1191).

A private sector body which believes that public authorities might hold information which is of commercial value to it should carefully target its requests, perhaps engaging the services of a surrogate data agency with experience of making requests. A useful technique is the so-called 'jigsaw' request – seeking by means of a number of co-ordinated requests to identify the missing pieces of the information jigsaw.

The useful information available under the FOIA could include:

- details of previous bids by competitors, including matters such as pricing, personnel levels and competency;
- contract compliance and performance data, which reveal how competitors' contracts have been performed;
- background information relating to procurement decisions and the regulatory climate, e.g. working parties' and consultants' reports;
- clients' evaluation criteria, which show exactly how previous bids have been evaluated and contract decisions reached;
- the health and safety records of competitors or reports of health inspectors.

It should be remembered that not all transactions between the public and private sectors are subject to contracts. Information relating to some of these more informal dealings will generally be less restricted. FOIA requests could be made in relation to subjects such as lobbying of government departments, or hospitality provided by competitors to public authorities.

6.6 CONCLUSION

Although the FOIA has no direct application to the private sector, it will often have a significant impact on the activities of any private body which has substantial dealings with the public sector. Suppliers of goods and services to the public sector must carefully consider the information which they have provided, and will provide in the future, in the course of contractual relationships or other dealings. In the absence of careful protective measures there is a serious risk that sensitive material may become available to competitors and the media. The provisions of the FOIA are complex and, in relation to commercially sensitive material, import complex private law concepts. Public authorities require careful guidance as to the types of information which they can properly disclose to applicants under the FOIA. Contracts should be drafted to identify the material which is sensitive and the reasons why it is sensitive. The consultation provisions of the Section 45 Code of Practice should be strengthened by express contractual mechanisms.

The FOIA also presents an important opportunity for the private sector to obtain commercially useful information from the public sector. A vast range of material is available in relation to both the activities and approach of government and the activities of commercial rivals.

CHAPTER 7

Freedom of information and the media

Keith Mathieson and Nick Wilcox, RPC

7.1 INTRODUCTION

The word 'media' appears nowhere in the Freedom of Information Act 2000 (FOIA). The FOIA does not on the face of things give the media any kind of preferential treatment. Newspapers, broadcasters and journalists would appear to have no greater rights of access than anyone else to information held by public authorities.

Why then bother with a chapter about freedom of information and the media? There are three principal reasons. First, the media collectively are among the biggest users of the FOIA. Lord Falconer, the Secretary of State for Constitutional Affairs at the time the Act came into force, said that in the first month of the FOIA's operation about half of the requests made of central government came from people identifying themselves as reporters.[1] There is no reason to think this was a flash in the pan or that journalists were playing with a new toy. A 2009 survey conducted by the University College London (UCL) Constitution Unit suggests that the three biggest categories of FOI requesters are members of the public, journalists and businesses. The research estimates that journalists originate 32 per cent of FOI requests, the public account for 31 per cent and businesses for 27 per cent.[2] Many people only hear of information obtained through the FOIA via the media. If the FOIA fails the media, it fails the public too.

The second reason for considering the position of the media is art.10 of the European Convention on Human Rights. That article enshrines the right to freedom of expression, which is expressed to include the right to receive information. The scope of the right to receive information has proved to be a vexed issue both here and in the European Court of Human Rights (ECtHR) in Strasbourg and is indeed currently the subject of an appeal to the Supreme Court in the case of *Kennedy* v. *Charity Commission* [2012] EWCA Civ 317. In that case a *Times* journalist sought

---

[1]   Lord Falconer, 'Freedom of information: the beginning of a new chapter in openness', Inaugural DCA/Constitution Unit lecture on freedom of information, 25 January 2005: **http:// webarchive.nationalarchives.gov.uk** and **www.dca.gov.uk/speeches/2005/lc250105.htm**.

[2]   UCL Constitution Unit (October 2010), 'FOI and local government: preliminary findings', University College London at **www.ucl.ac.uk/constitution-unit/research/foi/foi-and-local-government/tabs/preliminary-findings-oct-2010.pdf**.

to rely on art.10 in order to achieve an interpretation of the s.32 exemption that would have assisted his request for information about an inquiry into the affairs of a charity associated with George Galloway MP.

Third, some media organisations are themselves designated as public authorities under the FOIA, and it is therefore necessary to consider their position not as users of the FOIA but as organisations subject to it.

This chapter will first examine media experience of the FOIA since it came into force seven years ago. It will then consider the relevance of art.10, including the question of whether information sought for journalistic purposes merits any particular consideration under the Act. Finally, the chapter will consider the position of sections of the media, in particular the BBC, as public authorities.

7.2 MEDIA EXPERIENCE OF THE NEW FREEDOM OF INFORMATION REGIME

7.2.1 An overview

The media gave an unqualified welcome to the enactment of the FOIA. Their attitude to its operation since commencement has been rather less unqualified. In its written submission to the House of Commons Justice Select Committee's post-legislative scrutiny of the FOIA,[3] the Newspaper Society, which represents the UK's regional newspapers, put it as follows:

> ... the Freedom of Information Act 2000 has not dispelled the UK's culture of official secrecy, but is a helpful tool in extracting information from national, regional and local public bodies which would otherwise not be made public. However, improvements are still needed to the effectiveness, scope and operation of the Act and to encourage best practice by public bodies in its day to day implementation. (FOI 87)

There is no doubt that the media have made energetic use of the FOIA during the last seven years. The BBC has a section of its website[4] which shows the many occasions on which its journalists have deployed the FOIA to obtain information. They include information in the following areas: regional variation in ambulance response times, the Ministry of Transport failure rates for different makes of cars, the extensive cost of policing high profile football matches, the numbers of deaths from house fires despite the presence of smoke alarms, numbers of babies who missed their one-year health check due to staff shortages, details of which government phone helplines have the worst delays for answering calls, the amount of money raised by hospitals through parking charges, numbers of council homes which have been left unoccupied, and the increasing cost to councils of metal thefts.

David Higgerson, the head of multimedia for Trinity Mirror Regionals, one of the UK's largest regional newspaper publishers, runs a useful blog which contains a

---

[3] Post-legislative scrutiny of the Freedom of Information Act 2000: written evidence received (Justice Committee, February 2012); **www.publications.parliament.uk/pa/cm201012/cmselect/ cmjust/writev/foi/contents.htm**.
[4] **http://news.bbc.co.uk/1/hi/in_depth/uk/2006/foi/default.stm**.

weekly round up of FOI stories which have appeared, mainly but not exclusively, in the regional press.[5] In his evidence to the committee, Mr Higgerson says the following:

> For regional journalists, the Freedom of Information Act has become an indispensable tool when trying to hold increasingly secretive public bodies to account. At a time when most councils have adopted opaque 'cabinet style' structures, many health bodies have done away with public meetings when gaining 'Foundation Trust' status, and police forces are reluctant to release even basic details about their work, FOI has proved invaluable.
>
> However, it is never a journalist's first tool of choice when seeking to gain information. It is a slow process and, depending on the authority being questioned, can prove to be a frustrating process. Many of our journalists have very good relationships with FOI officers, but their ability to make effective use of FOI is often determined by the attitude towards openness set by senior officers and political figures. (FOI 59)

Mr Higgerson's concerns are echoed by the Newspaper Society, which in its submission to the committee proceeded to say that while more public authorities and public services now employed more press officers, editors felt that 'their proliferation has tended to obstruct rather than facilitate the flow of information to the public'. According to editors, the increasing number of press officers, many of whom are said to prioritise reputation management at the expense of the free flow of information, serves to:

> reduce direct contact between reporters and those actually responsible for policy areas or decision-taking or operational activities, detrimental to constructive discussion and provision of information. FOI rights therefore become more important – and some members say that press officers sometimes ask journalists to submit FOI requests rather than seek the information via the press office. (FOI 87)

The Newspaper Society notes that alongside the introduction of freedom of information legislation, legislative changes affecting the operation of public authorities and services and their practical consequences have also contributed to official secrecy, in addition to the development of data protection and related areas of law:

> For example, the changes in the way that local government is conducted, in cabinet rather than committee, the growth of contracting out, formation of companies and devolvement of public functions to others have effectively reduced public access to information rights, or opportunities for legally enforceable public scrutiny conferred by more specialized legislation. (FOI 87)

The Society of Editors, which has more than 400 members in national, regional and local newspapers, magazines, broadcasting and digital media, expresses similar views in its submission to the committee (FOI 92). While it says it has 'always supported the principles that underpin the Freedom of Information Act' and the Act has become 'an essential journalistic tool which has helped create a climate of genuine openness and transparency in British public life', it also says that the

---

[5] **http://davidhiggerson.wordpress.com/foi/**.

experience of its members and their journalists in using the Act 'has revealed a number of operational weaknesses'.

Among individual submissions to the committee, the editor of the *Financial Times* (FT) says that the FT 'strongly supports the principles behind the Freedom of Information Act and believes that while there is room for improvement, it is well constructed' (FOI 45). The managing editor of *The Independent* and *London Evening Standard* says his journalists:

> ... find regular frustration – with requests often dealt with as slowly as possible and exemptions cited as justification for not providing the requested information. There is a wide spectrum of approaches on the part of information controllers which itself high-lights the intransigence of some set against the good example of others. (FOI 32)

7.2.2 Specific media concerns about the operation of the FOIA

The written submissions from journalists and media organisations to the Justice Committee are perhaps the best existing guide to current media thinking about the FOIA. The submissions clearly demonstrate a significant sense of frustration on the part of journalists that public authorities are not 'playing the game': that instead of finding ways to promote the objectives of the Act, some public authorities are actively seeking ways of subverting it.

The following are some of the more widely expressed criticisms of current practices.

Different treatment of journalists compared with other requesters

The editor of the FT complains:

> The central problem for the press in using the Freedom of Information Act stems from the fact that our journalists are treated differently to other requesters: Press officers are informed about journalists' inquiries who monitor them for newsworthy returns. At the very least, this means that our replies come later than others. (FOI 45)

In the words of Mr Higgerson:

> It is not uncommon for our reporters to submit an FOI request and then be asked about it by the press officer. Coventry City Council even told a reporter its press office had to sign off on journalists' FOI request responses. This goes against the spirit of 'applicant blind' and could encourage a culture where reporters have to use fake names to get information. Press officers should have the same access to all FOI requests, and not treat press ones differently. (FOI 59)

According to the Newspaper Society:

Despite the intention that all FOI requests should be treated in the same way, whatever their origin, our members report that journalists' requests may well be accorded different treatment by some public bodies, possibly because of the perceived likelihood of public disclosure. (FOI 87)

Misplaced reliance on exemptions

The Newspaper Society observed:

Journalists feel that there is an over-readiness to apply and rely upon exemptions to refuse FOI requests. Exemptions are misunderstood, misinterpreted or misapplied. (FOI 87)

The FT notes the 'misuse of exemptions' (FOI 45). It criticises the assumption of the Act that 'so long as the right decision is reached eventually, little else matters', noting that the effect of misplaced reliance on an exemption can delay release of the information for more than a year. The FT goes so far as to recommend 'stern penalties' for 'deliberate or systematic misuse of exemptions'.

Inconsistency

It appears that there is inconsistency in the way public authorities deal with FOI requests. According to the Newspaper Society:

[Our members] typically cite a wide variation in their local public bodies' and public services' practice and culture. Some authorities within their areas are helpful and co-operative. Others appear more obstructive, albeit some of those might have helpful FOI officials battling against the less helpful prevailing culture of their organisation. (FOI 87)

Delay

The media note problems first with delay in responding to requests. The FT remarks that replies are often late and even when replies are on time, they 'almost always' come on the 20th day even when the information is readily to hand. It complains that there is little focus on combating delays in responding to requests.

Second, there are problems with the time taken over reviews of refusals and with any subsequent appeal to the Information Commissioner. The Newspaper Society notes that where information is refused, even on specious grounds, 'the requestors will persist and such problems will sometimes be overcome as a result of internal review or recourse to the ICO. However, this entails further delay' (FOI 87).

A non-media respondent to the select committee's call for evidence, David Holland, notes that 'disclosure delayed can be as bad as disclosure denied' (FOI 05). He observes that while an unsuccessful applicant for information is required to exhaust a public authority's complaints procedure, there is no statutory time limit for reconsideration of a refusal. The introduction of such a limit would be an obvious way of reducing delay.

225

Striking evidence of the delays that arise in relation to FOI requests has been provided by Ben Leapman of the *Sunday Telegraph* (FOI 33). Mr Leapman was one of the three journalists whose FOIA requests for details of MPs' expenses led to a High Court defeat for Parliament in 2008, forcing it to agree to publish full details of expenses claims – which, according to his evidence, 'led directly to the leak to *The Daily Telegraph* and the scandal of 2009'.

The brief timeline provided by Mr Leapman in his evidence is as follows:

- *January 2005*: The week FOIA came into force, he asked the House of Commons to disclose the full expenses claims, including receipts, submitted by six named MPs. Commons authorities rejected his request initially and again on internal appeal.
- *April 2005*: He appealed to the Information Commissioner, who joined his request with others submitted by Heather Brooke and Jonathan Ungoed Thomas.
- *June 2007*: After two years of consideration, the Commissioner issued a decision notice requiring the Commons to publish more detail of MPs' claims, but not the receipts.
- *Feb 2008*: The Commons appealed to the Information Tribunal, but its case was rejected and instead the Tribunal backed a cross-appeal by the journalists, ordering full publication including receipts.
- *May 2008*: The High Court rejected an appeal by the Commons authorities and ruled in favour of the three journalists, declaring: 'The expenditure of public money through the payment of MPs' salaries and allowances is a matter of direct and reasonable interest to taxpayers.' Consequently the Commons agrees to publish expenses claims in full and began to transfer paper records to electronic form.
- *May 2009*: Electronic records created as a result of journalists' High Court victory were leaked to *The Daily Telegraph* before their official release, prompting publication of the 'Expenses Files' investigation.

Mr Leapman, with some justification, describes the delays in his case as 'unacceptable'. Mr Higgerson observes:

> The ICO works very hard to resolve problems, but is not resourced to meet demand. It needs to have resource to respond to complaints quickly and be able to resolve them quickly. The current situation allow authorities keen not to release information to kick the problem into the long grass. (FOI 59)

Political interference in FOI

In Mr Higgerson's words:

> We have been alarmed by a number of cases where councillors or other politicians have become involved in FOI decisions. It is well documented that the leader of Kirklees Council vets many FOI requests before they are published, and has in some cases tweaked

the responses. This goes against the very spirit of FOI. A recent Welsh FOI decision was made by a first minister. The information sought – about problems at a Welsh hospital – would, we believe, have had the potential to cause a political issue. There need to be firmer rules detaching FOI from the political process. (FOI 59)

The editor of the FT has expressed his belief that political appointees 'push the use of sections 35 and 36' in order to frustrate requests from his journalists and he relates how certain information requested by an FT journalist was given in advance to a journalist of a rival newspaper because it was perceived by the government department in question that the rival newspaper would treat the information in a manner that was more sympathetic towards the department than the FT's manner would have been (FOI 45).

Mr Leapman accuses the Information Commissioner's office of deferring to politicians in the course of its consideration of his appeal against the refusal of his request for details of MPs' expenses claims. He criticises the then Information Commissioner for:

negotiating with the Parliamentary authorities over my FOIA request for MPs' expenses details, without ever discussing the issues with me or the other requesters. It was also unacceptable that the ICO went as far as drafting a decision notice, dated Oct 2006, which would have ordered the release of the full details of expenses claims; but then, following a meeting in Dec 2006 between Mr Thomas, Jack Straw and three other senior MPs, Mr Thomas changed his mind and eventually issued a quite different decision notice, which did not order disclosure (and was overturned by the Tribunal and the High Court). This meeting was kept secret at the time, and did not come to light until a whistleblower leaked details of it to me in 2009. (FOI 33)

Obstructiveness by public authorities

A common theme of media submissions to the committee is that public authorities simply do not do enough to assist those requesting information. Mr Higgerson suggests they are sometimes guilty of 'active misunderstanding' and relates an example which involved a reporter asking about bed blocking and being told the hospital trust in question did not suffer bed blocking. When asked under the FOIA about 'delayed discharges' a full breakdown followed. Mr Higgerson comments: 'It is unfair to expect members of the public to be experts in terminology when submitting FOI requests' (FOI 59).

The Society of Editors complains that the FOIA 'has proved to be feeble when applied to requests aimed at finding out specifically *why* certain decisions were taken. This is a fundamental element of bread-and-butter reporting – addressing the public's right to know how its money is being spent, and the reasons behind those decisions' (FOI 92).

The FT has noted strategies within certain departments aimed at avoiding scrutiny, including the use of non-departmental email accounts for departmental communications (meaning no information is held by the department itself) and the use of instant messaging (meaning no record even exists). It also reveals the existence of a senior official, described as an acting director at the Department for Education, who destroyed all his emails at the end of every month. The FT calls for a wider definition of the offence of evading FOI requests and stronger penalties.

Various media representatives express concern about what is seen as a growing tendency by public authorities to rubbish freedom of information on the ground that it is too costly. They point out that public authorities sometimes artificially inflate the cost of FOI by referring enquiries directed to the press office to the FOI officer and they observe that the authorities could in many cases reduce the cost of complying with FOI requests by better file administration and archiving processes.

There is almost universal media concern about possible changes to the cost limits. Mr Higgerson observes that factoring additional actions such as redaction into the costing of an FOI request 'would reward those authorities which make information hard to find' (FOI 59).

7.3   DOES ARTICLE 10 CONFER A RIGHT OF ACCESS TO INFORMATION?

The provisions of art.10 of the European Convention on Human Rights, incorporated into UK law by the Human Rights Act 1998, will be familiar to most readers:

> Everyone has the right to freedom of expression. This right shall include freedom to hold opinions *and to receive and impart information* and ideas without interference by public authority and regardless of frontiers. (emphasis added)

Does art.10 confer upon journalists or anyone else a 'right' to information such as to give them some sort of trump card when faced with a refusal by a public authority to provide information requested pursuant to the FOIA?

It has been generally thought that the right to receive information does not entail a corresponding right of *access* to such information. In other words, the right is a right to receive information free from interference in circumstances where others are willing to impart the information: it is not a right to compel the holder of information to provide that information in circumstances in which he is unwilling to provide it and/or has no legal obligation to do so. In *Leander* v. *Sweden* (1987) 9 EHRR 433, the point was expressed as follows:

> The Court observes that the right to freedom to receive information basically prohibits a Government from restricting a person from receiving information that others wish or may be willing to impart to him. Article 10 does not, in the circumstances such as those of the present case, confer on an individual a right of access to a register containing information about his personal position, nor does it embody an obligation on the Government to impart such information to the individual.

In later decisions, the ECtHR has, however, preferred a wider interpretation of the right to information. In *Tarsasag* v. *Hungary* (2011) 53 EHRR 3, the court said it had 'advanced towards the recognition of a right of access to information' and in *Kenedi* v. *Hungary* [2009] ECHR 786 (31475/05, 26 May 2009) the court decided that access to official documents for purposes of historical research was an essential element of the applicant's art.10 rights.

It seems correct in principle that art.10 should embrace the right to access certain kinds of information since without such a right, the right to freedom of expression is to an extent circumscribed. How can someone enjoy a right to freedom of expression if he is unable to access information about what the state is getting up to?

The English courts have nonetheless shown some reluctance to accept that art.10 includes a right of access to information. In 2010 the Supreme Court in *Re Guardian News and Media Ltd* [2010] UKSC 1 held that on the existing Strasbourg law as set out in *Leander* v. *Sweden*, there was no right under art.10 for the media to get access to information which would otherwise not be available to them. But then in *A* v. *Independent News & Media Ltd* [2010] EWCA Civ 343, the Court of Appeal used art.10 as the basis for its decision that the media should be permitted access to information about proceedings in the Court of Protection. It considered the law had moved on from *Leander*. In its view the more recent decisions of the ECtHR:

> . . . appear to provide support for the notion that article 10 is engaged in a case such as this, essentially for two reasons. First, the Strasbourg jurisprudence appears to have developed since *Leander* so that article 10 seems to have a somewhat wider scope; secondly, where the media are involved and genuine public interest is raised, it may well be that, at least in some circumstances, one is anyway outside the general principle laid down in *Leander* [41]

The Court of Appeal's decision seemed to suggest that the media's role as public watchdog entitled it to access to official information pursuant to art.10 (irrespective of its entitlement under the FOIA).

That interpretation is now seriously doubtful following the decision of the Supreme Court in *Sugar* v. *British Broadcasting Corporation* [2012] UKSC 4. In that case the applicant submitted that the BBC's failure to provide him with a copy of an internal report interfered with his art.10 right to receive information. Lord Brown bluntly dismissed that notion:

> There was no interference here with Mr Sugar's freedom to receive information. The Act not having conferred upon him any relevant right of access to information, he *had* no such freedom. [97]

Of the ECtHR decisions on which Mr Sugar relied, Lord Brown was no less blunt:

> In my judgment these three cases fall far short of establishing that an individual's article 10(1) freedom to receive information is interfered with whenever, as in the present case, a public authority, acting consistently with the domestic legislation governing the nature and extent of its obligations to disclose information, refuses access to documents. Of course, every public authority has in one sense 'the censorial power of an information monopoly' in respect of its own internal documents. But that consideration alone cannot give rise to a prima facie interference with article 10 rights whenever the disclosure of such documents is refused. Such a view would conflict squarely with the *Roche*[6]

---

[6]   *Roche* v. *United Kingdom* (2006) 42 EHRR 30.

approach. The appellant's difficulty here is not that Mr Sugar was not exercising 'the functions of a social watchdog, like the press.' (Perhaps he was.) The Jewish Chronicle would be in no different or better position. The appellant's difficulty to my mind is rather that article 10 creates no general right to freedom of information and where, as here, the legislation expressly limits such right to information held otherwise than for *the* purposes of journalism, it is not interfered with when access is refused to documents which *are* held for journalistic purposes. [94]

For the time being, this appears to be the last word on the matter. As will be seen, the Supreme Court's decision in *Sugar* put paid to the journalist Dominic Kennedy's freedom of information case against the Charity Commission. However, since Mr Kennedy has been given permission to appeal to the Supreme Court, it may not be too long before we have a further decision by the Supreme Court on the importance or otherwise of art.10 to media requests for information under the FOIA.

7.4   DO JOURNALISTS HAVE SUPERIOR RIGHTS UNDER THE FOIA?

The question has arisen, at least implicitly, in two important cases: *Kennedy* v. *Charity Commission* [2012] EWCA Civ 317 and *Cobain* v. *Information Commissioner and Crown Prosecution Service* (EA/2011/0112 and EA/2011/0113, 8 February 2012). As will be seen, the circumstances in which journalists will be able to get around exemptions on grounds that they interfere with their art.10 rights are likely, on the current state of the law, to be very limited.

7.4.1   Kennedy v. Charity Commission

The *Kennedy* case, has, to say the least, a somewhat complex history. Mr Kennedy is a journalist with *The Times* and made his request for information back in 2007. His request was for information relating to the Charity Commission's Inquiry into the Mariam Appeal, a fund-raising operation established in 1998 by George Galloway MP. Prior to Mr Kennedy's request the Charity Commission had concluded its inquiry. It had found, among other things, that the Mariam Appeal should have been registered with the Charity Commission as a charity; that some of its activities were political in nature; and that it had improperly received some of its funds from contracts made under the UN's Oil-for-Food Programme.

In response to Mr Kennedy's request the Charity Commission confirmed in July 2007 that it did hold information about the inquiry but said it was withholding it on grounds, among others, that it was covered by the s.32 exemption (information held for purposes of an inquiry).

Mr Kennedy complained to the Information Commissioner. His complaint was rejected (on 9 September 2008), so he appealed to the Information Tribunal.

In June 2009 the Information Tribunal ruled that although some of the material fell outside s.32, the bulk fell within it (EA/2008/0083, 14 June 2009). An appeal was then made to the High Court ([2010] EWHC 475 (Admin)). The appeal was dismissed, but permission was later given for Mr Kennedy to appeal on one ground only, namely that the judge had wrongly interpreted s.32 as conferring (a) a blanket exemption from disclosure that carried on for 30 years after a statutory inquiry has closed, regardless of content, regardless of the harmlessness of the disclosure, and regardless of the public interest in the disclosure; and (b) exemption in respect of documents held by a public authority prior to the commencement of a statutory inquiry.

The narrow issue that arose on Mr Kennedy's appeal to the Court of Appeal was, in the words of Ward LJ 'whether this exemption provided by section 32 subsists only for the duration of the inquiry or whether it continues after the inquiry has concluded' ([2011] EWCA Civ 367 at [14]). Following a scrupulously detailed consideration of the wording of s.32, Ward LJ concluded that the exemption continued after the inquiry had concluded.

Thus far, the case raises an interesting point of construction on the wording of s.32(2) but not any wider issue relating to freedom of expression or the right to access information (art.10). That wider issue arose in the following way.

When Mr Kennedy's legal team had addressed the Information Tribunal and the High Court, they had not raised any point specifically concerning his right to freedom of expression. The point had been raised for the first time in the Court of Appeal. Ward LJ had circulated to the parties a draft of his judgment which did not mention the point because the judge had taken the view that he should not deal with it as it had not been raised in the courts below and nor had Mr Kennedy addressed the issue in his evidence. However, as Mr Kennedy's counsel was, in Ward LJ's phrase, 'respectfully insistent' that the court should deal with the point, not least because the court was, as a public authority, bound by s.6 of the Human Rights Act 1998 to act compatibly with a Convention right, the Court of Appeal decided after circulating its draft that it should reconsider the case by reference to the art.10 argument. That argument was, essentially, that the court should give effect to s.32(2) in a way that is compatible with Convention rights, including the right to freedom of expression protected by art.10. In view of the opinion forcefully expressed by Ward LJ's fellow judge, Jacob LJ, that the construction favoured by the court (without regard to art.10) would lead to absurdity (because it would mean keeping information secret for 30 years, however harmless its disclosure would be and however great the public interest was in disclosing it), it was thought desirable for the court to hear further argument on the point before reaching a final judgment.

In May 2011 the Court of Appeal accordingly referred the human rights issue to the Tribunal for its determination, having taken such evidence and heard such further argument as it considered appropriate. In the meantime, the appeal was stayed pending the report from the Tribunal. The issue referred to the Tribunal (by now the First-tier Tribunal (Information Rights)) was:

> Whether s.32(2) of the Freedom of Information Act 2000 should in the circumstances be read down pursuant to s.3 of the Human Rights Act 1998 and art.10 of the European convention on Human Rights, so that the exemption that it provides from disclosure of information ends upon the termination of the relevant statutory inquiry.

([2012] EWCA Civ 317 at [8])

In November 2011 the Tribunal found in favour of Mr Kennedy on the art.10 issue (EA/2008/0083, 18 November 2011). It held (a) that on a 'conventional' interpretation of s.32(2) there had been an interference with his right to freedom of expression; (b) there was no justification for interfering with his rights; (c) s.32(2) should be construed consistently with art.10; and (d) by limiting s.32(2) to documents held by inquiries that have not been completed, Mr Kennedy's art.10 rights would not be interfered with in a disproportionate manner.

That was the somewhat tortuous background against which the case reached the Court of Appeal in 2012 on the Charity Commission's cross-appeal supported by the Secretary of State for Justice and the Information Commissioner. But as if matters were not complicated enough, a further factor was now in the mix in the form of the Supreme Court's judgment in the case of *Sugar* v. *British Broadcasting Corporation* [2012] UKSC 4, which had been handed down only a few days before the hearing in the Court of Appeal. That decision is the subject of separate analysis later in this chapter so far as it concerns the BBC's designation for the purposes of the FOIA. The current discussion relates only to what the Supreme Court said about the art.10 jurisprudence concerning the right to receive information.

As noted above, the Supreme Court considered the question of whether an individual's freedom to receive information is interfered with when a public authority, acting consistently with domestic legislation, refuses to provide access to documents. The court concluded that it is not. It followed that even if the Supreme Court was wrong to conclude that the BBC did not have to comply with Mr Sugar's information request, Mr Sugar could not go on to rely on his art.10 rights as a reason why he should nonetheless be entitled to the information he had requested.

In *Kennedy* v. *Charity Commission* [2012] EWCA Civ 317, the Court of Appeal took the straightforward line that in the light of *Sugar* the First-tier Tribunal had got it wrong: it now inevitably followed from *Sugar* that art.10 was simply never engaged by the Charity Commission's refusal to supply the information and documents that Mr Kennedy had requested. The Court of Appeal agreed. Being satisfied that the analysis and decision of Lord Brown in *Sugar* were part of the ratio of that case, which is binding on the Court of Appeal, Mr Kennedy's appeal was dismissed. The previous year's excursion into art.10 territory had in effect been a waste of time. The s.32 exemption did not have to be construed consistently with art.10 because art.10 was not engaged.

Nonetheless, Mr Kennedy may live to fight another day. As noted above, the Court of Appeal has granted him permission to appeal to the Supreme Court. Etherton LJ has explained his reasons as follows:

> The issues raised by Mr Kennedy's appeal are important ones. For reasons which Jacob LJ gave in his earlier judgment and were also given in the Tribunal's Article 10 Decision it appears difficult to justify the full extent of the restriction in s.32(2) after the conclusion of the inquiry. Lord Brown's qualification at the end of paragraph [95] of his judgment ('having regard to the particular relationship between the parties in this case') as well as

Lord Wilson's more relaxed approach to the limits of Article 10(1) in paragraph [58] of his judgment make this a suitable case for the Supreme Court to consider the precise boundaries of Article 10(1), particularly in a case where the applicant is taking the journalistic role of a social watchdog and, unlike the position in *Sugar*, the authority refusing disclosure has no journalistic functions. In that regard, I also note that Lord Mance expressed agreement with Lord Wilson's stated desire in paragraph [59] of his judgment for an appeal in which it is appropriate for the Supreme Court to consider whether, without acting extravagantly, it might usefully do more than to shadow the ECtHR. For those reasons, I would grant permission to appeal to the Supreme Court. [62]

7.4.2 Cobain v. Information Commissioner and Crown Prosecution Service

Only a month before the Court of Appeal decided *Kennedy*, the First-tier Tribunal (Information Rights) gave judgment in a similar case brought by a *Guardian* journalist, Ian Cobain, in respect of the refusal of an FOI request he had made in 2009 of the Crown Prosecution Service (CPS) (*Cobain v. Information Commissioner and Crown Prosecution Service* (EA/2011/0112 and EA/2011/0113, 8 February 2012)). The request was for papers relating to the 1998 prosecution for incitement of racial hatred of the right-wing politician Nick Griffin. The request was refused on various grounds, including, as in *Kennedy*, s.32 of the FOIA (though that exemption was not relied on initially).

At the time of the Tribunal's consideration, the First-tier Tribunal had only just ruled in *Kennedy* that s.32 had to be construed in a manner that was consistent with Mr Kennedy's art.10 rights. Not surprisingly, the Tribunal in *Cobain* took the same approach. It too ruled that it was an unjustifiable interference with Mr Cobain's right to freedom of expression for the CPS to be permitted to rely on the s.32 exemption in circumstances in which the case against Mr Griffin had been concluded years before. It held that limiting the restriction in s.32(1) so that it ends once a reasonable time has elapsed after the exhaustion or evident abandonment of the available appeal process would avoid a breach of art.10. The correctness of that judgment will of course now have to be reviewed in the light of the Court of Appeal's decision in *Kennedy* and the outcome of any appeal to the Supreme Court.

Before leaving *Cobain*, it may be worth mentioning the Tribunal's decision in relation to one of the other exemptions relied upon by the CPS and which was successfully appealed by Mr Cobain since it concerns the 'purposes of journalism' provision of the Data Protection (Processing of Sensitive Personal Data) Order 2000, SI 2000/417.

The FOIA exemption in question was the s.40(2) exemption for personal data. It was not disputed that much of the information sought by Mr Cobain constituted Mr Griffin's sensitive personal data as it related to his political opinions and information pertaining to the commission of an offence. Such information could, however, be disclosed to an applicant under the FOIA where the disclosure was fair and lawful and one of the relevant conditions of the Data Protection Act 1998 (DPA) was satisfied. One such condition (DPA, Sched.3, para.10) is that 'The personal data are processed in circumstances specified in an order made by the Secretary of

State for the purposes of this paragraph.' The Data Protection (Processing of Sensitive Personal Data) Order 2000 was enacted for this purpose. By art.2 of the Order, the circumstances specified in any of the paragraphs in the Schedule to the Order are circumstances in which sensitive personal data may be processed.

Paragraph 3(1) of the Schedule requires that:

> The disclosure of personal data –
>
> (a)   is in the substantial public interest;
> (b)   is in connection with –
>
>> (i)   the commission by any person of any unlawful act (whether alleged or established) [or],
>> (ii)   dishonesty, malpractice, or other seriously improper conduct by, or the unfitness or incompetence of, any person (whether alleged or established) … ;
>
> (c)   is for the special purposes as defined in section 3 of the Act; and
> (d)   is made with a view to the publication of those data by any person and the data controller reasonably believes that such publication would be in the public interest.

Section 3 of the DPA provides that the 'special purposes' include 'the purposes of journalism'.

In the Tribunal's view, disclosure of Mr Griffin's sensitive personal data was justified under para.3(1) of the Schedule, so the FOIA, s.40(2) exemption did not apply:

> Disclosure of the sensitive data would be 'in connection with' the commission of an unlawful act (hence the conviction), seriously improper conduct and arguably Mr Griffin's unfitness for political office. It would be for the purpose of journalism, Mr Cobain's occupation, and would be intended for publication in his newspaper and possibly thereafter, in a book. Given the issues involved, namely racial and/or religious hatred and the right to express even extreme views, we find that disclosure would be in the substantial public interest. We do not consider that the passage of eleven years before the request renders disclosure unfair, or unwarranted by reason of prejudice to Mr Griffin's interests nor likely to cause substantial damage or distress to him. In making that judgement we have regard to Mr Griffin's age (50 at the date of the request, 39 at the date of trial), his continuing political prominence and his apparent claim to be an educated, reasonable and responsible MEP and party leader who has rejected any racial extremism formerly associated with his party. (para.38)

7.5   THE MEDIA AS PUBLIC AUTHORITIES

Four media organisations are classed as 'public authorities' under the FOIA. They are the BBC, Channel Four, Sianel Pedwar Cymru (S4C) and the Gaelic Media Service. The Act applies to these organisations to a limited extent, however, and only in respect of 'information held for purposes other than those of journalism, art or literature' (Sched.1, Part VI).

These organisations are in the dual position of being significant beneficiaries in terms of use of information provided to them under the Act and also being the recipients of requests. Ensuring compliance with the obligations under the Act requires a significant allocation of resources for broadcasters. The BBC has a freedom of information compliance and advisory team within the BBC's legal department. This operates separately from journalistic activity and BBC News. From 2009 to 2011 the BBC dealt with an average of 1,700 requests per year.[7] The BBC also publishes on its website a selection of responses to previous FOIA requests handled under the Act.

The extent to which the FOIA applies to these organisations as a result of the phrase 'purposes other than those of journalism, art or literature', and the consequences in terms of the legal procedure for dealing with disputed requests for information, have been explored in a case arising from a request first made in 2005 which ran for seven years, taking in a trip to the House of Lords on a point of jurisdiction before returning to be decided by the Supreme Court in 2012.

The High Court also decided in 2009 a case concerning various items of financial information requested from the BBC, which proceeded as conjoined appeals from the Information Tribunal's decision that the information fell within the Act.

In January 2005, Mr Sugar made a request to the BBC for disclosure of a confidential and internal review of news coverage about the Middle East which had been prepared by a senior BBC editorial adviser. The report was a broad survey of the quality (including the impartiality) of the BBC's coverage of Middle Eastern affairs in certain programmes over a period and of the validity or otherwise of the themes of complaints about it. The report included certain practical suggestions for improvement of the quality of the BBC's coverage, including its impartiality. The BBC maintained that as at the date of Mr Sugar's request, the review was held for the purposes of journalism and so was exempt from the FOIA (and that accordingly the BBC was not a public authority for the purposes of the request). The Information Commissioner agreed and Mr Sugar appealed to the Information Tribunal (EA/2005/0032, 29 August 2006).

The Information Tribunal considered two main issues. First, did it have jurisdiction to hear the appeal at all, given that the BBC is listed as a public authority in the Act only 'in respect of information held for purposes other than those of journalism, art or literature'? Secondly, was the material held for such purposes?

The Tribunal decided that it had jurisdiction, and went on to find that whilst the review had been held initially for the dominant purposes of journalism, such purposes had changed to those of strategic policy and resource allocation when the document was later considered by a high-level, internal BBC management board. In reaching its decision the Tribunal applied a dominant purpose test.

The BBC appealed both decisions, in the first High Court action brought under the FOIA ([2007] EWHC 905 (Admin)). It explained that it was doing so not

---

[7] From the BBC's submission to the Justice Select Committee's post-legislative scrutiny of the FOIA (FOI 55).

because of the content of the review itself, but because the underlying principles had important resource implications.

Mr Justice Davis decided that the Tribunal did not have jurisdiction. He held that:

> it is only in respect of information held by the BBC otherwise than for the purposes of journalism, art or literature that the BBC is a public authority subject to the requirements of Part 1 to Part V of the FOIA. In respect of information not so held the BBC is not a public authority subject to Parts 1 to V of the FOIA. [37]

He went on to find that since the Information Commissioner had agreed with the BBC that the information was held for the purposes of journalism, no decision notice had been issued under the Act, meaning that the Tribunal did not have jurisdiction. Accordingly, both earlier decisions of the Information Tribunal were overturned.

The Court of Appeal ([2008] EWCA Civ 191) upheld Davis J's decision on the jurisdiction of the Information Tribunal but the House of Lords ([2009] UKHL 9), by a majority of three to two, overturned the decision. Clarifying the effect of the inclusion of the BBC and other public service broadcasters in the Act, the House of Lords ruled that even in relation to a request for information which lay outside the scope of the Act (because the broadcaster held the information for the purposes of journalism, art or literature), the broadcaster remained a public authority for the purposes of the Act (at [26]–[36] per Lord Phillips and [54] per Lord Hope).

The decision was significant for the BBC and other broadcasters listed in the Act, and those interested in their affairs. It means that even where a request is outside the scope of the FOIA, the BBC remains a 'public authority' and so has to comply with duties such as that under s.16 to provide advice and assistance in respect of the request. Where the Information Commissioner agrees that the FOIA does not apply, that decision will still constitute a decision notice under the Act (s.50) and the proper route to challenge it will be by way of appeal to the Information Tribunal (rather than the appellant requester's only route of challenge being by way of judicial review proceedings against the Commissioner's decision, with the associated risk in costs, which would have been the consequence if the High Court's decision on jurisdiction had stood).

Following the House of Lords decision on jurisdiction, the case went back down to the High Court for determination of the BBC's original appeal against the Tribunal's decision that the report had not been held at the time of the request for the dominant purpose of journalism ([2009] EWHC 2349 (Admin)).

In October 2009 Mr Justice Irwin allowed the BBC's appeal. He was concerned that the use by the Tribunal of a dominant purpose test was not correct. He concluded that 'the BBC has no obligation to disclose information which they hold to any significant extent for the purposes of journalism, art or literature, whether or not the information is also held for other purposes' (at [65]). He concluded that if the broadcaster holds the information at the time of the request for (anything more than de minimis) purposes of journalism, art or literature then the material would not fall within the ambit of the Act.

In a case heard separately but concurrently with the *Sugar* case, *British Broad-casting Corporation* v. *Information Commissioner* [2009] EWHC 2348 (Admin), Mr Justice Irwin held that various items of financial information that had been requested of the BBC did not fall within the Act, reversing decisions of the Information Tribunal in four cases that the material be disclosed (subject to reliance on any exemptions within the Act). The court held that information (among other things) about the costs referable to its broadcast of the popular soap *Eastenders*, the annual budgets of *Top Gear* and *Newsnight* and the cost of the broadcast rights for the 2006 Turin Winter Olympics and associated production costs for the games were held within the BBC at an operational level in order to assist the making of editorial and creative choices and so were held at least in part for the purposes of journalism. The court held that financial information which comes to be aggregated as it is passed up an organisation may, and was in this case, still be held at an operational level for journalistic, literary or artistic purposes.

The Court of Appeal ([2010] 1 WLR 2278) upheld the decision in respect of the report in June 2010 and gave some guidance in respect of the application of the test to be applied (the decision of the High Court in the financial information cases was not appealed).

The court indicated that 'journalism' should be given its natural meaning but that the question whether information, particularly financial information, is held for the purposes of journalism should be construed in a relatively narrow way.

The court (Lord Neuberger, Master of the Rolls) stressed that it is difficult to give guidance in general terms and that there will no doubt be cases where financial information is held for the purposes of journalism, art and literature, especially when it is closely related to programme making, but that it would not be sympa-thetic to claims that certain categories of financial information fall outside the Act, including for example advertising revenues, property ownership and outgoings, and financial debt.

The court also noted that journalism, especially news, is a perishable commodity and that there will be a point relatively quickly at which journalistic material stops being held for that purpose and is held for historical/archival purposes (thus falling within the scope of the Act).

Both the Court of Appeal ([2010] EWCA Civ 715) and the Supreme Court (see below) accepted the Tribunal's analysis of what constitutes 'journalism' for the purposes of the Act: including (1) collecting, writing and verifying pre-publication material; (2) editing of material and considering how and when it should be broadcast; and (3) the maintenance and enhancement of the standards of the output by reviews of its quality, in terms of accuracy, balance and completeness and the supervision and training of journalists. To this categorisation the Supreme Court added the actual act of broadcasting or publishing the material in question.

By unanimous decision the Supreme Court ([2012] UKSC 4) found the BBC to be under no duty to disclose the report (the BBC had earlier confirmed that if the report were held to fall within the Act it would not seek to rely on any exemptions under the Act). Whilst acknowledging that it is not without its difficulties, four of the judges agreed with the test approved by the High Court and upheld by the Court of Appeal: that information held to any significant degree for the purposes of journalism, art or literature does not fall within the ambit of the Act. The Supreme Court recognised that there is no 'unequivocal, bright-line' test (at [84]) and that the decision will still leave some difficult decisions for the Information Commissioner and, on appeal, the Tribunal.

From a review of the Act's legislative purpose the court held that the FOIA was enacted in order to promote an important public interest in access to information about public bodies. There is a strong public interest in the press and the general public having the right, subject to appropriate safeguards, to require public authorities to provide information about their activities. It adds to parliamentary scrutiny a further and more direct route to a measure of public accountability.

In this case there was, however, a powerful public interest pulling in the opposite direction. It is that public service broadcasters, no less than the commercial media, should be free to gather, edit and publish news and comment on current affairs without the inhibition of an obligation to make public disclosure of or about their work in progress. They should also be free of inhibition in reviewing their output in order to maintain standards.

A measure of protection might have been available under some of the qualified exemptions in Part II of the FOIA (s.36: prejudice to the effective conduct of public affairs, s.41: information provided in confidence, and s.43: commercial interests) but Parliament evidently decided that the important right to freedom of expression of the BBC and other broadcasters warranted a more general and unqualified protection for information held for the purposes of journalistic, artistic and literary output. The purpose of the immunity would have been lost if the co-existence of other non-journalistic purposes for holding the information deprived the broadcaster of the benefit of the immunity.

Lord Phillips and Lord Walker concluded that the protection is aimed at 'work in progress' and the BBC's 'broadcasting output'. Lord Walker underlined that regard ought to be had to the 'directness' of the purpose for which the information is held and the proximity between the subject matter of the request and the BBC's journalistic activities and end product. Information should only be found to be held for the purposes of journalism, art or literature if an 'immediate object' of holding the information is to use it for one of those purposes (Lord Phillips at [67]).

Lord Walker endorsed the comments of the Master of the Rolls in the Court of Appeal in respect of financial information that whilst such information 'may well affect journalism-related issues and decisions' it would not normally be held for the purposes of journalism (at [84]).

One issue of importance that remains to be considered by the courts is when material will with the passage of time no longer be held for the purposes of journalism but come to be held for archival or historical purposes only.

If a request were made today for the same 2004 report (or in a year or in five years' time) would the courts accept that it is still being held for the purposes of journalism? Is it still being used as a journalistic tool or a point of editorial reference or is it gathering dust in a drawer somewhere, its recommendations implemented and its observations no longer relevant to current issues?

Lord Philips (at [67]) noted that disclosure of material that is held only in the archives will not be likely to interfere with or inhibit the BBC's broadcasting functions such that it ought to be susceptible to disclosure under the Act. Lord Mance agreed but noted that a library maintained for current reference would in contrast contain material held for the purposes of journalism, art or literature. Each case will of course turn on its particular facts. Even if the information is judged to fall within the Act the broadcaster can still rely on any applicable exemptions to disclosure within the Act itself.

CHAPTER 8

Relationship between freedom of information and data protection

Antony White QC and Claire Darwin, Matrix Chambers

8.1 INTRODUCTION

At first blush, legislation concerned with data protection and legislation concerned with freedom of information (FOI) would seem to pull in opposite directions. The Data Protection Act 1998 (DPA) is a measure designed to safeguard individual privacy, whereas the Freedom of Information Act 2000 (FOIA) is a measure designed to secure open access to information. They have very different origins and objectives, yet they share a common regulator (the Information Commissioner) and have in many respects a similar enforcement regime (through decisions of the Information Commissioner and the Information Rights Tribunal). They deal with overlapping subject matter so there must of necessity be an interface between the two Acts. This chapter explores the differences between the two pieces of legislation and their interaction.

In this chapter, **8.2** explains the origins of the two Acts and the main ways in which they differ; **8.3** provides a brief overview of the DPA, drawing attention to the amendments introduced into that Act by the FOIA; **8.4** explores the manner in which the two Acts interact through the medium of the FOIA, s.40; and **8.5** discusses key recent decisions of the Information Rights Tribunal, and appellate courts.

8.2 LEGISLATIVE HISTORY OF THE TWO ACTS AND THE PRINCIPAL DIFFERENCES

8.2.1 History of the DPA

The political climate of the late 1960s and early 1970s which fostered the introduction of race and sex discrimination legislation also resulted in increasing concern about personal privacy. No fewer than eight Bills concerned with different aspects of privacy were introduced into Parliament during this period, but none received government support.[1] In 1972, the government-appointed Committee on Privacy, chaired by Kenneth Younger, produced its report (Cmnd 5012, 1972). The Younger Report set out a series of proposed guiding principles for the use of computers which manipulated personal data. In 1978, the government-appointed Data Protection Committee chaired by Sir Norman Lindop produced a further report recommending data protection legislation (Cmnd 7341, 1978). A government White Paper with proposals for legislation followed in April 1982 (Cmnd 8539, 1982). This led to the enactment of the Data Protection Act 1984. The 1984 Act was novel and complex legislation which had only limited impact.

On 24 October 1995 the European Parliament and the Council of the European Union adopted Directive 95/46/EC on the protection of individuals with regard to the processing of personal data and on the free movement of such data. As Brooke LJ observed in *Douglas* v. *Hello! Ltd* [2001] QB 967 at para.56, this Directive 'was self-avowedly concerned with the protection of an individual's Convention rights to privacy'.[2] This view of the Directive was echoed by Lord Phillips MR giving the judgment of the Court of Appeal in *Campbell* v. *MGN Ltd* [2002] EWCA Civ 1373; [2003] QB 633 where he stated at [73]:[3]

> The Directive was a response to the greater ease with which data can be processed and exchanged as a result of advances in information technology. Foremost among its aims is the protection of individuals against prejudice as a consequence of the processing of their personal data, including invasion of their privacy.

The DPA was passed to implement Directive 95/46/EC in domestic law (*Douglas* v. *Hello! Ltd* [2001] QB 967, para.56; *Campbell* v. *MGN Ltd* [2002] EWCA Civ 1373; [2003] QB 633, at [72]). The DPA largely follows the form of the Directive (*Campbell* v. *MGN Ltd*, para.72). It follows that in interpreting the DPA it is appropriate to look to the Directive for assistance. Lord Phillips MR explained in *Campbell* v. *MGN Ltd* at [97]:

> The Act should, if possible, be interpreted in a manner that is consistent with the Directive. Furthermore, because the Act has, in large measure, adopted the wording of the Directive, it is not appropriate to look for the precision in the use of language that is usually to be expected from the Parliamentary draftsman. A purposive approach to making sense of the provisions is called for.

---

[1]   Zinser, 'The United Kingdom Data Protection Act 1998: International Data Transfer and its Legal Implications' [2005] ICCLR 80, note 2.
[2]   For an analysis of the decision in the *Douglas* case, see *Privacy & Data Protection*, Vol.5, Issue 6, pp.9–12 (**www.pdpjournal.com**).
[3]   In a passage unaffected by the subsequent appeal in that case to the House of Lords: [2004] UKHL 22; [2004] 2 AC 457. See also para.3 of the decision of the Court of Justice of the European Union in *Tietosuojavaltuutettu* v. *Satakunnan Markkinapörssi Oy and Another* [2010] All ER (EC) 213.

It is also appropriate to look at its recitals, and it is noteworthy that the recitals refer to art.8 of the European Convention on Human Rights (ECHR), the right to respect for private and family life.[4]

In addition to informing its interpretation, the European origin of the DPA means that in applying the DPA the Information Commissioner, the Information Rights Tribunal and the ordinary courts must all be guided by the principle of proportionality. In particular, the principle of proportionality must govern any sanctions applied in the operation of the domestic legislation which implements the Directive (see *Criminal Proceedings against Lindqvist* (C-101/01) [2004] QB 1014, ECJ). This principle of proportionality is likely to be of particular importance in any situation where competing rights or societal values, enshrined in or recognised by the ECHR are in play – for example, competing rights of privacy and freedom of expression (as in *Campbell* v. *MGN Ltd* [2002] EWCA Civ 1373), or the competing privacy rights of two different individuals (as in *W* v. *Westminster City Council* [2005] EWHC 102 (QB)).

8.2.2 History of the FOIA

In contrast to the DPA, the FOIA has no European origin. The European Court of Human Rights has consistently declined to interpret art.10 of the ECHR as providing a right of access to officially held information (see *Leander* v. *Sweden* (1987) 9 EHRR 433, and *Guerra* v. *Italy* (1998) 26 EHRR 357). The same approach is evident in domestic cases in which reliance has been placed on art.10 in an attempt to obtain open access to government inquiries into foot and mouth disease and medical misconduct (*R (Persey)* v. *Secretary of State for Environment etc.* [2003] QB 794, *R (Howard)* v. *Secretary of State for Health* [2003] QB 830), or access to royal wills (*Brown* v. *Executors of the Estate of HM Queen Elizabeth the Queen Mother* [2007] EWHC 1607 (Fam) at [68] (reversed on other grounds by the Court of Appeal: [2008] EWCA Civ 56)). In *Sugar* v. *British Broadcasting Corporation* [2012] UKSC 4, the Supreme Court held that the art.10 right to receive information does not afford members of the public a specific right of access to information held by public authorities.[5] The position may be different where the press as the watchdog of the public seeks information from a court (and possibly other types of public authority) – see *A* v. *Independent News and Media* [2010] 1 WLR 2262 at paras.39–44.

A Freedom of Information Act was a 1997 manifesto commitment of the incoming Labour Government. A White Paper (Cm 3818, 1997) proposed radical changes with a view to promoting open government and transparent decision making. FOI legislation had been introduced elsewhere in the common law world at a much earlier stage (in the United States there has been a Freedom of Information

---

[4] See *R (on the application of Department of Health)* v. *Information Commissioner* [2011] EWHC 1430 (Admin), at [17].
[5] In *Kennedy* v. *Charity Commission* [2012] EWCA Civ 317, the Court of Appeal held that the Supreme Court's findings were part of the ratio of *Sugar*.

Act since 1966, and in Australia, Canada and New Zealand FOI legislation was enacted in 1982). The Freedom of Information Bill introduced by the government drew upon experience in other common law jurisdictions, as well as on the values protected by the rights introduced into domestic law by the Human Rights Act 1998. The government recognised that legislation required a delicate balance of the right to know against the right to privacy and confidentiality.[6]

The FOIA was passed on 30 November 2000 but most of its provisions were not brought into force until 1 January 2005. On the day it was brought into force, then Secretary of State for Constitutional Affairs, Lord Falconer, stated:

> We have caught up with other countries, and, in many cases, we have overtaken them. We have studied the experience of other countries to enable us to introduce one of the most generous freedom of information regimes in the world. The need to know culture has been replaced by a statutory right to know.

8.2.3 Similarities and differences between the two Acts

The fact that the DPA was passed to implement an EU Directive, whereas the FOIA has no European origin, might be thought to indicate a significant difference of approach in the two pieces of legislation. However, their difference in origin may not be particularly significant when it comes to their operation and application. Of course the DPA will be interpreted and applied in a manner consistent with the Directive which it implemented, whilst no such interpretative tool is available for the FOIA. However, the European principle of proportionality is rapidly becoming established in the field of English public law,[7] where the FOIA is located, and in the private law of confidentiality (see *Campbell* v. *MGN Ltd* [2004] 2 AC 457), with which the FOIA is necessarily concerned. In these circumstances the general approach to the interpretation and application of the two Acts is likely to be consistent. A consistent approach to their interpretation and operation is also called for by the fact that the FOIA introduces significant amendments into the DPA, and by the fact that s.40 of the FOIA expressly refers to and incorporates substantial parts of the DPA when dealing with personal information, as explained further below.

Two further important links between the two statutes should be emphasised. First, both Acts have at their core a right of access to information. This is self-evident in the case of the FOIA. In the case of the DPA, the primary right provided to data subjects is the right of access under s.7 of the DPA to personal data of which they are the subject. As Laddie J emphasised in *Johnson* v. *Medical Defence Union Ltd* [2005] WLR 750, para.19, the other rights provided to data subjects under ss.10–14 of the DPA are all dependent upon the data subject being able to discover, through the exercise of the right of access provided by s.7, whether and in what

---

6   Hansard, HL vol.612, cols.823–30, 20 April 2000.
7   See Fordham, *Judicial Review Handbook*, 5th edn (2008) section P58 and cases there discussed; *De Smith's Judicial Review*, 6th edn (2007), paras. 11–73 to 11–85.

fashion personal data are being processed by a data controller. The right of access under s.7 of the DPA is given special status by s.27(5) of the DPA which provides that it shall have effect 'notwithstanding any enactment or rule of law prohibiting or restricting the disclosure, or authorising the withholding, of information'.[8] Thus both Acts are fundamentally concerned with access to information. Secondly, as already noted, the two Acts share a common enforcement regime: the Information Commissioner and the Information Rights Tribunal.[9] The Information Commissioner was established under s.6 of the DPA for the purposes of both Acts (see DPA, s.6(1) as amended by the FOIA). The Information Rights Tribunal is now part of the First-tier Tribunal in the General Regulatory Chamber and is formally referred to as the First-tier Tribunal (Information Rights).[10]

There are, of course, also significant differences between the two Acts. The most significant of these are as follows:

- The DPA, in general terms, provides for rights against any data controller. A data controller may be a private individual, a small private company, a charitable organisation, a partnership, a large quoted company, or a public authority. By contrast, the FOIA provides rights only against public authorities.
- Under the DPA rights are, in general, provided only to data subjects, which are defined as living individuals. By contrast, the rights under the FOIA are conferred upon any person, which will include natural persons, companies, statutory or other bodies, and unincorporated associations.
- The information with which the DPA is concerned is confined, in general, to data relating to a living individual who can be identified from the data. The FOIA is concerned with all kinds of information.
- The DPA is, in general, concerned with information processed on computer equipment or contained in structured filing systems. The FOIA extends to information recorded in any form. (In certain specific situations the FOIA provides that information includes unrecorded information, see e.g. s.51(8).)

Further, it is apparent that a statute which entitles any person to request from a public authority any information recorded in any form has the potential to interfere with a measure designed to promote informational self-determination[11] for individuals. The manner in which these competing objectives are reconciled through s.40 of the FOIA is considered in **8.4**. It is first necessary to have a basic understanding of the operation of the DPA.

---

[8] Carey in *Data Protection: A Practical Guide to UK and EU Law*, 3rd edn (2009) observes at p.162 that this gives the subject information provisions special status.
[9] The Information Rights Tribunal was until recently known as the Information Tribunal.
[10] See the Transfer of Tribunal Functions Order 2010 (SI 2010/22, art.5(1)), Sched.2, paras.24, 25(b)).
[11] See Professor Ian Lloyd's *Guide to the Data Protection Act 1998* (1998, Butterworths), para.4.6.

8.3 OVERVIEW OF THE DPA

8.3.1 Key concepts

Sections 1–5 of the DPA define a number of key expressions and set the territorial limits of the Act.

'Data'

'Data' is defined by s.1(1), as amended by the FOIA 2000, to mean information which:

(a)   is being processed by means of equipment operating automatically in response to instructions given for that purpose,

(b)   is recorded with the intention that it should be processed by means of such equipment,

(c)   is recorded as part of a relevant filing system or with the intention that it should form part of a relevant filing system,

(d)   does not fall within paragraph (a), (b) or (c) but forms part of an accessible record as defined by section 68, or

(e)   is recorded information held by a public authority and does not fall within any of paragraphs (a) to (d)

In broad terms, paras.(a) and (b) of this definition of data refer to information which is or is intended to be processed on computer equipment. Paragraph (c) of the definition extends to information recorded as part of, or intended to form part of, a relevant filing system. A 'relevant filing system' means any set of information relating to individuals which, although not computerised, is structured either by reference to individuals or by reference to criteria relating to individuals in such a way that specific information relating to a particular individual is readily accessible (s.1(1)). In *Durant* v. *Financial Services Authority* [2003] EWCA Civ 1746 the Court of Appeal gave a narrow interpretation to the expression 'relevant filing system', concluding at [48] that 'Parliament intended to apply the Act to manual records only if they are of sufficient sophistication to provide the same or similar ready accessibility as a computerised filing system' (per Auld LJ, with whom Mummery and Buxton LJJ agreed). Paragraph (d) of the definition makes specific provision for health records, educational records and the accessibility of public records (see s.68 and Scheds.11 and 12).

Paragraph (e) of the definition of data was inserted by the FOIA. It extends the reach of the DPA to cover unstructured manual records held by public authorities (*Smith* v. *Lloyds TSB Bank plc* [2005] EWHC 246 (Ch), Laddie J at [27]), but not other data controllers.

'Data subject', 'personal data' and 'sensitive personal data'

Section 1(1) of the DPA also defines a 'data subject' as an individual who is the subject of personal data. 'Personal data' is defined as data which relate to a living individual who can be identified from such data or from such data and other information which is in the possession of, or is likely to come into the possession of, the data controller. It includes any expression of opinion about the individual and any indication of the intentions of the data controller or any other person in respect of the individual.

The leading case on the meaning of 'personal data' is the decision of the House of Lords in *Common Services Agency* v. *Scottish Information Commissioner* [2008] UKHL 47.[12] The House of Lords held that depending on the extent to which it was anonymised, information about the physical health or condition of children diagnosed with leukaemia might constitute personal data within s.1(1) of the DPA or indeed 'sensitive personal data' within s.2(e) of the DPA, since it was data about the physical health of living children who might be identified by the public from data released in response to the request when taken together with other information in the possession of, or likely to come into the possession of, the data controller.[13]

In *Common Services Agency,* the House of Lords emphasised the importance of looking at the definition of 'personal data' in the context of what Member States were expected to achieve when implementing Directive 95/46/EC. Accordingly, the House of Lords held that 'personal data' is data from which the individual to whom the data relate can be identified by the public, whether from that information alone or when that information is combined with other information. If it is impossible for the recipient of the data (or indeed anyone to whom he or she might pass on the data) to identify the individuals to whom the data relate, then the information does not constitute 'personal data'.[14] This is the case even if the original data controller can identify the individuals to whom the data relate.[15]

Some types of personal data are identified as 'sensitive personal data' in relation to which particularly stringent requirements are applied. As was observed by Lord Rodger of Earlsferry in *Common Services Agency*, the classification of data as 'sensitive personal data' rather than 'personal data' matters because the regulation of the processing of sensitive personal data is, understandably, tighter than the regulation of the processing of other personal data.

Section 2 of the DPA identifies sensitive personal data as personal data in relation to the data subject consisting of information as to:

(a)   the racial or ethnic origin of the data subject,
(b)   his political opinions,
(c)   his religious beliefs or other beliefs of a similar nature,
(d)   whether he is a member of a trade union . . .,

---

[12]   This was an appeal from the Court of Session and concerned the Freedom of Information (Scotland) Act 2002. However, much of the wording of s.38 of that Act, which addresses the overlap between rights of access under that Act and rights of access under the DPA 1998, is reproduced in the FOIA, s.40, which addresses the same problem.
[13]   At [35].
[14]   See the discussion of the *Common Services Agency* decision in *Craigdale Housing Association and Others* v. *Scottish Information Commissioner* [2010] CSIH 43.
[15]   *R (on the application of Department of Health)* v. *Information Commissioner* [2011] EWHC 1430 (Admin) (at [52]).

(e)   his physical or mental health or condition,
(f)   his sexual life,
(g)   the commission or alleged commission by him of any offence, or
(h)   any proceedings for any offence committed or alleged to have been committed by him, the disposal of such proceedings or the sentence of any court in such proceedings.

A noteworthy omission from this list is any reference to finance, taxation or similar matters.

In *Common Services Agency*, the House of Lords held that 'sensitive personal data is a subset, or a species, of "personal data"',[16] and that the DPA requires the definition of 'personal data' to be read into the definition of 'sensitive personal data'.[17] So, for example, information contained in a prosecution file is not sensitive personal data unless it was personal data in the first place (*Cobain* v. *Information Commissioner and Crown Prosecution Service* (EA/2011/0112 and EA/2011/0113, 8 February 2012)).

'Data controller' and 'data processor'

In general the rights provided by the DPA are rights against a 'data controller', meaning a person who (either alone or jointly or in common with other persons) determines the purposes for which and the manner in which any personal data are, or are to be, processed. A 'data processor' is any person other than an employee of a data controller who processes data on behalf of the data controller.

'Processing'

The expression 'processing', in relation to information or data, is defined extremely widely. It embraces the obtaining, recording or holding of information or data or the carrying out of any operation or set of operations on the information or data including:

- organisation, adaptation or alteration of the information or data;
- retrieval, consultation or use of the information or data;
- disclosure[18] of the information or data by transmission, dissemination or otherwise making it available; or
- alignment, combination, blocking, erasure or destruction of the information or data.

The width of the definition of processing was emphasised by the Court of Appeal in *Campbell* v. *MGN Ltd* [2002] EWCA Civ 1373; [2003] QB 633. However, the

---

[16]   At [37].
[17]   At [40].
[18]   In *Campbell* v. *MGN Ltd* [2002] EWCA Civ 1373; [2003] QB 633 the Court of Appeal held that publication of data in a newspaper amounted to processing where the information in question had previously been processed on computer equipment (at [106]).

apparent width of the definition of processing must now be read in the light of the later decision of the Court of Appeal in *Johnson* v. *Medical Defence Union Ltd* (2007) 96 BMLR 99. In that case the Court of Appeal held by a majority that the carrying out of a 'risk assessment review' by the Medical Defence Union, following which the claimant's membership was terminated, had not involved the 'processing' of his personal data within the terms of the DPA. The majority judgments take a much narrower view of the concept of 'processing' under the DPA from that taken by the Court of Appeal in the *Campbell* case. The majority in *Johnson* divided the series of operations involved into three phases. The first and third phases (retrieval of information from a computer and recording of the review outcome on a computer) amounted to processing, although this was not complained of or unfair. The second phase (the exercise of individual judgment in relation to information retrieved from the computer) did not amount to processing even where the result of the review was subsequently recorded electronically. Arden LJ dissented, holding that the operation as a whole amounted to processing. The majority view is (as Arden LJ points out) difficult to reconcile with the *Campbell* case.

The 'special purposes'

The special purposes, which are relevant to certain exemptions and remedies, are defined in s.3 of the DPA as any one or more of the following:

(a)   the purpose of journalism,
(b)   artistic purposes, and
(c)   literary purposes.

The 'data protection principles'

Section 4(4) of the DPA sets out the basic statutory duty of all data controllers, which is to comply with the data protection principles in relation to all personal data. The data protection principles are set out in Part I of Sched.1 to the DPA (s.4(1)). Part II of Sched.1 provides guidance on the interpretation of the data protection principles (s.4(2)). Schedule 2 (which applies to all personal data) and Sched.3 (which applies only to sensitive personal data) set out conditions applying for the purposes of the first data protection principle (s.4(3)).

The eight data protection principles set out in Part I of Sched.1 are as follows:

1.   Personal data shall be processed fairly and lawfully and, in particular, shall not be processed unless:

(a)   at least one of the conditions in Schedule 2 is met, and
(b)   in the case of sensitive personal data, at least one of the conditions in Schedule 3 is also met.

2.   Personal data shall be obtained only for one or more specified and lawful purposes, and shall not be further processed in any manner incompatible with that purpose or those purposes.

3. Personal data shall be adequate, relevant and not excessive in relation to the purpose or purposes for which they are processed.
4. Personal data shall be accurate and, where necessary, kept up to date.
5. Personal data processed for any purpose or purposes shall not be kept for longer than is necessary for that purpose or those purposes.
6. Personal data shall be processed in accordance with the rights of data subjects under this Act.
7. Appropriate technical and organisational measures shall be taken against unauthorised or unlawful processing of personal data and against accidental loss or destruction of, or damage to, personal data.
8. Personal data shall not be transferred to a country or territory outside the European Economic Area unless that country or territory ensures an adequate level of protection for the rights and freedoms of data subjects in relation to the processing of personal data.

Part II of Sched.1 to the DPA contains important guidance on the interpretation of the first, second, fourth, sixth, seventh and eighth principles. Paragraphs 1 and 2 of Part II of Sched.1 are of particular significance in that they impose requirements of fairness in relation to the obtaining of data.[19] It is also important to understand how the sixth principle operates. Paragraph 8 of Part II of Sched.1 provides that a person is to be regarded as contravening the sixth principle only if he or she contravenes one or more of ss.7, 10, 11, 12 of the DPA. Such contraventions can only occur if a data subject has invoked the rights provided by those sections.

Schedules 2 and 3 each contain a list of conditions. At least one of the Sched.2 conditions must be met before the first data protection principle can be satisfied in relation to any processing of personal data. If the personal data in question are sensitive personal data, the first data protection principle will not be satisfied unless, in addition, at least one of the conditions in Sched.3 is also met.[20]

8.3.2 Territorial limits

Section 5 sets out the territorial limits of the application of the DPA. In general it applies to a data controller in respect of any data only if:

---

[19] In *Campbell* v. *MGN Ltd* at first instance ([2002] EMLR 30) and again in *Douglas* v. *Hello! Ltd (No.3)* [2003] 3 All ER 996 it was held that data obtained by means of surreptitious photography had not been fairly obtained. In each case the court placed reliance on *R* v. *Broadcasting Standards Commission, ex p. British Broadcasting Commission* [2001] QB 885 where the Court of Appeal recognised that surreptitious photography is regarded as objectionable. See also *R* v. *Loveridge* [2001] EWCA Crim 973. Contrast *Murray* v. *Express Newspapers plc and Another* [2007] EWHC 1908 (Ch) at [73] where Patten J appears to have held that surreptitious photography in the street was not of itself an unfair obtaining of data. This point was not considered in the subsequent appeal to the Court of Appeal in that case: [2009] Ch 481.

[20] These requirements, together with the requirement of the first data protection principle that personal data shall be processed fairly and lawfully are cumulative, see *Campbell* v. *MGN Ltd* [2002] EMLR 30, paras.102, 119. The Court of Appeal did not disagree with this part of the trial judge's analysis: see [2003] QB 633, para.88.

- the data controller is established in the UK[21] and the data are processed in the context of that establishment;[22] or
- the data controller is established neither in the UK nor in any other state of the European Economic Area (EEA) but uses equipment in the UK for processing the data otherwise than for the purposes of transit through the UK.

Export of data to a country or territory outside the EEA may contravene the eighth data protection principle. Note, however, that a person does not transfer data to a country or territory outside the EEA simply by loading the data on to an internet page which may be accessed from other countries (see *Criminal Proceedings against Lindqvist* (C-101/01) [2004] QB 1014, ECJ at p.1038, paras.69–71).

8.3.3 Part II of the DPA: data subject rights

Part II of the DPA provides for the rights of data subjects and others. These are:

- the right of access to personal data (ss.7–9A);
- the right to prevent processing likely to cause damage or distress (s.10);
- the right to prevent processing for purposes of direct marketing (s.11);
- rights in relation to automated decision taking (s.12);
- entitlement to compensation for failure to comply with certain requirements (s.13);
- rectification, blocking, erasure and destruction (s.14).

It is a noteworthy feature of the rights provided by ss.7–12 (although not ss.13 or 14) that the first step in enforcing the rights is the service of a written notice by the data subject. In the case of such rights the court can only have a role if such self-help proves ineffective.

Right of access to personal data

As already noted, the right of access to personal data may be seen as the primary right conferred on data subjects by the DPA. The nature of the right was described in the following terms by Laddie J in *Johnson* v. *Medical Defence Union Ltd* [2005] 1 WLR 750, paras.20–21:

> [S]ection 7(1)(a) allows the individual to find out *whether* personal data about him are being processed and section 7(1)(b) allows him to find out how they are being processed *if* section 7(1)(a) is answered in the affirmative. There is no precondition that the individual believes or can demonstrate a prima facie case that the data controller has any of his

---

21 See s.5(3) of the DPA. An individual is established in the UK if ordinarily resident here. A company is established in the UK if incorporated under the law of any part of the UK. A partnership or unincorporated association is established in the UK if formed under the law of any part of the UK. Any other person who maintains in the UK an office, branch or agency through which he or she carries on any activity, or a regular practice, is also established here.

22 This requirement may give rise to difficult questions where data are processed by the UK office of a multinational concern.

personal data nor is there a precondition that, if any such personal data are held, the individual believes or can demonstrate a prima facie case that they are being processed improperly. Section 7 is not concerned with whether the data controller is acting improperly.

Therefore the purpose of these provisions is to make the processing of personal data transparent. Because there is nothing in this to limit applications to cases where the data controller has acted in some way improperly, he may charge a fee for complying with a data request under this section: section 7(2)(b). Section 7 also contains provisions which allow the data controller to refuse requests for information, at least in part, where compliance might disclose the identity of third parties.

The right of access to personal data is exercised, in the first instance, by a data subject serving on a data controller a request in writing and, if required, paying a fee up to a prescribed amount (s.7(2)). Unless the data controller reasonably requires further information in order to satisfy himself or herself of the identity of the data subject or in order to locate the information which the data subject seeks, and has informed the data subject of that requirement, the data controller must comply with the request within 40 days (s.7(3), (8) and (10)).

Where the data controller cannot comply with the request without disclosing information relating to another individual who can be identified from that information he or she may be able to refuse to comply with the request, either wholly or in part, if that other person does not consent to the disclosure (ss.7(4)–(6) and 8(7)). A data controller who has previously complied with a request by an individual is not obliged to comply with a subsequent identical or similar request by that individual unless a reasonable interval has elapsed since compliance with the previous request (s.8(3)).

Subject to the matters referred to in the preceding paragraph, a data subject is entitled in response to a request made under s.7(1):

(a)   to be informed by any data controller whether personal data of which that individual is the data subject are being processed by or on behalf of that data controller,

(b)   if that is the case, to be given by the data controller a description of –

    (i)   the personal data of which that individual is the data subject,
    (ii)   the purposes for which they are being or are to be processed, and
    (iii)   the recipients or classes of recipients to whom they are or may be disclosed,

(c)   to have communicated to him in an intelligible form –

    (i)   the information constituting any personal data of which that individual is the data subject, and
    (ii)   any information available to the data controller as to the source of those data, and

(d)   where the processing by automatic means of personal data of which that individual is the data subject for the purpose of evaluating matters relating to him such as, for example, his performance at work, his creditworthiness, his reliability or his conduct, has constituted or is likely to constitute the sole basis for any decision significantly affecting him, to be informed by the data controller of the logic involved in that decision-taking.

Under s.7(9) if a court is satisfied that a data controller has failed to comply with a request in contravention of the provisions of s.7, the court may order him or her to comply with the request. Under s.15(2) the court may inspect the information which the data subject has requested in order to see whether s.7 has been complied with, but it shall not, unless it determines that question in the data subject's favour, require the information to be disclosed to him or her. In *Johnson v. Medical Defence Union Ltd* [2005] 1 WLR 750 Laddie J held that s.15(2) did not prevent a data subject whose application to the court under s.7(9) had failed from obtaining disclosure of documents relating to the processing of his or her personal data in subsequent substantive proceedings for breach of the data protection principles. Section 8 contains supplementary provisions relating to the operation of s.7, and s.9 modifies the operation of s.7 where the data controller is a credit reference agency.

Section 9A, which was introduced by the FOIA, provides an important modification to the operation of s.7 where the information requested by a data subject is unstructured personal data held by a public authority. In such a case the public authority is not obliged to comply with s.7(1) in relation to any unstructured personal data unless the request contains a description of the data (s.9A(2)). Even if the data are described by the data subject in his or her request, the public authority is not obliged to comply with s.7(1) if it estimates that the cost of complying with the request in relation to those data would exceed the appropriate limit (s.9A(3)).[23] The effect of s.9A is to increase significantly the right of access to personal data held by public authorities. Whereas other data controllers will only have to search structured manual filing systems which meet the narrow definition of a relevant filing system laid down by the Court of Appeal in *Durant v. Financial Services Authority* [2003] EWCA Civ 1746, public authorities will have to conduct much more extensive searches. The burden imposed upon public authorities in relation to unstructured personal data held by them is limited, outside the operation of s.7, by s.33A of the DPA.

Right to prevent processing likely to cause damage or distress

By s.10(1) an individual is entitled by notice in writing to a data controller to require the data controller at the end of a reasonable period to cease, or not to begin, processing any personal data in respect of which he or she is the data subject, on the ground that, for specified reasons:

(a)   the processing of those data or their processing for a particular purpose or in a particular manner is causing or is likely to cause substantial damage or substantial distress to [the data subject] or to another, and

(b)   that damage or distress is or would be unwarranted.

---

[23]   See the Freedom of Information and Data Protection (Appropriate Limit and Fees) Regulations 2004, SI 2004/3244, reg.3. The appropriate limit is £600 in the case of a government department, the House of Commons or House of Lords, the Northern Ireland Assembly or the National Assembly for Wales, or the armed forces of the Crown. In the case of any other public authority the appropriate limit is £450.

The right to serve a notice under s.10(1) does not apply if the data subject has given consent to the processing, or if the processing is necessary for the performance of a contract with the data subject or for the taking of steps at the request of the data subject with a view to entering into a contract, or if the processing is necessary for compliance with any legal obligation of the data controller (other than an obligation imposed by contract), or if the processing is necessary in order to protect the vital interests of the data subject (see s.10(2) and Sched.2, paras.1–4).

The data controller must respond within 21 days of receiving a notice under s.10(1) stating whether he or she has complied or intends to comply with the request, and if not, why not (s.10(3)). If the data controller fails to comply with the notice, a court may order him or her to take such steps for complying with it as the court thinks fit (s.10(4)).

Right to prevent processing for purposes of direct marketing

Section 11(1) entitles a data subject to serve a notice in writing on a data controller requiring the latter at the end of a reasonable period to cease, or not to begin, processing personal data for the purposes of direct marketing. If the data controller fails to comply with the notice the court may order him or her to do so (s.11(2)).

Rights in relation to automated decision taking

Section 12(1) entitles a data subject to serve a notice in writing on a data controller requiring the data controller to ensure that no decision taken by or on behalf of the data controller which significantly affects the data subject is based solely on the processing by automatic means of personal data for the purpose of evaluating matters such as, for example, performance at work, creditworthiness, reliability or conduct. The data controller must respond within 21 days stating whether he or she intends to comply with the notice (s.12(3)). Certain types of automated decision taking are exempt (s.12(4)–(7)). A court may order a data controller who has failed to comply with a notice under s.12(1) to reconsider his or her decision or take a new decision which is not based solely on automatic processing of personal data (s.12(8)).

Compensation for failure to comply with certain requirements

Section 13 provides that an individual who suffers damage by reason of any contravention by a data controller of any of the requirements within the DPA is entitled to compensation (s.13(1)). An individual who suffers distress as well as damage is entitled to compensation from the data controller for that distress (s.13(2)(a)). Even if the individual does not suffer damage, he or she is entitled to compensation for distress if the contravention of which he or she complains relates to the processing of personal data for the special purposes (s.13(2)(b)). It was under this provision that Morland J awarded damages for distress in *Campbell* v. *MGN Ltd* [2002] EMLR 617.

However, the DPA should not be construed so as to afford an individual a remedy when damaging information has been published about him or her which is not defamatory or malicious. Nor does the DPA empower a court to order someone to publish a correction or apology when the person concerned does not believe he or she has published anything untrue (*Quinton* v. *Peirce and Another* [2009] EWHC 912 (QB)).

Rectification, blocking, erasure and destruction

A data subject may apply to the court where personal data of which he or she is the subject is inaccurate, and the court may order the data controller to rectify, block, erase or destroy such data and any expression of opinion which appears to the court to be based on the inaccurate data (s.14(1)). Specific provision is made for situations in which the data controller has obtained the inaccurate data from the data subject or a third party (s.14(2)), and for informing third parties of the court's decision (s.14(3)). The court also has a power, which is not limited to inaccurate data, to require the rectification, blocking, erasure or destruction of data in relation to which there has been a contravention by a data controller of any of the requirements of the DPA which has caused damage to the data subject entitling him or her to compensation where there is a substantial risk of further contravention (s.14(4)).

8.3.4 Part III – notification and registration requirements

Sections 16–26 of the DPA make provision for the registration of data controllers. Under s.17, processing without prior registration is prohibited. Breach of that prohibition is a criminal offence (see s.21), but it has been held that failure to register does not, of itself, give rise to a private law cause of action: *Murray* v. *Express Newspapers plc and Another* [2007] EWHC 1908 (Ch). Supplementary provision is made in relation to fees and other matters.

8.3.5 Part IV – exemptions

The provisions of Part IV of the DPA, read together with regulations made thereunder and with Sched.7 to the DPA, provide a number of important exemptions from the requirements of the Act. These provisions are extremely complex and in a work of this nature it is impossible to provide more than a bare summary.

The first point to note is that s.27(1), which introduces the exemptions which follow, explains that the exemptions may relate either to data or to processing. The distinction between exempting data, and exempting the processing of it, was significant in relation to the interpretation of the media exemption in s.32 by the Court of Appeal in *Campbell* v. *MGN Ltd* [2003] QB 633.

The various exemptions make either data or processing of different sorts exempt from different provisions or sets of provisions. Throughout Part IV two expressions are used as shorthand formulae for different sets of provisions. These two expressions are:

- 'the subject information provisions', which means:

  (a) the first data protection principle to the extent to which it requires compliance with Sched.1, Part II, para.2 (one of the requirements relating to fairness in the obtaining of data from the data subject or other sources); and

  (b) s.7 (the right of access to personal data);

- 'the non-disclosure provisions', which means:

  (a) the fair and lawful requirement of the first data protection principle;

  (b) the second, third, fourth and fifth data protection principles; and

  (c) ss.10 and 14(1)–(3).

Notwithstanding the introduction of these two shorthand formulae, some of the exemptions make data or processing exempt from a wider set of provisions – see, for example, the exemption in relation to national security under s.28. Other exemptions apply only in relation to s.7 – see, for example, the exemption in relation to personal data processed for research purposes provided by s.33(4). Other exemptions refer to Part II of the DPA (which includes s.7) without referring specifically to s.7 – see, for example, s.33A.

The types of data and/or processing of data exempt from some or all of the provisions of the DPA are as follows:

- s.28 – national security;[24]
- s.29 – crime and taxation;
- s.30 – health, education and social work;[25]
- s.31 – regulatory activity (the definition of 'relevant regulatory functions' in s.31(2) is extremely wide) (s.31 is amended and the exemption extended by s.200 of the Local Government and Public Involvement in Health Act 2007);
- s.32 – journalism, literature and art;[26]
- s.33 – research history and statistics;

---

[24] Provision is made for a conclusive ministerial certificate subject to review on administrative law principles by the Information Rights Tribunal. See s.28(2)–(7) and *Baker* v. *Secretary of State for the Home Department* [2001] UKHRR 1275.

[25] See the Data Protection (Subject Access Modification) (Health) Order 2000, SI 2000/413; the Data Protection (Subject Access Modification) (Education) Order 2000, SI 2000/414; the Data Protection (Subject Access Modification) (Social Work) Order 2000, SI 2000/415; Data Protection (Subject Access Modification) (Social Work) (Amendment) Order 2005, SI 2005/467; Data Protection (Subject Access Modification) (Social Work) (Amendment) Order 2011, SI 2011/1034.

[26] See *Sugar* v. *British Broadcasting Corporation* [2012] UKSC 4. Under s.32(4)–(5) there is a complete bar on pre-publication injunctive relief. Under s.32(1)–(3) there is a public interest exemption which applies both to pre-publication processing and to publication itself (*Campbell* v. *MGN Ltd* [2003] QB 633).

- s.33A – manual data held by public authorities;[27]
- s.34 – information available to the public by or under any enactment (such enactments do not include the FOIA; this exclusion is necessary in order to avoid circularity);
- s.35 – disclosure required by law or made in connection with legal proceedings;
- s.35A – parliamentary privilege;
- s.36 – domestic purposes;
- s.37 – miscellaneous exemptions. These are:

    - Sched.7, para.1 – confidential references given by the data controller;
    - Sched.7, para.2 – prejudice to combat effectiveness of the armed forces;
    - Sched.7, para.3 – data processed for the purposes of judicial appointments, the appointment of Queen's Counsel or the conferring of any honour or dignity;
    - Sched.7, para.4 – Crown employment and Crown or ministerial appointments (see the Data Protection (Crown Appointments) Order 2000, SI 2000/416);
    - Sched.7, para.5 – management forecasts and management planning;
    - Sched.7, para.6 – corporate finance information to the extent that information might emerge which would be price sensitive or might damage the economic or financial interests of the United Kingdom (see the Data Protection (Corporate Finance Exemption) Order 2000, SI 2000/184);
    - Sched.7, para.7 – negotiations with the data subject;
    - Sched.7, para.8 – examination marks;
    - Sched.7, para.9 – examination scripts;
    - Sched.7, para.10 – legal professional privilege;
    - Sched.7, para.11 – privilege against self-incrimination;

- s.38 – further exemptions made by Order of the Secretary of State. These are (see the Data Protection (Miscellaneous Subject Access Exemptions) Order 2000, SI 2000/419 and Data Protection (Miscellaneous Subject Access Exemptions) (Amendment) Order 2000, SI 2000/1865):

    - adoption records and reports;
    - statement of a child's special educational needs;
    - parental orders, records and reports.

---

[27] In the case of personal data relating to appointments or removals, pay, discipline, superannuation or other personnel matters this exemption extends to all of the provisions in Part II: s.33A(2). In relation to other personal data held in manual form by public authorities the exemption is more limited, and in particular the fourth data protection principle (which requires data to be accurate and up to date) and the sixth data protection principle so far as it relates to the rights conferred by ss.7 and 14, remain in effect: s.33A(1).

8.3.6 Part V – enforcement

Sections 40–50 of the DPA contain provisions relating to enforcement by the Information Commissioner and appeals to the Information Rights Tribunal.

Section 40 empowers the Information Commissioner to serve an enforcement notice if satisfied that a data controller has contravened or is contravening any of the data protection principles. An enforcement notice may require the data controller to take specified steps or to refrain from any processing of personal data or specified personal data, and may require the data controller to rectify, block, erase or destroy inaccurate data and to notify third parties.

Section 41A empowers the Information Commissioner to serve government departments who are data controllers with an assessment notice, in order to determine whether the data controller has complied or is complying with the data protection principles. An assessment notice can require a data controller to permit the Information Commissioner to enter any specified premises, direct the Information Commissioner to any documents, equipment or other material on the premises that are of a specified description, or even make available a specified number of persons who process personal data on behalf of the data controller for interview. The Secretary of State is empowered to make an order which designates public authorities or other persons to be data controllers covered by section 41A (s.41A(2)(b) and (c)).

Section 42 provides that any person who believes himself or herself to be directly affected by any processing of personal data may request the Information Commissioner to assess whether it is likely or unlikely that the processing has been or is being carried out in compliance with the DPA. On receiving such a request the Information Commissioner shall decide how to proceed, taking into account, in particular, whether or not the person making the request is entitled to make an application for access to the personal data under s.7. This tends to emphasise again that the right of access under s.7 is the primary right afforded by the DPA.

Section 43 empowers the Information Commissioner to serve an information notice on a data controller in order to pursue a request under s.42 or in order to obtain information for the purpose of determining whether the data controller has complied or is complying with the data protection principles. Such an information notice will require the data controller to furnish the Information Commissioner with 'specified information', namely information the form and content of which will be determined by the Information Commissioner.

Sections 44–46 make specific provision relating to enforcement where the personal data are, or are claimed to be, being processed for the purposes of journalism, art or literature, including provision for service of a special information notice which may be served with a view to ascertaining whether data are being processed only for such purposes.

Section 47 makes a failure to comply with an enforcement notice, information notice or special information notice a criminal offence.

Sections 48–49 provide that a person served with an enforcement notice, an assessment notice, an information notice or a special information notice may appeal to the Information Rights Tribunal against the notice. The appeal is a full appeal on facts and law and may involve the fresh exercise of discretion. A further appeal on a point of law lies to the Upper Tribunal Administrative Appeals Chamber.

Section 50 and Sched.9 provide the Information Commissioner with powers of entry and inspection, subject to the issue of a warrant by a circuit or district judge.

Monetary penalties

Sections 55A–55E provide that the Information Commissioner may serve a data controller with a monetary penalty notice if the Information Commissioner is satisfied that there has been a serious contravention of the data protection principles, the contravention was deliberate or the data controller failed to take reasonable steps to prevent the contravention, and it was of a kind likely to cause substantial damage or substantial distress. A data controller can appeal to the Information Rights Tribunal against the issue of the monetary penalty notice, or the amount of the monetary penalty (s.55B(5)).

8.3.7 Part VI – miscellaneous and general provisions

Sections 51–54A and ss.58–59 make further provision relating to the functions of the Information Commissioner and the Information Rights Tribunal. Section 51 imposes general duties on the Information Commissioner to promote good practice, disseminate information, give advice and issue codes of practice. By s.52 the Information Commissioner's reports and codes of practice must be laid before Parliament. Section 52A requires the Commissioner to prepare a code of practice which contains practical guidance in relation to the sharing of personal data in accordance with the DPA and other relevant guidance. This is to be known as the Data-Sharing Code (s.52E(4)). The code must be submitted to the Secretary of State for approval (s.52B). A breach of the Data-Sharing Code itself is not actionable in any court or tribunal (s.52E(1)). However, the code will be admissible as evidence in any legal proceedings (s.52E(2)). Further, any relevant provision of the code must be taken into account by the Information Commissioner (s.52E(3)(c)), or by a court or tribunal when determining a question arising in legal proceedings (whether or not under the DPA) or in connection with the exercise of that jurisdiction (s.52E(3)(a) and (b)).

Section 53 gives the Information Commissioner power to grant legal assistance in cases of substantial public importance. Section 54 sets out the Information Commissioner's role in relation to international co-operation and obligations in the area of data protection. Section 54A provides that the Information Commissioner may inspect any personal data recorded in the Schengen information system, the Europol information system and the Customs information system. Section 58 prevents any enactment or rule of law from prohibiting the provision of information to the Information Commissioner or the Information Rights Tribunal. Section 59 imposes obligations of confidentiality on the Information Commissioner and his staff in relation to information obtained under the DPA or under the FOIA.

Section 55 creates the criminal offence of unlawfully obtaining personal data. It is subject to a public interest defence (s.55(2)). There is also a defence open to those who act for the special purposes, with a view to the publication by any person of any journalistic, literary or artistic material (s.55(2)(ca)).[28] However, both defences depend upon it being established that the processing actually is in the public interest (s.55(2)(d)), which is surprising given that the exemption for the media from most types of civil liability under s.32 only requires a reasonable belief that the processing is in the public interest. Parliament passed s.78 of the Criminal Justice and Immigration Act 2008 to remove this anomaly but that section has not been brought into force, for reasons which have been under consideration by the Leveson Inquiry.

Section 56 prohibits an employer and/or a person concerned with the provision of goods, facilities or services to the public or a section of the public (whether or not this is done in exchange for payment) from requiring other persons or third parties to supply him or her with certain data which he or she could obtain from a data controller. Section 57 renders ineffective any contractual term which purports to require an individual to provide any other person with information contained in any health record. In essence these provisions are designed to prevent an employer from obliging an employee to disclose criminal records, health records or other details.

8.4 INTERFACE BETWEEN THE DPA AND THE FOIA: SECTION 40 AND EXEMPTION BY INCORPORATION

8.4.1 The purpose and structure of s.40

Section 40 of the FOIA contains strikingly complex provisions which govern the interaction between that Act and the DPA. The complexity arises as a result of the legislative technique used in s.40 to establish sets of potential exemptions from the duties imposed on a public authority under s.1 of the FOIA by incorporating substantial parts of the DPA. The key to understanding the provisions of s.40 is to bear in mind three points:

1. Where a living individual makes a request to a public authority for personal data (within the meaning of s.1(1) of the DPA) of which he or she is the data subject (again within the meaning of s.1(1) of the DPA), that request cannot be dealt with by the public authority under the FOIA, but must be dealt with by the public authority under the DPA.

2. Where, however, (a) a living individual requests personal data of which he or

---

[28]   These provisions have not yet come into effect. See the Criminal Justice and Immigration Act 2008, s.153(7).

she is not the data subject (i.e. information relating to another living individual); or (b) a request for personal data is made by a person who is not a living individual (e.g. a company, partnership or unincorporated association), the request must be dealt with by the public authority under the FOIA but will be subject to potential exemptions (absolute and/or qualified) arising from the provisions of the DPA which are incorporated by reference into s.40(3) and (4).

3. A separate provision (s.40(5)) provides for exemptions in relation to the public authority's duty to confirm or deny under s.1 of the FOIA. There is an absolute exemption from this duty where a request for personal data is made by a living individual who is the data subject. In other cases the exemption from the duty to confirm or deny is qualified, even if there is an absolute exemption from the duty to communicate the information requested.

Bearing these three points in mind, the provisions of s.40 may be broken down into four component parts as outlined below.

Section 40(1)

> Any information to which a request for information relates is exempt information if it constitutes personal data [as defined in DPA, s.1(1) – see FOIA, s.40(7)] of which the applicant is the data subject [as defined in DPA, s.1(1) – see FOIA, s.40(7)].

This is the provision which prevents a living individual using the FOIA to request personal data of which he or she is the data subject from a public authority. It provides for an absolute exemption (s.2(3)(f)(i)). The policy of the legislation is that such requests are outside the scope of the FOIA and must be pursued under s.7 of the DPA. In furtherance of this policy the definition of data (and hence of personal data) in s.1(1) of the DPA was amended by the FOIA to extend to any recorded information held by a public authority. In practice, in accordance with the requirements of good public administration, any request under the FOIA falling within s.40(1) will be dealt with by the public authority as a data subject access request under s.7 of the DPA. The public authority will be under no duty even to confirm or deny under the FOIA (s.2(1)(a) and s.40(5)(a)), but will be obliged to respond to the request in accordance with s.7 of the DPA.

Section 40(2)–(4)

(2) Any information to which a request for information relates is also exempt information if –

(a) it constitutes personal data which do not fall within subsection (1), and
(b) either the first or the second condition below is satisfied.

(3) The first condition is –

(a) in a case where the information falls within any of the paragraphs (a) to (d) of the definition of 'data' in section 1(1) of the Data Protection Act 1998, that the disclosure of the information to a member of the public otherwise than under this Act would contravene –

(i)   any of the data protection principles, or

(ii)   section 10 of that Act (right to prevent processing likely to cause damage or distress), and

(b)   in any other case, that the disclosure of the information to a member of the public otherwise than under this Act would contravene any of the data protection principles if the exemptions in section 33A(1) of the Data Protection Act 1998 (which relate to manual data held by public authorities) were disregarded.

(4)   The second condition is that by virtue of any provision of Part IV of the Data Protection Act 1998 the information is exempt from section 7(1)(c) of that Act (data subject's right of access to personal data).

These subsections contain the absolute and qualified exemptions which may apply where information which constitutes personal data (as defined in DPA, s.1(1) – see FOIA, s.40(7)) is requested from a public authority by a living individual who is not the data subject (i.e. the person to whom the personal data relate), or by a legal person such as a company, firm or unincorporated association. The operation of these potential exemptions is considered further below. It is, however, worth noting at the outset that where s.40(3)(a)(i) or (b) applies an absolute exemption is conferred (see s.2(3)(f)(ii)), whereas if s.40(3)(a)(ii) or s.40(4) applies, a qualified exemption is conferred.

Section 40(5)

The duty to confirm or deny –

(a)   does not arise in relation to information which is (or if it were held by the public authority would be) exempt information by virtue of subsection (1), and

(b)   does not arise in relation to other information if or to the extent that either –

(i)   the giving to a member of the public of the confirmation or denial that would have to be given to comply with section 1(1)(a) would (apart from this Act) contravene any of the data protection principles or section 10 of the Data Protection Act 1998 or would do so if the exemptions in section 33A(1) of that Act were disregarded, or

(ii)   by virtue of any provision of Part IV of the Data Protection Act 1998 the information is exempt from section 7(1)(a) of that Act (data subject's right to be informed whether personal data being processed).

This part of s.40 confers a qualified exemption in relation to the duty to confirm or deny. It confers a qualified exemption because s.40(5) is not one of the provisions listed in s.2(3). However, although in general the effect of s.40(5) is to confer qualified exemptions, the combined effect of s.40(5)(a) and s.2(3)(f)(i) is to confer an absolute exemption from the duty to confirm or deny where a request for information falls within s.40(1).

Section 40(6)

> In determining for the purposes of this section whether anything done before 24th October 2007 would contravene any of the data protection principles, the exemptions in Part III of Schedule 8 to the Data Protection Act 1998 shall be disregarded.

As noted above, Part III of Sched.8 to the DPA relates to the processing during the second transitional period (24 October 2001 to 23 October 2007 – see DPA, Sched.8, Part 1, para.1(2)) of manual data which was held prior to 24 October 1998. The effect of s.40(6) is to re-impose, for the purposes of s.40, restrictions on the processing of such data during the second transitional period which are disapplied by para.14(2) or para.14A of Part III of Sched.8 to the DPA. This will not impact on the rights of data subjects under the DPA, but will impact upon the rights of living individuals who are not the data subject or other persons to obtain personal data relating to others under the FOIA.

8.4.2   The operation of s.40(2)–(4)

The threshold requirement

The potential exemptions provided by subsections (2)–(4) of s.40 of the DPA are only engaged where a public authority receives a request for information which constitutes personal data from a living individual who is not the data subject or from a legal person such as a company, firm or unincorporated association. This threshold requirement is set out in s.40(2)(a). In simple terms it requires a request for personal data relating to a living individual who is not the person making the request. If the information to which a request relates crosses this threshold, it will be exempt information if either the first condition (set out in s.40(3)), or the second condition (set out in s.40(4)) is satisfied.

The first condition

The first condition, set out in s.40(3), has two limbs, (a) and (b). Limb (a) is itself subdivided into two parts, (i) and (ii). As already noted, part of the first limb (s.40(3)(a)(i)) and the second limb (s.40(3)(b)) of the first condition confer absolute exemptions; the second part of the first limb (s.40(3)(a)(ii)) confers a qualified exemption.

The difference between the two limbs of the first condition is that the first limb (s.40(3)(a)) applies where the information requested falls within any of paras.(a)–(d) of the definition of data in s.1(1) of the DPA. This is a reference to the definition of data prior to its amendment by the FOIA. As explained in **8.3.1**, paras.(a) and (b) of the definition of 'data' refer to information which is or is intended to be processed by means of computerised equipment, para.(c) refers to information recorded or to be recorded as part of a relevant filing system,[29] and para.(d) is limited to accessible records defined by s.68(1) of the DPA.

The second limb of the first condition, contained in s.40(3)(b), relates only to information falling within para.(e) of the definition of data in s.1(1) of the DPA. It will be recalled from **8.3.1** that para.(e) of the definition of data was inserted by the FOIA and extended the definition of data to include all recorded information held by a public authority not falling within paras.(a)–(d) of the definition. In essence, para.(e) covers unstructured manual records held by public authorities.

The first part of the first limb of the first condition (s.40(3)(a)(i)), and the second limb of the first condition (s.40(3)(b)) confer an absolute exemption (s.2(3)(f)(ii)). That absolute exemption applies where the disclosure of the information in question to a member of the public[30] otherwise than under the FOIA would contravene any of the data protection principles. For the purposes of the second limb of condition 1, when assessing whether such disclosure would contravene any of the data protection principles the exemptions contained in s.33A(1) of the DPA are disregarded (s.40(3)(b)). For the purposes of the first part of the first limb there is no comparable disapplication of any of the exemptions from the data protection principles contained in the DPA, from which it would appear that the assessment required under that part of the first limb is whether the disclosure to a member of the public would contravene any of the data protection principles in so far as they are applied by the DPA to the kind of data in question.

The data protection principles are contained in Part I of Sched.1 to the DPA and are set out in **8.3.1**. Guidance on the interpretation of the data protection principles is provided in Part II of Sched.1 to the DPA. Since the data protection principles cover all aspects of processing of data, and processing is widely defined to include obtaining, recording, holding, organising, adapting, altering, retrieving, consulting or using the data as well as disclosing it, only certain parts of certain of the data protection principles would appear to have an impact on an assessment of whether there should be disclosure of the information in question to a member of the public.

The data protection principles most likely to apply to the first part of the first limb, and to the second limb, of the first condition are those following below.

---

[29] See **8.3.1** – in *Durant* v. *Financial Services Authority* [2004] FSR 28 the Court of Appeal gave a narrow interpretation to the expression 'relevant filing system', limiting it to structured filing systems with their own internal indexation or search facility, i.e. manual records only if they are of sufficient sophistication to provide the same or similar ready accessibility as a computerised filing system (para.48).

[30] The focus in s.40(3)(b) on disclosure to a member of the public can be significant. In *York Hospitals NHS Trust* (FS50069257, 7 November 2005), disclosure of information provided by third parties in relation to the investigation of a grievance was refused even though certain of the third parties had consented to the disclosure of the information to the applicant. The question was not whether disclosure to the applicant would involve a breach of the data protection principles but whether disclosure to a member of the public would do so. See also *Bristol North Primary Care Trust* (FS50066908, 10 April 2006) which determined that where disclosure to the public of CCTV footage would be an unwarranted interference with privacy rights, disclosure of that footage would not be ordered.

- *The first data protection principle* – Personal data shall be processed fairly and lawfully and, in particular, shall not be processed unless:

  (a) at least one of the conditions in Sched.2 is met; and

  (b) in the case of sensitive personal data, at least one of the conditions in Sched.3 is also met.[31]

  As explained above, the first data protection principle imposes three cumulative requirements: the data must be processed fairly and lawfully; at least one of the conditions in Sched.2 must be met; and, in the case of sensitive personal data, at least one of the conditions in Sched.3 must also be met. As to the first of these requirements, although the provisions of s.40 of the FOIA will be capable of rendering disclosure of the information to a member of the public lawful, such disclosure will not be treated as fair unless the data controller complies with para.2 of Part II of Sched.1 to the DPA. In essence this paragraph requires certain information to be provided to the data subject where the data have been obtained from that data subject, and, with limited exceptions, requires the same information to be provided to the data subject where the information has been obtained from another source. The practical consequence of these requirements is that the disclosure of personal data by a public authority is unlikely to be fair unless the public authority has taken all reasonably practicable steps to contact the data subject and provide him or her with the requisite information. So far as the second and third requirements of the first data protection principle are concerned, the focus in the cases to date has tended to be on para.6 of Sched.2 to the DPA. In cases involving sensitive personal data it is possible that the condition in para.7(1)(b) of Sched.3 to the DPA will be met.[32]

- *The second data protection principle* – Personal data shall be obtained only for one or more specified and lawful purposes, and shall not be further processed in any manner incompatible with that purpose or those purposes.

  It is likely that this data protection principle may be contravened by disclosure of information to a member of the public, on the basis that information obtained for one purpose (e.g. medical treatment, social service functions, education or rating) will be disclosed to a stranger in a manner incompatible with that purpose. Paragraph 6 of Part II of Sched.1 to the DPA suggests that there may be a contravention of the second data protection principle where information is disclosed to a person who intends to use it for a purpose other than that for which the public authority obtained it.

- *The third data protection principle* – personal data shall be adequate, relevant and not excessive in relation to the purpose or purposes for which they are processed.

---

[31] See, for example, *Smith* v. *Information Commissioner and Devon and Cornwall Constabulary* (EA/2011/0006, 15 September 2011).

[32] For a contrary view see Coppel, *Information Rights*, 3rd edn (2010), pp.730–2. Coppel suggests that at least one of the conditions in Sched.3 will be met.

The disclosure of irrelevant or excessive personal data would contravene this principle. However, provided a public authority limits the disclosure to that which is relevant and necessary it will not contravene this principle.

- *The sixth data protection principle* – personal data shall be processed in accordance with the rights of data subjects under the DPA.

  This principle might be contravened if the data subject had served a notice on the public authority under s.10 of the DPA requiring it not to disclose personal data relating to him or her on the ground that such disclosure would be likely to cause the data subject or another person substantial damage or substantial distress which would be unwarranted.

- *The eighth data protection principle* – personal data shall not be transferred to a country or territory outside the EEA unless that country or territory ensures an adequate level of protection for the rights and freedoms of data subjects in relation to the processing of personal data.

  Although it has been suggested[33] that this principle is unlikely to have particular relevance to disclosure of information under the FOIA, it is not safe to assume this will be the case. In a press release issued on 1 January 2005 to coincide with the coming into force of the FOIA, the then Secretary of State for Constitutional Affairs, Lord Falconer, pointed out that 'anyone, of any nationality, and living anywhere in the world, will be able to make a written request for information'.[34] If a public authority receives a request for personal data from a country outside the EEA, there is no reason why a transfer of the data in question to that person will not be covered by this principle. The public authority must consider the matters listed in para.13 of Part II of Sched.1 to the DPA when deciding whether an adequate level of protection for the rights and freedoms of data subjects in relation to the processing of personal data exists in the country or territory from which the request was received and to which the data are to be transferred.

The second part of the first limb of the first condition (set out in s.40(3)(a)(ii)) confers a qualified exemption where the information falls within paras.(a)–(d) of the definition of data in s.1(1) of the DPA and the disclosure of the information to a member of the public would contravene s.10 of the DPA. Such a contravention could only occur where the data subject had served a notice in writing under s.10(1) of the DPA requiring the data controller to cease, or not to begin, processing of personal data in respect of which he or she is the data subject on the ground that the processing was causing or was likely to cause substantial damage or distress to the data subject or to another which was or would be unwarranted. It should be a simple matter for the public authority to check whether such a written notice has been received from the data subject.

---

[33] Coppel, *Information Rights* (2010), p.732.
[34] Department for Constitutional Affairs press release, 1 January 2005, para.25.

The second condition

The second condition, set out in s.40(4) of the FOIA, is that by virtue of any provision of Part IV of the DPA the information is exempt from s.7(1) of that Act. This confers a qualified exemption. When considering the provisions of Part IV of the DPA (which are summarised in **8.3.5**) it is important to bear in mind that information is exempt from s.7(1) where the relevant exemption refers:

(a) to Part II of the DPA (where s.7 appears); or
(b) to the subject information provisions (defined in s.27(2) of the DPA) (which includes s.7); or
(c) specifically to s.7.

The relevant exemptions are:

- s.28 – national security;
- s.29 – crime and taxation;
- s.30 – health, education and social work;
- s.31 – regulatory activity;
- s.32 – journalism, literature and art;
- s.33 – personal data processed for research purposes including historical or statistical purposes;
- s.33A – manual data held by public authorities;
- s.35A – parliamentary privilege;
- s.36 – domestic purposes; and
- s.37 – the following paragraphs of Sched.7:

   (1) confidential references given by the data controller;
   (2) information prejudicial to the combat effectiveness of the armed forces;
   (3) judicial appointments/appointments of Queen's Counsel/honours and dignities;
   (4) Crown employment and Crown or ministerial appointments;
   (5) management forecasts and management planning;
   (6) corporate finance;
   (7) negotiations with the data subject;
   (8) examination marks;
   (9) examination scripts;
   (10) legal professional privilege;
   (11) privilege against self-incrimination.

- s.38 – miscellaneous exemptions made by Order of the Secretary of State:

   – adoption records and reports;
   – statement of a child's special educational needs;
   – parental orders, records and reports.

A public authority, even if it acts in perfectly good faith in performing what it understands to be its obligations under the FOIA, may if it errs in its approach to the law, be held liable for infringing the art.8 (ECHR) rights of affected individuals (compare *R (Robertson)* v. *City of Wakefield Metropolitan Council* [2002] QB 1052 and *W* v. *Westminster City Council* [2005] EWHC 102 (QB)). It is therefore important for public authorities to adopt a methodical, structured approach to the operation of s.40.

Persons requesting information under the FOIA, and public authorities responding to such requests, may find it helpful to adopt the following step-by-step approach to the operation of s.40.

1. Consider first whether the information to which the request relates constitutes personal data as defined by s.1(1) of the DPA, in the light of the interpretation given to that definition by the House of Lords in *Common Services Agency* v. *Scottish Information Commissioner* [2008] UKHL 47. If the information requested does not constitute personal data, s.40 will not apply.

2. If the information to which the request relates constitutes personal data, consider whether the applicant is the data subject of the data for the purposes of s.1(1) of the DPA. If so, s.40(1) confers an absolute exemption, and there is no obligation on the public authority to confirm or deny or to communicate information. However, the public authority should, consistently with the principles of good public administration, process the request as a subject access request under s.7 of the DPA.

3. If the information to which the request relates constitutes personal data, but the applicant is not the data subject of the data, consider whether either the first part of the first limb of the first condition (set out in s.40(3)(a)(i)), or the second limb of the first condition (set out in s.40(3)(b)) applies to make the information exempt on the grounds that disclosure of the information to a member of the public otherwise than under the FOIA would contravene any of the data protection principles.

4. If that is not the case, consider whether the second part of the first limb of the first condition (set out in s.40(3)(a)(ii)) applies on the grounds that disclosure of the information to a member of the public otherwise than under the FOIA would contravene s.10 of the DPA. If so, consider the usual public interest test required in the case of a qualified exemption.

5. If neither of the limbs of the first condition is satisfied, move on to consider whether the second condition (set out in s.40(4)) is satisfied on the grounds that the information in question is exempt from s.7(1) of the DPA by any provision of Part IV of that Act. If so, a qualified exemption is conferred and again the usual public interest balancing exercise must be conducted.

8.5 SIGNIFICANT RECENT DECISIONS OF THE COURTS AND INFORMATION RIGHTS TRIBUNAL

In a work of this nature it is not possible to provide a detailed digest of all of the decisions which consider s.40, but certain themes emerging from the cases can be identified.

Readers wishing to keep fully up to date with decisions of the Information Commissioner are referred to the regular periodical *Freedom of Information* (**www.foij.com**).

Decisions of the courts

In terms of the general approach to s.40, the House of Lords held in *Common Services Agency* v. *Scottish Information Commissioner* [2008] UKHL 47 that while the FOIA should be construed in as liberal a manner as possible since its whole purpose is the release of information, the courts should not apply this proposition too widely and ignore the way the FOIA is intended to interact with the DPA (as per Lord Hope of Craighead at [4]).[35] In particular, the courts must give special consideration to the release of personal information relating to individuals.

The House of Lords held that the conditions contained in s.40 of the FOIA,

> require careful treatment in the context of a request for information under [the Freedom of Information (Scotland) Act] 2002. It must be borne in mind that they were not designed to facilitate the release of information. They were designed for ... the protection of personal data from processing in a way that might prejudice the rights and freedoms or legitimate interests of the data subject.[36]

Many of the decisions on s.40 have involved requests for information relating to employees of public authorities. The Information Rights Tribunal has consistently held that the interests of data subjects are not paramount where the data in question relate to their public lives. The Information Rights Tribunal has at times declined to disclose the names of public employees. For example, in *McGonagle* v. *Information Commissioner and Ministry of Defence* (EA/2011/0104, 4 November 2011), the Information Rights Tribunal declined to disclose the names of former employees who had had responsibility for matters relating to unidentified flying objects. However, the disclosure of the names of senior civil servants will generally be fair (*Dun* v. *Information Commissioner and National Audit Office* (EA/2010/0060, 18 January 2011)). Similarly, in the MPs' expenses case, the Divisional Court dismissed an appeal against the disclosure of the private addresses of the MPs, finding that there was a legitimate public interest well capable of such justification.[37]

---

[35] That case concerned the interpretation of the Freedom of Information (Scotland) Act 2002.

[36] At [28].

[37] *Corporate Officer of the House of Commons* v. *Information Commissioner and Others* [2008] EWHC 1084 (Admin), at [42].

Generally compromise agreements or information relating to out-of-court settlements with former public employees are not disclosable; however, the issue is fact specific. In *Gibson* v. *Information Commissioner and Craven District Council* (EA/2010/0095, 22 February 2011), the Information Rights Tribunal ordered the disclosure of a compromise agreement with a very senior employee. Further, in *Sikka* v. *Information Commissioner and Commissioners of Her Majesty's Treasury* (EA/2010/0054, 11 July 2011) the Information Rights Tribunal held that the names of senior employees involved in the BCCI collapse should be disclosed. The Tribunal placed importance on the criticism of BCCI employees voiced in the Sandstorm Report, and the importance of employee competence and honesty to future employers in the banking sector. However in *Beckles* v. *Information Commissioner* (EA/2011/0073 and EA/2011/0074, 7 September 2011), the Information Rights Tribunal held that Cambridge University did not have to disclose information relating to out-of-court settlements entered into with four former employees, because it was readily foreseeable that those individuals would be identified.

In *Greenwood and Bolton Metropolitan Borough Council* v. *Information Commissioner* (EA/2011/0131 and EA/2011/0137, 17 February 2012), the Information Rights Tribunal considered a request for information contained in a register of interests completed by senior employees employed by Bolton Metropolitan Borough Council. The Information Rights Tribunal decided that the names, departments, sections and job titles of all employees who had made entries on the register should be disclosed, as well as details of their other professional commitments.

Finally, in a recent case, the Information Rights Tribunal held that information relating to a local authority's recruitment of a new chief executive officer which related to all applicants for that role was exempt from disclosure because it would break the first data protection principle. The Tribunal held that the fact that individuals had applied for a position with the authority did not amount to the discharge of public functions by those individual applicants. However, the Tribunal held that the authority had been wrong not to disclose information which did not amount to personal data such as a blank version of the application form (*Bolton* v. *Information Commissioner and East Riding Yorkshire Council* (EA/2011/0216, 26 March 2012)).

8.6 CONCLUSION

Both the DPA and the FOIA have at their core a right of access to information. In the case of personal biographical information liable to impact on an individual's right of privacy, the individual to whom the information relates has a right of access under the DPA but not under the FOIA. If other individuals or legal persons seek access to information relating to another living individual they must do so under the FOIA, and their right of access to such information is subject to a large number of exemptions which s.40 of the FOIA incorporates by reference from the DPA. In this way, the two Acts seek to balance respect for a living individual's autonomy and dignity by giving access to and control over personal data, against the public interest in the free flow of information held by public authorities with a view to promoting greater participation in the democratic process and transparency of public decision making. The balancing mechanism is complex and a methodical, step-by-step approach to s.40 will be required in practice if the mechanism is to operate in the manner intended by Parliament. The decisions discussed above provide practical guidance on the application of the s.40 exemption.

CHAPTER 9

The Environmental Information Regulations 2004

Nusrat Zar and Anna Condliffe, Herbert Smith LLP

9.1 INTRODUCTION

Although the main focus of this book is the right of access to information provided by the Freedom of Information Act 2000 (FOIA), it is important for readers to note that where the information requested by an applicant is 'environmental information' the provisions of the FOIA do not apply. Instead there exists a parallel legal regime of access to information under the Environmental Information Regulations 2004, SI 2004/3391 (EIR). As will become apparent in this chapter, the access regime under the EIR differs in significant ways from that contained in the FOIA.

The EIR came into operation on 1 January 2005, implementing EU Council Directive 2003/4/EC on public access to environmental information. They supersede earlier regulations dating from 1992 (SI 1992/3240, subsequently amended by SI 1998/1447), themselves implementing an earlier EU measure (Council Directive 90/313/EEC on freedom of access to information on the environment).

The purposes of this chapter are to describe the main features of the EIR, and to draw attention to the more important differences between rights of access to environmental information and the rights of access under the FOIA to other kinds of information.

9.2 WHY A SEPARATE AND DIFFERENT REGIME?

In relation to rights of access to environmental information, the UK is subject to particular obligations under international law – namely, the 1998 UNECE Convention on Access to Information, Public Participation in Decision-making and Access to Justice in Environmental Matters (Aarhus Convention),[1] and also under EU law – Council Directive 2003/4/EC on public access to environmental information.

---

[1] Ratified by the UK in February 2005. For the text, see **www.unece.org/env/pp/treatytext.html**.

Rather than draft the FOIA so that access to all information would be governed by rules equivalent to the Aarhus Convention/EU rules which only apply to environmental information, the approach adopted by the government was to create two separate legal regimes.

9.2.1 Mutual exclusivity of the two regimes

In any case where a request for information involves or includes a request for environmental information, the rules set out in the EIR will apply. In so far as the requested information may also include information which is not environmental information, the provisions within the FOIA will apply to that other information (this is the practical effect of s.39 of the FOIA, as modified by reg.20 of the EIR).

9.2.2 How do the two regimes compare?

As the discussion which follows will demonstrate, there are many differences between the two regimes. Some provisions within the respective regimes which may seem broadly similar differ quite significantly in terms of detail; and on certain matters the rules differ starkly in content.[2] It should never be assumed that the answer to any particular question will be the same under each of the two regimes.[3]

It may be useful here to flag two of the key differences:

- The EIR are broader in scope, in that they apply to a larger range of bodies than FOIA as a result of the broad definition of 'public authority' in reg.2 (discussed further at **9.2.5**).

- The exemptions to the duty to disclose (called 'exceptions' under the EIR) are broadly similar within the two regimes but are by no means identical. It is essential to look closely at the detailed formulation of each exemption/exception within each regime. In general, however, it may be said that exceptions are more narrowly drawn under the EIR than are the exemptions under the FOIA (but not always: see reg.12(4)(e) protecting internal communications where the exception under the EIR appears on its face to be broader than any equivalent under the FOIA).[4]

---

[2]   Compare, for example, FOIA, s.44 with EIR, reg.5(6) (contrary approaches to effect of statutory prohibitions on disclosure). Note also that there is no specific provision in the EIR permitting non-disclosure on grounds of the cost of compliance; compare with FOIA, s.12.

[3]   In a case where the public authority or the Information Commissioner may have proceeded on a wrong conclusion as to whether information is or is not 'environmental information', no appeal will succeed if the same conclusion would have followed had the correct categorisation of the information been made. See *Robinson* v. *Information Commissioner and East Ridings Yorkshire Council* (EA/2007/0012, 9 October 2007).

[4]   The nearest equivalent in the FOIA to the exception in reg.12(4)(e) of the EIR relating to internal communications is the exemption in s.35, which applies where disclosure would inhibit the free and frank exchange of views or provision of advice, or would otherwise prejudice the effective conduct of public affairs.

At the same time as stressing significant differences between the FOIA and the EIR it should be noted that some attempt has been made to 'marry up' the procedural and enforcement aspects of the two regimes. So, for example, time periods for disclosure are broadly the same, and jurisdiction in relation to disputes has been conferred in relation to both regimes upon the Information Commissioner and the First-tier and Upper Tribunals.

9.2.3   Breadth of the definition of 'environmental information'

The key concept of environmental information is a broad one. It extends well beyond what might in common parlance be thought to fall within that phrase, as has been evident from the number of cases in which public authorities have dealt with information requests under the wrong legal regime. The breadth of the concept of environmental information can best be demonstrated by setting out the definition within the EIR. Regulation 2(1) provides that 'environmental information' means:

> . . . any information in written, visual, aural, electronic or any other material form on –
>
> (a)   the state of the elements of the environment, such as air and atmosphere, water, soil, land,[5] landscape and natural sites including wetlands, coastal and marine areas, biological diversity and its components, including genetically modified organisms, and the interaction among these elements;
>
> (b)   factors, such as substances, energy, noise, radiation or waste, including radioactive waste, emissions, discharges and other releases into the environment, affecting or likely to affect the elements of the environment referred to in (a);[6]
>
> (c)   measures (including administrative measures), such as policies, legislation, plans, programmes, environmental agreements, and activities affecting or likely to affect the elements and factors referred to in (a) and (b) as well as measures or activities designed to protect those elements;
>
> (d)   reports on the implementation of environmental legislation;
>
> (e)   cost-benefit and other economic analyses and assumptions used within the framework of the measures and activities referred to in (c); and
>
> (f)   the state of human health and safety, including the contamination of the food chain, where relevant, conditions of human life, cultural sites and built structures inasmuch as they are or may be affected by the state of the elements of the environment referred to in (a) or, through those elements, by any of the matters referred to in (b) and (c).

This definition of environmental information is identical to that in art.2(1) of Directive 2003/4/EC, which itself is drawn closely from the definition contained within the Aarhus Convention (see art.2(3)). Recital 10 to the Directive provides:

---

[5]   For a broad construction of the notion of information relating to the state of land, see *R* v. *British Coal Corporation, ex p. Ibstock Building Products Ltd* [1995] Env LR 277, decided under the Environmental Information Regulations 1992.

[6]   Note that where information covered by para.(b) is made available, the public authority is required, upon request, in so far as it is possible so to do, to refer the applicant to where information can be found on the measurement procedures used in compiling that information: see reg.5(5).

> The definition of environmental information should be clarified so as to encompass information in any form on the state of the environment, on factors, measures or activities affecting or likely to affect the environment or designed to protect it, on cost-benefit and economic analyses used within the framework of such measures or activities and also information on the state of human health and safety, including the contamination of the food chain, conditions of human life, cultural sites and built structures in as much as they are, or may be, affected by any of those matters.

The ambit of this definition is significant. As indicated above, if information is environmental information it may be requested of a broader range of bodies than other information; and if information is environmental information it may be that exemptions which would apply to other kinds of information (so as to protect from disclosure) will not apply.

The broad interpretation to be given to the meaning of environmental information can be illustrated by reference to examples from the case law.

- Information about a proposal to introduce tolling on a new bridge over the River Mersey. There was no dispute that the construction of the bridge would have a significant environmental impact and the disputed information therefore related to a 'measure' which would affect elements of the environment (reg.2(1)(c)). This included information about tolling since this was an integral part of the project and its viability (*Mersey Tunnel Users Association* v. *Information Commissioner and Halton Borough Council* (EA/2009/0001, 24 June 2009)).

- Information in minutes of meetings between the Department for Business, Enterprise and Regulatory Reform and the Confederation of British Industry covering energy policy and climate change (*Department for Business, Enterprise and Regulatory Reform* v. *Information Commissioner and Friends of the Earth* (EA/2007/0072, 29 April 2008)).

- Information held by Ofcom on the location, ownership and technical attributes of mobile phone cellular base stations. The Tribunal found that the information sought fell within reg.2(1) as being information on energy, radiation or emissions affecting or likely to affect the air or atmosphere (see *Office of Communications* v. *Information Commissioner and T-Mobile (UK) Ltd* (EA/2006/0078, 4 September 2007) at paras.21–29). Further, the Tribunal held that the names of base station operators should be regarded as 'environmental information', as it would be artificial to hold that whereas information about, for example, radiation was environmental information the identity of its producer was not (see para.31).[7]

- Legal advice relating to the enforceability of a s.106 planning agreement and other planning matters, in the context of proposed night-time flights at Kent

---

[7] This decision has been appealed up to the Supreme Court (and considered on a reference to the Court of Justice of the European Union) on other points of law (see [2010] UKSC 3 on appeal from [2009] EWCA Civ 90 and [2008] EWHC 1445 (Admin)) but the discussion regarding 'environmental information' in the Information Tribunal decision is still of interest.

International Airport (*Kirkaldie* v. *Information Commissioner and Thanet District Council* (EA/2006/0001, 4 July 2006).

- Information relating to an equality impact assessment carried out by a local authority in relation to its policy on the disposal of land. This included the names of the individuals responsible for the drafting of the document. The information fell within reg.2(1)(c) because policy on the disposal of land was a 'measure likely to affect the land and landscape' (*Omagh District Council* v. *Information Commissioner* (EA/2010/0163, 20 May 2011)).

- Names and addresses of a local authority's commercial clients which had their waste collected from the street in sacks. The Information Commissioner found that waste disposal is a measure having a direct impact on the environment and information identifying the clients was information 'about' that measure (*Camden Council* (FS50255077, 19 April 2010)).

- Information relating to sales figures for silica sand extracted from a quarry – the sales figures reflected the amount of sand extracted, and the amount of sand extracted affected the land from which it was taken (*Staffordshire County Council and Sibelco (UK) Ltd* v. *Information Commissioner* (EA/2010/0015, 22 November 2010)).

- Information about achievement and management reviews of progress reports of the units carrying out compulsory purchases in relation to the Crossrail project – Crossrail was a 'major civil engineering project' with a major impact on the environment and the information therefore related to a 'measure' likely to affect the environment (*Transport for London* (FS50298330, 23 February 2011)).

What happens where a request is made which covers documents containing a mixture of environmental and other information? This was the situation considered by the tribunal in *Department for Business, Enterprise and Regulatory Reform* v. *Information Commissioner and Friends of the Earth* (see above). In that case, the requested information covered minutes of meetings at which a range of issues were discussed, including some which were environmental. The Tribunal considered whether the disputed information should be considered on a document by document basis to decide which regime applied (paras.28–32). It noted that although this would be a convenient approach, it did not reflect that the definition under the EIR covers 'information' rather than 'documents'. It found that where a document divides easily into parts containing environmental and non-environmental information, it should be considered in parts. Where this is not the case, it is necessary to decide whether the predominant purpose of the document covers environmental information – if it does, then the whole document may be considered under the EIR. Where there is no single predominant purpose then the public authority will have no choice but to review the contents of the document in detail.[8]

---

[8] See also *Milford Haven Port Authority* (FER0072936, 28 March 2007) in which the Information Commissioner analysed two risk assessments in relation to proposed liquid natural gas terminals at

In the First-tier Tribunal decision of *Nottinghamshire County Council* v. *Information Commissioner, Veolia ES Nottinghamshire Ltd and UK Coal Mining Ltd* (EA/2010/0142, 29 December 2010) the disputed information included financial information contained in parts of a PFI contract under which the council was to outsource certain waste management services to Veolia. The Tribunal held that there was within the thousands of pages of contractual documentation core financial information which had no bearing on the environment. It was particular to the specific contract in question in terms of pricing and other factors and it could be adjusted over a broad commercial range of negotiation without having any effect on environmental issues. This brought that information firmly within the FOIA regime and outside the EIR.[9]

9.2.4 Bodies subject to obligations under the EIR: the EU legislative background

The definition of 'public authority' under the EIR is based closely on the wording of Directive 2003/4/EC (see art.2(2)), which in turn reflects the definition contained in the Aarhus Convention (see art.2(2)).

Whereas the FOIA has adopted an approach of listing by name the bodies to which the Act's obligations apply, the approach as regards environmental information has been to describe entities not by name but by reference to certain characteristics set out in a definition.

Although there is no doubt that the concept of 'public authority' is significantly broader under the EIR than under the FOIA, there has been, and remains, some uncertainty as regards just how broadly the definition within the EIR should be interpreted.

Early differences of view as to the breadth of the concept of 'public authority' under the EIR can be explained, at least in part, by examination of the legislative history of the EU Directive which those regulations are intended to implement.

In summary, the legislative history shows that within the European Commission's initial Proposal for the Directive the definition of 'public authority' was substantially broader in scope than that which emerged in the final text of the adopted Directive.

In the initial Proposal the definition suggested was:

Public authority shall mean:

(a)   government or other public administration at national, regional or local level;

(b)   any legal or natural person having public responsibilities or functions, or providing public services, relating directly or indirectly to the environment under the control of a body or person falling within (a);

Milford Haven, and concluded that they comprised 'environmental information' even though some of the content was not environmental.

[9] On appeal to the Upper Tribunal (see *UK Coal Mining Ltd* v. *Information Commissioner and Others* [2012] UKUT 212 (AAC)) this point was not in issue, the focus being on which information in the contracts fell within the scope of s.43(2) of the FOIA.

(c) any legal person entrusted by law, or under arrangements with a body or person falling within (a) or (b), with the operation of services of general economic interest which affect or are likely to affect the state of elements of the environment.

This Proposal was acknowledged by the Commission to go further than was necessary in order to meet Aarhus Convention requirements. In particular, the Proposal's reference to bodies entrusted 'with the operation of services of general economic interest which affect or are likely to affect the state of elements of the environment' would have produced a Directive which would have been clearly applicable to public utility services generally, across the fields of water, waste, electricity, nuclear power and so on.

When the matter came before the European Parliament's lead Committee on this Directive (its Environment Committee) an amendment to the definition of 'public authority' was immediately proposed with a view to aligning the wording of the Directive more closely with that of the Aarhus Convention. At first reading, the European Parliament adopted this proposed amendment.

At this point the Commission produced an amended Proposal (June 2001) in which it accepted the Parliament's approach that the Directive should adopt the same definition of 'public authority' as contained in the Aarhus Convention. In particular the definition in the amended Proposal no longer referred to bodies whose functions were likely to 'affect' the environment. Rather, the definition was now couched in significantly narrower terms: in terms, that is, of bodies having public responsibilities or functions 'in relation to the environment'.

The definition contained in that amended Commission Proposal was to all intents and purposes the same as that which was adopted in the final Directive.

Given the significant changes which occurred to the definition of 'public authority' during this EU legislative process it is important to be wary of early statements about what the Directive was intended to achieve, since these may better reflect the Commission's original intentions than its intentions when putting forward the amended Proposal.

With these remarks in mind we can turn to the definition of 'public authority' within the EIR.

9.2.5 Meaning of 'public authority' within the EIR

Regulation 2(2) of the EIR defines 'public authority' to mean:

(a) government departments;
(b) certain other public authorities as defined in s.3(1) of the FOIA (with some exceptions);
(c) any other bodies or other persons which carry out functions of public administration; and
(d) any other bodies or other persons which are under the control of a person falling within (a), (b) or (c) above, and:

    (i) have public responsibilities relating to the environment;

> (ii) exercise functions of a public nature relating to the environment; or
>
> (iii) provide public services relating to the environment.

Public authorities within categories (a) and (b)

Categories (a) and (b) seem reasonably self-explanatory.

Public authorities within category (c)

Category (c) serves to bring squarely within the scope of the EIR a variety of entities which perform what may legitimately be regarded as functions of public administration notwithstanding that they may be organisationally independent of governmental entities falling within (a) or (b). This would seem to cover those branches of government which have over past decades been hived off to executive agencies. Note, moreover, that the functions of public administration performed by these bodies need not be functions which are in any respect environmental.

That a body can only fall within category (c) if it performs *administrative* functions was emphasised by the Information Tribunal in *Network Rail Ltd* v. *Information Commissioner* (EA/2006/0061 and EA/2006/0062, 17 July 2007). It was not sufficient for a body to be a 'public body'[10] or to 'perform functions of a public nature', or to 'perform public functions' (formulae relevant in other contexts, such as having obligations under the Human Rights Act 1998 or being amenable to judicial review under the Civil Procedure Rules 1998 (CPR) rule 54.1).

The Tribunal looked closely at the functions of Network Rail Ltd and concluded that:

> even if [Network Rail Ltd] is a body which carries out public functions, it is not a body which carries out public administrative functions. (para.27)

In so concluding, the Tribunal was influenced by statements made by Blackburne J in *Griffin* v. *South West Water Services Ltd* [1995] IRLR 15:

> [South West Water] is no more an 'administrative body' because it 'administers' a service (the supply of water and sewerage services) than is a company carrying on a business, manufacturing and distributing sweets because such a company 'administers' that enterprise . . . [South West Water's] primary function, as a supplier of water and provider of sewerage services, is to be contrasted with administrative functions such as town planning, court administration, and any of the myriad functions of the civil service. (para.123, quoted in *Network Rail Ltd* at para.26)

Referring to Network Rail Ltd, the Tribunal commented that it:

---

[10] Indeed, the Information Tribunal concluded later in its decision that applying the tests laid down in cases such as *Parochial Church Council for the Parish of Aston Cantlow and Wilmecote and Billesley* v. *Wallbank* [2004] 1 AC 546 and *YL* v. *Birmingham City Council* [2007] UKHL 27, Network Rail should not be regarded as a 'public body' (see para.48).

runs a railway system, just as [South West Water] ran a water supply and sewerage service. It does not administer anything, save in the sense that it runs its own business. It is not a regulator; that is the role of the [Office of Rail Regulation]. Unlike its predecessor, it does not set rail safety standards. (para.28)[11]

Smartsource Drainage & Water Reports Ltd v. *Information Commissioner and A Group of 19 Water Companies* (GI/2458/2010, 23 November 2010); [2010] UKUT 415 (AAC) is another significant decision relating to the definition of 'public authority'. In considering whether water and sewerage companies carried out 'functions of public administration' so as to bring them within part (c) of the definition, the Upper Tribunal acknowledged that they were not 'ordinary' companies, in that they had certain residual statutory regulatory functions, were subject to a comprehensive statutory regime and were obliged to provide a universal service. However, it found that these features were ancillary to their primary commercial purpose of supplying water and/or sewerage services to the public for profit. That commercial activity did not become a 'function of public administration' just because there was an obvious and significant public interest in securing a clean water supply and safe sewerage system. The companies were therefore not 'public authorities' within reg.2(2)(c). Interestingly, the Upper Tribunal approved the Information Tribunal's decision in *Network Rail Ltd* but doubted the relevance of the *Griffin* case in the context of the EIR.

See also the Information Tribunal decision in *Bruton* v. *Information Commissioner and Duchy of Cornwall* (EA/2010/0182, 3 November 2011).[12] In that case, the Tribunal followed the approach adopted in *Smartsource* and considered a number of factors. It concluded that, taking particular account of the Duchy's status and obligations as a statutory harbour authority, the preponderance of factors pointed to the fact that it was performing functions of public administration and was therefore subject to the EIR. Its role as a statutory harbour authority was independent and unrelated to its property management business and could not be said to be 'ancillary' to that primary function. It was noted that in *Smartsource* the Upper Tribunal had also found that a body cannot be a 'hybrid' public authority for the purposes of the EIR, meaning that it cannot be a public authority in respect of some of its functions but not others. It therefore followed that because the functions performed by the Duchy in its capacity as statutory harbour authority were 'functions of public administration' this was sufficient to bring information relating to all of its functions within the scope of reg.2(2)(c).

---

[11] See also *Port of London Authority* v. *Information Commissioner and Hibbert* (EA/2006/0083, 31 May 2007) in which the Information Tribunal concluded that the Port of London Authority (PLA) was, in contrast to Network Rail, a body performing functions of 'public administration'. In forming that view the tribunal focused, among other things, on the nature of the statutory duties imposed on the PLA, and the powers conferred on the PLA to regulate others.
[12] Permission to appeal the decision in *Bruton* to the Upper Tribunal had been granted at the time of writing.

Public authorities within category (d)

Category (d) is more controversial. It brings within the scope of the EIR a variety of entities which are not government bodies and which do not perform functions of public administration.

The aim of category (d) appears to be to ensure that private law entities which perform certain functions that at one time may have been regarded as functions of the state shall not, simply as a consequence of the privatisation of that function, fall outside the scope of the EIR.

It is important to note, however, that category (d) does not purport to bring all privatised industries within the scope of the EIR. For an entity to fall within category (d) it must satisfy both of the following conditions:

- it must be *under the control of* a body which is a public authority within one of categories (a), (b) or (c); *and*
- it must have public responsibilities relating to the environment, or exercise functions of a public nature relating to the environment, or provide services relating to the environment.

Unfortunately, none of the above phrases is defined in the EIR, the Aarhus Convention or the EU Directive. It would appear to be the intention of the Convention, the Directive and the EIR that companies exercising what are essentially environmental functions shall be subject to the duties of disclosure of environmental information in cases where those companies have been afforded only a very limited degree of operational freedom from governmental control.

In contrast, companies which do not perform environmental functions, or which do perform such functions but do so with some substantial operational freedom from governmental prescription, would seem not to fall within the EIR.

In interpreting the key phrases it would seem probable that the mere fact that a company's activities have significant impacts on the environment should not be regarded as the same as the company having responsibilities in relation to the environment, providing services in relation to the environment or having public functions in relation to the environment.[13]

Further, the concept of 'under the control of' a governmental body would seem to suggest something rather more than merely that a company operates in a field of activity which is, in the general public interest, closely regulated by government. It would seem to import the notion of government having some rather substantial degree of managerial control over the running of the company.[14]

---

[13] The *Environmental Information Regulations 2004 Detailed Guidance* (Defra, revised July 2010) states that: 'Examples of bodies that may be covered by EIR limb (d) are private companies or Public Private Partnerships with obvious environmental functions such as waste disposal, water, energy, transport regulators. Public utilities, for example, are involved in the supply of essential public services such as water, sewerage, electricity and gas and may fall within the scope of the EIRs' (para.2.22). Note, however, that this guidance predates the Upper Tribunal decision in *Smartsource*.
[14] Paragraphs 2.19–2.20 of the *Environmental Information Regulations 2004 Detailed Guidance* (Defra, revised July 2010) suggest: 'control could mean a relationship constituted by statute,

The scope of limb (d) of the definition of 'public authority' was considered by the Upper Tribunal in the *Smartsource* case (see above) in the context of water and sewerage companies. It found that there was an important distinction to be made between 'regulation' and 'control' – the latter connoting a greater degree of influence than the former. It was accepted that the water companies were subject to a detailed regulatory regime. However, it was important to have proper regard to the free market principles underpinning that regime. The companies enjoyed a high level of commercial freedom and independence from 'decisive' regulatory interference, such that they were not to be considered to be under the control of any licensing or regulatory body. It will clearly be necessary for companies to consider, limb by limb, whether they fall within the scope of the definition of public authority within the EIR. Where there is room for argument a company may well opt to withhold information requested, putting the onus on the applicant to refer the matter to the Information Commissioner for resolution, with further recourse later perhaps to the tribunals and ultimately the courts.

For the moment the message should be that:

- the notion of public authority under the EIR is clearly broader than the equivalent concept under the FOIA;
- the concept certainly extends to a range of companies which might be surprised to find themselves so described;
- the concept does not extend as broadly as intended initially by the European Commission;
- each case should be taken on its merits, looking to see how far the characteristics of the company in question match the key statutory tests described above.

9.2.6 Regulations not applicable to public authorities exercising certain functions

The rights of access and the public authority obligations summarised below are expressly stated not to apply in relation to any public authority to the extent that that authority is acting in a judicial or a legislative capacity (reg.3(3)).

9.2.7 The Houses of Parliament

The EIR do not apply to either House of Parliament to the extent that this is required to avoid an infringement of the privileges of either House (reg.3(4)).

---

regulations, rights, license, contracts or other means which either separately or jointly confer the possibility of directly or indirectly exercising a decisive influence on a body. Control may relate, not only to the body, but also to control of the services provided by the body. It is important to note that the level of control needs to be sufficient to exert a decisive influence on the body – the simple existence of a contract with a public authority does not necessarily provide this control ... Each case will need to be considered on its merits and a range of factors would need to be taken into account.'

9.2.8   General duty to disseminate information

In addition to duties to respond to particular requests for environmental information, public authorities to which the EIR apply are under a general duty progressively to make the environmental information which they hold available to the public by electronic means which are easily accessible. Further, each public authority must take steps to organise the environmental information relevant to its functions with a view to active and systematic dissemination to the public of that information (reg.4(1)(a) and (b)). (By virtue of reg.4(2) the use of electronic means to make information available or to organise information is not required in relation to information collected before 1 January 2005 in non-electronic form.) This obligation does not, however, extend to any information covered by the exceptions to the duty to disclose information, as set out in reg.12 (reg.4(3)).

For the purposes of this and other provisions of the EIR, under reg.3(2) environmental information is held by a public authority if the information:

(a)   is in the authority's possession and has been produced or received by the authority; or

(b)   is held by another person on behalf of the authority.

The *Environmental Information Regulations 2004 Detailed Guidance* (Defra, updated July 2010) suggests that:

> Any information in the 'possession' of the public authority or which is stored elsewhere and is held by a natural or legal person on behalf of a public authority is 'held' by it. (para.3.10)

In *Doncaster Metropolitan Borough Council* (FS50102786, 21 November 2007) it was held that information about aircraft noise at Robin Hood Airport which was available to a local authority as a matter of contractual right from a third party computer and was accessible via a telephone line was information 'in the authority's possession' within reg.3(2)(a).

Under reg.4(4)(a), the information which is required by the EIR to be disseminated must include at least the information referred to in art.7(2) of Directive 2003/4/EC, which includes:

(i)   texts of international treaties, conventions or agreements, and of Community, national, regional or local legislation on the environment or relating to it;

(ii)   policies, plans and programmes relating to the environment;

(iii)   progress reports on the implementation of the items referred to in (i) and (ii) above when prepared in electronic form by public authorities;

(iv)   national (and where appropriate, regional and local) reports on the state of the environment published at regular intervals not exceeding four years – such reports to include information on the quality of, and pressures on, the environment;

(v)   data or summaries of data derived from the monitoring of activities affecting, or likely to affect, the environment;

(vi) authorisations with a significant impact on the environment and environmental agreements (or a reference to the places where such information can be requested or found);

(vii) environmental impact studies and risk assessments concerning the environmental elements referred to within the definition of 'environmental information'.[15]

Under reg.4(4)(b) public authorities must also disseminate 'facts and analyses of facts which the public authority considers relevant and important in framing major environmental policy proposals'.

9.2.9 The general duty to make environmental information available on request

Regulation 5 imposes a general duty that public authorities should upon request make available to an applicant environmental information which it holds (or which is held by another on its behalf) (reg.5(1)). The duty does not apply where the environmental information is 'personal data of which the applicant is the data subject' (reg.5(3)). There is no requirement that the request should be in writing, and certainly the request does not need to be a request explicitly for access under one or other of the statutory access regimes. No obligations apply in relation to information no longer held by the public authority or by any person on its behalf, save in the case where the public authority has passed the information over to a different public authority (see **9.2.12**). Where information was not held by the public authority at the time of the request but is acquired by the authority prior to its decision regarding disclosure, the Information Commissioner will regard it as good practice for the public authority to regard that information as disclosable (subject to the operation of an exception).

Under the EIR the general duty to make environmental information available on request applies notwithstanding any enactment or rule of law that would prevent the disclosure of information in accordance with the EIR (reg.5(6)). This rule, it should be noted, is directly the opposite of the principle found in the FOIA. Section 44 of the FOIA provides an absolute exemption from disclosure for information that is prohibited from being disclosed by another Act or Community obligation.

Requests for environmental information may be made by any person (the applicant is not required to demonstrate any particular interest in the matter), and unless one of the exceptions described below applies, public authorities are required to make requested information available as soon as possible, and no later than 20 working days after receipt of a request. This 20-day period may, however, be extended by the public authority to 40 working days in cases where this is reasonably believed by the public authority to be necessary in the light of the complexity and volume of the information requested. The necessity in question

---

[15] Note that art.7(2) of Directive 2003/4/EC also requires that such information 'shall be updated as appropriate'. This requirement does not expressly appear within the EIR.

may here relate either to the business of actually providing the information requested within the 20-day period, or to the difficulty within that period of making a decision that the information should not be disclosed (reg.7(1)). Any decision to extend the 20-day period must be taken by the public authority and notified to the applicant within that 20-day period (reg.7(3)).

Prima facie the public authority must make the information available in such form or format as the applicant requests. However, this presumption is displaced where it is reasonable for the public authority to make the information available in some other form or format or the information is already publicly available and accessible to the applicant in another format (reg.6(1)).

There is also a potentially far-reaching obligation under the EIR that the information 'shall be up to date, accurate and comparable, so far as the public authority reasonably believes' (reg.5(4)). It is presently unclear how proactive public bodies must be to ensure on an ongoing basis that information in their possession meets these requirements. For example, what are the obligations imposed on a public authority where the authority is aware that its latest information is out of date or inaccurate? Is it sufficient merely to make these shortcomings clear, or is there an obligation to correct the shortcoming by updating or securing more accurate information? If the information is not made available in the form or format requested, the public authority must explain (in writing if requested) the reason for this as soon as possible and no later than 20 days from the receipt of the request for the information, and inform the applicant of his or her rights to make representations under reg.11 and to take advantage of applicable appeal and enforcement mechanisms (see reg.6(2)).

9.2.10 Charging

Charging is dealt with in reg.8. In relation to charging for the provision of information, a distinction is drawn in the EIR between recoupment by a public authority of the costs it incurs in providing the information requested by an applicant, and recoupment of costs incurred merely in affording on-site access to that information.

A public authority may not make any charge for allowing an applicant access to any public registers of environmental information which it holds, nor may it make any charge in relation to the examination of requested information at the place which the public authority makes available for that examination (reg.8(2)). In *Kirklees Council* v. *Information Commissioner and PALI Ltd* (GI/258/2011, 10 March 2011); [2011] UKUT 104 (AAC), the Upper Tribunal considered the application of reg.8(2) to a request from a company engaged in the business of obtaining information from local authorities to complete local search enquiries (on standard form Con29) in connection with conveyancing. The company requested the local authority to make available for inspection any information which it would need to complete the form. The information was held on various registers by the local authority, and the company therefore claimed that it was entitled to inspect it free of charge under reg.8(2). The Upper Tribunal agreed.

However, outside the two situations referred to in reg.8(2), a public authority may charge the applicant for making the requested information available (reg.8(1)). (It seems clear that no charge may be made in relation to refusals of information.) It was not initially clear whether the expression 'making the information available' related only to the cost of copying and transmitting retrieved information to the applicant, or whether it also embraces the cost of retrieving that information internally. The matter seemed finely balanced as a matter of interpretation. However, in *Markinson* v. *Information Commissioner* (EA/2005/0014, 28 March 2006) the Information Tribunal made clear that the costs of locating and retrieving information were not relevant to a public authority's assessment of its charge for making that information available once located and retrieved (see para.33(c)). This approach is reflected in the guidance *Charging for Environmental Information Under the Environmental Information Regulations 2004* (Defra, July 2010).

The charge imposed by a public authority must not exceed an amount which the public authority is satisfied is a reasonable amount (reg.8(3)).[16] The concept of reasonableness of charge is not further defined. In *Commission of the European Communities* v. *Federal Republic of Germany* (Case C–217/97, 28 January 1999) the European Court of Justice took the view, in relation to the reasonable charge for supplying information criteria of the earlier EU Directive (Directive 90/313/EEC), that charges set at a level which would serve to deter persons from seeking access to information would frustrate the main aims of the Directive, and so would not qualify as reasonable.

This is of particular significance in the light of the fact that, unlike under the FOIA, there is no specific provision under the EIR permitting a public authority to refuse to disclose information because of the disproportionate expense likely to be involved. (Under the FOIA an exception exists where the cost of complying with a request will exceed the 'appropriate limit' (currently £600 for central government and £450 for local government) within the meaning of the Freedom of Information and Data Protection (Appropriate Limit and Fees) Regulations 2004, SI 2004/3244 made under ss.9, 12 and 13.) In certain circumstances a request involving a public authority in very substantial expense may fall within the 'manifestly unreasonable' exception (see further **9.2.15**). However, there may be circumstances where the public interest in the matter being disclosed is sufficiently great to render the request not manifestly unreasonable, despite the fact that disclosure may be at substantial public expense.

---

[16] The wording of recital 18 to Directive 2003/4/EC may be instructive in interpreting notions of reasonable charge: 'Public authorities should be able to make a charge for supplying environmental information, but such a charge should be reasonable. This implies that, as a general rule, charges may not exceed actual costs of producing the material in question. Instances where advance payment will be required should be limited. In particular cases where public authorities make available environmental information on a commercial basis, and where this is necessary in order to guarantee the continuation of collecting and publishing such information, a market-based charge is considered to be reasonable'.

In *Markinson* (see above) the Information Tribunal considered an appeal on the part of an individual who had been charged £6 for a copy of each planning or building control decision he requested, and 50p for each sheet within the planning file which he wanted photocopied. In his decision the Information Commissioner had noted the subjective wording of reg.8(3) – 'an amount which the public authority is satisfied is a reasonable amount' – and felt therefore unable to substitute his own judgment as to reasonableness for that of the local authority. On appeal the Tribunal drew attention to the wording of art.5(2) of Directive 2003/4/EC:

> Public authorities may make a charge for supplying any environmental information but such charge shall not exceed a reasonable amount.

The Tribunal declined to accede to an argument that reg.8(3) should be interpreted in any way other than its ordinary meaning in order that it should be rendered consistent with the EU Directive. Instead the Tribunal concluded that the 'subjective' wording of the regulation was consistent with the EU Directive:

> It seems to us that the UK Government was not obliged to re-state the precise language of Article 5(2) in the Regulations, it was left with some discretion, or margin of appreciation (para.30)

On that basis the role of the Information Commissioner and the Information Tribunal was not to ask whether the sums charged in any particular case were or were not reasonable sums, rather it was to ask whether any reasonable public authority could have regarded such sums as reasonable: applying the standard of review applicable in irrationality-based challenges to the decisions of public bodies in judicial review cases.

The Tribunal therefore asked two questions: (i) did the local authority honestly believe its charges to be reasonable, and if so (ii) whether that belief was a belief that a reasonable local authority, properly directing itself to the relevant law and facts, could have held.

On close examination of the reasoning processes which had, it seemed, led the council to the level of charges which it had set, the Tribunal found that all relevant considerations had not been taken into account by the local authority: for example, there was guidance on such charges issues by the Office of the Deputy Prime Minister (ODPM), and this appeared to have been ignored by the local authority. The Tribunal indicated in its final decision that the ODPM's indicative figure of 10p per page for photocopying charges should apply unless an authority could show good reason why this sum should be exceeded.

Public authorities are required to publish and make available to applicants a schedule of their charges, and also information on the circumstances in which a charge may be made or may be waived (reg.8(8)). A public authority may require payment of its proposed charge in advance of making the environmental information available to the applicant. Where the public authority opts to do so it must inform the applicant of this fact, and also of the amount of the charge, within 20 working days of receipt of the request for the information (reg.8(4)). In calculating the 20 working days within which the public authority must disclose the information the period from the date of such notification and the payment of the advance charge is ignored (see reg.8(6)). In such circumstances the applicant has 60 working days from the date of such notification within which to pay the charge, and trigger the duty to disclose the information (reg.6(5)). Although the duty to disclose will lapse if the charge is not paid within this 60-day period, there is no reason why a further, albeit identical, request could not be made by the applicant – triggering a new duty to disclose.

9.2.11 Advice and assistance

Public authorities are required to provide advice and assistance to applicants so far as it is reasonable to expect them to do so (reg.9(1)). For example, where the public authority considers that an applicant has formulated a request in too general a manner (so that the 'too general' exception from disclosure may apply) the authority is required to ask the applicant for more particulars and also to assist the applicant in providing those particulars (reg.9(2)). In *Keston Ramblers Association* v. *Information Commissioner and London Borough of Bromley* (EA/2005/0024, 26 October 2007) it was held that where a public authority has collated information in response to a request and offers to copy it in return for a fee, the duty to advise and assist would 'in general' require the authority to offer the documents for inspection, thereby enabling the applicant to avoid having to pay the fee.

9.2.12 Transfers of requests

Where a public authority receives a request for environmental information which it does not hold but it believes that the information is held by another public authority, the former public authority is required either to transfer the request to the other public authority or to supply the applicant with the name and address of the transferee authority (reg.10(1)). For the purpose of the 20-day rule the transferee authority has 20 working days from the date on which it receives the transferred request (see reg.10(2)).

9.2.13 Exceptions to the duty to disclose environmental information

A public authority may refuse (i.e. there is no express duty not to disclose information just because an exception applies) to disclose environmental information in circumstances where the following two conditions are satisfied:

- the information falls within one of the categories listed below; and
- in all the circumstances the public interest in non-disclosure outweighs the public interest in disclosing the information (reg.12(11)).

Note that both of the above conditions must be satisfied before a request for disclosure may be refused, and also that in weighing the two facets of public interest within the second bullet point the public authority must apply a presumption in favour of disclosure (reg.12(2)).[17] In *Archer* v. *Information Commissioner and Salisbury District Council* (EA/2006/0037, 9 May 2007) the Tribunal explained, correctly, that 'the result, in short, is that the threshold to justify non-disclosure is a high one'.

In relation to the application of the public interest test, it is important to note the decision of the Court of Justice of the European Union (CJEU) in *Office of Communications* v. *Information Commissioner* [2011] EUECJ C-71/10, on a reference from the Supreme Court (see footnote to **9.2.3** for citations of previous hearings in the domestic courts). The CJEU held that when a public authority is considering the application of more than one exception under the EIR, if the public interest factors supporting each exception separately are not sufficient to outweigh the public interest in disclosure, the public authority may undertake a further exercise in which the cumulative public interest in maintaining the exceptions is considered.

Under reg.12(5) a public authority may, applying the above conditions, refuse to disclose environmental information to the extent that such disclosure would adversely affect:[18]

(a) international relations, defence, national security [in relation to which a ministerial certificate of adverse effect is conclusive – see reg.15(1) and (3)][19] or public safety;

(b) the course of justice, the ability of a person to receive a fair trial or the ability of a public authority to conduct an inquiry of a criminal or disciplinary nature;

(c) intellectual property rights;

(d) the confidentiality of the proceedings of that or any other public authority where such confidentiality is provided by law;

(e) the confidentiality of commercial or industrial information where such confidentiality is provided by law to protect a legitimate economic interest;

(f) the interests of the person who provided the information where that person –

    (i) was not under, and could not have been put under, any legal obligation to supply it to that or any other public authority;

    (ii) did not supply it in circumstances such that that or any other public authority is entitled apart from [under the EIR] to disclose it; and

    (iii) has not consented to its disclosure; or

(g) the protection of the environment to which the information relates.

---

[17] But note that in *Staffordshire County Council and Sibelco (UK) Ltd* v. *Information Commissioner* (EA/2010/0015, 22 November 2010) the First-tier Tribunal stated that following the Court of Appeal's judgment in *Veolia ES Nottinghamshire Ltd* v. *Nottinghamshire County Council* [2010] EWCA Civ 1214: 'The presumption in favour of disclosure … in Regulation 12(2) EIR 2004 must now be read subject to an exception in the case of any such information which is held by the public body subject to a legal duty of confidentiality' (para.151).

[18] The phrase 'would adversely affect' seems a more onerous pre-condition than its equivalent under the FOIA, that is, 'would be likely to prejudice'.

[19] A Minister may designate another person to certify such matters on his or her behalf (reg.15(2)).

Emissions

A special rule of some substantial potential significance applies in relation to information which relates to 'emissions'. The exceptions in reg.12(5)(d)–(g) above do not apply to information relating to emissions (reg.12(9)). The concept of 'emissions' is not specifically defined in either Directive 2003/4/EC or the EIR. Initial guidance from the Information Commissioner and Defra suggested that the concept should be afforded a meaning consistent with its defined usage in other EU Environmental Directives, so that it would be construed as including both direct and indirect releases of substances, vibrations, heat or noise from individual or diffuse sources to the atmosphere, to water and on to land. This approach was, however, regarded by the Information Tribunal as perhaps being unduly cautious in *Office of Communications* v. *Information Commissioner and T-Mobile (UK) Ltd* (EA/2006/0078, 4 September 2007). The Tribunal noted that exceptions to disclosure should be narrowly interpreted, and in consequence exceptions to exceptions should be broadly interpreted. As such the word 'emissions' should bear its plain and natural meaning even if that gave it a broader meaning than that afforded by other EU Directives. In the particular case, radiation from a mobile phone base station could be properly categorised as an 'emission' (this finding was not challenged in the further appeals in the case).

In *Milford Haven Port Authority* (FER0072936, 28 March 2007) the Information Commissioner held that the concept of 'emissions' does not extend to emissions which have not yet occurred. Accordingly, in relation to a document dealing with future risks of liquid natural gas escapes, the exceptions referred to above were not excluded (see paras.32–36).

9.2.14 The reg.12(5) exceptions

There is now a substantial body of case law from the Information Commissioner, First-tier and Upper Tribunals and the courts illustrating how the EIR exceptions are being applied in practice. Some examples are given below.

International relations, defence, national security and public safety (reg.12(5)(a))

In *Sinclair* v. *Information Commissioner and Department for Energy and Climate Change* (EA/2011/0052, 8 November 2011) the First-tier Tribunal held that the Department for Energy and Climate Change (DECC) was not required to disclose information relating to the costs of the UK meeting its climate change commitments following negotiations with other EU Member States at the Copenhagen conference in 2009. DECC relied on reg.12(5)(a), arguing that premature publication of the UK's estimates would significantly prejudice its position in the ongoing negotiations and its relationship with other countries. The Tribunal found that 'international relations' for the purpose of reg.12(5)(a) covers all aspects of relations between the UK and other states or international organisations. On the application of the public interest test, the Tribunal, impressed by the strength of the evidence adduced by DECC in relation to the harm that disclosure would cause, found that the public interest in disclosure was outweighed.

The Information Commissioner applied this exception in *Health and Safety Executive* (FS50102202, 30 August 2007) in upholding a decision of the Health and Safety Executive not to release information relating to computer modelling exercises carried out to examine the likely impact of a terrorist attack on a major nuclear facility in the UK. The Commissioner was satisfied that the information would be of great use to a potential attacker in choosing targets and planning an operation. In balancing the public interest in favour of and against disclosure:

> [the Commissioner] is satisfied that release of that information into the public domain, where it would be accessible to anybody, would be of immeasurable assistance to anyone contemplating a terrorist attack ... the nature of the information is such that its release might in fact help to precipitate such an action, or at least help attackers to maximise their impact. He also accepts the view that it would not be possible to produce a redacted version of the information that would contain any information useful to the complainant that would not also be helpful to the potential terrorist. Taking all these factors into account, the Commissioner is therefore of the view that on this occasion – despite the presumption – the public interest in maintaining the exception clearly outweighs the public interest in disclosing the information. (para.20)

The course of justice, the ability of a person to receive a fair trial or the ability of a public authority to conduct an inquiry of a criminal or disciplinary nature (reg.12(5)(b))

This exception has been held, notwithstanding the absence of clear words to such effect, to give some protection to information which is covered by legal professional privilege. See *West* v. *Information Commissioner* (EA/2010/0120, 25 October 2010) in which the First-tier Tribunal questioned whether reg.12(4)(b) has the same scope as the exemption in s.42 of the FOIA, or whether the EIR exception may only cover material attracting litigation privilege, as opposed to legal advice privilege. In *Woodford* v. *Information Commissioner* (EA/2009/0098, 21 April 2010) the Information Tribunal held that it extends to cover legal advice given by in-house lawyers (paras.28–29). In *Kirkaldie* v. *Information Commissioner and Thanet District Council* (EA/2006/0001, 4 July 2006) the Information Tribunal stated that:

> The purpose of this exception is reasonably clear. It exists in part to ensure that there should be no disruption to the administration of justice, including the operation of the courts and no prejudice to the rights of individuals or organisations to a fair trial. In order to achieve this it covers legal professional privilege, particularly where a public authority is, or is likely, to be involved in litigation. (para.21)

In *Burgess* v. *Information Commissioner and Stafford Borough Council* (EA/2006/0091, 7 June 2007) the Information Tribunal held that the exception was equally applicable to advice given to a local authority even where the request was made after the legal proceedings in relation to which the advice was sought were concluded. This was the case, at any rate, where the advice was of a sufficiently general nature that it might be relevant to guide the local authority at some future juncture. In *Burgess* the local authority argued for non-disclosure on the grounds that disclosure would render it difficult for the local authority to maintain any other position on the particular point in future dealings with the public, and that as the advice was simply a view of the law from one lawyer, the local authority was entitled not in that way to become constrained to that interpretation. On the facts, in *Burgess* the Information Tribunal concluded that the public interest in maintaining the exception outweighed the public interest in disclosure. See also Information Tribunal decisions in *Boddy* v. *Information Commissioner and North Norfolk District Council* (EA/2007/0074, 23 June 2008); *Rudd* v. *Information Commissioner and Verderers of the New Forest* (EA/2008/0020, 28 September 2008); *Mersey Tunnel Users Association* v. *Information Commissioner and Halton Borough Council (Stage 2)* (EA/2009/0001, 11 January 2010).

A further issue in *Burgess* related to an argument that the advice should no longer be regarded as privileged because the privilege had been waived either by disclosure of the advice by the council to council members, or by an offer of disclosure (not followed up by actual disclosure) of the advice by a council member to an individual. The Information Tribunal held that legal advice is obtained for the very purpose of helping a council to take decisions, and disclosure of the advice to members is a necessary part of that process. Such disclosure does not involve waiver of privilege. The Tribunal also held that a mere unconsummated offer of disclosure was not something which could be equated with waiver of privilege (para.24).

By contrast in *Kirkaldie* (see above), privilege was held on the facts to have been waived, by dint of statements indicating the tenor of that advice made by a councillor at a council meeting (paras.40–41). The Tribunal explained that for there to be waiver of privilege there must be something more than disclosure that legal advice has been taken, there must be reference to the content of that advice: the content of that advice must be summarised or quoted.

In practice, orders to disclose privileged information in the public interest are rare, as the public interest in protecting the doctrine of privilege is given much weight. However, for an example of a case in which privileged environmental information had to be disclosed, see the Information Tribunal decision in *Maiden* v. *Information Commissioner and Borough Council of King's Lynn and West Norfolk* (EA/2008/0013, 15 December 2008). In that case, the Tribunal held that a legal opinion obtained from a barrister should be disclosed in the public interest. The council had relied on largely generic arguments to support its position and had failed to address properly the facts of the case, including the fact that its legal services director had disclosed other pieces of advice on related issues.

Intellectual property rights (reg.12(5)(c))

This exception was considered in *Office of Communications* v. *Information Commissioner and T-Mobile (UK) Ltd* (EA/2006/0078, 4 September 2007). Ofcom argued that disclosure of information about mobile phone base stations would adversely affect the intellectual property rights of mobile network operators. The Information Commissioner held that, although copyright and database rights applied, there was no 'adverse effect' such as to trigger the exception. The Information Tribunal disagreed and identified a number of potential adverse effects on intellectual property rights; however, it held that the public interest in disclosure should prevail. On appeal to the Court of Appeal, the focus of the case shifted to the significant issue of whether public interest factors relating to more than one exception under the EIR could be aggregated.

The confidentiality of the proceedings of that or any other body where such confidentiality is provided by law (reg.12(5)(d))

In *Local Government Ombudsman* (FS50094124, 22 May 2007) this exception was applied so as to uphold non-disclosure of information relating to a confidential investigation by the local government ombudsman into a complaint of maladministration made by the applicant. Although under the EIR the bar on disclosure of such information under the Local Government Act 1974, s.32(2) was not determinative (compare with the position under the FOIA), the balance of public interest here lay in favour of non-disclosure. See also the First-tier Tribunal's decision in *Dalley* v. *Information Commissioner* (EA/2011/0180, 15 February 2012).

The confidentiality of commercial or industrial information where such confidentiality is provided by law to protect a legitimate economic interest (reg.12(5)(e))

It is clear from the case law relating to reg.12(5)(e) (and the equivalent exemptions under the FOIA) that persuasive evidence of the alleged harm caused by the disclosure of confidential commercial information will be required to support non-disclosure. For example, in *Elmbridge Borough Council* v. *Information Commissioner* (EA/2010/0106, 4 January 2011) the First-tier Tribunal dismissed the local authority's reliance on reg.12(5)(e) (and (f)), commenting that the exceptions were not engaged because the authority had failed to provide independent and objective evidence of the alleged adverse effect. It found that the 'evidence' in support of the exceptions was no more than assertions and speculation. See also *North Western and North Wales Sea Fisheries Committee* v. *Information Commissioner* (EA/2007/0133, 8 July 2008).

In *Chichester District Council* v. *Information Commissioner* (EA/2010/0153, 16 March 2011) a request was made for information about a valuation produced by the council relating to land which it owned and proposed to sell as part of a development. The council refused to disclose the information on the basis that it would have an adverse effect on its ability to sell the land for the best possible price. Although the valuation dated from 2007 the council claimed that it was still an accurate reflection of the value of the land. The First-tier Tribunal, substantially upholding the decision of the Information Commissioner, ordered that most of the information should be disclosed. It found that the exception in reg.12(5)(e) could not apply because the information had been generated internally by the council and so there was no duty of confidentiality provided by law that could be enforced by a third party. The council could not 'self-generate' confidentiality. This approach reflects the position in s.41 of the FOIA, which expressly requires that confidential information must have been obtained by the public authority from a third party. In relation to the difference between s.41 of the FOIA and reg.12(5)(e), see also *Mersey Tunnel Users Association* v. *Information Commissioner and Halton Borough Council (Stage 2)* (EA/2009/0001, 11 January 2010).

See also *Bath and North East Somerset Council* v. *Information Commissioner* (EA/2010/0045, 5 October 2010) in which the disputed information was a developer's financial model and independent viability reports prepared for the council in the context of a co-operation agreement between the developer and the council. The focus of the First-tier Tribunal's decision was the application of the public interest test. Under the terms of the agreement, the developer had agreed to work on an 'open book' basis, so that the council could look at the financial assumptions underlying the proposals. As part of that process the developer provided its detailed financial models which included commercially sensitive information about fees, cash flow and anticipated land values. It was common ground that this information fell within the scope of the exception but, overruling the Information Commissioner, the Tribunal held that the models could be withheld in the public interest. The viability assessments, however, should be disclosed subject to the redaction of commercially sensitive information. In support of the public interest in non-disclosure, the Tribunal was persuaded that disclosure would have prejudiced the developer's negotiating position and given its competitors a material advantage at a time when it was in active discussions regarding a competitive restructuring of its finances.

The interests of the person who provided the information where that person was not under a legal obligation to supply it and did not supply it in circumstances such that any public authority is entitled to disclose it (apart from under the EIR) and has not consented to disclosure (reg. 12(5)(f))

This exception is often relied on in conjunction with reg.12(5)(e) – for example, it was (unsuccessfully) relied on by the local authority in the *Elmbridge Borough Council* case referred to above.

Note also that in *Dainton* v. *Information Commissioner and Lincolnshire County Council* (EA/2007/0020, 10 September 2007) the Information Tribunal referred to the fact that where an anonymous provider of information fears that disclosure of a document will allow identification by handwriting, this exception will not apply because the public authority should discharge its disclosure duties by way of a typed manuscript (see para.36).

9.2.15   The reg.12(4) exceptions

In addition to the exceptions listed above, within reg.12(4) the EIR provide more generally that a public authority may refuse to disclose environmental information in circumstances where the public interest in non-disclosure outweighs the public interest in disclosure, and:

(a)   it does not hold the information when the applicant's request is received (note here the duties imposed on a public authority where that body is aware that the requested information is held by another public authority; see **9.2.12**);

(b)   the request for information is manifestly unreasonable (the Information Commissioner's advice on vexatious requests under the FOIA is also likely to be a useful guide to interpretation of this 'manifestly unreasonable' exception (see *When Can a Request Be Considered Vexatious or Repeated?*, version 5 (ICO, June 2012));

(c)   the request is formulated in too general a manner (note here the public authority's obligation under reg.9 to assist the applicant in providing particulars which may render the request less general);

(d)   the request relates to material which is still in the course of completion, to unfinished documents or to incomplete data;[20] or

(e)   the request involves the disclosure of internal communications (including communications between government departments).[21]

It is worth noting that, like all exceptions under the EIR, the 'manifestly unreasonable' exception is subject to the public interest test. In practice, the test under the EIR is similar to that applicable to 'vexatious or repeated requests' under s.14 of the FOIA. The first case relating to this provision to be considered at the Information Tribunal level was *Carpenter* v. *Information Commissioner and Stevenage Borough Council* (EA/2008/0046, 17 November 2008) in which the Information Tribunal considered the case law under s.14 of the FOIA and concluded that the

---

[20]   Where this exception is relied upon the written decision refusing disclosure must specify, if known, the estimated time in which the information will be finished or completed (see reg.14(4)). See, by way of example of the application of this exception, the Information Tribunal decision in *Secretary of State for Transport* v. *Information Commissioner* (EA/2008/0052, 5 May 2009) in which the tribunal rejected the Information Commissioner's argument that draft reports could not fall within the 'unfinished documents' exception once there was a final version.

[21]   Reg.12(4) and (8). The intent here appears to be to provide some protection in relation to communications which do not yet constitute the settled view within government on a particular matter.

public interest in protecting local authority staff from the 'wholesale abuse' represented by the information requests in this case clearly outweighed any public interest in disclosure. Specifically, reg.12(4)(b) may cover cases where complying with a request would incur unreasonable costs for the authority or where responding would be an unreasonable diversion of resources. Each case will turn on its facts. In *Mersey Tunnel Users Association* v. *Information Commissioner and Halton Borough Council* (EA/2009/0001, 24 June 2009) the Information Tribunal rejected the authority's reliance on reg.12(4)(b), specifically finding that a request which would involve exceeding the costs threshold for the purposes of s.12 of the FOIA, had the information not been environmental, would not necessarily be 'manifestly unreasonable'. See also *Little* v. *Information Commissioner* (EA/2010/0072, 30 December 2010) in which reliance on reg.12(4)(b) was upheld.

The last of these exceptions – that the request involves the disclosure of internal communications, including communications between government departments – has been considered in several cases before the Information Commissioner and the Information Tribunal.

At first glance this exception would appear to be of very wide scope. Is it not the case that a high proportion of documents sought from public authorities will fall within the general rubric 'internal communications'? The key point to note, however, is that this set of exceptions only applies where the request falls within that ambit, *and in addition* the public interest in non-disclosure outweighs the public interest in disclosure (with the presumption being always in favour of disclosure). In other words, taking the last example on the list, there is no blanket exception in relation to internal communications – there is simply an exception in relation to internal communications in respect of which a clear case can be made out that in the circumstances of the case the public interest in protecting the confidentiality of that disclosure outweighs the public interest in such disclosure.

The public interest in non-disclosure of such internal communication has generally been described in terms of the concept of 'private thinking space'. A typical statement may be found in *Pesticides Safety Directorate* (FER0082566, 11 October 2007) where the applicant sought 'internal communication' documents relating to the consideration by Defra of responses to a consultation on pesticide crop spraying matters. The decision notice states:

> The Commissioner recognises that frank and honest debate is necessary for high quality policy formulation and that there is a public interest, in certain circumstances, in maintaining private space for such discussion away from public scrutiny. That is, the EIR will protect internal communications when it is sufficiently in the public interest to do so. (para.23)

On the facts of the case, however, the Commissioner held that the public interest in disclosure (allowing the public to understand the way in which government had reached decisions, and allowing more informed participation by the public in debates with government) outweighed the public interest (outlined above) which lay behind this exception.

This approach to the public interest may be seen also in a number of Information Tribunal cases. In *Chichester District Council* v. *Information Commissioner* (EA/2010/0153, 16 March 2011) it was held that reg.12(4)(e) applied to the disputed information but concluded that the greater public interest lay in disclosure.

In *Friends of the Earth* v. *Information Commissioner and Export Credits Guarantee Department* (EA/2006/0073, 20 August 2007) (upheld on appeal to the High Court, see [2008] EWHC 638 (Admin)) a request for inter-departmental correspondence in relation to an application for export credit for the 'politically sensitive' Sakhalin II oil and gas project was resisted on the grounds that reg.12(4)(e) applied, and that there was a strong public interest in the full and frank provision and discussion of advice within government, because that makes for better quality decision making. Moreover, it was argued that such disclosure would be contrary to the public interest as undermining the convention of collective responsibility. Friends of the Earth countered, *inter alia*, that given the environmentally controversial nature of the project in question (e.g. its threats to the already endangered grey whale species) there was a strong public interest favouring disclosure so that the reasons for any public funding support for the project could be discerned. On appeal, the Information Tribunal overturned the decision of the Information Commissioner and held that the balance of public interest lay in favour of disclosure: that on a balance of probabilities the Export Credits Guarantee Department had failed to prove a sufficiently demonstrable public interest requiring protection from disclosure, such as to overturn the clear legal presumption in favour of disclosure. The Tribunal referred to the:

> onus which clearly rests on a public authority in the context of the EIR whenever it chooses to rely on an exception ... that onus being to *specify clearly and precisely the harm of harms that would be caused were disclosure to be ordered.* (para.53, emphasis added)

The Tribunal made clear that each case must accordingly be assessed on its own merits, and that there could be no 'immutable' principle that, for example, the convention of ministerial collective responsibility should operate in all cases as some form of 'trump card' against applications for disclosure.

Having looked at the documents in question and having weighed the controversial nature of the project against the quite ill-defined, and generic rather than specific, assertions of the harm that disclosure would entail, the Tribunal ordered disclosure.[22] See also *Cabinet Office* v. *Information Commissioner* (EA/2010/0027, 4 October 2010).

---

[22] For an apparently rather different approach to the weighing of public interests in relation to reg.12(4)(e) compare *Archer* v. *Information Commissioner and Salisbury District Council* (EA/2006/0037, 9 May 2007).

9.2.16   Power to neither confirm nor deny

Where a request for environmental information is for information which, if held by a public authority, might fall within one of the various exceptions referred to above, and the public authority holding such information forms the view that the information should not be disclosed under one of the exceptions, the public authority is empowered in certain situations to respond to the request by neither confirming nor denying whether such information exists and is held by the authority. The situations where the refusal to disclose will legitimately incorporate a statement neither confirming nor denying that the information exists and is held by the authority are where such confirmation or denial would itself adversely affect international relations, defence, national security or public safety, and the public interest in such confirmation and denial would be outweighed by the adverse effect in question (reg.12(6) and (7)).

9.2.17   Personal data[23]

We noted earlier that the general duty of disclosure under the EIR does not apply to the extent that the environmental information is personal data of which the applicant is the data subject (reg.5(3)). Applications for such data must instead be treated as subject access requests made under the Data Protection Act 1998 (DPA) (see, in particular, s.7 of the DPA).

In contrast, to the extent that the requested environmental information may comprise personal data of which the applicant is not the data subject, the information is subject to the provisions of the EIR. Although requests for this category of environmental information do not fall under the DPA, some of the protections afforded by that Act to personal data are replicated in the EIR.

The EIR provide that such requested personal data must not be disclosed where either one of the two conditions set out in reg.13 is satisfied (reg.12(3)).

The first of those conditions deals separately with two distinct situations depending on whether or not the information falls within the first four categories of data in s.1(1) of the DPA.[24] Where the information falls within those categories of data the information must not be disclosed where such disclosure would *either*:

---

[23]   This concept is defined in s.1(1) of the DPA as data which relate to a living individual who can be identified (a) from those data; or (b) from those data and other information which is in the possession of, or is likely to come into the possession of, the data controller, and includes any expression of opinion about the individual and any indication of the intentions of the data controller or any other person in respect of the individual. For a restrictive interpretation of the scope of this definition see *Durant* v. *Financial Services Authority* [2003] EWCA Civ 1746; *Harcup* v. *Information Commissioner and Yorkshire Forward* (EA/2007/0058, 5 February 2008); and also *Dainton* v. *Information Commissioner and Lincolnshire County Council* (EA/2007/0020, 10 September 2007), in which it was held that answers given in a local authority questionnaire by users of a disputed footpath about their use of the path, what has happened to them when using the footpath, and their opinions about its legal status, amounted to 'personal data' (see at para.19).

[24]   'Data' within the meaning of s.1(1) of the DPA consist of information which: (i) is being processed by means of equipment operating automatically in response to instructions given for that purpose; (ii) is recorded with the intention that it should be processed by means of such equipment;

- contravene one or more of the data protection principles (reg.13(2)(a)(i));[25] *or*
- contravene s.10 of the DPA (i.e. where the data subject has given notice that disclosure would cause unwarranted substantial damage or distress to the data subject), *and* the public interest in not disclosing outweighs the public interest in disclosing the information (reg.13(2)(a)(ii)).[26]

In *Cobain* v. *Information Commissioner and Crown Prosecution Service* (EA/ 2011/0112 and EA/2011/0113, 8 February 2012) the requester, a journalist, had asked the Crown Prosecution Service (CPS) for information relating to the prosecution, trial and conviction of British National Party leader Nick Griffin for breaches of the Public Order Act 1986. The CPS withheld the information. The Information Commissioner upheld the CPS's decision to withhold the information on the basis of the exemption for personal information (FOIA, s.40(2)) (finding that it was 'sensitive personal data') and the requester appealed. The Tribunal overruled the Commissioner on the application of s.40(2), finding that although the information was sensitive personal data, in the particular circumstances of the case disclosure was justified as some of the grounds set out in Sched.2 or Sched.3 to the DPA were satisfied. See also *Greenwood and Bolton Metropolitan Borough Council* v. *Information Commissioner* (EA/2011/0131 and EA/2011/0137, 17 February 2012) in which the disputed information related to the register of interests of the local authority's councillors and senior officers. The Information Commissioner ordered disclosure of some of the information, holding that although it was personal data, processing would not breach the data protection principles because it would not be unfair and condition 6 of Sched.2 to the DPA (legitimate interests of third parties) would be satisfied. The council appealed and the First-tier Tribunal found that when deciding whether disclosure would be 'fair and lawful' a distinction should be made between the position of individuals at different levels of seniority. It held that for the less senior officers, it would be fair to disclose their names, department/section and job title, but no more. Disclosure of information relating to their membership of other organisations/associations and other professional activities would be unfair, taking into account their level of responsibility and the corresponding checks and balances of line managers and internal monitoring. The same considerations did not apply to chief officers, given their seniority and responsibility for decision making.

(iii) is recorded as part of a relevant filing system or with the intention that it should form part of a relevant filing system; (iv) does not fall within paragraph (i), (ii) or (iii) but forms part of an accessible record as defined by s.68 of the DPA; or (v) is recorded information held by a public authority and does not fall within any of paras.(i)–(iv).

[25] The data protection principles are set out in Sched.1 to the DPA and further elaborated in Scheds.2, 3 and 4. They include the principle that 'personal data shall be obtained only for one or more specified and lawful purposes, and shall not be further processed in any manner incompatible with that purpose or those purposes'. In *Tunbridge Wells Borough Council* (FER0086785, 10 October 2007) the Information Commissioner held that personal data should be released under condition 6 of Sched.2 to the DPA (see paras.47–51).

[26] The public interest criterion applies only to the s.10 ground, so that where disclosure would contravene one of the data protection principles no such balancing of public interests arises.

However, information about their memberships and associations, being of a more private nature, could be withheld.

Where the information does not fall within the first four categories of data in s.1(1) of the DPA (i.e. it is recorded information held by a public authority not falling within the first four categories of data listed in s.1(1) of the DPA) the information must not be disclosed where the disclosure of that information would contravene any of the data protection principles (reg.13(2)(b)).[27]

The second condition is that requested information must not be disclosed where the information is exempt from the disclosure requirements of s.7 of the DPA by virtue of any of that Act's exemptions (see Part IV of the DPA) – in other words, generally speaking, a requester who is not the data subject cannot access information under the EIR which the data subject himself or herself could not access under the DPA – and in all the circumstances of the case the public interest in not disclosing the information outweighs the public interest in disclosing it (reg.13(3)).

9.2.18 Reasoned decisions

Decisions by public authorities to refuse to disclose information under any of the various exceptions, or under the personal data provisions, must be communicated in writing and within 20 working days of the receipt of the request (reg.14(1)). (For power to extend this period, see **9.2.10**.) The decision must indicate the particular exception(s) relied upon, and must indicate the matters the public authority took into consideration in reaching its decision that the public interest favoured non-disclosure rather than disclosure (reg.14(3)).

The written refusal must also inform the applicant of the right to make representations to the public authority under the reg.11 internal review procedure, and of the enforcement and appeal provisions applicable to the decision.

9.3 ENFORCEMENT AND APPEALS

At the outset of this chapter it was emphasised that although the new EIR came into force on the same day as the FOIA, their pedigrees are quite different: one a home-grown measure, the other a measure designed to meet requirements set at

---

[27] For these purposes the exemptions from the data protection principles for the fifth category of data in s.1(1) of the DPA, i.e. recorded information held by public authorities, should be disregarded. The exemptions referred to, and to be disregarded, are those contained in s.33A(1) of the DPA (added by FOIA, s.70). In *Dainton v. Information Commissioner and Lincolnshire County Council* (September 2007) the Information Tribunal held – in relation to disclosure of personal information contained in responses to a local authority questionnaire – that the first data protection principle would have been breached by disclosure of such information. The requirement of 'fairness' would not have been met because those completing the questionnaire would have anticipated that their answers would not be disclosed unless and until a later stage in the statutory 'rights of way modification' process had been reached (see para.30).

international multilateral treaty level and at EU level. As such a warning was sounded that in significant ways their substantive breadths of operation are by no means identical.

One area, however, where a close link has been achieved between the two regimes lies in the fields of enforcement and appeals. Regulation 18 provides that, subject only to certain modifications (e.g. Part IV of the FOIA (enforcement) does not apply where a certificate has been issued by a Minister under reg.15), the enforcement and appeal provisions of the FOIA (Parts IV and V) apply also for the purposes of the EIR.

The relevant provisions of the FOIA are dealt with in **Chapter 10**. In briefest summary, a person who has made a request may make an initial complaint (this should follow the internal review process provided for by reg.11) to the Information Commissioner if he or she considers that the request has not been handled (the complaint may for example be as regards level of fee charged, or time taken to determine the request) or determined in accordance with the EIR. The Information Commissioner has power to issue an information notice as a means of gaining the information the Commissioner will need in order to determine the complaint. The Information Commissioner also has powers of entry, search and seizure, and offences exist with respect to any obstruction of the Information Commissioner in the exercise of these functions. Given the ubiquity within the EIR of the need for the balancing of public interests it will generally be necessary for the Information Commissioner to review documents sought in order to decide whether a correct decision has been reached by the public body in question. The Information Commissioner will issue a decision notice giving his decision on the merits of the application.

From decisions of the Information Commissioner, appeal lies at the suit of the applicant for information or at the suit of the public authority as the case may be, to the First-tier Tribunal (Information Rights) and from there to the Upper Tribunal. There then lies a further right of appeal on a point of law to the High Court (and beyond).

9.3.1 Offences (reg.19)

Where a request has been made to a public authority for environmental information and that request is one which does not fall within the scope of the above-mentioned exceptions (including the provisions restricting access to personal data) an offence is committed by any person who, with the intention of preventing the disclosure of all or part of the information, alters, defaces, blocks, erases, destroys or conceals any record held by the authority. The offence is triable summarily and the maximum penalty is a fine not exceeding level 5 on the standard scale.

No proceedings in relation to this offence may be instituted except by the Information Commissioner, or by or with the consent of the Director of Public Prosecutions (reg.19(4)).

CHAPTER 10

Enforcement and appeals

Jeremy Ison, Deutsche Bank AG

10.1 INTRODUCTION

> Life after FOIA has changed and had to change.

So said the Information Tribunal when deciding to grant an appeal brought by Friends of the Earth, which was seeking disclosure of information passing between government departments in relation to the controversial Sakhalin II oil and gas project. The Tribunal remained 'unimpressed' by the arguments that a disclosure order would create a 'chilling effect' in Whitehall such that civil servants would be fearful of documenting their views candidly and meetings would no longer be minuted (*Friends of the Earth* v. *Information Commissioner and Export Credits Guarantee Department* (EA/2006/0073, 20 August 2007), para.61). On appeal the High Court endorsed the Tribunal's conclusion.

Thus, decisions of the Information Commissioner and the appellate tribunals and courts have played a key role in delivering the promised transparency of officialdom since the Freedom of Information Act 2000 (FOIA) came into force at the start of 2005. Yet change has come too to the very structure of the regime within which the scope of the new information rights is determined. In January 2010 the Information Tribunal's work was transferred to the First-tier Tribunal (Information Rights) in the General Regulatory Chamber. Appeals from there were no longer to the High Court but to the newly created Upper Tribunal Administrative Appeals Chamber. Freedom of information appeals have been pursued right up to the House of Lords and, since that court was rebaptised, to the Supreme Court.

One thing that remains constant is the dynamism of this area of law. The numbers of appeals to the Information Rights Tribunal have been increasing year on year, and the jurisprudence may develop in one direction but then is liable to change. While all those with an interest in freedom of information scrutinise the constant stream of adjudications, the concept of 'precedent' is an elusive one. Each case is decided on its own facts, and merely because an earlier case concerned a similar situation, that does not mean that the outcome of the later case will inevitably be the same; time will have moved on and considerations as to the application of the exemptions and the public interest test may well be materially different.[1]

Primary responsibility for enforcement of the FOIA lies with the Information Commissioner, who monitors public authorities and can issue notices directing them to take action so as to comply with their statutory obligations. Failure to comply with the Information Commissioner's notices can be punished as if it were a contempt of court. The enforcement and appeals regime under the FOIA applies also to the Environmental Information Regulations 2004, SI 2004/3391 (EIR),[2] which govern access to environmental information. With some adjustments the same regime applies to the INSPIRE Regulations 2009, SI 2009/3157 (INSPIRE Regulations), which came into force on the last day of 2009 and overlap to some extent with the EIR, as they cover access to location-specific environmental information held by public authorities (see **10.5.7**).[3]

The FOIA, EIR and INSPIRE Regulations apply in England, Wales and Northern Ireland only. In Scotland the enforcement regime under the Freedom of Information (Scotland) Act 2002, the Environmental Information (Scotland) Regulations 2004, SSI 2004/520, and the INSPIRE (Scotland) Regulations 2009, SSI 2009/440, is broadly similar but there is no equivalent of the tribunals north of the border. The regulator is the Scottish Information Commissioner (see **www.itspublicknowledge.info** for links to the law and guidance). The only appeal from the Scottish Commissioner is to the Court of Session, and only on a point of law rather than a full merits-based review as elsewhere in the UK.

At the heart of the enforcement regime lies the complaints process. This is the route (outlined in Figure 10.1) which an applicant must follow if the applicant considers that his or her request for information has been turned down or dealt with improperly.

This chapter will first review the UK Information Commissioner's role and the various notices he can serve, before looking in detail at the complaints process at **10.5–10.9**, including appeals to the Information Rights Tribunal and beyond. Finally, it will turn to the position of interested third parties (such as private sector

---

[1]   In June 2012 an Upper Tribunal judge put it this way: 'there are dangers in paying too close a regard to previous [First-tier Tribunal] decisions, as this may elevate issues of fact into issues of law or principle … This warning applies with even greater force, if that were possible, when one is concerned with the Commissioner's previous Decision Notices', (*UK Coal Mining Ltd* v. *Information Commissioner and Others* [2012] UKUT 212 (AAC), para.28).

[2]   The enforcement provisions of the FOIA (contained in Part IV of the Act, including Sched.3) and its appeals provisions (contained in Part V) are applied to the EIR, with the necessary modifications, by reg.18 of the EIR. Similarly, the Information Commissioner's powers and duties under ss.47 and 48 (the latter dealing with practice recommendations) are applied, as modified, to the EIR by reg.16(5) and (6). References in this chapter to the FOIA are to be taken to include a reference to the EIR and references to exemptions include a reference to exceptions under the EIR – unless clearly inappropriate in the context. See **Chapter 9** for a full discussion of the EIR.

[3]   The INSPIRE Regulations implement EU Directive 2007/2/EC. INSPIRE stands for Infrastructure for Spatial Information in the European Community. For ease of reading, all references in this chapter to a 'public authority' are to be taken to include a participating third party in the context of the INSPIRE Regulations where not expressly stated.

companies that do business with the public sector) and their somewhat limited opportunities to restrain disclosure of information which affects them.

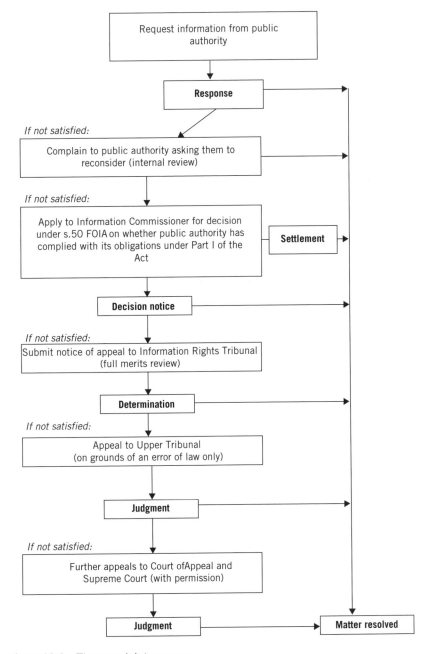

Figure 10.1 The complaints process

10.2   THE INFORMATION COMMISSIONER'S ROLE

Although appointed by the Crown and answerable to Parliament, the Information Commissioner is independent of government. It may be more accurate to say 'largely' independent, as his budget is set by the Ministry of Justice (MoJ), a matter which the incoming Commissioner said in the 2009–10 Annual Report he was keen to alter, so that he would be accountable to Parliament only.

The regulator is charged with ensuring that the rights and duties contained in the FOIA and the EIR are widely known about and respected. He has a similar role in relation to the Data Protection Act 1998 (DPA). He investigates complaints and has the power to instruct bodies to disclose information. In practice, his primary focus in this regard is to consider whether the exemptions in Part II of the FOIA have been properly applied by public bodies and to ensure that, in doing so, those bodies have had due regard to the public interest in disclosure.

He is supported by a staff of over 300 people, including two Deputy Commissioners and a legal department. The Information Commissioner's Office (ICO) is based in Wilmslow, near Manchester, with satellite offices in Cardiff, Edinburgh and Belfast.

10.2.1   Duties

The Information Commissioner's duties are outlined as follows under Parts III and IV of the FOIA and under the EIR:

- to promote the following of good practice by public authorities generally, and in particular to carry out his work in such a way as to promote the observance by public authorities of the requirements of the legislation and the provisions of the codes of practice made under the FOIA and the EIR (FOIA, s.47(1); EIR, reg.16(5))[4] – good practice in this context is stated not to be limited to following the provisions of the FOIA and the codes of practice made under ss.45 and 46 of the FOIA;
- to publish information about the operation of the legislation, good practice and other matters relating to his statutory functions (FOIA, s.47(2); EIR reg.16(5));
- to lay an annual report before both Houses of Parliament containing a general report on the exercise of his statutory functions (s.49(1));
- (save in certain circumstances) to determine, when asked to do so by an applicant under s.50(1), whether or not a public authority has complied with its

---

[4]   Two codes of practice have been issued under the FOIA: the code issued by the Secretary of State for Constitutional Affairs under s.45 giving guidance to public authorities on the practice which he judges it desirable they should follow in order to satisfy their obligations under Part I of the Act (Section 45 Code of Practice, sometimes referred to as the Access Code), and the Lord Chancellor's code under s.46 of the FOIA containing guidance for public authorities on record management (Section 46 Code of Practice). Under reg.16 of the EIR the Secretary of State for Environment, Food and Rural Affairs issued a code of practice in February 2005 for public authorities in respect of their obligations under the EIR.

obligations under Part I of the FOIA, or Parts 2 and 3 of the EIR, in responding to a request for information (FOIA, s.50(2); EIR, reg.18), or whether the actions of a public authority are compatible with its obligations under regs.7(4)(c) or 9 of the INSPIRE Regulations (INSPIRE Regulations, reg.11(4)).

In addition, the Information Commissioner is subject to the same public law duties of any executive decision maker, and his decisions may be challenged, where appropriate, by means of judicial review. The High Court has held expressly that the Information Commissioner is 'under a broad duty to act fairly' in his handling of complaints (*British Broadcasting Corporation* v. *Sugar* [2007] EWHC 905 (Admin), at [52]).

10.2.2 Powers

In order to assist him in carrying out these duties, the legislation gives the Information Commissioner the following powers:

● to advise anyone on the operation of the legislation, good practice and other matters relating to his functions (FOIA, s.47(2); EIR, reg.16(5));[5]
● to assess whether a public authority is following good practice, subject to that authority's consent (FOIA, s.47(3); EIR, reg.16(5));
● to issue a written practice recommendation to a public authority, specifying the steps which it should take to remedy the situation where he considers that its practice does not conform to the codes of practice (FOIA, s.48; EIR, reg.16(5));
● to charge for any services with the agreement of the Secretary of State (currently not used) (FOIA, s.47(4); EIR, reg.16(5));
● to lay reports before both Houses of Parliament from time to time as he thinks fit, in addition to the obligatory annual report referred to above (FOIA, s.49(2));
● to approve a public authority's publication scheme, or to refuse to approve it or revoke his approval for it (giving reasons); and to approve a model publication scheme, or to refuse to approve it or revoke his approval for it (again, giving reasons) (FOIA, ss.19–20);
● to issue decision notices, information notices and enforcement notices (FOIA, ss.50–52; EIR, reg.18; INSPIRE Regulations, reg.11);
● to obtain a warrant to enter and search premises so as to obtain evidence where he suspects a public authority of failing to comply with its obligations under the legislation or the notices referred to in the previous bullet point, or where he

---

5 By virtue of this section anybody (including public authorities or applicants for information) can contact the ICO for advice on the operation of the FOIA or the EIR, including on compliance issues, such as an authority's obligations with regard to access requests or the effect of particular exemptions. They will be advised by staff in a separate section of the ICO from those dealing with enforcement or complaints handling. Advice will be generalised, however, and staff will not advise on particular cases.

suspects an offence under s.77 of the FOIA or reg.19 of the EIR (obstructing disclosure of requested information) (FOIA, s.55 and Sched.3; EIR, reg.18; INSPIRE Regulations, reg.11(9), which apply to public authorities in respect of their obligations under regs.7(4)(c) or 9, and under which there is no equivalent of the s.77 offence of altering/concealing records to prevent disclosure);

• to certify to the court that a public authority has failed to comply with a decision notice, an information notice or an enforcement notice, so that the court can investigate and punish the non-compliance as a contempt of court if appropriate (FOIA, s.54; EIR, reg.18; INSPIRE Regulations, reg.11).

It should be noted that the Information Commissioner has no power to impose fines on public authorities for a breach of their duties under the FOIA, the EIR or the INSPIRE Regulations, which contrasts with his relatively new power to impose civil monetary penalties of up to £500,000 for serious breaches of the DPA. Nor does he have the power to award compensation to complainants or to make costs orders against the parties involved in a complaint which is directed to him for determination. It is also important to be aware that the Information Commissioner is not empowered to adjudicate formally on, and issue decision notices about, complaints against public authorities by anyone other than a person who has sought information from them under s.1 of the FOIA or reg.5 of the EIR. By contrast, anyone may apply for a decision by the Information Commissioner on whether a public authority or participating third party is acting compatibly with their obligations under regs.7(4)(c) or 9 of the INSPIRE Regulations (reg.11(4)).

10.3 THE INFORMATION COMMISSIONER'S NOTICES IN MORE DETAIL

10.3.1 Decision notices

Decision notices are only issued in the context of a complaint by someone who is dissatisfied with a public authority's response to his or her request for information and has applied to the Information Commissioner under s.50(1) for a decision on whether the authority has met its obligations under Part I of the FOIA, or Parts 2 or 3 of the EIR. (With regard to the INSPIRE Regulations, see the previous paragraph.) Following his determination of the matter, the Information Commissioner must either notify the complainant of his reason for not adjudicating on the complaint or serve a decision notice on the complainant and the public authority (s.50(3)). Where he decides that the public authority failed to comply with its obligations under ss.1(1), 11 or 17 of the FOIA or regs.5(1), 6, 11 or 14 of the EIR, or where he finds a public authority has not acted compatibly with its obligations under regs.7(4)(c) or 9 of the INSPIRE Regulations,[6] the notice must set out the steps he requires it to take

---

[6] FOIA, s.1(1) requires public authorities to confirm or deny that they hold the information requested and to provide any such information, and EIR, reg.5(1) requires authorities to make environmental information available on request. FOIA, s.11 and EIR, reg.6 require an authority to

to be in compliance and by when they must be taken (s.50(4)). There is no bar on the decision notice containing such steps in other cases, however. The Information Commissioner may also make reference in a decision notice to any provisions of the Section 45 Code of Practice which the public authority has breached and with which it is to comply (see the Foreword to the Section 45 Code of Practice at para.9).

Either the complainant or the public authority may appeal to the Information Rights Tribunal against a decision notice under s.57 and notices must contain details of that right of appeal (s.50(5)). The deadline for taking the steps specified in the notice cannot expire before the end of the period within which the public authority is entitled to appeal – namely 28 days from the date the Information Commissioner sends it to the appellant (the Tribunal Procedure (First-tier Tribunal) (General Regulatory Chamber) Rules 2009, SI 2009/1976, rule 22). Further, if the authority does challenge the Information Commissioner's decision, it is not obliged to take any action affected by the appeal until the appeal's determination or withdrawal (s.50(6)). Failure to comply with a decision notice is ultimately punishable in the High Court as if for contempt of court (s.54). It can also lead to the Information Commissioner obtaining a warrant to search premises to find evidence of non-compliance (FOIA, s.55 and Sched.3; EIR, reg.18; INSPIRE Regulations, reg.11). There is no provision permitting the Information Commissioner to cancel a decision notice once issued, as is possible with other notices. However, a decision notice under the FOIA or the EIR (but not the INSPIRE Regulations) can be overridden by the so-called ministerial veto (see **10.3.5**) For details of the Information Commissioner's approach to handling complaints and issuing decision notices see **10.6.1**.

10.3.2   Information notices

If the Information Commissioner has received an application for a decision notice or otherwise reasonably requires any information to determine whether a public authority has complied with, or is complying with, any of the requirements of Part I of the FOIA (or Parts 2 and 3 of the EIR, or regs.7(4)(c) or 9 of the INSPIRE Regulations) or the codes of practice under ss.45 and 46 of the FOIA and reg.16 of the EIR, he may serve an information notice on the authority requiring any information relevant to those matters and he may specify how and by when he is to receive it (s.51(1)(b)).[7] By contrast with an information-seeker's right of access, the

---

give effect to an applicant's preferred means of receiving the information where reasonably practicable, or to say why it is not. FOIA, s.17 and EIR, reg.14 contain the requirements for the sending and content of refusal notices, such as explaining why an exemption applies or why the greater public interest lies in withholding the information. EIR, reg.11 requires an authority to review its decision following representations from the applicant. Reg.7(4)(c) of the INSPIRE Regulations requires access to relevant datasets to be user-friendly, while reg.9 sets out the various grounds on which it is permissible to limit public access to the datasets.

[7]   An information notice cannot be issued by the Commissioner to assess whether a public authority or third party is acting compatibly with any code of practice issued under the INSPIRE Regulations.

notice can call for unrecorded information (s.51(8)). If the Information Commissioner serves the information notice in response to a request for a decision under s.50(1), the notice must say so. Otherwise, the notice must state that the Information Commissioner regards the information sought as relevant for the purposes mentioned above and reasons must be given (s.50(2)).

The public authority (but not a complainant) may appeal against the notice to the Information Rights Tribunal under s.57 of the FOIA and notices must contain details of that right (s.51(3)). The deadline for providing the Information Commissioner with the information he specifies cannot expire before the end of the period within which the public authority is entitled to appeal, which is 28 days from the date the Information Commissioner sends it to the appellant (Tribunal Procedure (First-tier Tribunal) (General Regulatory Chamber) Rules 2009, rule 22). Further, if the authority does challenge the notice, it is not obliged to furnish the Information Commissioner with the information before the appeal's determination or withdrawal (s.51(4)). The Information Commissioner may cancel an information notice by written notice to the relevant public authority (s.51(7)). (An authority could thus seek cancellation of the notice where it was for some reason no longer appropriate but the time for appealing had expired and no extension of the deadline was likely to be available.) Failure to comply with an information notice is ultimately punishable in the High Court as if it were a contempt of court. The same is true where, in purported compliance with an information notice, a public authority makes a statement which is false in a material respect, either with knowledge of its falsity or else recklessly (s.54), i.e. not caring whether it is true or false. Failure to comply with the notice can also lead to the Information Commissioner obtaining a warrant to search premises to find evidence of non-compliance (s.55 and Sched.3).

In responding to the notice, the public authority is under no obligation to provide the Information Commissioner with information in respect of any legally privileged communications containing legal advice on a client's rights, obligations or liabilities under the FOIA, the EIR or the INSPIRE Regulations or made in connection with, or in contemplation of, proceedings arising out of that legislation (s.51(5)). This provision was at the centre of an Information Tribunal case which ruled that the Information Commissioner was not permitted to issue an information notice requiring the Department for Constitutional Affairs to provide him with legal advice from the Attorney General regarding the public interest test and its interpretation under the FOIA (*Ministry of Justice (previously the Department for Constitutional Affairs)* v. *Information Commissioner* (EA/2007/0016, 6 August 2007)).

For further details of the Information Commissioner's practice concerning information notices, see under **10.6.1**.

10.3.3   Enforcement notices

If the Information Commissioner is satisfied that the public authority is in breach of any of its obligations under Part I of the FOIA or Parts 2 and 3 of the EIR or regs.7(4)(c) or 9 of the INSPIRE Regulations, he may serve an enforcement notice requiring the public authority to take particular steps by a particular time to comply with those obligations. An enforcement notice cannot be issued purely in relation to a breach of a code of practice unrelated to a breach of the FOIA or the EIR. Code breaches can be the subject of practice recommendations (see **10.3.6**).

An enforcement notice must specify those obligations with which the Information Commissioner is satisfied the public authority has failed to comply, and his reason for reaching that conclusion. It must also give details of the right to appeal against the notice under s.57 (s.52(2)). Only a public authority may appeal, not any complainant with an interest in the matter. As with the notices considered above, the deadline for taking the steps specified in an enforcement notice cannot expire before the end of the period within which the public authority is entitled to appeal – 28 days from the date the Information Commissioner sends it to the appellant (Tribunal Procedure (First-tier Tribunal) (General Regulatory Chamber) Rules 2009, rule 22). Again, the authority is not obliged to comply with it pending the determination or withdrawal of any appeal (s.52(4)). The Information Commissioner may cancel an enforcement notice by written notice to the public authority (s.52(4)). (Again, an authority could thus ask him to cancel the notice where it was for some reason no longer appropriate but the time for appealing had expired and no extension of the deadline was likely to be available.) An enforcement notice can also be overridden by ministerial veto, except in the case of the INSPIRE Regulations (see **10.3.5**). Failure to comply with a notice can be punished in the High Court as a contempt of court (s.54) and can also lead to the Information Commissioner obtaining a warrant to search premises to find evidence of non-compliance (s.55 and Sched.3).

The distinction in practice between enforcement and decision notices is that the latter arise in the context of specific complaints, whereas the former are more likely to be issued where there have been systemic failures or repeated non-compliance with the FOIA, the EIR or the INSPIRE Regulations. Examples of where an enforcement notice might be issued include:

- systemic, repeated or serious non-compliance with the legislation (for instance as regards meeting the time limits for responding to information requests or conducting internal reviews, or as regards issuing refusal notices in the correct form, i.e. specifying the relevant exemptions/exceptions and explaining why they apply);
- as a means of grouping together several similar complaints against the same public authority;
- failure to adopt a publication scheme or to make information available in accordance with the scheme;
- where an authority subject to the EIR does not have an internal complaints process as the regulations require.

Consonant with the Information Commissioner's declared aim of adopting a proportionate approach to taking regulatory action, the Information Commissioner will not issue an enforcement notice where he is satisfied that the risk can be addressed appropriately through less formal means. This might involve the public authority consenting to a practice assessment under s.47(3) or a period of performance monitoring by the ICO, or signing undertakings to comply with the legislation (see below). When considering whether an enforcement notice is appropriate the Information Commissioner will consider:

- the severity and/or repetition of the breach;
- whether there is evidence that obligations are being deliberately or persistently ignored;
- whether there would be an educative or deterrent effect;
- whether it would help clarify or test an issue; and
- whether an example needs to be created or a precedent set.[8]

Few enforcement notices have been issued to date. The first one, however, attracted a great deal of attention, concerning as it did several requests by different people for the Attorney General's advice to the Prime Minister in 2003 on the legality of military intervention in Iraq (enforcement notice dated 22 May 2006 addressed to the Legal Secretariat to the Law Officers).

10.3.4 Undertakings

Although there is no provision for them in the FOIA, the Information Commissioner has adopted a policy of inviting senior officers of public authorities to sign formal undertakings which commit the authority to a particular course of action in order to improve its compliance with the Act. Such documents are signed as the outcome of a negotiation with the Commissioner under which he agrees not to take formal action, such as issuing a practice recommendation or an enforcement notice, in return for the statement of commitment. Although undertakings are published, and hence can be the source of adverse publicity for a public authority, the advantage for the authority is that they allow it to demonstrate a positive attitude towards compliance and to take some comfort in the fact that breach of the undertaking would not render the authority liable to committal for contempt of court, as would be the case with the breach of an enforcement notice. A key advantage for the ICO is that it does not have to devote resources to dealing with the otherwise inevitable appeals against enforcement notices. In various ways, then, the policy fits well with the Information Commissioner's commitment to proportionate regulation. Naturally, though, a serious or repeated breach of an undertaking, as well as being personally embarrassing for the chief executive or other signatory, is likely to be followed by the issue of an enforcement notice (see *Freedom of Information Regulatory Action Policy*, version 2.0 (ICO, updated December 2010), p.5: **www.ico.gov.uk/what_we_cover/taking_action/foi_eir.aspx**).

---

[8] See *Freedom of Information Regulatory Action Policy*, version 2.0 (ICO, updated December 2010).

To illustrate, around March 2012 Dame Gill Morgan DBE, Permanent Secretary of the Welsh Assembly, signed an ICO undertaking stating that the Welsh Government would allocate sufficient resources to the handling of FOI and EIR requests and internal reviews in an endeavour to be consistent in meeting the relevant timescales, and would provide appropriate training to staff. This followed concerns raised by the Information Commissioner and a period of monitoring of the public authority's performance to see if it would improve sufficiently to avoid the need for any enforcement step. The undertaking documents the fact that it did not and that the Information Commissioner considered it was appropriate to 'formalise the Welsh Government's commitment to openness and compliance with the legislation' by way of the undertaking.

10.3.5 Ministerial veto

Under the controversial s.53 of the FOIA, a decision notice or an enforcement notice served on a government department – or the Welsh Assembly Government or any public authority designated by the Secretary of State – can be overridden by a politician. This applies equally to such notices issued under the EIR (reg.18(6)) but not to notices issued under the INSPIRE Regulations (reg.11(2)). The notice ceases to be of effect if within 20 working days of its service by the Information Commissioner (or of the withdrawal or determination of any appeal to the Information Rights Tribunal or the Upper Tribunal under s.57, or any further appeal) an accountable person in relation to the public authority in question gives the Information Commissioner a signed certificate stating that he or she has, on reasonable grounds, formed the opinion that in respect of the request(s) concerned there was no failure:

- to comply with s.1(1)(a) of the FOIA in respect of information which falls within any provision of Part II of the Act stating that the duty to confirm or deny does not arise; or
- to comply with s.1(1)(b) in respect of exempt information.

What this rather opaque drafting means is that where the Information Commissioner (or appeal tribunal) has decided that the information falls within a qualified exemption but that the public interest requires the authority to disclose the information (or at least confirm whether or not it holds such information), the accountable person can trump the Information Commissioner's view on the public interest analysis (or the tribunal's view) and prevent disclosure.

As soon as practicable after delivering the certificate, the accountable person must lay a copy of it before both Houses of Parliament, and the Northern Ireland or Welsh Assembly too, if relevant to those bodies. Further, where the certificate overrides a decision notice, as soon as practicable after delivering the certificate, the accountable person must also inform the complainant of the reasons for his or her opinion but need not, in so doing, provide any exempt information.

An accountable person is in most cases a Cabinet Minister or the Attorney General, but in relation to a Northern Ireland department or public authority would be the First Minister and Deputy First Minister of Northern Ireland acting jointly, or the First Secretary of the Welsh Assembly regarding that body or any designated Welsh public authority.

There is no statutory appeal to the Information Rights Tribunal or the Upper Tribunal against such a certificate. The ministerial decision would, however, be subject to judicial review on the application of a party with the requisite standing – the most obvious candidates being the complainant or the Information Commissioner. To succeed in the Administrative Court, however, would generally mean showing that the Minister had acted irrationally or in a way that no one in his or her position reasonably could have done, which will often be a difficult test to meet.[9] The complainant and even the Information Commissioner may in addition be largely ignorant of the relevant detail lying behind the government's decision, as it would no doubt be withheld, being allegedly exempt and possibly made the subject of a claim to public interest immunity. There would also be the risk of being ordered to pay the government's costs if the application for review was unsuccessful.

When the FOIA first came into force, Lord Falconer, the then Lord Chancellor, sought to allay fears that the government would actually resort to the 'executive override', by indicating that it would only be used very exceptionally and subject to the approval of the entire Cabinet.[10] For his part, the Information Commissioner expressed the view that it was desirable for the credibility of the FOIA, and indeed likely, that the veto would only be used rarely. Indeed in the first four years after the Act came into force, the veto was not resorted to at all. However, between 2009 and the time of writing, it has been deployed five times to block disclosures ordered by the Information Commissioner or the Information Rights Tribunal. In four out of the five cases the power was used to block the release of minutes of Cabinet committee meetings (the relevant exemption being that in s.35 of the FOIA). The first two occasions took place under a Labour administration, regarding (i) minutes from 2002 on the decision to go to war in Iraq and (ii) minutes from 1997 on the issue of Scottish and Welsh devolution. The Conservative/LibDem coalition subsequently exercised the override, again on meetings from 1997 and 1998 on devolution, and also to stop publication of the Department of Health's assessment of the risks posed by its planned overhaul of the NHS. In July 2012 the coalition Attorney General overruled the Information Commissioner's decision in respect of a fresh

---

[9]   In 2009, the Information Commissioner obtained and published legal advice about the prospects of challenging the first such veto. The advice concluded that there was little chance of a successful challenge by way of judicial review (see Annex 1 to *Ministerial Veto on Disclosure of Cabinet Minutes Concerning Military Action against Iraq: Information Commissioner's Report to Parliament*, Stationery Office, HC 622, 10 June 2009): **www.ico.gov.uk/upload/documents/library/ freedom_of_information/research_and_reports/ ico_report_on%20iraq_minutes_ministerial_veto.pdf**.
[10]   See Lord Falconer's comments in 'Falconer rejects risk to information act' (Travis and Evans, *The Guardian*, 1 January 2005); available at: **www.guardian.co.uk/uk_news/story/ 0,,1381649,00.html**.

request for disclosure of the Iraq war meeting minutes. The Attorney General noted in his Statement of Reasons for issuing the veto[11] that in spite of the passing of time and changes in circumstances since the initial request, there remained a need to protect a 'safe space' for Cabinet discussions relating to such highly sensitive matters. Disclosure, he concluded, would have seriously damaged the principle of collective Cabinet responsibility and would have had a detrimental effect on the quality of future Cabinet decision-making.

Following each use of the veto, the Information Commissioner has laid a special report before Parliament, under s.49(2), in which he reflects on the use of the veto. In the third of these, in February 2012, he commented as follows:

> I am particularly disappointed that the Attorney General has overruled the decision before the public interest conclusions that we came to in this case could be properly tested at the Information Rights Tribunal. If the Government want Cabinet minutes to be exempt from freedom of information and not be subject to potential disclosure on public interest grounds, they can propose a change in the law.[12]

However, in July of the same year, following a detailed review of the functioning of the FOIA, the Justice Committee of the House of Commons chose not to recommend a new class-based exemption for information related to policy formation. This was principally due to the absence of compelling evidence that the FOIA was having a significant 'chilling effect' on the decision-making process within government. The Committee did acknowledge, though, that the 'realities of Government' meant the veto would need to be resorted to 'from time to time' to protect the safe space for Cabinet discussion and policy formation.[13] It also suggested that it might be appropriate for the government to revise its stated position[14] that the exercise of the veto would only be appropriate in 'exceptional circumstances' if in reality it was to be used more systematically to protect Cabinet discussions.[15]

10.3.6 Practice recommendations

If it appears to the Information Commissioner that the practice of a public authority does not conform to provisions of the codes of practice issued under ss.45 and 46 of

---

[11] 'Exercise of the Executive Override under section 53 of the Freedom of Information Act in respect of the decision of the Information Commissioner dated 4 July 2012' (ref: FS50417514), 31 July 2012: **www.cabinetoffice.gov.uk/sites/default/files/resources/Statement_of_Reasons-31July2012_0.pdf**.

[12] 'The Information Commissioner presents Ministerial veto report to Parliament' (ICO news release, 29 February 2010). The Information Commissioner's reports to Parliament on the uses of the veto can be accessed via the ICO news archive: **www.ico.gov.uk/news/latest_news.aspx**.

[13] 'The House of Commons Justice Committee's Report on its post-legislative scrutiny of the Freedom of Information Act 2000, First Report of Session 2012–13', HC 96-1, 26 July 2012, Volume I, Chapter 6, paras.200–201: **www.parliament.uk/business/committees/committees-a-z/commons-select/justice-committee/news/foi-report**.

[14] 'Statement of HMG Policy: Use of the executive override under the Freedom of Information Act 2000 as it relates to information falling within the scope of section 35(1)' (Ministry of Justice); available at: **www.justice.gov.uk/downloads/publications/moj/2011/foi-veto-policy.pdf**.

[15] 'House of Commons Justice Committee's Report', note 13 above, para.179.

the FOIA and reg.16 of the EIR, he may give the authority a recommendation specifying the steps which ought in his opinion to be taken for promoting such conformity (FOIA, s.48(1); EIR, reg.16(5)). The Information Commissioner has no jurisdiction to make a practice recommendation in the context of the INSPIRE Regulations.

A practice recommendation differs from the notices discussed above as there are no sanctions for non-compliance with it, nor is there any statutory right of appeal against it. This difference is reflected by the fact that the notices are dealt with in Part IV of the FOIA (entitled 'Enforcement') and practice recommendations in Part III, which is concerned with the general functions of the Information Commissioner. A failure to take account of a practice recommendation will not be subject to formal sanctions but the Information Commissioner's policy is now to publish and publicise all practice recommendations. The Information Commissioner has said that a public authority's failure to take account of a practice recommendation may also be referenced in the annual report he makes to Parliament (see p.5 of the *Freedom of Information Regulatory Action Policy* referred to above). Also worth bearing in mind is that an authority which receives a practice recommendation is by definition at risk of breaching the FOIA itself, so it serves as a warning that procedures need to be addressed in order to avoid a more formal sanction. In the absence of an appeal mechanism, the Information Commissioner's decision to issue a practice recommendation is likely to be amenable to judicial review if one can show grounds, namely, that the decision was irrational, unlawful or procedurally unfair, or else a breach of the Human Rights Act 1998.

Practice recommendations are more likely to be issued in response to grave breaches of the codes than minor breaches. However, repeated poor practice could also be a ground for serving a public authority with a practice recommendation. The ICO may become aware of poor practice when investigating complaints from requesters or items in the media, or else when carrying out a practice assessment under s.47(3) of the FOIA, or when contacted by a public authority for assistance in carrying out its obligations under the FOIA or the DPA. Where the poor practice in question is also a breach of the FOIA or the EIR – such as the provision of inadequate advice and assistance to requesters – the Information Commissioner is more likely to investigate using his enforcement powers and the result will be a decision notice or an enforcement notice rather than a practice recommendation.

The sort of issues likely to be the subject of practice recommendations under the Section 45 Code of Practice include a public authority's failure to do the following:

- provide an internal review procedure;
- complete internal reviews within the appropriate timescales;[16]
- transfer or redirect requests appropriately;
- consult with relevant third parties;

---

[16] In December 2009 the ICO issued practice recommendations to Cardiff Country Council and the UK Border Agency to help them improve the way their internal reviews were conducted.

- make its FOIA obligations clear when entering into contracts with third parties and hence agree to excessive confidentiality obligations inconsistent with FOIA disclosure requirements.

In the case of the Section 46 Code of Practice,[17] practice recommendations can only be made after consultation between the Information Commissioner and the Keeper of Public Records (or the Deputy Keeper in cases concerning Northern Ireland) (s.48(3) and (4)) and this consultation process operates under a Memorandum of Understanding dated 21 March 2005. Issues that might be the subject of a practice recommendation under the Section 46 Code of Practice include a public authority's failure to:

- have in place organisational arrangements that support records management;
- have in place a records management policy;
- retain the records needed for business, regulatory, legal and accountability purposes;
- have in place systems that enable records to be stored and retrieved as necessary;
- know what records are held, where they are and ensure that they remain usable;
- ensure that records are stored securely and that access to them is controlled;
- define how long records should be kept for, and to dispose of them when no longer needed;
- ensure that records shared with other bodies or held on their behalf are managed in accordance with the Code;
- monitor compliance with the Code.

The Information Commissioner may agree an action plan with the public authority that is designed to help it implement the recommendations set out in the practice recommendation. The ICO will then monitor the authority's progress and, after an appropriate interval, may review the authority and publish its findings.

By way of example, Liverpool City Council was issued with a practice recommendation on 8 May 2007 as a result of its repeated failures to handle FOI requests appropriately or in a timely manner, and its failures to respond to the Information Commissioner's investigations. (This included failing to respond to an information notice, leading the Information Commissioner to threaten High Court proceedings.) His concerns about the council had been sparked during his investigation of a complaint from someone who had made a request for information (and by a separate data protection prosecution) and he therefore audited all complaints which the ICO had received about the council. These totalled 18. Among other failings, it was apparent that the council had failed to explain in refusal notices why exemptions applied, and its responses to applicants were inadequate. Upon finding that the council was falling short of good practice in its provision of advice and assistance to requesters (and that a 10-week internal review process was unreasonably lengthy),

---

[17] Lord Chancellor's Code of Practice on the Management of Records Issued under Section 46 of the Freedom of Information Act 2000.

the Information Commissioner recommended action on various fronts, including conducting a review of the resources allocated to dealing with FOI requests, and providing all staff with relevant training (ICO case ref: FPR0152907; see also the connected decision notice in *Liverpool City Council* (FS50079486, 10 January 2007)).

10.4 ADDITIONAL SUPPORT FOR THE INFORMATION COMMISSIONER'S ENFORCEMENT POWERS

10.4.1 Non-compliance with notices punishable as if contempt of court

A public authority which has been served with a decision notice, information notice or enforcement notice might, deliberately or otherwise, fail to comply with the steps specified in the notice within the required deadline.[18] Once the time for compliance has expired, and likewise the time for appealing against the notice (within 28 days of it being sent by the Information Commissioner), or else after an unsuccessful appeal, then assuming that the notice has not been overridden by ministerial veto (see **10.3.5**), the Information Commissioner can take further enforcement action. In many cases the prompt for him to do so will be another complaint from the applicant who is waiting to receive the requested information. The Information Commissioner can certify the non-compliance in writing to the High Court (the Court of Session in Scotland), upon which the court may inquire into the matter and, after hearing any witness who may be produced against or on behalf of the public authority, and after hearing any statement that may be offered in defence, deal with the public authority as if it had committed a contempt of court (s.53(3)). A failure by the Information Commissioner to take this step can only be challenged by way of judicial review (or possibly a complaint to the Parliamentary and Health Service Ombudsman – see **10.6.4**). It cannot form the basis of an appeal to the Information Rights Tribunal: *Charman* v. *Information Commissioner and Olympic Delivery Authority* (EA/2011/0210, 27 April 2012).

The principal sanctions for contempt are an unlimited fine and a fixed-term prison sentence of up to two years (Contempt of Court Act 1981, s.14) but the court can also order sequestration of assets,[19] or issue an injunction (*Elliot* v. *Klinger* [1967] 3 All ER 141). Committal and sequestration, being drastic penalties, are only imposed in serious cases, where there is an element of fault or misconduct (*Fairclough & Sons* v. *Manchester Ship Canal Co. (No.2)* (1897) 41 Sol Jo 225). They will not often feature in the context of the FOIA. The amount of any fine imposed must take account of the seriousness of the contempt and the damage to the public

---

[18] In the case of an information notice, non-compliance includes cases where, in purported compliance with the notice, a public authority makes a statement which is false in a material respect either knowingly or recklessly (s.54(2)).

[19] RSC Order 45, rule 5, contained in Sched.1 to the CPR.

interest.[20] Where a public authority accidentally fails to comply with the Information Commissioner's notice, the court will often simply make an order for costs against it, although this can be on the indemnity basis (e.g. *Stancomb* v. *Trowbridge Urban District Council* [1910] 2 Ch 190).

In principle, only the party bound by an order can be liable for civil contempt (breach of a court order – in this case the Information Commissioner's notice). As s.54(3) provides that the authority can be dealt with as if it had committed a contempt, it seems unlikely that the court could impose sanctions on the individual officers and employees by whom it acts (and who were in fact responsible for breaching the notice), unless it made a further order requiring named individuals to act or refrain from acting in a certain way and they then breached that order. On an application for committal brought by the Information Commissioner over Allerdale Borough Council's failure to adopt a publication scheme and to respond to an enforcement notice, the court ruled that the contempt proceedings should have been instituted against the council rather than its CEO, as they had been (*Information Commissioner* v. *Chief Executive of Allerdale Borough Council*, QBD (Chester), 24 June 2004, unreported).

Where the public authority is a corporate body, however, an order for sequestration or committal could possibly be made against any director or other officer aware of the terms of the notice if they wilfully fail to take adequate steps to ensure compliance, by virtue of RSC Order 45, r.5(1), contained in Sched.1 to the Civil Procedure Rules 1998 (CPR) (see Attorney General for *Tuvalu* v. *Philatelic Distribution Corp. Ltd* [1990] 2 All ER 216, CA). Thus there is the potential for senior officers of a public authority to be fined or in an extreme case imprisoned. There is perhaps in addition a risk that any employee of a public authority who knowingly assists it in breaching a notice issued by the Information Commissioner could be liable for criminal contempt, on the basis that this constituted an interference with the administration of justice. That could certainly be the case in relation to a breach of any subsequent order from the court to comply with the notice (*Marengo* v. *Daily Sketch and Sunday Graphic Ltd* [1948] 1 All ER 406). An intention to interfere with the course of justice would need to be proved, however, with mere recklessness not sufficing (*R* v. *Runting* (1989) 89 Cr App R 243, 247, CA, per Lord Lane LCJ). While it is not possible for the Crown to be held in contempt, a government Minister can be (*M* v. *Home Office* [1994] 1 AC 377).

Procedure regarding orders for committal is dealt with in RSC Order 52 (CPR Sched.1) and the accompanying Practice Direction. Even with civil contempt the criminal standard of proof applies, i.e. the case would need to be proved beyond reasonable doubt (*Dean* v. *Dean* [1987] 1 FLR 517, CA). That said, it is not necessary to prove that the authority intended to breach the Information Commissioner's notice (see *Stancomb*, above, at 194), merely that it knew of its existence (*Z*

---

[20]   *Re Agreement of the Mileage Conference Group of the Tyre Manufacturers' Conference Ltd* [1966] 2 All ER 849 at 862; [1966] 1 WLR 1137 at 1162–3, per Megaw P; *Re Supply of Ready Mixed Concrete* [1991] ICR 52 at 70–2, RPC, per Anthony Lincoln J (*affirmed* [1995] 1 AC 456; [1995] 1 All ER 135, HL).

Ltd v. *A-Z and AA-LL* [1982] QB 558, 580 per Eveleigh LJ) and intended to do the acts or omissions which constituted the contempt (i.e. the failure to comply); an argument by the authority that it was simply negligent in overlooking the notice may well not suffice to avoid liability (*VDU Installations Ltd* v. *Integrated Computer Systems and Cybernetics Ltd* [1989] 1 FSR 378, 394 per Knox J). On the other hand, if breach of the notice is accidental, the authority may well face costs but no additional sanctions (see *Fairclough & Sons*, above). If the Information Commissioner's notice does not express in clear terms what steps the authority must take to comply with it, that might give the authority scope to argue against the making of an order for committal. Any order punishing a contempt, whether civil or criminal, can be appealed to the Court of Appeal (see Administration of Justice Act 1960, s.13(2)(b), as amended by the Courts Act 1971, s.56(4) and Sched.11, Part II and CPR rule 52.3(1)(a)(i)).

Public authorities ought to bear in mind that even where contempt proceedings are not brought, an authority which fails to comply with a notice from the Information Commissioner opens itself up to negative publicity and reputational damage beyond that surrounding the publication of the Information Commissioner's determination, as its non-compliance is likely to be included in a report to Parliament, by way of either a special report or the Information Commissioner's regular annual report under s.49 of the FOIA, or both.

10.4.2 Prosecution of offences under s.77 (obstructing disclosure)

Where a public authority has been asked for information, it is an offence under s.77 of the FOIA for the authority or any of its officers, employees or anyone under its direction to alter, deface, block, erase, destroy or conceal any record which it holds, with the intention of preventing disclosure of any information to which the applicant would have been entitled under s.1 of the FOIA (subject to payment of any fee). The offence is punishable in the magistrates' court by a fine of up to level 5 on the standard scale (currently £5,000 (Criminal Justice Act 1982, as amended, s.37)). Government departments are not liable to prosecution under this section but a person in the public service of the Crown can be (s.81(3)). This offence applies equally under reg.19 of the EIR but not under the INSPIRE Regulations.

The Information Commissioner is a prosecuting authority for these purposes and a prosecution under this section can only be started in England, Wales and Northern Ireland by him or by, or with the consent of, the Director of Public Prosecutions. One limiting factor is that under s.127 of the Magistrates' Court Act 1980, proceedings for this offence have to be commenced within six months of the offence occurring but the ICO might not be aware of the offence in sufficient time to do so. If on the facts the offence is found to be a continuing one, perhaps in a case involving concealment, the six-month period could in effect be extended.

10.4.3 Exchange of information with other ombudsmen

Schedule 7 to the FOIA (which is given effect by s.76(2), as amended) provides that certain ombudsmen[21] can make available to the Information Commissioner any information which they obtain in the exercise of their statutory functions if it appears to them to relate to a matter in respect of which the Information Commissioner could exercise any power conferred by Part IV of the FOIA (which includes the issuing of enforcement, information and decision notices and the powers of entry and inspection) or s.48 of the FOIA (practice recommendations) or the commission of a s.77 offence. Information relevant to enforcement under the EIR and INSPIRE Regulations would also be covered by these provisions.[22]

10.4.4 The Information Commissioner's powers of entry and inspection

Where the Information Commissioner has reasonable grounds to suspect that a public authority has failed to comply with any requirement of Part I of the FOIA or of one of his notices (not including practice recommendations), or similarly where he has reasonable grounds to suspect an authority of committing an offence under s.77 of the FOIA (see **10.4.2**), he can apply to a circuit judge for a warrant authorising entry to any premises[23] and search, inspection and seizure of materials which may be evidence of such breaches. The warrant may in addition authorise the Information Commissioner to inspect, examine, operate and test any equipment found there in which information held by the public authority may be recorded. This will give the Information Commissioner access to computer files. These powers are granted under s.55 of and Sched.3 to the FOIA and apply equally in the context of the EIR (EIR, reg.18(2)(a)) and the INSPIRE Regulations (INSPIRE Regulations, reg.11(2)(e)).

Except where urgent or where a warning might prevent seizure of relevant evidence, the judge will need to be satisfied before he grants the warrant that:

---

[21] The Parliamentary Commissioner for Administration, the Commissioners for Local Administration in England, the Health Service Commissioners for England, the Public Services Ombudsman for Wales, the Northern Ireland Commissioner for Complaints and the Assembly Ombudsman for Northern Ireland.

[22] Similarly, s.76 of the FOIA (as amended) provides that the Information Commissioner may disclose to those same ombudsmen (plus the Scottish Public Service Ombudsman and the Commissioner for Older People in Wales) any information which he has obtained under the FOIA or the DPA if it appears to him that it relates to matters investigable by them in accordance with their functions under the statutes tabulated in s.76 of the FOIA. Similarly, the Information Commissioner may make appropriate disclosures to the Scottish Information Commissioner (FOIA, s.76A). The same applies to information which the Information Commissioner obtains under the EIR (reg.18(10)) and the INSPIRE Regulations (reg.11(11)).

[23] Not only premises owned or occupied by the public authority in question but any premises at which the Information Commissioner reasonably suspects there to be relevant evidence (FOIA, Sched.3, para.1). The term also applies to any vessel, vehicle, aircraft or hovercraft, in which case references to the occupier of the premises mean the person in charge of that vehicle (FOIA, Sched.3, para.13).

(i)   the Information Commissioner gave seven days' written notice to the occupier of the premises demanding access;

(ii)   either access was demanded at a reasonable hour but unreasonably refused or entry was granted but the occupier unreasonably refused to comply with a request of the Information Commissioner or his staff; and

(iii) the occupier has been notified by the Information Commissioner of the application for the warrant and has had an opportunity of being heard by the judge in relation to whether it should be issued or not.

Schedule 3 to the FOIA contains provisions for the manner of execution of such a warrant which include the following:

- a person executing the warrant may use such reasonable force as may be necessary (para.4);
- the warrant must be executed at a reasonable hour unless the person executing it considers that he or she has grounds to suspect that to do so would prevent finding the evidence which is sought (para.5);
- the warrant must be shown to an officer or member of staff of the occupier of the premises (whether the occupier is a public authority or not), if present, and a copy must be given to him or her or left in a prominent place (para.6(1) and (2));
- the person executing the warrant must on request give a receipt for any item seized (para.7(1));
- if requested by the occupier of the premises, and if the person executing the warrant considers it is possible without causing undue delay, he or she must give a copy of anything seized under the warrant (para.7(2));
- anything seized under the warrant can be retained for as long as is necessary in all the circumstances (para.7(2)).

Certain information is exempt from inspection or seizure under the warrant. This applies first to any national security-related information falling within the exemptions in s.23(1) or s.24(1) in Part II of the FOIA (Sched.3, para.8) or reg.9(5)(a) of the INSPIRE Regulations (INSPIRE Regulations, reg.11(9)(b)) and, in the context of the EIR, any information whose disclosure would adversely affect national security (EIR, reg.18(4)(h)). Secondly, a warrant cannot authorise inspection or seizure of any legally privileged communication held by a client or his or her legal adviser which contains legal advice relating to the FOIA, the EIR or the INSPIRE Regulations or is made in contemplation of proceedings under or arising out of such legislation (Sched.3, para.9). This does not extend to any material held in furtherance of a criminal purpose or held by anyone other than the lawyer and client or client's representative. Where the occupier of the premises objects to inspection or seizure on the ground that some of the material contains matters which are covered by these exemptions, he or she must nevertheless give the person exercising the warrant a copy of the remaining material if the latter so requests (Sched.3, para.10).

10.4.5 Related criminal offences: obstruction of execution of a warrant

The following offences are created by para.12 of Sched.3 to the FOIA, and apply equally in the context of the EIR and the INSPIRE Regulations:

- intentionally obstructing a person in the execution of a warrant issued under Sched.3;
- failing without reasonable excuse to give any person executing a warrant such assistance as he or she may reasonably require for its execution.

10.5 INTERNAL REVIEW FOLLOWING A COMPLAINT

Where an applicant has requested information from a public authority and is dissatisfied with the result (perhaps because it has been refused or he or she suspects that there is additional disclosable information which has not been produced, or he or she considers that the authority has not satisfied particular procedural requirements imposed by the FOIA), his or her first step must in most cases be to complain to the authority itself, asking it to reconsider its decision. Unlike the Freedom of Information (Scotland) Act 2002 (s.20) and the EIR (reg.11), the FOIA does not require authorities to have a procedure for reviewing decisions but the guidance in the Section 45 Code of Practice is that they ought to (para.36).

Not only is a complaint to the authority in question likely to be the most straightforward way of resolving the matter but it is also virtually required by the FOIA by virtue of s.50(2)(a), which permits the Information Commissioner not to entertain a complaint where the complainant has not exhausted any internal complaints procedure which the public authority provides in conformity with the codes of practice under s.45 of the FOIA or reg.16(1) of the EIR, or with reg.13 of the INSPIRE Regulations.

From an applicant's point of view, it is worth bearing in mind that the more wide-ranging the request (and the larger the public authority in question), the more likely it is in practice that relevant information will have been missed first time around and thus a different result might be reached when the request is looked at by a fresh pair of eyes, which will often be those of a more senior person, who may have a better or broader view of the work of the organisation.

10.5.1 The Section 45 Code of Practice

The Section 45 Code of Practice contains guidance for public authorities from the Secretary of State for Constitutional Affairs (now the Secretary of State for Justice) on practice which he thinks it desirable for them to follow in connection with the discharge of their functions under Part I of the FOIA. Breach may result in the Information Commissioner issuing a practice recommendation but cannot form the basis of a s.50(1) complaint by an applicant unless it also constitutes a breach of the FOIA. Paragraph 36 of the Section 45 Code of Practice suggests that in the first instance a complaint should, if possible, be resolved informally. If this cannot be achieved swiftly or satisfactorily, however, the public authority ought to give the applicant details of its internal complaints procedure, and of how to contact the Information Commissioner about the matter, should he or she wish to. Complaints procedures are to be as clear and simple as possible and to encourage prompt determination of complaints (para.39).

Similarly, when communicating a decision to refuse a request on the grounds that an exemption in Part II of the FOIA applies or that the request is vexatious or repetitious or that the estimated cost of complying with the request exceeds the free-provision ceiling, public authorities are obliged, under s.17(7) of the FOIA, to give applicants details of their internal complaints procedure, or else state that they do not have one. In doing so, para.37 of the Section 45 Code of Practice says they should also inform the applicant of his or her right to complain to the Information Commissioner under s.50 if he or she is still dissatisfied following the authority's review.

Applicants wishing to submit a complaint to a public authority should therefore request details of the authority's complaints procedure, if not already provided, and follow it. Details of the complaints procedure will often be published under a public authority's publication scheme and may be available on its website.

Applicants should put their complaints in writing or confirm them in writing if made initially by telephone or in person. (Complaints – 'representations' – under the EIR must be made in writing: reg.11(2).) Providing a clear, dated record of the complaint will assist its resolution by the public authority and also any subsequent complaint to the Information Commissioner. It also obliges the authority to deal with it properly because para.38 of the Section 45 Code of Practice advises authorities to treat as a complaint any written communication from the applicant (which includes faxes and emails) expressing dissatisfaction with its response to a request for information, as well as any written communication from a person who considers that the authority is not complying with its publication scheme. Such communications are to be handled in accordance with the authority's complaints procedure, even if the applicant does not expressly state his or her desire for the authority to review its decision or handling of the request. Nonetheless it would be advisable to mark the envelope or entitle the email, 'Request for internal review under FOIA/EIR', to ensure it is dealt with promptly. In urgent or significant cases which are likely to be appealed to the Information Commissioner, it would also be prudent to send any letters by recorded delivery in order to have proof of posting and evidence of receipt by the authority. Similarly, to obtain a speedier result it will be worth making a telephone call to find out the name of the FOI officer or other appropriate person to direct the request to.

10.5.2 Formulating arguments for and against the complaint

Even if not required by the relevant public authority's complaints procedure, it will usually help an applicant to set out in as much detail as possible the grounds for disputing the authority's notice refusing disclosure of the requested information. Not only is a well argued case more likely to succeed in the first instance, but it may well draw out more detailed reasons for any further refusal. This would be of value to the applicant, first in evaluating whether it is worth referring the matter to the Information Commissioner, and second in knowing what issues and arguments to deal with when putting together a complaint to the Information Commissioner.

An applicant requesting an internal review would thus be well advised to consider the reasons for non-disclosure given in the authority's refusal notice against the detail of the exemption provisions in Part II of the FOIA or the exceptions in reg.12 of the EIR (legislation available at **www.ico.gov.uk/ what_we_cover/legislation.aspx**). Helpful interpretation of how those provisions (and the public interest test) should apply in practice is provided not only in books such as this but also in the ICO's *Guide to Freedom of Information* and more detailed guidance notes and the specialist FOI Policy Knowledge Base available on the ICO website (see: **www.ico.gov.uk/for_organisations/ freedom_of_information.aspx**), as well as the guidance for public authorities produced by the Ministry of Justice (see **www.justice.gov.uk/information-access-rights/foi-guidance-for-practitioners**). Similarly, the Department for Environment, Food and Rural Affairs (Defra) has published guidance on the EIR (*Environmental Information Regulations 2004 Detailed Guidance* (revised July 2010): **http://archive.defra.gov.uk/corporate/policy/opengov/eir/index.htm**). The applicant may be able to support the argument for disclosure further by pointing to cases where information was supplied in response to comparable requests, and could usefully consider:

- reported rulings of the Information Rights Tribunal (see **www.justice.gov.uk/ tribunals/information-rights/decisions**), the Upper Tribunal (**www.judiciary.gov.uk/media/tribunal-decisions/osccs-decisions**), and the courts (**www.bailii.org**);
- published decisions of the Information Commissioner (see **www.ico.gov.uk**) – note that the site permits searches by section number of the legislation and by public authority);
- any disclosure log published by the authority in question, which will show whether it has granted similar requests in the past (see, for example, details of information released by Defra at **http://archive.defra.gov.uk/corporate/ policy/opengov/defra/available/inforelease/index.htm**); and
- disclosure logs kept by similar organisations.[24]

---

[24] Anyone with a need for more comprehensive research might wish to consider also public interest arguments drawn from the freedom of information case law of comparable jurisdictions, and also the decisions of the UK Parliamentary Ombudsman under the non-statutory Code of Practice on Access to Government Information, which was in force from 1994 to 2004. See, for example, *Balancing the Public Interest: Applying the Public Interest Test to Exemptions in the UK Freedom of Information Act 2000* (Cook, August 2003), a study carried out by the University College London Constitution Unit at the request of the Information Commissioner (available at: **www.humanrightsinitiative.org/**

In addition, assistance with complaints under the EIR can sometimes be obtained from the EU Directive which it sought to implement – Council Directive 2003/4/EC on public access to environmental information. The Directive has been successfully used by an applicant to challenge the reasonableness of fees charged for providing photocopies of planning documents (*Markinson* v. *Information Commissioner* (EA/2005/0014, 28 March 2006)). In *Office of Communications* v. *Information Commissioner* [2010] UKSC 3, a case under the EIR, the Supreme Court found that it was necessary to refer a question to the European Court of Justice (ECJ) for a preliminary ruling about the proper interpretation of Directive 2003/4/EC in order to determine whether a public authority could weigh the public interest in different exceptions together against the public interest in disclosure, rather than having to weigh the balance for each exception separately. The response from the ECJ was that public authorities do have to take this cumulative approach ([2011] EUECJ C-71/10). This accorded with the Court of Appeal's judgment and the 3–2 majority view in the Supreme Court but against the earlier decisions of the Information Tribunal and the Administrative Court.

Public authorities would of course also be well advised to have regard to such sources of guidance and authority, and they are likely to find that giving as detailed reasons as they can for turning down requests (supported by reference to any cases from the above list) is the best way of reducing the number of complaints to the Information Commissioner that they are forced to deal with. As stated in **10.1**, however, and as the Information Commissioner has underlined, 'it would be a mistake to regard one decision as setting a binding precedent in other circumstances'.[25] The Information Rights Tribunal also frequently notes that it is free to depart from its own earlier decisions, a principle that was confirmed by the Upper Tribunal in *London Borough of Camden* v. *Information Commissioner and Yiannis Voyias* [2012] UKUT 190 (AAC) at [20] where it was also said that in order to aid consistency in decision making the Information Rights Tribunal is nevertheless to regard its own earlier decisions as of 'persuasive authority'. However, the Information Commissioner does follow the rulings of the Information Rights Tribunal, which in turn follows any FOIA-related rulings of the Upper Tribunal and the Court of Appeal.

10.5.3 A fair, thorough and independent review

The Section 45 Code of Practice provides that an authority's complaints procedure should constitute a fair and thorough review of the handling of the request and of decisions taken pursuant to the FOIA, including decisions about where the public

---

programs/ai/rti/international/laws_papers/uk/public_interest_MCook_Aug03.pdf); and *Parliamentary Ombudsman Monitoring of the Non-statutory Codes of Practice 1994–2005* (HC 59, Parliamentary Ombudsman, May 2005) (details at: **www.ombudsman.org.uk/about-us/media-centre/press-releases/2005/pr2004-04**).
[25] *Regulation under the Freedom of Information Act 2000 and the Environmental Information Regulations 2004* (ICO, March 2005), para.41.

interest lies in respect of exempt information (para.39). There should be a full reconsideration of the case and where the complaint concerns a request for information the review should be undertaken, where reasonably practicable, by somebody senior to the person who took the original decision (para.40). The Information Commissioner has glossed this as 'someone independent of the original decision making process'.[26]

10.5.4 Timescales

No time limit for the submission of requests for internal review under the FOIA is specified in the FOIA or the Section 45 Code of Practice but complainants ought to consult the procedures of the relevant public authority to see what regulations it imposes in this regard. The position is different with complaints under the EIR and the Freedom of Information (Scotland) Act 2002 (see **10.5.6**). If the authority refuses to accept a complaint, saying it is out of time, the applicant should apply direct to the Information Commissioner.

As for public authorities' responses, the Section 45 Code of Practice states that complaints should be acknowledged promptly and that the complainant should be informed of the authority's target date for determining the complaint. Where it is apparent to the authority that a complaint will take longer than estimated to deal with, it should inform the applicant and explain the reason for the delay (para.41). Authorities are encouraged to set their own target times for dealing with complaints but these are required to be reasonable and subject to regular review. They must also be published, together with details of how successful the authority is in meeting them (para.42).

Following complaints that public authorities were abusing the review process to stymie the progress of complaints for weeks or months, the Commissioner introduced guidance on what he considers a reasonable period for dealing with requests for review. He advises that public authorities should respond substantively to such a request within 20 working days of the request in most cases (the same period as appears in the Freedom of Information (Scotland) Act 2002, s.21(1)) and within 40 days in exceptional circumstances.[27]

Where a public authority does not meet these deadlines, the Commissioner is likely to exercise his discretion under s.50(2)(a) to entertain a complaint from a requester even though the internal review has not been completed. Significant or repeated unreasonable delays in dealing with internal reviews can result in monitoring by the Commissioner's enforcement team and possibly the issuing of a practice recommendation (see **10.3.6**).

---

[26] Ibid., para.10.
[27] See the ICO's *Guide to Freedom of Information*: **www.ico.gov.uk/for_organisations/ freedom_of_information/guide/refusing_a_request.aspx.**

10.5.5 Outcomes

The Section 45 Code of Practice provides, naturally enough, that the complainant ought always to be informed of the outcome of the complaint (para.40). Where the outcome of a complaint is a decision that information should be disclosed which was previously withheld, the information in question should be disclosed as soon as practicable and the applicant should be informed how soon this will be (para.44). Where the internal review reveals that the procedures within an authority have not been properly followed, the authority is to apologise to the applicant and take appropriate steps to prevent similar errors occurring in future (para.45).

Where the outcome of a complaint is that an initial decision to withhold information is upheld, or is otherwise in the authority's favour, the applicant is to be informed of the right to ask the Information Commissioner for a determination on whether the request for information has been dealt with in accordance with the requirements of Part I of the FOIA, and is to be given details of how to do so (para.46).

Public authorities are required to maintain records of all complaints and their outcome. They are also supposed to have procedures in place for monitoring complaints and for reviewing, and, if necessary, amending, procedures for dealing with requests for information where such action is indicated by more than occasional reversals of initial decisions (para.43).

10.5.6 EIR

Public authorities are obligated by reg.11 of the EIR to conduct an internal review, free of charge, where the applicant makes written representations about the handling of his or her request within 40 working days of the date on which he or she believes the public authority has failed to comply with a requirement of the EIR. (This is essentially the same time period as applies under the Freedom of Information (Scotland) Act 2002, s.20(5)). In most cases this will mean within 40 working days of receipt of the refusal notice turning down the original request. The Code of Practice on the Discharge of the Obligations of Public Authorities under the Environmental Information Regulations 2004, issued under reg.16 of the EIR (Regulation 16 Code of Practice) states, as with the Section 45 Code of Practice under the FOIA, that any written expression of dissatisfaction should be treated as a complaint. The public authority must reply as soon as possible, within 40 working days in any event. Notification of any revised decision by the authority must include a statement of its failure to comply with the EIR, the action it has decided on in order to comply with the relevant requirement and the period within which that action is to be taken (reg.11). Where the decision is taken to release information this should be actioned immediately (Regulation 16 Code of Practice, para.65). Where an authority fails to provide an internal review in spite of these requirements, the applicant can complain to the Information Commissioner, who will generally issue a decision notice requiring the authority to do so.[28]

10.5.7 INSPIRE Regulations

The INSPIRE Regulations require public authorities (and participating third parties) to make certain information available in a common format regarding any electronic datasets they hold containing defined categories of location-specific environmental information (e.g. map data), and to create services for accessing these datasets. The objective of the EU Directive 2007/2/EC which the INSPIRE Regulations implement is to enforce data sharing so as to facilitate the development of better environmental policy across EU Member States.

The FOIA and EIR codes of practice do not apply to public authorities in the context of the INSPIRE Regulations. However, the INSPIRE Regulations themselves require relevant public authorities and third parties to establish an internal complaints procedure for dealing with complaints relating to the performance of any aspect of their functions under the INSPIRE Regulations (reg.13). Such complaints might for example cover: the way they have provided (or restricted access to) relevant data or services to the public or other public authorities; the way they have charged for such access and services; how they have dealt with the technical standards set by the INSPIRE Regulations; or how they have handled personal data.

Anyone wishing to complain about these or other matters must do so in writing and follow the procedure published by the relevant public authority or third party. The INSPIRE Regulations require the public authority/third party to determine complaints within a reasonable time and notify the complainant of its response without delay. Guidance issued by Defra adds that reasons must be given in support of that response (*A Guide to the INSPIRE Regulations* (Defra, December 2009): see **www.defra.gov.uk**). Where the complainant is not satisfied with the response, he or she can refer the matter to the Information Commissioner under s.50(1) of the FOIA (which is applied to the INSPIRE Regulations by reg.11) if it relates to the public authority's, or the third party's, obligations under regs.7(4)(c) or 9. These provisions deal with, respectively, user-friendliness of access and validity of any limitations to access which have been claimed, for instance on grounds of national security. Although the guidance is not clear on how to deal with complaints on other aspects of the INSPIRE Regulations, they would perhaps best be referred to Defra, given that the Secretary of State has the function of enforcing the requirements of reg.6 (metadata) and reg.7 (network services), other than reg.7(4)(c) (see reg.14(3)). Contact details as follows: Chief Information Officer Directorate, Defra, Area 1D Ergon House, Horseferry Road, London, SW1P 2AL; email: inspire@defra.gsi.gov.uk

---

[28] See further in the FOI Policy Knowledge Base, reference LTT 191 on the ICO website: **www.ico.gov.uk/foikb/index.htm**.

Where the Secretary of State investigates the matter he or she may be obliged to publish his or her findings (see reg.14(3)(b)).

10.6   COMPLAINING TO THE INFORMATION COMMISSIONER

10.6.1   Complaints about individual requests for information

The term 'complaints' when used in this context is convenient shorthand for what is in fact an application to the Information Commissioner under s.50(1) of the FOIA, by a person who requested information from a public authority, for a decision on whether that request was dealt with by the authority in accordance with its obligations under Part I of the FOIA (or Parts 2 and 3 of the EIR or regs.7(4)(c) and 9 of the INSPIRE Regulations). An application under s.50(1) cannot be made merely because a public authority has breached a code of practice provision.

Those obligations include, most significantly, the obligation under s.1(1) of the FOIA to confirm or deny whether the authority holds information requested by the applicant and to communicate it to him or her (subject, most importantly, to the exemptions in Part II). However, it also includes many obligations of a more procedural nature, so that a complaint could, for instance, be made to the Information Commissioner where the applicant believes:

- the public authority has charged excessive fees for responding to his or her request (FOIA, ss.9 and 13; EIR, reg.8);
- the authority took longer to respond to the request than it should have (FOIA, s.10; EIR, regs.5(2), 7 and 14);
- the authority was unreasonable in not complying with his or her preference for how he or she wished to receive the information (FOIA, s.11; EIR, reg.6);
- the authority was wrong to say the cost of complying with the request meant that it was not obliged to comply (FOIA, ss.12 and 13; EIR, reg.8);
- the authority was wrong to label the request vexatious or repetitious and refuse to deal with it (FOIA, s.14; EIR, reg.12(4)(b));
- the authority failed to offer him or her appropriate advice and assistance in formulating (or refining) his or her request (FOIA, s.16; EIR, reg.9);
- the authority should have given reasons for claiming that the information sought was exempt (FOIA, s.17(1), (3) and (4); EIR, reg.14(3)).

The typical stages through which a complaint to the Information Commissioner will pass are described below. Certain aspects of this procedure are set out in the FOIA but much of the detail is a matter of discretion for the Information Commissioner. This detail can be found in various ICO publications, including: (i) *Guide to Freedom of Information*; (ii) *How We Deal with Complaints – A Guide for Public Authorities* (September 2011); and (iii) *How We Deal with Complaints – A Guide for Complainants* (November 2011) (see **www.ico.gov.uk**).

How to submit a complaint

Applications for a decision under s.50(1) should be submitted to the ICO in writing either by post to First Contact Team, Information Commissioner's Office, Wycliffe House, Water Lane, Wilmslow, Cheshire SK9 5AF; or by fax to 01625 524 510. A complaint can be submitted by email to casework@ico.gsi.gov.uk but given the need to send accompanying documents, which an applicant may not have in electronic form, it may be easier to do so by post (in which case retain a copy for reference) or by fax. A complaint form can be printed off from the ICO website but it is not necessary to use it. Queries can be made via the telephone helpline on 0303 123 1113.

The applicant must be identified, i.e. complaints submitted anonymously will not be considered. This does not preclude the submission of requests by a named person on behalf of another whose identity is not disclosed. An address must also be provided, and it can be helpful for the applicant to give his or her telephone number and/or email address as well.

Only the person who submitted the original request (or a person acting on his or her behalf) may apply to the Information Commissioner under s.50(1) of the FOIA. Third parties cannot apply (see **10.10**).

In order to consider the complaint, the Information Commissioner will expect to receive the following, as appropriate:

- brief details of the issues the applicant wishes the Information Commissioner to consider;
- a copy of the original request for information, and any acknowledgement of receipt from the authority (e.g. an automated email response);
- a copy of the refusal notice issued by the public authority;
- a copy of the applicant's complaint to the public authority concerning that initial refusal of information (i.e. the applicant's request for an internal review), or if no such complaint was made, an explanation why not;
- a copy of the public authority's response following its reconsideration of the request, or if no response has been provided, any acknowledgement of receipt from the authority in respect of the request for internal review (e.g. an automated email response);
- any other information the applicant believes relevant. This could include, for example, the complainant's arguments as to why the information does not fall within the exemptions claimed by the authority, or why the public interest favours disclosure if a qualified exemption is relevant. Although there is no requirement for an applicant to set out any arguments in support of the access request, it may well be in his or her interests to do so, both in order to persuade and to make decision making as speedy as possible. (For sources of help in formulating such arguments, see **10.5.2**.) If the applicant needs the information urgently, it would be relevant to say so and why. There is no guarantee, however, that the complaint will be expedited as a result.

Applications must be submitted without undue delay or the Information Commissioner is entitled not to consider them (s.50(2)(b)). 'Undue delay' is not defined in the FOIA but whereas the Information Commissioner indicated in the early years of the FOI regime that complaints should be submitted within two months of receipt of the public authority's final refusal to disclose the information, i.e. following any internal review, he has now extended that to six months from the final refusal. This longer period mirrors that in the Freedom of Information (Scotland) Act 2002 (s.47(4)). Complaints submitted later than this might still be considered if there is a good reason for the delay. Equally, complaints should not be submitted to the ICO too soon, which normally means no earlier than the public authority's response to a request for internal review or, if no response has been received, 40 days after submitting that request for a review of the original decision.

There is no fee to pay on submission of a complaint to the ICO and neither the applicant nor the public authority can be ordered by the Information Commissioner to pay the other's costs. In some cases, parties (especially public authorities) will want to obtain expert evidence and/or legal advice in order to argue their case before the Information Commissioner. Such costs will potentially be recoverable only if the matter goes on appeal to the tribunals (see **10.7.1** and **10.7.2**).

The Information Commissioner decides whether to deal with the complaint

The ICO must first consider whether the complaint is an appropriate one to deal with. Under s.50(2) of the FOIA, the Information Commissioner has a duty to make a decision on all complaints about the way a public authority has handled a request for information under s.1, except in the four specific situations listed below. There is no duty to make a decision on a complaint:

1. Where the complainant has not exhausted any complaints procedure provided by the public authority in conformity with the Section 45 Code of Practice, i.e. by requesting an internal review (see **10.5.1**). The Information Commissioner might, however, be prepared to take on such a complaint where, for example, the public authority has simply not responded to the applicant's request for information, or where there is nobody suitable to undertake the internal review because there is no one on the authority's staff who is independent of, and more senior to, the original decision maker.
2. Where there has been undue delay in making the application (in most cases this means anything later than six months after the public authority's final decision).
3. Where the application is frivolous or vexatious. These terms are not defined in the FOIA but a good insight into the Information Commissioner's approach can be obtained from his guidance on s.14 of the FOIA, under which public authorities do not have to comply with 'vexatious' information requests. In that guidance (*When Can a Request Be Considered Vexatious or Repeated?*,

version 4 (ICO, December 2008)), the Information Commissioner notes that deciding whether a request is vexatious is a balancing exercise, taking into account the context and history of the request. 'The key question is whether the request is likely to cause unjustified distress, disruption or irritation.' The following questions will guide the Commissioner in reaching a conclusion:

- Could the request fairly be seen as obsessive?
- Is the request harassing the authority or causing distress to staff?
- Would complying with the request impose a significant burden in terms of expense and distraction?
- Is the request designed to cause disruption or annoyance?
- Does the request lack any serious purpose or value?

These criteria are arguably capable of covering a situation where the breach complained of is trivial (e.g. a complainant had received all the information requested within 21 days rather than 20).

4.   Where the application has been withdrawn or abandoned. An FOI complaint might be withdrawn after it has been settled informally (see below). In other situations, where an individual submits a complaint to the Information Commissioner but stops replying to the ICO's letters during the course of the investigation, the Information Commissioner may have to conclude that the individual has abandoned his or her application for a decision and may close the case without issuing a decision notice.

Even where there is no duty to determine a complaint, the Commissioner may exercise his discretion to do so nonetheless.

An applicant whose application for a decision under s.50(1) is not proceeded with on one of the four s.50(2) grounds discussed above could challenge the Information Commissioner's decision in that regard by way of judicial review – there is no appeal to the Information Rights Tribunal in these circumstances (see *Day* v. *Information Commissioner and Department for Work and Pensions* (EA/ 2006/0069, 24 September 2007), para.8). The bar to success would be set high, however, as the applicant would need to show that nobody in the Information Commissioner's position could reasonably have come to the same decision.

It had seemed that there was also a ground upon which the Information Commissioner would have to decline to entertain a complaint purportedly made under s.50(1). This was where the complaint related to a request to a body that was only subject to the FOIA in respect of some of its information and where the requested information fell outside that category. The House of Lords decided, however, in a majority judgment, that requests to such 'hybrid' bodies are validly made under s.50(1) and the Information Commissioner does have jurisdiction to issue a decision notice in response, which can thus be appealed to the Information Rights Tribunal as normal rather than being subject to challenge by way of judicial review (*Sugar* v. *British Broadcasting Corporation* [2009] UKHL 9).

The Information Commissioner's investigation

Where a complaint is appropriate for the Information Commissioner to deal with, the ICO will send an acknowledgement to the complainant and a case officer will be assigned to investigate the complaint and act as the contact point for both complainant and public authority, keeping them up to date with progress on the matter. The case officer provides a complaint reference number and their direct contact telephone number. The ICO communicates with parties not only by post, but also by telephone and email. By 2008 the extent of the backlog of cases meant that a newly submitted complaint could languish for several months before the investigation started. Happily that is no longer the situation, although it remains true that while the ICO aims to deal with all complaints within six months, complex cases still take longer (see **10.6.2**).

In all but the clearest of cases the Information Commissioner asks the public authority for information so he can make his assessment. The authority is given 20 working days to provide a detailed explanation about the grounds on which it withheld the information from the requester or, as the case may be, why it believes it does not hold the requested information, or how it calculated the fee charged, or why it did not provide advice and assistance or why it treated the information request as vexatious or a repeat of a recent request. A public authority that cannot meet the deadline must contact the case officer immediately to discuss this. The Commissioner's guidance advises that a public authority's submission should include the following:

- what information the complainant requested, why an exemption applies and, where applicable, how the public interest in maintaining that exemption outweighs the public interest in disclosure;
- information about the context of the request, and the role of any staff named within the information provided or withheld;
- copies of documents that support the points made in the submission;
- background to help the ICO understand the context and sensitivity of the information sought by the complainant;
- relevant legal advice (although there is no obligation to provide this);
- a view on whether it might be possible to release the information in a redacted version;
- a view on whether the case may be open to informal resolution, such as if the authority might be willing to release some or all of the information to the complainant or whether there is some other possible action that would satisfy him or her; and
- a description of any information in the submission which the authority would prefer the Information Commissioner not to disclose to other parties making a FOIA request to the ICO (which is itself a public authority subject to the FOIA) and an explanation why not.

The Information Commissioner may also want to see any information that was withheld from the applicant or redacted (blanked out). He is entitled to ask for relevant unrecorded information too, such as what officials know of the relevant matter beyond what is documented (FOIA, s.51(8)). He may also wish the authority to tell him any views on the access request expressed by an interested third party, such as on the potential for prejudice to arise from disclosure or the relative public interests in disclosing or withholding the information. If he judges that any such third party's views are potentially relevant but have not been provided, the Information Commissioner will in some cases approach the third party himself and in other cases invite the public authority to do so.

It is worth noting in passing that a public authority cannot refuse to disclose any information to the Information Commissioner or the Information Rights Tribunal which is 'necessary for the discharge of their functions' on the grounds that in doing so it would be making itself civilly or criminally liable – by breaching a confidence, for example (DPA, s.58 as amended by FOIA, Sched.2, para.18). Nor will a claim of legal privilege permit the public authority to withhold information from the Information Commissioner except where it concerns FOIA-related communications (s.51(5) and (6)). Public authorities can at least take comfort that it is an offence for current or former Commissioners or ICO staff to disclose non-public information obtained in the course of their duties unless they have lawful authority to do so (s.59 of the DPA).

If the public authority does not volunteer this information promptly, the Information Commissioner could issue a formal information notice or decide the case on the basis of the information before him. He would normally warn of his intention to serve an information notice. If the Information Commissioner considers he has not received all the information he requires from a public authority following service of an information notice, he can seek a warrant to obtain access to any premises where he might find such information (see **10.4.4**). If the public authority claims it does not hold the information requested but the ICO is not satisfied with the quality of the searches already carried out, the case officer will ask the authority to make further searches so that the Information Commissioner can determine, on the balance of probabilities, whether the relevant information is held (or was held at the time of the request) or not.[29] Where relevant documents are identified that proved difficult to locate initially, the Information Commissioner may consider making a practice recommendation to ensure the public authority is in compliance with the Section 46 Code of Practice on records management.

In sensitive cases and where the security of the public authority's information is a particular issue, government departments (and potentially other public authorities) can ask the Information Commissioner himself or named staff to go and inspect papers *in situ* rather than sending them to the ICO. In other cases, the Information

---

[29]   For a review of cases on whether requested information was held by a public authority or not, and the adequacy of its search, see the FOI Policy Knowledge Base, reference LTT 121 on the ICO website.

Commissioner may agree it is mutually beneficial for his staff to inspect information at the public authority's premises rather than being provided with it, such as where the papers are voluminous or need technical explanation by officials.

The public authority should consider whether to submit evidence in support of its argument that a certain exemption applies. For example, where a public authority is relying on the exemption under s.29(1)(a) in respect of disclosures which would be likely to prejudice the economic interests of the UK or part of it, the authority's arguments might be bolstered by presenting the Information Commissioner with a report prepared by a suitably qualified economist or industry expert. Similarly, in the context of the exemption under s.41, an authority may wish to obtain professional legal advice on whether the disclosure of requested material would breach a duty of confidence owed to a third party and whether there would be a defence of public interest or not. (The Information Commissioner may sometimes appoint his own expert to advise on the validity of the arguments presented to him in relation to the exemptions.) The costs of seeking external advice would not be recoverable from the other party by order of the Information Commissioner. Even if the case went to the Information Rights Tribunal, the recoverability of costs is limited (see **10.7.1** and **10.7.2**).

Late-claimed exemptions

It is best practice and is likely to reduce costs if a public authority can correctly identify all relevant exemptions on which it relies at the outset of the request process. However, an authority is free to argue before the Information Commissioner that it can lawfully withhold the requested information on the basis of an exemption which it did not rely on when turning down the applicant's request for information originally or at internal review stage. Although the Commissioner had previously ruled that new exemptions could only be relied upon where there was a reasonable justification to do so, the Court of Appeal in *Birkett* v. *Department for Environment, Food and Rural Affairs* [2011] EWCA Civ 1606 confirmed that public authorities have an unfettered right to do so. Note, however, that the same principle does not apply to late claims to rely on s.12, i.e. that compliance with the request would exceed the cost limit – see further at **10.7**).

In such a case, the Information Commissioner's guidance is that the public authority should explain to the complainant and the ICO why the new exemption applies, and the case officer will generally give the complainant an opportunity to respond to the new arguments. Even if the public authority's refusal to provide the information is vindicated on the newly claimed grounds, the Information Commissioner's decision notice will usually rule that the public authority was in breach of the s.17 (or EIR, reg.14) refusal notice provisions and order it to issue an amended refusal letter citing the relevant exemption and grounds. The same applies where the public authority dealt with a request under the FOIA when it related to environmental information and thus should have been dealt with by reference to the exceptions under the EIR, or vice versa (*Archer* v. *Information Commissioner and Salisbury District Council* (EA/2006/0037, 9 May 2007)).

Unclaimed exemptions and grounds for complaint

The question arises whether the Commissioner has a duty, or a discretion, to consider complaints or arguments against disclosure which are not advanced by the parties themselves.

The Information Tribunal ruled in *Bowbrick* v. *Information Commissioner and Nottingham City Council* (EA/2005/0006, 28 September 2006) that the Information Commissioner has no positive duty to consider the applicability of exemptions not relied upon by the public authority (para.46). On the other hand, the Information Tribunal acknowledged that he has discretion to do so, though seemingly only 'in some exceptional cases'. Examples given (at paras.49–51) were:

- where he finds that the authority misidentified the applicable exemption (e.g. the s.30 exemption (investigations and proceedings) instead of the closely related s.31 exemption (law enforcement));
- where he finds that the authority mistakenly identified an exemption under the FOIA in a case where the EIR apply (or vice versa) and there is a corresponding exemption (see *Kirkaldie* v. *Information Commissioner and Thanet District Council* (EA/2006/0001, 4 July 2006));
- where he believes the authority has failed to identify the applicability of the s.40 exemption (personal information) and the rights of data subjects ought to be protected.

The last situation was given in the light of the Information Commissioner's statutory responsibilities regarding data protection under the DPA.

The Information Tribunal has also indicated that, even where a complainant does not mention this in his or her complaint, the Information Commissioner should be ready to consider whether a public authority has breached its s.16 duty to provide the applicant with advice and assistance with his or her request for information (*Barber* v. *Information Commissioner* (EA/2005/0044, 11 November 2005), paras.17–19). However, according to the Information Tribunal in *Fitzsimmons* v. *Information Commissioner and British Broadcasting Corporation* (EA/2008/0043, 3 December 2008), para.47, where any such breach is identified in a decision notice, the Information Commissioner has no power to specify steps to comply with s.16 under s.50(4) and is limited to issuing a practice recommendation. The Information Commissioner refutes this view (see reference LTT142 in the ICO's FOI Policy Knowledge Base: **www.ico.gov.uk/foikb/index.htm**).

Mixed FOIA and EIR cases

Where the information that falls within the scope of a request includes but is not limited to environmental information, the Information Commissioner's approach, largely based on the Information Tribunal case of *Department for Business, Enterprise and Regulatory Reform* v. *Information Commissioner and Friends of the Earth* (EA/2007/0072, 29 April 2008), is as follows. Where a document can be easily divided between environmental and other information then it should be considered in parts to decide which information is caught by the EIR and which by the FOIA. Where a document cannot be easily divided in this way, then a 'predominant purpose test' may be applied to determine whether the entire document, or sections of it, can be taken to be environmental information despite the fact that some of the information within that document/section, when taken in isolation, might not be regarded as environmental information. Where there is no predominant purpose, public authorities are to undertake a detailed review of the contents of the document, considering relevant items of information under the applicable regime. According to the Information Commissioner, this may also be the right approach where the predominant purpose is not environmental, as information seekers may otherwise be disadvantaged by having their request for environmental information considered under the less liberal access regime of the FOIA (see reference LTT122 in the ICO's FOI Policy Knowledge Base: **www.ico.gov.uk/ foikb/index.htm**).

Informal resolution

In the early days of the FOI regime, applicants and public authorities alike were understandably keen to obtain rulings from the Information Commissioner (and the Information Tribunal) in order to obtain clarity on the practical application of the FOIA and establish points of principle. As time goes on, parties are increasingly prepared to settle complaints prior to a formal ruling, so that all involved can enjoy the savings of time, money and effort and the increased regulatory efficiency that this brings. Alternatively, after the involvement of the ICO, a public authority may quickly realise that its initial view was mistaken, or a complainant may see that his or her complaint has little chance of success. In other cases a public authority may prefer to avoid the publicity of a decision notice and may therefore encourage the complainant to drop his or her complaint by offering more rapid access to some of, if not all, the information requested if he or she agrees to do so. Nearly half of all complaints to the ICO in 2011–12 were resolved in this way, or by the complainant accepting advice from the ICO that his or her complaint was unlikely to be upheld. In his guidance the Information Commissioner encourages the parties to speak directly even during the ICO's investigation to see if some agreement can be reached. Where a compromise is struck by the parties independently, or any further information is disclosed, they are required to inform the case officer, and the complainant will normally be invited to withdraw the complaint. If the complainant agrees, the Information Commissioner no longer has a duty to make a decision on the complaint by virtue of s.50(2)(d) and thus the matter can be closed. If the complainant refuses to withdraw the complaint, the Commissioner normally will issue a short decision notice, merely recording the fact that the information was provided but out of time in breach of the FOIA, s.10(1), or the EIR, reg.5(2). There will be no detailed consideration of whether the requester was actually entitled to the information under s.1, nor whether the refusal notice complied with s.17 (see reference LTT188 in the ICO's FOI Policy Knowledge Base: **www.ico.gov.uk/foikb/index.htm**). This approach is attractive to the regulator in terms of its ability to deal efficiently with its caseload, as it avoids having to spend time considering the applicability of exemptions, including the public interest test. However, a finding of a breach of s.10(1) without first establishing that there was in fact a duty to disclose under s.1 would appear to invite a challenge from the public authority. In an extreme case, a complainant who refuses to withdraw his or her complaint after the information is provided could find that the Information Commissioner will in turn refuse to issue a decision notice at all on the grounds that the complaint is then frivolous or vexatious under s.50(2)(c).

If the Information Commissioner refuses to issue a decision notice, there are no grounds for appeal to the Information Rights Tribunal. The only means of challenging the decision would be by way of judicial review or else by invoking the ICO complaints procedure and then appealing to the Parliamentary and Health Service Ombudsman (see **10.6.4**).

Details of informally settled complaints are in general not posted on the ICO website, thus providing an incentive to public authorities wishing to avoid the public censure of a decision notice. It is possible, however, that occasionally – such as where the case highlights a point of principle – the Information Commissioner might exercise his discretion to issue a decision notice in any event, in compliance with his s.47 duty to publish information about the operation of the FOIA and about good practice.

Hearings

The Information Commissioner does not hold hearings.

Burden of proof and standard of proof

In effect, the public authority bears the burden of proving that any information it withholds has been lawfully withheld. This is clear under the EIR, as public authorities are subject to an express presumption of openness (reg.12(2)), and thus bear the burden of rebutting that presumption. Accordingly, should there be doubt as to whether an exception applies or where the greater public interest lies, there will be an order for disclosure.

While there is no express burden of proof under the FOIA, the High Court in *Office of Government Commerce* v. *Information Commissioner* [2008] EWHC 737 (Admin) (at (at [71]) approved the following statement of the Information Tribunal in *Secretary of State for Work and Pensions* v. *Information Commissioner* (EA/2006/0040, 5 March 2007) at para.29:

It can be said, however, that there is an *assumption* built into FOIA that the disclosure of information by public authorities on request is in itself of value and in the public interest, in order to promote transparency and accountability in relation to the activities of public authorities. What this means is that there is always likely to be some public interest in favour of the disclosure of information under the Act. The strength of that interest, and the strength of the competing interest in maintaining any relevant exemption, must be assessed on a case by case basis: section 2(2)(b) requires the balance to be considered 'in all the circumstances of the case'.

There is certainly no burden on the applicant to show that the public interest in disclosure outweighs that in the maintenance of the exemption. This is a question for the Information Commissioner or the Tribunal to determine on the basis of the evidence and the relevant circumstances of the case (*Kessler* v. *Information Commissioner and HM Commissioners for Revenue and Customs* (EA/2007/0043, 29 November 2007), paras.56–57). Furthermore, when applying the public interest test, it follows from the wording of s.2(2)(b) that information must be disclosed where the public interests in disclosure and maintenance of the exemption are evenly balanced.

Evidence presented by the public authority will need to come up to the normal civil standard, namely that the facts alleged are, on the balance of probabilities, true. Rather than relying on generalised arguments, a public authority must therefore show why, on the particular facts of the case, a particular exemption is engaged or the public interest favours non-disclosure (see the failure to evidence this in *Home Office and Ministry of Justice* v. *Information Commissioner* [2009] EWHC 1611 (Admin)). Unsupported assertions of harm will not suffice where a public authority is relying on a prejudice-based exemption. The authority has an evidential burden on it to show that the relevant harm would be 'real, actual or of substance', causally linked to the disclosure of the information, and sufficiently likely to occur to meet the requirements of the exemption claimed (see *Hogan and Oxford City Council* v. *Information Commissioner* (EA/2005/0026 and EA/2005/0030, 17 October 2006), paras.30 and 34).

Similarly, it is not enough under the EIR for a public authority merely to assert that it does not hold the information requested; it must advance adequate evidence to overturn the presumption of disclosure. This could be done by providing evidence of the search carried out, or of the authority's document destruction policy, or of an explanation as to why the information is not, or is no longer, held (*Fowler* v. *Information Commissioner and Brighton and Hove City Council* (EA/2006/0087, 6 November 2007), paras.22–24).

Exceptionally, the legislation provides five instances where a government Minister may serve a conclusive evidence certificate, which precludes the Information Commissioner from assessing the evidence himself. For example, under reg.15 of the EIR a Minister can assert conclusively that disclosure of certain information would adversely affect national security and would not be in the public interest (see **10.8.2**).

The Information Commissioner's decision

It certain situations, the ICO's practice is to not investigate a complaint fully and instead to issue a short decision notice which does not specify any breaches but requires the public authority to reconsider the request. This can arise where the public authority:

- rejects the request (or part of it) but fails to identify the exemptions/exceptions it is relying on;
- responds under the FOIA but the request (or part of it) should be considered under the EIR, or vice versa;
- incorrectly claims not to be subject to the FOIA in relation to a particular request (or part of it).

This puts the complaints process back to square one. Thus, where the public authority reconsiders the request in accordance with the decision notice but then refuses disclosure, the correct approach is for the applicant to apply for an internal review before submitting a complaint to the Information Commissioner. As discussed above, however, the Commissioner does have discretion to deal with complaints even where there has been no internal review where he considers it appropriate. (See reference LTT190 in the ICO's FOI Policy Knowledge Base: **www.ico.gov.uk/foikb/index.htm**.)

Where the case has been investigated fully and the matter cannot be resolved informally, the Information Commissioner issues a decision notice setting out any steps required of the public authority, such as what information is to be disclosed, how soon (often within 35 days) and by what means. He might order disclosure of all or just part of the requested information, or else he might endorse the authority's claim that the information is exempt from disclosure.

It may happen that although a complaint is upheld because the Information Commissioner finds that the public authority should have provided the information in response to the request, the Commissioner will exercise his discretion not to order the authority to disclose the information because circumstances have changed since the time the request was made and disclosure would now be undesirable. Such circumstances might include cases where court proceedings have been commenced since the date of the request and disclosure would prejudice the fairness of the trial, or where a statutory bar would now apply to disclosure of such information, or where it would now be unfair to reveal personal data (see the High Court case of *Office of Government Commerce* v. *Information Commissioner* [2008] EWHC 737 (Admin); and the Upper Tribunal case of *Information Commissioner* v. *Her Majesty's Revenue and Customs and Gaskell* [2011] UKUT 296 (AAC)).

The decision notice is sent to the complainant by post (and on request by email) and at the same time to the chief executive of the public authority. Served with the decision notice there is a statement of reasons summarising the Information Commissioner's rationale for the decision. This provides a basis for the parties to consider an appeal. In view of the fact that public authorities may wish to appeal against the decision to the Information Rights Tribunal and that a statement of reasons may include references to, or quotations from, material which an authority considers exempt, the version given to the complainant is not always identical to that given to the public authority. The parties are given a few days to digest the contents of the decision notice before they are made public. Either party (or both) may appeal to the Information Rights Tribunal within 28 days of the ICO sending out the decision notice (see **10.7**). If the public authority fails to comply with the steps specified in the decision notice, the Information Commissioner may ask the High Court to look into the case and deal with the authority as if it had committed a contempt of court (see **10.4.1**).

As to the requirements in the legislation regarding the content of decision notices, whether they can be appealed, the potential for ministerial override, and the consequences of non-compliance, see **10.3.1** and **10.3.5**.

At the end of a case, if the public authority wishes to recover any documents which it has provided to the ICO, it must ask for them within six months, as otherwise documents other than originals are generally destroyed.

Publicity

All decision notices and enforcement notices are publicly available and are posted on the ICO website, excluding any exempt information. Both a case summary and the full text of the decision appear. The database of decisions has a useful function which allows you to search, *inter alia*, by reference to individual public authorities or section numbers of the legislation. Whereas the public authority which is the subject of a complaint will always be identified, complainants' names are not released.

There might be the occasional exception to this, such as where the requester is a journalist who has publicly referred to his or her complaint.[30] Where appropriate, parties should consider notifying the ICO of any preference they may have not to be identified in case reports.

Owing to the sensitive nature of their contents, information notices are not normally published but they can receive publicity where this would help an investigation or the matter is already in the public domain. Indeed, the ICO states it aims to get media coverage for enforcement activities.[31] It also puts out news releases via social media channels, such as Twitter, Facebook and LinkedIn. Certain cases (whether resulting from complaints or the ICO's own monitoring) may receive additional publicity where this would illustrate the Information Commissioner's approach to enforcement and any lessons to be learned (as in the guidance *When Can a Request Be Considered Vexatious or Repeated?*, version 4 (ICO, December 2008)).

---

[30] Personal communication from Assistant Information Commissioner with responsibility for complaints resolution (April 2005).
[31] See *Communicating Enforcement Activities* (ICO, February 2010).

Timescales

Whereas the Scottish Information Commissioner is required to reach a decision within four months of receiving the application, or such other period as is reasonable in the circumstances (Freedom of Information (Scotland) Act 2002, s.49(3)(b)), no time limit is prescribed under the FOIA. The time taken to resolve complaints will obviously vary, depending on the complexity of a case, the speed and adequacy of response of the public authority and the workload of ICO staff. Procedural cases can be dealt with relatively quickly but cases involving the application of the exemptions take longer. The length of time taken by the ICO to resolve complaints was raised as a subject of concern before the House of Commons Constitutional Affairs Select Committee (Seventh Report of Session 2005–6, HC 991, 28 June 2006) and also in decisions of the Information Tribunal (e.g. *Spurgeon* v. *Information Commissioner and Horsham District Council* (EA/2006/0089, 29 June 2007), paras.18 and 31) but new procedures and an increase in staff headcount within the ICO have meant that the issues of delay and a burgeoning case backlog have now been brought under control. Most cases are dealt with in under six months, with the rest largely being disposed of within a year.

10.6.2 Case-handling statistics

Table 10.1 FOIA/EIR case-handling statistics for the ICO

Number of new cases received by the ICO per month	386
Number of cases closed by the ICO per month	397
Time from start to finish of a case (% of caseload)	
0–30 days	27%
1–3 months	37%
3–6 months	18%
6–9 months	11%
9–12 months	4%
12–18 months	1%
18–24 months	0%
Proportion of cases resulting in decision notices	24%
Proportion of cases resolved informally	45%
Of decision notices issued, proportion upheld or partially upheld	50%
Of decision notices issued, proportion not upheld	50%
Proportion of ICO decision notices appealed to the Information Rights Tribunal*	25%
Proportion of those appeals granted at least in part (i.e. ICO decision stands in large majority of cases)	19%

The figures above are drawn from the Information Commissioner's Annual Report 2011/12, other than the items marked with an asterisk, which come from the Annual Report 2010/11 as they were not specifically reported in 2011/12, at: **www.ico.gov.uk/about_us/performance/annual_reports.aspx**.

10.6.3   Complaints relating to a publication scheme

A person seeking to obtain information from a public authority which is supposedly available under its publication scheme may be concerned at the amount of money he or she has been asked to pay for it or at the near impossibility of obtaining access to it in practice. In another situation a company or an individual whose reputation has been damaged by information released by a public authority under its publication scheme may be irate that they were not consulted prior to the disclosure. An application under s.50(1) for a decision of the Information Commissioner cannot be made, however, in relation to a complaint about a public authority's publication scheme. Nevertheless, were these people to bring their grievances to the Information Commissioner's attention, he would be able to investigate the matter under his general duties to promote authorities' observance of the FOIA and the codes of practice (ss.47 and 48). The outcome may be that he issues the public authority with a practice recommendation or an enforcement notice but, unlike a decision notice, a copy is not required to be served on the person who initially complained. In some circumstances, it may be open to an aggrieved party to take legal action in respect of disclosures under a publication scheme, such as for judicial review, breach of confidence or under the DPA (see **10.10.5**).

10.6.4   Complaints about the ICO

A party dissatisfied with the content of the Information Commissioner's ruling should appeal to the Information Rights Tribunal. However, if a party wishes to complain about the way in which an assessment was conducted (e.g. rudeness of staff) he or she should – within six months of the incident – set out his or her concerns on the ICO's case review and service complaint form, which is available via the website or the helpline. If the complainant remains dissatisfied after the ICO has responded, he or she can appeal the decision and ultimately complain to the Parliamentary and Health Service Ombudsman through an MP (see **www.ombudsman.org.uk/make-a-complaint**).

10.7   APPEALS TO THE INFORMATION RIGHTS TRIBUNAL

Where a requester or a public authority wishes to overturn a decision notice issued by the Information Commissioner (or an information or enforcement notice in the case of public authorities), they can apply to the Information Rights Tribunal (FOIA, s.57). A notice of the Commissioner can even be challenged by a party in some aspects if it is otherwise broadly in favour of that party (see the Upper Tribunal decision in *Shephard* v. *Information Commissioner and West Sussex County Council* (GIA/1681/2010 and JR/2013/2010, 19 September 2011)). The Information Rights Tribunal's website is at: **www.justice.gov.uk/tribunals/information-rights**.

When the FOIA came into force in January 2005 all appeals against decisions of the Information Commissioner were heard by the Information Tribunal (formerly the Data Protection Tribunal). A further appeal from the Information Tribunal on a point of law lay to the High Court. As part of a major restructuring of the Tribunals Service, in January 2010 the Information Tribunal in effect became the Information Rights Tribunal, more accurately referred to as the First-tier Tribunal (Information Rights). In the new structure, it is one of the tribunals within the General Regulatory Chamber, along with, for example, the Consumer Credit Tribunal. There are five other chambers comprising the First-tier Tribunal, which clusters together tribunals on related areas, such as the Health, Education and Social Care Chamber. The Information Rights Tribunal is administered by the Tribunals Service, an executive agency of the Ministry of Justice, and is independent of the Information Commissioner. Appeals from decisions of the Information Rights Tribunal lie to the newly created Upper Tribunal (Administrative Appeals Chamber) on the grounds of an error of law.[32]

Not all appeal cases are heard at first instance before the Information Rights Tribunal. Where information has been withheld in reliance on a ministerial certificate asserting that it is covered by a national security exemption, any appeal is automatically transferred from the First-tier Tribunal to the Upper Tribunal (see **10.8.2**). (Such appeals used to be heard by a specialist panel of the Information Tribunal.) In addition, the Information Rights Tribunal has discretion to apply for any other type of case (or a preliminary issue within a case) to be heard at first instance in the Upper Tribunal. This could be appropriate where a case is of considerable public importance or involves complex or unusual issues.[33] *All Party Parliamentary Group on Extraordinary Rendition* v. *Information Commissioner and Ministry of Defence* [2011] UKUT 153 (AAC) was just such a case, given that the information sought from the Ministry of Defence related to the treatment of people detained in the conflicts in Iraq and Afghanistan.

The Information Rights Tribunal will allow the appeal or substitute its own notice for that of the Commissioner where it finds that the Information Commissioner's notice was 'not in accordance with the law' or where the Commissioner should have

---

[32] The new tribunals were brought into being by the Tribunals, Courts and Enforcement Act 2007, s.3. Appeals under s.57 of the FOIA against notices of the Information Commissioner still lie to 'the Tribunal' but under the 2010 reorganisation that term was redefined, substituting a reference to the First-tier Tribunal and the Upper Tribunal for the reference to the Information Tribunal: see the Transfer of Tribunal Functions Order 2010 (SI 2010/22), arts.1(1), 5(1), Sched.2, para.71.

[33] The Tribunal Procedure (First-tier Tribunal) (General Regulatory Chamber) Rules 2009, SI 2009/1976, rule 19. For more information, see the two office notes on mandatory and discretionary transfers on the Information Rights Tribunal website: **www.justice.gov.uk/tribunals/information-rights/appeals/how-to-appeal**.

exercised his discretion differently. In reaching its determination, the Information Rights Tribunal is entitled to review any findings of fact on which the Information Commissioner's notice was based (FOIA, s.58). Points to note about this framework are as follows:

- A decision notice would be 'not in accordance with the law' where, for example, the Information Commissioner misinterpreted or misapplied the law, or his decision was flawed in public law terms (e.g. because it was illogical or irrational or he ignored a material fact or consideration, as in, for example, *Burgess* v. *Information Commissioner and Stafford Borough Council* (EA/2006/0091, 7 June 2007), para.49)).

- An appeal to the Information Rights Tribunal lies as of right (there is no requirement for permission to appeal) and amounts to a rehearing of all significant matters of law and fact. It is thus free to consider evidence that was not put before the Information Commissioner (*Bowbrick* v. *Information Commissioner and Nottingham City Council* (EA/2005/0006, 28 September 2006), para.27). This can be fresh evidence put forward voluntarily by the parties; but since the Information Rights Tribunal also has an investigatory role it can also call for witnesses or particular evidence to be provided. In consequence, a decision of the Information Commissioner may be found to be unlawful not because of any error of legal reasoning on his part but because the Information Rights Tribunal has fresh evidence before it and makes different findings of fact (*Guardian Newspapers Ltd (1) and Heather Brooke (2)* v. *Information Commissioner and British Broadcasting Commission* (EA/2006/0011 and EA/2006/0013, 8 January 2007), para.14(4) and (6)). The Information Rights Tribunal is entitled to enter a merits-based judgment and is not restricted merely to a review of the lawfulness of the Information Commissioner's decision-making process, as the Administrative Court would be in a judicial review case.

- Where an appeal is brought on the basis that the Information Commissioner exercised his discretion wrongly, the Information Rights Tribunal considers how it would exercise its discretion on the issue, taking account of any fresh evidence (*Guardian Newspapers*, above, para.14(7)). Note that the Information Commissioner's analysis of the public interest test in the context of qualified exemptions (or the EIR) is not a question of discretion but a matter of law, or mixed law and fact (*Guardian Newspapers*, above, para.14(5)).

- A public authority is freely entitled to base its appeal to the Information Rights Tribunal on FOIA exemptions or EIR exceptions which it did not raise previously either in responding to the request for information or before the Information Commissioner. This principle was established by the Upper Tribunal and confirmed on appeal by the Court of Appeal in *Birkett* v. *Department for Environment, Food and Rural Affairs* [2011] EWCA Civ 1606. An earlier line of cases had proceeded on the basis that late claiming of exemptions was subject to the Tribunal's discretion and that the authority had to show reasonable justification to raise the exemption at a late stage (as in the First-tier Tribunal appeal of the *Birkett* case: *Birkett* v. *Information Commissioner* (EA/2009/0106, 13 May 2010)). Note, however, that the Court of Appeal in *Birkett* found that the entitlement only applies up to notice of appeal stage in the First-tier Tribunal; any request by a public authority to amend its notice of appeal to rely on a new exemption after the appeal has been lodged will be subject to the Information Rights Tribunal's case management powers, including the overriding objective to deal with cases fairly and justly. Clearly it is better to raise all relevant exemptions when first responding to a request for information, both to save time and expense and – where the late claiming of exemptions has become a pattern – to avoid the risk of criticism by the Information Commissioner either in a practice recommendation or a report to Parliament (see **10.2** and **10.3.6**).

- The principle in the previous bullet point is likely to apply in cases where a public authority seeks to rely for the first time before the Information Rights Tribunal on an exception under the EIR where the dispute had earlier been fought, mistakenly, on the basis of provisions in the FOIA. Again, this was previously a matter of discretion, which was more likely to be exercised in the public authority's favour where the FOIA exemption was similar to the EIR exception (see *Archer* v. *Information Commissioner and Salisbury District Council* (EA/2006/0037, 9 May 2007) and *Kirkaldie* v. *Information Commissioner and Thanet District Council* (EA/2006/0001, 4 July 2006)).

- By contrast, a public authority which fails to invoke s.12 (the exemption for dealing with requests which would exceed the cost limit) in its refusal notice under s.17 of the FOIA or reg.14 of the EIR may not rely on that argument for the first time before either the Information Commissioner or the Information Rights Tribunal without permission (*All Party Parliamentary Group of Extraordinary Rendition* v. *Information Commissioner and Ministry of Defence* [2011] UKUT 153 (AAC) and *Sittampalam* v. *Information Commissioner and British Broadcasting Corporation* (EA/2010/0141, 4 July 2011)).

- The Information Rights Tribunal is under no general duty to consider whether there are any relevant exemptions not raised by a public authority in an appeal (*Bowbrick*, above, para.56).

As to remedies, the Information Rights Tribunal is not able to award compensation or impose fines in connection with breaches of the FOIA or the EIR. The question of costs is dealt with below. Unlike the Information Commissioner, the Information Rights Tribunal has no power to issue recommendations to public authorities on how they might better comply with the codes of practice under ss.45 and 46 of the FOIA or reg.16 of the EIR. It has, however, been prepared to issue a decision notice in which it invited the Commissioner to make a practice recommendation under his s.48 powers, an invitation which he took up (see *Bowbrick*, above, para.1(D)) and see the Information Commissioner's practice recommendation of 13 February 2007 issued to Nottingham City Council).

10.7.1 Procedure

The Information Rights Tribunal process is more formal than that encountered during the Information Commissioner's investigation. In common with other tribunals and in contrast to the courts, however, the Information Rights Tribunal adopts an inquisitorial approach, asking questions of the parties rather than simply relying on them to present their case. Although the Information Commissioner is typically represented by a lawyer (whether solicitor or barrister, in-house or external), it is possible and indeed common for individual appellants not to have legal representation. The Information Rights Tribunal has published useful guidance for such litigants-in-person.[34] It is also possible for an appellant or other party to appoint a representative, who does not have to be legally qualified, to conduct its case or represent it at a hearing. There is no legal aid for Information Rights Tribunal cases. Some organisations may, however, be willing to offer individual appellants free legal advice and support.[35]

The Information Tribunal not only gained a new name in January 2010, it also became subject to a new set of procedural rules: the Tribunal Procedure (First-tier Tribunal) (General Regulatory Chamber) Rules 2009, SI 2009/1976 (FTT Rules 2009), which replaced the 2005 Rules.[36] These rules are made under the Tribunals, Courts and Enforcement Act 2007. The key procedural steps and features are described below. One innovation under the new rules was the articulation of an 'overriding objective' (rule 2), akin to that which applies in the civil courts under the CPR. The thrust of the overriding objective is to require the Information Rights Tribunal to operate fairly and justly, dealing with cases in ways which are proportionate to the importance of the case, the complexity of the issues, the anticipated costs and the resources of the parties, as well as avoiding unnecessary formality and seeking flexibility in the proceedings, and avoiding delay without unduly prejudicing a proper consideration of the issues. All parties to an appeal are under an obligation to assist the Information Rights Tribunal in furthering the overriding objective and to co-operate with the Tribunal generally. To illustrate, in *Edwards* v. *Information Commissioner and Ministry of Defence* (EA/2010/0056, 2 December 2010), the Tribunal found that the appeal had become academic because the public

---

[34] *Guidance Notes for Individuals Representing Themselves in Freedom of Information Appeals in the General Regulatory Chamber of the First-tier Tribunal* (General Regulatory Chamber, June 2011): **www.justice.gov.uk/downloads/tribunals/information-rights/how-to-appeal/6-guidance-notes-for-individuals-representing-themselves-June2011.pdf**.

[35] See the references at: **www.justice.gov.uk/tribunals/information-rights/appeals/how-to-appeal**, including one body specifically for EIR cases.

[36] The FTT Rules 2009 have since been amended by SI 2010/43, SI 2010/2653 and SI 2011/651. A consolidated version is available via the Information Rights Tribunal website: **www.justice.gov.uk/tribunals/information-rights/rules-and-legislation**. The 2005 Rules were contained in the Information Tribunal (Enforcement Appeals) Rules 2005, SI 2005/14, as amended by the Information Tribunal (Enforcement Appeals) (Amendment) Rules 2005, SI 2005/450.

authority had already disclosed the requested information. The Tribunal held that by virtue of the overriding objective to deal with cases proportionately and its rule 5 power to regulate its own procedure (which included the ability to give a direction regarding the conduct or disposal of proceedings at any time) it was entitled to strike out the appeal even if the specific grounds for strike out under rule 8 had not been made out (see below).

Todd v. *Information Commissioner and British Broadcasting Corporation* (EA/ 2010/0107, 6 September 2010) was another case where the Information Rights Tribunal took a broad view of its powers by reference to the overriding objective (rule 2) and its case management powers (rule 5). Here it concluded, in the face of the contrary argument by the BBC, that in the absence of any specific guidance in the rules it did have the power to make an order permitting the unrepresented appellant, Mr Todd, to publish online the Information Commissioner's and the BBC's responses to his notice of appeal. Mr Todd had sought permission to do so in order to obtain free advice on his case. The Tribunal allowed his request, seeming to acknowledge, however, that it would need to consider any similar requests in future on a case-by-case basis.

Another new addition to the rules is the requirement for First-tier Tribunals to inform the parties about any alternative dispute resolution procedure that is available. The parties cannot be required to use such procedures, however; whether they do so is a matter for them to decide (rule 3).

10.7.2 How to appeal

To lodge an appeal a party must ensure that the Information Rights Tribunal receives a written notice of appeal, enclosing the decision appealed against and setting out the grounds for appeal, within 28 days of the date when the Information Commissioner's notice was sent to it, i.e. the date of the notice or covering letter or email by which the notice was sent (rule 22). Note that the appeal is always brought against the Information Commissioner (the respondent) and not against the public authority or the information seeker.

A party can apply for an extension of time to lodge the appeal, under rule 5(3)(a) of the FTT Rules 2009. Where possible, the application should be made within the 28-day period, and should provide good reasons for the delay and a reasonable date by which the notice of appeal will be lodged, minimising any further delay. As an alternative to making an advance application for more time, an appellant may submit their notice of appeal after the ordinary 28-day deadline (or any extension already granted) has passed, together with a retrospective request for a time extension, supported by reasons for the delay. In *Information Commissioner* v. *PS* [2011] UKUT 94 (AAC), the Upper Tribunal held that the key issue for the Tribunal in determining whether to grant permission for a notice of appeal to be lodged out of time was whether this would be 'fair and just' under rule 2. It acknowledged that the First-tier Tribunal had set out factors that could provide guidance in reaching this decision when it had considered the application at first instance (see *Sikka* v.

Information Commissioner (EA/2010/0054, 11 July 2011)). Those factors – which the Upper Tribunal said were not to be seen as a rigid checklist – include: how late the application is; whether the delay was due to a holiday, ill health or other causes largely beyond the appellant's control; the complexity of the decision being appealed; whether the appellant is represented or familiar with the appeal process; whether the appellant had contacted the Information Rights Tribunal or the ICO about appealing before the deadline; and, finally, the public interest in the disputed information. In the instant case, Professor Sikka's notice of appeal was held to be valid, albeit submitted 46 days late.

It is not necessary to use the Information Rights Tribunal notice of appeal form on its website[37] but it is helpful to do so, or at least to review it, in order to ensure that all the information which the Tribunal requires is provided. The website also contains a guidance note on how to complete the notice of appeal. Suffice it to say here that it is better to keep it focused, by clearly delineating the information which remains the subject of dispute, identifying the parts of the Commissioner's notice that are being challenged and summarising why those elements of the notice were wrongly decided. Detailed arguments covering relevant facts and law can be left for development in witness statements and skeleton arguments. The notice of appeal should be sent to the Information Rights Tribunal, whose contact details are as follows:

First-tier Tribunal (Information Rights)
General Regulatory Chamber
Arnhem House Support Centre
PO Box 9300
Leicester LE1 8DJ
email: informationtribunal@hmcts.gsi.gov.uk
tel: 0300 123 4504
fax: 0116 249 4253

The Information Rights Tribunal then sends a copy of the notice of appeal to the Information Commissioner and any other respondent. It is therefore important that an appellant informs the Tribunal if there is any material in its appeal papers which it does not wish those other parties to see (e.g. because the appellant argues such material is exempt from disclosure under the FOIA).

The Information Commissioner has 28 days from receipt of the notice of appeal to send his response to the Information Rights Tribunal and the appellant in which he sets out his grounds for opposing the appeal. (This gives the Commissioner a week longer than under the old rules.) As with the appellant, the Information Commissioner may seek to apply for an extension of the ordinary deadline.

The appellant is then permitted to make a written submission and provide further documents in reply to the Information Commissioner's response. The appellant must send the reply to the Information Rights Tribunal and the Information

---

[37] See **www.justice.gov.uk/tribunals/information-rights/appeals/how-to-appeal**. The form is of course also available by contacting the Information Rights Tribunal by telephone or in writing.

Commissioner (and any other party to the appeal) within 14 days of the date on which the Information Commissioner sent his response to the appellant. Again, if the deadline cannot be met, the appellant may make an advance application for extra time or simply submit its reply together with a retrospective request for an extension of time and the reason why the reply was not provided in time (rule 24).

Where two or more cases deal with related issues of law or fact the Information Rights Tribunal can direct that they be heard together (consolidated), or else treat one case as a lead case whose outcome would be binding on the other cases, which are stayed in the meantime (rules 5(3)(b) and 18). Equally, the Information Rights Tribunal, at its own initiative or on request by a party, can direct that the case (or part of it) be referred to the Upper Tribunal, for instance on grounds of the case's complexity or public importance. The outcome of such a request is ultimately in the hands of the President of the Administrative Appeals Chamber of the Upper Tribunal, following discussions with the President of the General Regulatory Chamber, but all parties will first be given an opportunity to give their views on the request to refer the case up (rule 19).[38]

10.7.3 Strike out

Having reviewed the parties' written submissions, or at any other time, the Information Rights Tribunal can strike out a party's case (or part of it) without a hearing, so bringing the matter (or that party's involvement in the case) to an early conclusion (rule 8), where:

- the Information Rights Tribunal has no jurisdiction to hear the case;
- there is no reasonable prospect of the relevant party's case (or a specific aspect of it) succeeding;
- a party has failed to co-operate with the Tribunal to such an extent that the Tribunal cannot deal with the proceedings fairly and justly;
- a party has failed to comply with a direction which specified that failure to comply would, or could, result in that party's case being struck out (however, reinstatement of the case may be possible in such cases).

Any party can apply to the Tribunal to strike out another party's case, or part of it, under this rule. The Tribunal may also strike out a case where this is justified for reasons of proportionality under the overriding objective (see the reference to *Edwards* v. *Information Commissioner and Ministry of Defence* at **10.7.1**).

---

[38] See *Joint Office Note: Discretionary Transfers of Information Rights Appeals* (General Regulatory Chamber and Administrative Appeals Chamber, revised November 2010) on the Information Rights Tribunal website: **www.justice.gov.uk/tribunals/information-rights/appeals/how-to-appeal**.

10.7.4 Between written submissions and the hearing

Once initial submissions are in, the Information Rights Tribunal will write to the parties suggesting appropriate directions, that is, the steps required to prepare the case for its full hearing and the timetable that will operate. This will include setting a date for the hearing, which might typically be some three months later. If directions cannot be agreed through correspondence, there will need to be a directions hearing. This hearing may be in person or by telephone or video conference, and is usually conducted by a judge sitting alone rather than by a tribunal of three. Under a typical set of directions, the parties will be asked to prepare and exchange a list of documents relevant to the case and then exchange those documents, subject to the ordinary rules of privilege (i.e. minus any confidential legal correspondence). They may be asked to prepare a chronology charting the key events surrounding the dispute, and a statement of matters which are agreed and thus about which it is not necessary to hear further argument. Similarly, the parties will be asked to prepare and then exchange witness statements containing the evidence of individuals who can shed light on the relevant issues in the case.[39] Witness statements must be signed by the witness and accompanied by a statement that the witness believes the matters stated to be true. The parties may also seek permission from the Information Rights Tribunal (or be asked by it) to obtain expert evidence, potentially using a single joint expert.

Owing to the nature of information rights access cases, it often happens that in order to adjudicate upon a matter, the Tribunal needs to receive information or documents from the public authority or the Information Commissioner which it would not (at least at that stage) be appropriate for that party or the Tribunal to disclose to the requester in full or perhaps at all. Under a new Practice Direction, one party can only withhold material from another party in such circumstances where it has applied for and been granted a direction permitting it to do so (see generally the Practice Note on Closed Material in Information Rights Cases, May 2012, and especially the guidance on drafting such applications[40] at para.6). Such a direction, made under rule 14(6), will only be granted to the extent necessary to avoid disclosing information part-way through proceedings whose very purpose is to determine whether or not such information has to be disclosed. Under rule 14(10) the Tribunal must conduct proceedings in such a way as not to undermine such a direction, so parties are expected to work with it to ensure that such information is not inappropriately disclosed during hearings or in 'open' versions of witness statements, skeleton arguments or written decisions. It should be noted that the Information Rights Tribunal has indicated elsewhere that when parties prepare an open and a closed version of a document, its preference is to receive a copy of the full document with the closed (i.e. redacted) passages highlighted and annotated

---

[39] A party will not be permitted to summons a witness where there is no real possibility that the person will be able to give relevant evidence that will assist the Tribunal to determine the appeal (*Keston Ramblers Association* v. *Information Commissioner and London Borough of Bromley* (EA/2005/0024, 7 June 2006)).

[40] See **www.justice.gov.uk/tribunals/information-rights/appeals/how-to-appeal**.

with the exemption relied upon as justifying the omission (*Gradwick* v. *Information Commissioner and Cabinet Office* (EA/2010/0030, 5 August 2010), paras.35–40).

The Information Rights Tribunal has other powers to prohibit publication or disclosure of information or documents, such as where this could lead to the undesirable identification of a person by members of the public, or else to serious harm to an individual (rule 14(1)–(2)). Where the Tribunal directs that certain information is not to be disclosed to one of the parties, it can nevertheless order that the information be disclosed to that party's representative on terms that the representative may not disclose the matter to his or her client. Similarly, in *Campaign Against the Arms Trade* v. *Information Commissioner and Ministry of Defence* (EA/2007/0040, 26 August 2008), the Tribunal considered that it had power to direct the appointment of a security-cleared special advocate to represent the appellants' interests in hearings from which the appellants were to be excluded and to consider evidence which the appellants were not permitted to see (para.21). The Tribunal commented that this step was justified due to the volume and nature of the 'closed' evidence but that ordinarily the Tribunal would be well able to appraise such evidence itself, in view of its independent, inquisitorial role.

The Information Rights Tribunal can give directions specifying the evidence it wishes to receive from the parties. It may compel a person anywhere in the UK to appear at an appeal hearing, answer any questions and produce any relevant documents under his or her control as it specifies (rule 16). A witness summonsed in this way is entitled to have his or her expenses paid if he or she is not a party to the appeal. Where appropriate the Tribunal can also make an 'entry direction', requiring the occupier of any premises, on seven days' notice, to permit specified persons to enter the premises at a specified time and inspect, examine, operate or test any equipment or materials which store information (rule 18A). Privileged documents are immune from inspection, examination or testing.

In some cases the Information Rights Tribunal, whether on request or at its own initiative, will consider it appropriate to bring forward a hearing on one particular aspect of a case (a preliminary issue) that may help decide the whole case or cut down the time and effort required to prepare for the full hearing. Whether the case will proceed to an oral hearing or be decided by means of the Tribunal simply reviewing the papers, it may often be that detailed legal submissions are required in writing in advance (e.g. skeleton arguments before an oral hearing). The directions hearing may also specify who must prepare the files of relevant documents for the full hearing (the bundle), although this is normally the Information Commissioner where the appeal is brought by an individual without legal representation.

A party can always apply for a new direction, such as to request permission to amend its written submissions or to alter or set aside any initial direction given by the Information Rights Tribunal, such as the deadlines set down for the various steps (rule 6). Applications must be accompanied by reasons, and a party would be well advised to support its request by reference to the overriding objective (rule 2) because when deciding what directions to make, the Tribunal will need to consider whether they would assist it in dealing fairly and justly with the case. The Information Rights Tribunal can also issue directions on matters not specifically mentioned in the rules. For example, a party could request an expedited hearing if it needed its case to be heard in a shorter timeframe than usual, perhaps due to the existence of interrelated legal proceedings. Unless there is an issue of confidentiality, it is good practice to send a copy of an application for a direction to the other participants in the appeal.

A party that fails to comply with a direction of the Information Rights Tribunal risks having their appeal, or their reply, wholly or partially struck out (rule 7). Further information about the directions stage of the process can be found in guidance notes prepared by the Information Rights Tribunal, which are of particular use to non-lawyers.[41]

Note that, should the parties be prepared to settle the matter at any stage, the Information Rights Tribunal may, at their request and if it considers it appropriate, make a consent order disposing of the proceedings and making such other appropriate provision as the parties have agreed. No hearing need take place in this case and the Tribunal does not have to provide reasons for the order (rule 37).

10.7.5 Third parties

One other matter of importance often dealt with at the directions stage is whether the Information Rights Tribunal should invite, or order, anyone else to become a party to the appeal (under rule 9) on the basis that they have an interest in the proceedings or can assist the Tribunal to determine the case because they can provide relevant evidence or assistance with the legal arguments.[42]

The non-appealing party may wish to be involved in the appeal so it can make its insights available to support the Information Commissioner in opposing the appeal, for instance, to give its own account of why it considers the relevant information exempt or else to explain the precise steps it took in searching for information which it concluded it did not hold. Other third parties with an interest in the case may include a relevant pressure group, or else the subject of the information being sought, such as a party providing commercial services to a public authority. The Tribunal can use this power to call its own expert witnesses to assist it in determining appeals. Where the Tribunal makes an order joining a third party to the proceedings it will give directions as appropriate, generally allowing the new 'respondent' to make a written submission (its reply) and permitting the appellant

---

[41] See (1) *Guidance Notes for Individuals Representing Themselves in Freedom of Information Appeals in the General Regulatory Chamber of the First-tier Tribunal* (General Regulatory Chamber, June 2011) and (2) *First-tier Tribunal Directions, Information Rights, Explanatory Notes* (General Regulatory Chamber, January 2010), both available at: **www.justice.gov.uk/tribunals/information-rights/appeals/how-to-appeal**.

[42] The Practice Note on Confidential Information stated that judges are required to keep this matter under review as cases progress (paras.19–20) but this document was removed from the Information Rights Tribunal's website in early 2012 and the point has not been taken up again in further guidance to date.

and the Information Commissioner to respond or else to amend their earlier submissions. (For further discussion of the position of third parties, see **10.10**.)

10.7.6 Hearings

Appeals to the Information Rights Tribunal are adjudicated upon by a tribunal of three, comprising a judge and two non-legal, 'lay' or 'wing' members. The latter are generally from a professional, business, charity or public sector background and are required to have 'substantial experience' of information rights. In order to provide a balanced panel, they are grouped, based on their experience, into those who reflect the interests either of public authorities or of information seekers.[43]

An oral hearing must take place unless all parties consent and the Tribunal is satisfied that it can properly determine the issues by considering the papers alone. (This reverses the default position that applied under the 2005 Rules.) The Tribunal will favour an oral hearing where there are disagreements over the facts (so that witnesses can give evidence and be questioned) or where there are complicated legal arguments which require further exploration. Papers-only hearings are suitable where all the main facts are agreed and the dispute comes down to a question of interpretation of law where the arguments can be satisfactorily explained in writing.

Oral hearings are generally held in public – usually in London but elsewhere in the UK if this is requested and convenient. (Thus an appellant unfamiliar with the workings of the Information Rights Tribunal might like to arrange to attend the hearing of another case as preparation for his or her own experience. He or she should also refer to the Information Rights Tribunal's guidance notes for individuals representing themselves, referred to above.) The Tribunal may direct, however, that a hearing is to be partly or wholly held in private or that particular individuals are to be excluded in certain circumstances, such as to protect national security. These are referred to as 'closed hearings' or 'closed sessions'. Parties to the appeal should consider asking the Tribunal to make such an order where they are concerned about safeguarding commercially sensitive information or any information which they argue is exempt under the FOIA, or where they have a good reason for not wishing to be identified to the public. The opposing party may be able to argue against the making of such an order (or at least its breadth) by reference to the overriding objective, which requires the Tribunal to ensure 'so far as practicable, that the parties are able to participate fully in the proceedings' (rule 2(2)(c)). Public authorities may be criticised by the Tribunal for including in 'closed' documents evidence which should in fact be dealt with openly because it is not sensitive, as this may amount to an infringement of the art.6 right to a fair trial under the ECHR.

---

[43]   See the Qualifications for Appointment of Members to the First-tier Tribunal and Upper Tribunal Order 2008, SI 2008/2692; and the *Practice Statement: Composition of Tribunals in Relation to Matters that Fall to Be Decided by the General Regulatory Chamber on or after 1 September 2010* (Senior President of Tribunals, 1 October 2010): **http://www.judiciary.gov.uk/publications-and-reports/practice-directions/tribunals/tribunals-statements**.

Should a party fail to attend a hearing, the hearing may go ahead if the Tribunal is satisfied that reasonable steps have been taken to notify the party of the hearing and it is in the interests of justice to proceed (rule 36).

In an oral hearing there may be a short opening statement from each side to outline its case. First the appellant and then the Information Commissioner (and any other parties) can then call their own witnesses, who will be questioned by the opposing party and the Tribunal. The selection of the right witness, particularly by a public authority, is important: he or she needs to be senior enough to speak with authority, yet not so senior that he or she is not sufficiently aware of operational matters to be able to answer the factual questions put to him or her. Any evidence may be adduced even if not admissible in a court (rule 15). Hearsay and documentary evidence is therefore admissible (but would potentially carry less weight than direct oral evidence). The Tribunal may allow parties to adduce evidence that was not available to the Information Commissioner. Equally, it may exclude evidence that is submitted after the relevant deadline or where it would otherwise be unfair to admit the evidence.

After the witness evidence has been heard, the appellant and Information Commissioner (and any other parties) make submissions to the Tribunal, explaining what decision they think the Tribunal should reach, and why, making reference to the facts of the case, the provisions of the FOIA or the EIR and any relevant previous cases. Regarding the sources and challenges of precedent decisions, see **10.1** and **10.5.2**.

10.7.7 The decision

The Information Rights Tribunal may be able to give the parties a decision at the end of the hearing, with written reasons to follow. Typically, however, the parties learn of the outcome around three weeks later when they are sent the decision setting out the Tribunal's findings of fact and the reasons for its determination. Sometimes a decision will indicate that certain information has been protected in a confidential annex, which could be necessary to protect an individual's privacy or matters which are commercially sensitive or exempt under the FOIA or the EIR. The decision will be published on the Information Rights Tribunal website a few days later (**www.justice.gov.uk/tribunals/information-rights/decisions**), once the parties have had a chance to draw the Tribunal's attention to any clerical errors or omissions, and once the relevant party (usually the public authority) has had an opportunity to say whether any information that ought to be in the confidential annex has been included in the open part of the decision.

Unlike in the published decisions of the Information Commissioner, the names of individual claimants do generally appear. The Information Rights Tribunal may, however, assent to a request for anonymity where it deems it appropriate (e.g. *S* v. *Information Commissioner and General Register Office* (EA/2006/0030, 9 May 2007)).

A public authority which loses an appeal will commonly be ordered by the Information Rights Tribunal to disclose the disputed information within 35 days. Any further appeal needs to be made within 28 days (see below).

In 2012, most cases were taking an average of six or seven months to progress from service of the appeal notice to a final decision. A small number of complex cases, however, ran for more than a year.

10.7.8 Costs

The usual rule in the Information Rights Tribunal is that all parties bear their own legal costs regardless of who wins or loses. However, any party can make an application for costs (expenses in Scotland), or the Tribunal may of its own initiative make an order in respect of costs, as follows:

- against any party which in the Tribunal's view has acted unreasonably in bringing, defending or conducting the proceedings;
- against the Information Commissioner where the Tribunal considers the Commissioner's original decision was unreasonable;
- against the legal or other representative of a party in respect of any or all 'wasted costs'. This means that where costs are incurred by a party as a result of any improper, unreasonable or negligent act or omission by its own or another party's representative, the Tribunal can order the representative to meet those costs, or at least not require the costs to be paid by the other party. The Tribunal can also make such an order in respect of costs incurred by a party *prior* to an improper act or omission by its own or the other side's representative where it would be unreasonable to expect the party to pay in the light of the representative's subsequent conduct (see the FTT Rules 2009, rule 10, and the Tribunals, Courts and Enforcement Act 2007, s.29(4)).

An application for costs must be made in writing to the Information Rights Tribunal, with a copy to the person against whom the order is sought, accompanied by a schedule of the costs or expenses claimed. The application must be made no later than 14 days after the date on which the Tribunal sends the final decision notice to the person seeking a costs order. Prior to making an order the Tribunal must allow the party against whom the order is to be made an opportunity to make representations and, if this is an individual, the Tribunal must consider that person's financial means.

The Tribunal may itself summarily assess the amount of costs to be paid or permit the paying and receiving party to agree the sum, or else direct that the costs be assessed by the court. In that situation the receiving party would apply to the county court under the CPR for costs to be assessed, on either the standard basis or the indemnity basis as specified by the Tribunal.

In the rather extreme circumstances of *Bowbrick* v. *Information Commissioner and Nottingham City Council* (EA/2005/0006, 28 September 2006), the Information Tribunal (which operated under a costs regime broadly similar to that of the

355

Information Rights Tribunal) ordered the public authority to pay the whole of the applicant's costs (to be taxed). Nottingham City Council had effectively told Dr Bowbrick that it held none of the information which he had requested. The Information Tribunal concluded, however, that the council knew all along that it did hold relevant information. Indeed, by the end of the appeal, the council had disclosed, in a piecemeal and drawn out fashion, around 1,000 pages of information. Even then it was ordered to release additional information by the Information Tribunal, which declared itself 'dismayed' at the public authority's conduct, commenting that it 'appears to have misled [the applicant] and then the Information Commissioner in his investigation'. In drafting its decision, the Information Tribunal took the opportunity to assess its powers in relation to costs orders, and found that while it could not award a punitive (rather than compensatory) sum, it could make an award in respect of costs incurred prior to the Information Tribunal proceedings, provided they were incurred 'in connection with the proceedings' (paras.71–102). However, a later Information Tribunal case, *Milford Haven Port Authority* v. *Information Commissioner* (EA/2007/0036, 6 November 2007), stated as follows:

> In our view rule 29 [Tribunal's power to impose a costs order] only relates to the conduct of a party in relation to proceedings before the Tribunal and not before the IC. This is accepted by the Appellant and 1st Additional Party. (para.14)

Where a public authority is itself in breach of the legislation, any claim for costs against an appellant who is acting unreasonably in pursuing the appeal will be materially undermined (*Fowler* v. *Information Commissioner and Brighton and Hove City Council* (EA/2006/0087, 6 November 2007), paras.42–43).

10.7.9 Challenging a decision of the Information Rights Tribunal

A further distinction between the 2005 Rules and the new rules governing the tribunals is the number of avenues provided by the latter for challenging a decision of the Information Rights Tribunal. There are now seven possibilities expressly catered for.[44]

(i) Correction of clerical errors

If a party notices a significant typographical error or other mistake in a decision, it can draw this to the attention of the Information Rights Tribunal, which may correct it and amend any published document relating to that decision (rule 40). This 'slip rule' is only to correct editorial errors and may not be used to alter decisions where

---

[44] These arise under the rights of review and appeal established by the Tribunals, Courts and Enforcement Act 2007, ss.9 and 11.

the Tribunal 'has changed its mind and had further thoughts' (*London Borough of Camden* v. *Information Commissioner and Yiannis Voyias* [2012] UKUT 190 (AAC), para.24).

(ii) Setting aside a decision in light of procedural unfairness

A party can apply for the Information Rights Tribunal's final decision in a case to be wholly or partly set aside on the grounds that it is in the interests of justice to do so and at least one of the following conditions applies:

(a)   a party or the Tribunal did not receive a document relating to the proceedings at an appropriate time;

(b)   a party, or its representative, was not present at a hearing relating to the proceedings; or

(c)   there has been some other procedural irregularity in the proceedings.

Any such application must be made within 28 days of the date when the Tribunal sent the decision notice to the party making the application. If necessary an extension of this deadline could be sought under rule 5(3)(a). No further hearing is necessary. If satisfied that the grounds are made out, the Information Rights Tribunal may set the original decision (or part of it) aside and re-make it (rule 41).

(iii) Review of its decision by the Information Rights Tribunal

A party can apply to the Information Rights Tribunal in writing for permission to appeal to the Upper Tribunal against the decision of the former on the grounds that it contained one or more errors of law. In essence, this includes failings by the First-tier Tribunal in the following respects:

- it applied the wrong law (e.g. the FOIA rather than the EIR, or by overlooking applicable case law), or it misinterpreted the law or else misapplied it to the facts;
- it made its decision on the basis of insufficient or irrelevant evidence or findings of fact, or by misinterpreting or overlooking relevant evidence;
- it failed to give adequate reasons for its decision;
- its conclusions were illogical or irrational in view of the evidence and relevant law;
- it failed to follow applicable procedural rules or to give a party an appropriate opportunity to make representations, or it displayed apparent bias;
- it acted incompatibly with the European Convention on Human Rights as domesticated by the Human Rights Act 1998.

The application has to identify the alleged error(s) of law and state the result the applicant seeks (rule 42(5)). Where it receives such an application, the Information Rights Tribunal must first consider, taking into account the overriding objective in rule 2, whether to review its decision (rules 43–44). The Tribunal will often consider it fair and just to carry out a review where the application to appeal on the face of it discloses a reasonable case. If the case is made out the Tribunal may revise its decision but only after giving all parties a chance to make representations.

The written application for permission to appeal must be received by the Information Rights Tribunal no later than 28 days after it sends the applicant its written reasons for the decision (or 28 days after a corrected or revised decision after a review, or notification that an application for the decision to be set aside – if brought in time – has been unsuccessful) (rule 42).

Once again, additional time for lodging an application for permission to appeal may be sought either in advance under rule 5(3)(a), or retrospectively at the time when the application is submitted late, supported by reasons for the delay in either case.

(iv) Request to Information Rights Tribunal for permission to appeal

Where an application for permission to appeal has been made as described under (iii) above but the Information Rights Tribunal decides not to review its original decision, or reviews it but does not revise it, the Tribunal must next consider whether to grant the applicant's request for permission to appeal against the decision (rule 43). Where it refuses permission to appeal it has to give written reasons. The FTT Rules 2009 do not indicate the basis on which permission to appeal is to be granted or refused. In practice, Tribunal judges may adopt a similar approach to that of the courts set out in CPR rule 52.3, under which permission to appeal may be given only where the court considers that the appeal would have a real (as opposed to a fanciful) prospect of success or where there is some other compelling reason why the appeal should be heard.[45]

(v) Request to Upper Tribunal for permission to appeal

If a party has been refused permission to appeal under (iv) above, it can apply direct to the Upper Tribunal for permission to appeal to the Upper Tribunal, provided it does so within one month of the First-tier Tribunal sending the refusal notice. It is possible for the party to request extra time where it has a good reason – again, either in advance of the deadline or retrospectively on submitting the application late (see below, rule 21(3)(b) of the Tribunal Procedure (Upper Tribunal) Rules 2008, SI

---

[45]   See, for example, these comments of Judge Wikeley when considering an application to the Upper Tribunal for permission to appeal to the Upper Tribunal: 'I should grant permission to appeal if I think it is arguable that there is a material error of law in the First-tier Tribunal's decision not to admit the late appeal. I do not have to be satisfied at this stage that the applicant will probably win any appeal if permission is given … I have to be satisfied that it was a material error of law (see *R (Iran)* v. *Secretary of State for the Home Department* [2005] EWCA Civ 982) and moreover that a grant of permission is an appropriate exercise of the Upper Tribunal's discretion. As Brooke LJ observed in the Iran case, "Errors of law of which it can be said that they would have made no difference to the outcome do not matter"' (*Shephard* v. *Information Commissioner and West Sussex County Council* (GIA/1681/2010, 19 September 2011), paras.19 and 21).

2008/2698 (UT Rules 2008)). The application will normally be treated as the notice of appeal and the Upper Tribunal will send a copy of it to all the other parties (UT Rules 2008, rule 22(2)(b)).

Again, the UT Rules 2008 do not indicate the basis on which permission to appeal will be granted or refused but see the comments in paragraph (iv) above as to their approach. There is no appeal from a decision of the Upper Tribunal on an application for permission to appeal against a First-tier Tribunal decision (Tribunals, Courts and Enforcement Act, s.13(8)(c)) but see the following paragraph.

(vi) Request to the Upper Tribunal to reconsider a refusal of permission to appeal

If following a review of the papers, the Upper Tribunal refuses permission to appeal or grants permission to appeal but subject to certain conditions or limitations, the appellant can apply for the decision to be reconsidered at a hearing. Such a request must be made within 14 days of the Upper Tribunal sending the appellant its decision regarding the application to appeal (UT Rules 2008, rule 22(4)–(5)).

(vii) Application for judicial review

Where there is no right of appeal against a procedural decision of the Information Rights Tribunal it is nevertheless possible to apply for that decision to be judicially reviewed by the Upper Tribunal Administrative Appeals Chamber (see **10.8.3**). That might be applicable for example in relation to the First-tier Tribunal's decision not to review a case, or to review but not to revise it, or its decision to set aside its own decision (Tribunals, Courts and Enforcement Act 2007, s.11(5)(d)).

Given the potentially confusing number of alternatives for challenging a decision listed above, it is just as well that the Information Rights Tribunal may treat an application for a decision to be corrected, set aside or reviewed, or for permission to appeal against a decision, as an application for any other one of those things.

Any challenges to an Information Rights Tribunal decision will generally be decided by a single judge but where the President of the General Regulatory Chamber thinks it appropriate, a case may be determined by the same members of the Tribunal as gave the substantive decision or a differently constituted tribunal.[46]

---

[46] See *GRC Guidance Note 2: Permission to Appeal on or after 18 January 2010* (General Regulatory Chamber, 9 February 2010), available at: **www.justice.gov.uk/tribunals/information-rights/appeals/how-to-appeal**.

10.8 APPEALS BEFORE THE UPPER TRIBUNAL

10.8.1 Appeals against decisions of the Information Rights Tribunal

As discussed above, appeals against notices issued by the Information Commissioner are usually heard by the Information Rights Tribunal. Under the Tribunals, Courts and Enforcement Act 2007, s.11(2), a further appeal against the Information Rights Tribunal's decision lies to the Upper Tribunal Administrative Appeals Chamber (referred to below simply as the Upper Tribunal: see **www.justice.gov.uk/tribunals/aa**) on the grounds that it contained one or more errors of law (as to which, see alternative (iii) under **10.7.9**). (The appeal framework prior to January 2010 was that appeals from notices of the Information Commissioner were heard by the Information Tribunal, from where a further appeal lay to the High Court on a point of law under FOIA, s.59.)

The appellant must overcome the threshold hurdle of obtaining permission to appeal to the Upper Tribunal. Such permission must be sought in the first place from the Information Rights Tribunal, failing which, permission may be sought from the Upper Tribunal itself (see **10.7.9**). The Upper Tribunal can suspend the effect of the Information Rights Tribunal's substantive ruling pending its determination of the application for permission to appeal and the appeal itself.

These cases are usually determined by a single judge, without an oral hearing, who reviews the First-tier Tribunal's decision and generally does not consider new evidence or permit parties to re-argue questions of fact and judgement which have been properly adjudicated upon by the First-tier Tribunal.[47]. By contrast, cases referred directly to the Upper Tribunal by the Information Rights Tribunal – namely, national security certificate cases (see **10.8.2**) and other complex or significant cases – will be heard by a panel of three, often with an oral hearing, and with full evidence submitted by the parties.[48]

The procedural rules that apply in the Upper Tribunal are the UT Rules 2008, as amended,[49] which are largely similar to the FTT Rules 2009. For an overview of those rules see **10.7**. In addition, here are some key points to note about the UT Rules 2008, including ways in which they differ from the FTT Rules 2009:

- Where the Information Rights Tribunal has given permission to appeal to the Upper Tribunal, the appellant must submit a notice of appeal within one month. Where the First-tier Tribunal has refused permission, the application can be

---

[47] See for example comments of Judge Wikeley in *UK Coal* v. *Information Commissioner and Nottinghamshire County Council and Veolia ES Nottinghamshire Ltd* [2012] UKUT 212 (AAC), para.27.

[48] See art.3 of the First-tier Tribunal and Upper Tribunal (Composition of Tribunal) Order 2008, SI 2008/2835 and paras.3(d) and (e) of *Practice Statement: Composition of Tribunals in Relation to Matters that Fall to Be Decided by the Administrative Appeals Chamber of the Upper Tribunal on or after 1 October 2010* (Senior President of Tribunals, 1 October 2010): **www.judiciary.gov.uk/ publications-and-reports/practice-directions/tribunals/tribunals-statements**.

[49] The Tribunal Procedure (Upper Tribunal) Rules 2008, SI 2008/2698 as amended by SI 2009/274, SI 2009/1975, SI 2010/43, SI 2010/44, SI 2010/747, SI 2010/2653, SI 2011/651, SI 2011/2343, SI 2012/500 and SI 2012/2007. Consolidated rules available at: **www.justice.gov.uk/tribunals/rules**.

renewed within one month to the Upper Tribunal and this will normally be treated as the notice of appeal. The respondent may submit a written response within one month of that (rule 24). Time extensions are available in justifiable cases. The appellant then has a further month in which to submit a reply (rule 25).

- A person or entity that is not a party to an appeal before the Upper Tribunal can apply to be joined (rule 9).
- The Upper Tribunal is entitled to make all decisions without a hearing but must consider any preferences for a hearing expressed by the parties (rule 34).
- The Upper Tribunal must support its decisions with written reasons, unless the parties agree otherwise or a consent order has been made.
- Where the Upper Tribunal finds that the Information Rights Tribunal's decision involved the making of an error on a point of law, it may – but does not have to – set aside that decision. If it chooses to do so, the Upper Tribunal must either remit the case to the First-tier Tribunal with directions for its reconsideration (by the same or a differently constituted tribunal) or remake the decision itself (Tribunals, Courts and Enforcement Act 2007, s.12).
- A decision of the Upper Tribunal can be challenged within one month, either by asking the Upper Tribunal to set it aside for reasons of procedural irregularity, or by asking the Tribunal for permission to appeal to the Court of Appeal on the grounds of one or more errors of law (see rules 43 and 44(4) and the Tribunals, Courts and Enforcement Act 2007, s.13(2)). Permission will only be granted if the proposed appeal would raise some important point of principle or practice or there is some other compelling reason to allow an appeal to be heard (see the Appeals from the Upper Tribunal to the Court of Appeal Order 2008, SI 2008/2834, art.2).
- Where a party applies for permission to appeal to the Court of Appeal, the Upper Tribunal may (but does not have to) review its decision but only if it previously overlooked a legislative provision or binding authority which could have had a material effect on the decision, or if a court has in the meantime made a decision that, had it been made before the Upper Tribunal's decision, could have had a material effect on the decision. If it does not review or revise the decision it must however go on to consider the application for permission to appeal. A complete or partial refusal of permission to appeal must be accompanied by reasons (rule 45).
- There is no appeal against a decision of the Upper Tribunal in relation to the review of (or decision not to review or not to set aside) its own decision on a case (Tribunals, Courts and Enforcement Act 2007, s.13). Such decisions would in principle be subject to judicial review in the High Court.
- Parties again generally bear their own costs regarding appeals before the Upper Tribunal, although the Upper Tribunal has powers to award costs similar to those of the First-tier Tribunal (see rule 10 and **10.7.8**). Applications for costs can be submitted up to one month after the date on which the Upper Tribunal sends its final determination or after a notice of a withdrawal under rule 17

which ends the proceedings. If the Upper Tribunal makes an order for costs but does not summarily assess those costs, costs will be subject to detailed assessment in the High Court or the Costs Office of the Supreme Court.

10.8.2 Appeals against national security certificates

A government Minister is entitled under the legislation to issue a certificate that provides conclusive evidence of matters which, in effect, show that the national security exemptions of the FOIA or the EIR apply to certain information (the FOIA, s.23 exemption and the EIR, reg.12(5)(a) exception) or apply subject to the public interest test (the FOIA, s.24 exemption). Where an individual's request for information is blocked by a public authority relying on such a certificate, the only means of challenging the validity or applicability of the certificate is by appealing direct to the Information Rights Tribunal under s.60 of the FOIA (or as that section is applied to the EIR under reg.18). The Information Commissioner has no jurisdiction to determine such complaints. In fact, the Information Rights Tribunal cannot hear the appeal either, and must refer it instead to the Upper Tribunal. On the other hand, it is possible that a certificate will only be adduced by the public authority after the Information Commissioner has already become involved in a complaint lodged under s.50(1) of the FOIA, and the Commissioner is also entitled to appeal under s.60 to challenge the certificate. Indeed, where timing allows it may be prudent for an applicant to seek the involvement of the Information Commissioner, as a way of protecting himself or herself against costs (see below).[50]

There are in fact two categories of national security appeals under s.60 of the FOIA.

Section 60(1) appeals

A government Minister can issue a certificate under s.23(2) of the FOIA asserting that particular information falls within the s.23 exemption because it was directly or indirectly supplied by, or relates to, one of the bodies dealing with security matters listed in s.23(3). That list includes MI5, MI6, GCHQ and the National Criminal Intelligence Service. On an appeal brought under s.60(1), however, the Upper Tribunal can quash the certificate if it finds that the Minister was wrong.

Similarly, a Minister can issue a certificate under s.24(3) of the FOIA or reg.15(1) of the EIR asserting that particular information is exempt under s.24 of the FOIA or reg.12(5)(a) of the EIR because (broadly) its disclosure would prejudice national

---

[50] By contrast, the FOIA does not provide for any appeal against the conclusive evidence certificates that can be issued by the Speaker of the House of Commons or the Clerk of the Parliaments in relation to the House of Lords under s.34(3) in respect of parliamentary privilege or s.36(7) in respect of prejudice to effective conduct of public affairs resulting from disclosure of information held by Parliament. In the absence of a statutory appeal, the only remaining avenue of challenge to these certificates would be by way of a judicial review but the courts are most unlikely to intervene, both because of the way the clauses are drafted and out of reluctance to interfere with parliamentary privilege.

security and (in the case of the EIR exception only) the public interest test favours non-disclosure. Again, on an appeal brought under s.60(1), the Upper Tribunal may quash the certificate where it finds that there were no reasonable grounds for issuing it. The standard applied is the same as in judicial review cases, i.e. that no one standing in the Minister's shoes could reasonably have concluded that it was appropriate to issue the certificate.

Note that because s.24 provides a public authority with a qualified exemption only, regardless of whether a related ministerial certificate has been quashed or not, it is still open to the person making the request for information to submit a complaint to the Information Commissioner arguing that the information should be disclosed because the public interest in withholding it does not outweigh the public interest in disclosure.

Section 60(4) appeals

It is permissible for certificates issued under s.24(3) of the FOIA or reg.15(1) of the EIR to be framed in general terms. Where a public authority claims that a generally worded certificate applies to the specific information requested, the Tribunal can, on an appeal under s.60(4), determine that the certificate does not in fact cover that information. It is possible that the Minister would then issue a fresh certificate more tailored to the information in question, although that certificate too would be subject to appeals under s.60.

Procedure

The procedural rules for challenging ministerial conclusive evidence certificates are not dissimilar to those which applied before the reorganisation of the tribunals system.[51] It is notable, however, that the public authority can participate formally now (as the respondent), an involvement which authorities were denied under the previous regime where the Minister was the respondent.

An appellant starts proceedings by sending a notice of appeal so that it is received by the Information Rights Tribunal within 28 days of the date on which the claim was made by the public authority that a generally worded ministerial certificate applies to the information in question for appeals under s.60(4) of the FOIA, or at any time during the currency of the ministerial certificate in question for appeals under s.60(1) of the FOIA (see FTT Rules 2009, rule 22(6)).

The Information Rights Tribunal's role is limited to transferring the case to the Upper Tribunal (FTT Rules 2009, rule 19(1A)). At that point the applicable rules become the UT Rules 2008. Rule 14(10) of those rules places the Upper Tribunal under a general obligation to ensure that in the course of such appeals information is

---

[51] The old rules were contained in the Information Tribunal (National Security Appeals) Rules 2005, SI 2005/13.

not disclosed contrary to the interests of national security. A special procedure therefore applies with appropriate protections built in (rule 26A and Sched.2).

Following the transfer, the Upper Tribunal has to provide a copy of the notice of appeal to the respondent, the relevant Minister and the Information Commissioner. The Minister has 42 days from receipt of the notice of appeal to send the Upper Tribunal a response and a copy of the relevant certificate (Sched.2, para.3). The response includes the Minister's grounds for supporting or opposing the appeal and the evidence to support those grounds. In an appeal under s.60(1) of the FOIA (or as that section is applied to the EIR by reg.18) the response must also give reasons for the issue of the certificate.

Subject to the Minister's right to object on national security grounds, the Upper Tribunal provides the response of the Minister and any other party to the appellant, the Information Commissioner and any respondent, and sends a copy of any other response to the relevant Minister (Sched.2, para.6). Where the Minister does raise such an objection, he or she must do so at the time he or she submits the response, support it with reasons and, to the extent that it is possible to do so, provide a version of the response in a form that can be shown to the other parties (Sched.2, paras.7–8).

Where any other party submits a response to the notice of appeal, the Upper Tribunal must first provide it to the Minister, who is given 42 days in which to object to its being shared with the Information Commissioner or another party (Sched.2, para.7(b)). Any objection must again be supported by reasons.

Another protective element of the procedure is that before the Upper Tribunal gives any direction, issues a summons or citation, or produces or publishes a written record of, or reasons for, a decision, the rules require it to notify the Minister of the proposed action first. If the Minister considers that the proposal would result in disclosure of information that is or would be exempt by virtue of a provision in Part 2 of the FOIA (or Part 3 of the EIR), he or she may object to the proposal by lodging a notice with the Upper Tribunal within 14 days of being notified of the proposal (Sched.2, para.9).

The Upper Tribunal is not required to hold a hearing to decide whether to uphold a ministerial objection but if it does, this takes place in the absence of the appellant, the public authority and any other parties to the appeal. If the Upper Tribunal is minded to overrule the Minister's objection, or to require the Minister to provide a version of his or her response in a form other than one already provided, the Upper Tribunal must invite the Minister to make representations. If the Upper Tribunal overrules an objection in relation to the disclosure of a response, the Tribunal may only disclose material which was the subject of the objection if the Minister is relying on that material in opposing the appeal (Sched.2, para.10).

Subject to the above, the Upper Tribunal can make such directions as it deems appropriate for the handling of the appeal, for example, as to document disclosure, the calling of witnesses and so on (rule 26A). The Tribunal is permitted to decide the appeal without a hearing but must have regard to the views of the parties in this respect (rule 34). If there is a hearing it will be held in public unless the Tribunal determines that it should take place partly or wholly in private – a decision to be taken bearing in mind the interests of national security (rule 37(2A)). The Tribunal is empowered to exclude any individual from a private session, including a party to the appeal. The Minister, however, is entitled to attend any hearing (rule 35).

The Tribunal must give a copy of its decision notice and any supporting statement of reasons to the Minister and the Information Commissioner if they are not parties (rule 40(5)).

The opportunities to challenge an Upper Tribunal decision on a national security certificate are far more limited than is the case with Information Rights Tribunal decisions or decisions of the Upper Tribunal on appeal from decisions of that First-tier Tribunal. Specifically, the Upper Tribunal has no power to review (correct, amend or set aside) its decisions on national security certificate appeals (Tribunals, Courts and Enforcement Act 2007, s.10(1)). Nor can such decisions be appealed to the Court of Appeal (s.13(8)(b) of the same Act). The only way to challenge such a decision would therefore be by way of judicial review in the High Court.

It should be noted that for constitutional reasons the bar will be set high as regards challenges to ministerial certificates under s.60(1) – both on the initial appeal to the Upper Tribunal or in a judicial review before the High Court – as the judges will extend a considerable degree of deference to the Minister. This is because decisions on matters of national security are regarded largely as the province of the executive rather than the judiciary (see Lord Steyn in *Secretary of State for the Home Department* v. *Rehman* [2001] UKHL 47 at [31]).

Costs

In national security certificate appeals, the Upper Tribunal can make the following orders for costs:

- on an appeal under s.60(1) of the FOIA (and as applied to the EIR), against the relevant Minister and in favour of the appellant if the Upper Tribunal allows the appeal and quashes the certificate to any extent or the Minister withdraws the certificate;
- on an appeal under s.60(4) of the FOIA (and as applied to the EIR),
    - (i) against the appellant and in favour of any other party if the Upper Tribunal dismisses the appeal to any extent; or
    - (ii) in favour of the appellant and against any other party if the Upper Tribunal allows the appeal to any extent;
- in respect of wasted costs under s.29(4) of the Tribunals, Courts and Enforcement Act 2007 (for the detail on this see **10.7**);
- against a party or its representative if the Upper Tribunal considers either has acted unreasonably in bringing, defending or conducting the proceedings.

Prior to making any adverse order, the Tribunal must give the paying party the opportunity to make representations, and must consider his or her financial means if he or she is an individual (UT Rules 2008, rule 10).

10.8.3 Judicial review in the Upper Tribunal

Decisions of the Information Rights Tribunal in relation to which no statutory right of appeal is provided are nevertheless subject to challenge by way of judicial review in the Upper Tribunal on the same basis as in the High Court (Tribunals, Courts and Enforcement Act 2007, s.15).[52] Thus, under this jurisdiction, the Upper Tribunal reviews the process by which the Information Rights Tribunal reached its decision and assesses whether it was fair and lawful. If the Upper Tribunal finds the decision was flawed, it can quash the decision and remit the matter to the Information Rights Tribunal, with a direction to reconsider the matter and reach a decision in accordance with the findings of the Upper Tribunal. Alternatively, the Upper Tribunal may substitute its own decision for that of the Information Rights Tribunal, but only if the decision is quashed due to an error of law and without that error there is only one decision that the Information Rights Tribunal could have made (Tribunals, Courts and Enforcement Act 2007, s.17). The Upper Tribunal may also hear claims for damages within its judicial review jurisdiction (Tribunals, Courts and Enforcement Act 2007, s.16).

Anyone with a 'sufficient interest' in the subject matter of the application may apply for judicial review. The first step is to apply to the Upper Tribunal for permission ('leave' in Northern Ireland) to bring a judicial review. This must be done promptly and generally within three months of the relevant decision, act or omission (UT Rules 2008, rule 28). The Upper Tribunal may refuse to grant permission, or any substantive relief, where it considers there has been undue delay in making the application and granting the relief sought would be likely to cause substantial hardship to, or substantially prejudice the rights of, any person, or would be detrimental to good administration. The information that has to be included in the application is specified in rule 28 of the UT Rules 2008.

An interested party who wants to be involved in the permission application must submit an acknowledgment of service within 21 days of being served with the application for permission (rule 29). A permission hearing, if any, may be held on just two working days' notice. The Upper Tribunal will serve all interested parties with its decision on the permission application, and, if permission is granted, they must submit detailed responses within 35 days (rule 31). The Upper Tribunal can decide the case without a hearing, although it must consider the parties' views on this (rule 34).

Where the Upper Tribunal rejects an application for permission to bring a judicial review, the applicant can appeal against that decision to the Court of Appeal. Where

---

[52] This was confirmed by a Practice Direction given by the Lord Chief Justice entitled *Upper Tribunal: Judicial Review Jurisdiction* [2009] 1 WLR 327. The direction satisfies the somewhat obscurely drafted Condition 3 referred to in s.18 of the Tribunals, Courts and Enforcement Act 2007, which determines the scope of the Upper Tribunal's judicial review jurisdiction. There are two cases where judicial review is not available: (i) decisions of the Information Rights Tribunal on national security appeals (but anyway the Information Rights Tribunal does not make substantive decisions on these); and (ii) any class of decision specified in an order made by the Lord Chancellor (currently no such orders have been made).

the Court of Appeal grants permission to bring the judicial review application, the Court of Appeal may hear the substantive application (Tribunals, Courts and Enforcement Act 2007, s.16(8)).

An applicant can appeal to the Court of Appeal on a point of law in relation to an Upper Tribunal decision on the substantive judicial review application. It would be necessary to apply first to the Upper Tribunal for permission within one month of the final decision being sent by the Upper Tribunal (rule 44), and if this were rejected, then to apply to the Court of Appeal direct. It would be necessary to argue that the proposed appeal would raise some important point of principle or practice, or that there is some other compelling reason for the court to hear the appeal (see the Appeals from the Upper Tribunal to the Court of Appeal Order 2008, SI 2008/2834).

The procedure on judicial review cases is set out in Part 4 of the UT Rules 2008.

10.9 APPEALS TO THE COURT OF APPEAL AND BEYOND

If a request for permission to appeal to the Court of Appeal against an Upper Tribunal decision on a point of law is refused by the Upper Tribunal, a would-be appellant can apply to the Court of Appeal direct for permission to appeal. Permission to appeal will not be granted unless the Court of Appeal considers that the proposed appeal would raise some important point of principle or practice or there is some other compelling reason for it to hear the appeal. Should the Court of Appeal refuse to grant permission to appeal to it, that refusal cannot be appealed to the Supreme Court (Access to Justice Act 1999, s.54(4)).

Where the Court of Appeal finds that an Upper Tribunal decision involved the making of an error on a point of law, the Court of Appeal may (but is not obliged to) set aside the Upper Tribunal's decision and either remake the decision itself or remit the matter to the Upper Tribunal (or the Information Rights Tribunal if heard there at first instance) with directions for its reconsideration. It may direct that the case be considered by a different panel from that which made the original decision (Tribunals, Courts and Enforcement Act 2007, s.14). Where the Court of Appeal remits the decision to the Upper Tribunal, the Upper Tribunal can, rather than remaking the decision itself, remit the decision to the Information Rights Tribunal (together with the directions of the Court of Appeal), and can itself direct a change of panel and issue further procedural directions. As for the procedural rules governing appeals to the Court of Appeal, see the CPR Part 52 and accompanying Practice Direction ◄www.justice.gov.uk/courts/procedure-rules/civil).

Following a decision of the Court of Appeal, a dissatisfied party could ask the court for permission to appeal to the Supreme Court. If that request were turned down the party could apply for such permission direct from the Supreme Court (see s.40 of the Constitutional Reform Act 2005 and the Supreme Court Rules 2009, SI 2009/1603, together with the Practice Directions that accompany the latter).

10.10   THIRD PARTIES

10.10.1   Limited rights of intervention under the FOIA

In the context of the FOIA and the EIR a third party is anyone other than the applicant requesting access under s.1(1) and the public authority to which he or she addresses that request. A third party might have an interest in an access request (or in information which an authority proposes to publish under its publication scheme) because it supplied that information, or is the subject of the information, or would be affected by its disclosure. It could be another public authority, an individual, or a private sector company providing services to the authority under contract. There are many reasons why such persons or entities might be reluctant to see the information disclosed: to protect their confidential information, their reputation or their privacy, to name but the most obvious. To an extent, their interests are protected by the exemptions under the FOIA but they are still dependent on the public authority choosing to invoke the exemption (the FOIA does not prohibit authorities from disclosing exempt material but doing so may of course bring criminal or civil consequences under other laws such as the Official Secrets Act 1989 or the law of confidence). They also face the risk that the public authority may not appreciate that the requested information is exempt, or may disclose it without meaning to. The third party will often have knowledge which puts them in a better position than the public authority to know, for example, that certain information is a trade secret or that its disclosure would prejudice their commercial interests or the national or regional economy, or to appreciate the relevant public interest arguments in favour of maintaining the exemption and withholding information. More generally, a third party may well have a stronger impulse to shield from public view information concerning it than the public authority which has been asked to disclose it.

In spite of all this, it is a notable (and in the eyes of many, lamentable) difference between the FOIA and freedom of information regimes in many other countries that in the UK (the position under the Freedom of Information (Scotland) Act 2002 is the same) interested third parties have no statutory right to be notified about requests made for information which affects them, nor is there an effective procedure under the FOIA by which they can maintain an objection to its disclosure (sometimes known as 'reverse FOI'). They have no standing to apply to the Information Commissioner under s.50(1) to complain about the authority's proposed or actual disclosure of information. Nor can they lodge an appeal against a decision notice of the Commissioner with the Information Rights Tribunal.

10.10.2   Participation in appeals before the tribunals

On the other hand, both the Information Rights Tribunal and the Upper Tribunal are empowered to direct third parties to be joined to an appeal before them. It is by no means certain, however, that the third party will be aware of the appeal in order to be able to apply to participate. A practice note which was until early 2012 available on

368

the Information Rights Tribunal website required Information Rights Tribunal judges to keep in mind during a case the appropriateness of joining a third party in the appeal. The practice note gently suggested the following as one of the factors a judge 'might consider' as relevant to such a decision:

> where it appears that an appeal may determine the rights or liabilities of a person who is not a party to an appeal, the desirability of that person having the opportunity to make representations. (para.20)

The problem is that in many cases this right of participation in the complaint comes too late in the day, in that disclosure might have occurred at an earlier stage, following a decision of the public authority or the Information Commissioner.

Further, where the third party is not party to the appeal, the Information Tribunal (as it then was) has shown reluctance to give weight to public authorities' arguments about prejudice to that party's commercial interests (the s.43 exemption) if there is no evidence that such arguments would be espoused by the third party itself (see *Derry City Council* v. *Information Commissioner* (EA/2006/0014, 11 December 2006), para.24, where the absent third party was Ryanair; and *Keene* v. *Information Commissioner and Central Office of Information* (EA/2008/0097, 14 September 2009), para.39).

On a more positive note, in a case in the Upper Tribunal there was judicial recognition of the importance of allowing third party interests to be fully taken into account in FOI decisions. The Tribunal pointed to this factor as justifying its establishment of the principle that up to and including the stage of lodging an appeal before the Information Rights Tribunal, public authorities do not require permission from the Information Commissioner or the Information Rights Tribunal to base their case on an exemption which they had not raised at an earlier stage (*Department for Environment, Food and Rural Affairs* v. *Information Commissioner and Birkett* [2011] UKUT 39 (AAC), paras.28–29). The judge said that because third parties 'have no role in the information rights process', their interests might be overlooked initially, and hence would go unprotected unless there was full freedom for public authorities to invoke exemptions belatedly. The judge also gave his view of the responsibilities of the Information Commissioner when handling complaints under s.50 of the FOIA: 'As to third parties, the Commissioner must always be alert to their interests if they are not being protected by the complainant or the public authority' (para.50).

10.10.3   Rights to be consulted when request first made

Interested third parties have a limited entitlement to be consulted by a public authority when it receives a request for information. This is provided by the non-statutory guidance in Part IV of the Section 45 Code of Practice, whose provisions are not binding obligations but constitute practice which, in the opinion of the Secretary of State, is desirable for public authorities to follow in connection with the discharge of their functions under Part I of the FOIA. Even where consultation takes place, however, ultimate responsibility for deciding whether or not to disclose the information requested lies with the public authority. An authority is thus not bound to withhold information simply because a relevant third party asks it to do so or argues that it should.

It is worth pointing out in passing that the Section 45 Code of Practice provisions on consultation with affected third parties appear to be applicable also in the context of information which a public authority is proposing to release under its publication scheme, even though the Code makes no express reference to publication schemes in the section on consultation. Although the ICO's *Guide to Freedom of Information* advises public authorities that they are not required to publish documents under their publication schemes which are exempt under the FOIA, they are not actually prevented by the FOIA from releasing such material if they so wish. They may also not always realise that, or be certain whether, the information in question is exempt. Consultation may well be required in such cases under the Section 45 Code of Practice. There is no mechanism in the FOIA for the making of complaints about publication schemes (but see comments in **10.6.3**).

The Section 45 Code of Practice indicates first that consultation with an interested third party will in some cases be necessary, either for the public authority to know whether the information requested is covered by an exemption or to determine whether the obligations in s.1 of the FOIA arise in relation to it (para.27). This last phrase seems likely to mean that it may also be necessary for a public authority to consult a third party on how the public interest test should be applied where information is potentially exempt. (It could also mean such consultation may be necessary to know whether the authority is even required to confirm or deny that it holds the information requested.) However, this begs the question: when will consultation be necessary for those purposes? The word 'necessary' in this context is assumed to mean: practically needed in order for the public authority to form a view on whether an exemption applies or on the relative public interests at stake, rather than required by law. It is arguable, however, that consultation could be required in some cases because of a public authority's obligations under public law (see **10.10.5**). In addition, any contract between the authority and the third party may require consultation in certain circumstances. Some help with deciding when consultation is necessary can perhaps be drawn from what was para.37 of the original text of the Section 45 Code of Practice (issued November 2002) even though it has been removed from the current edition (November 2004). The earlier edition explained that consultation would not be necessary where: (i) the authority proposes to oppose disclosure on other grounds; (ii) the third party's views could be of no effect, for instance, because disclosure is required or prevented by other legislation; and (iii) where no exemption is relevant (which presumably meant, where none was even potentially relevant).

A second category of cases which the Section 45 Code of Practice contemplates is those where consultation is not necessary but would still be good practice. This applies 'in a range of … circumstances' and it gives the example of where an authority proposes to disclose information which relates to a third party or which is likely to affect its interests. Here, though, the Code does not appear to be recommending consultation in the ordinary meaning of the word: authorities are merely to take 'reasonable steps ... where appropriate, to give [third parties] advance notice, or failing that, to draw it to their attention afterwards' (para.28).

Thirdly, public authorities are advised that, in some cases, it may also be appropriate to consult interested third parties about other sorts of question, such as whether the applicant ought to be given any explanatory material or advice, such as any copyright (or other) restrictions as there might be on the applicant's further use of the material (para.28).

The requirement to consult in all three categories of cases appears to be further qualified where the information to be disclosed relates to, or affects, a number of third parties. Where these share a representative organisation, the authority may consider whether it would be sufficient to notify or consult with that organisation or, in other cases, to notify or consult with a representative sample of the third parties (para.30).

The Section 45 Code of Practice, in addition, highly recommends that public authorities ensure that third parties are made aware of the authorities' duties of disclosure under the FOIA (para.26). An authority could comply with this, however, by making a general statement to this effect on first dealing with a particular person or entity rather than in connection with a specific request for information. In summary, the position as to when consultation is required or will take place is uncertain and third parties can take only limited comfort from the provisions of the Section 45 Code of Practice. In the context of the EIR, the Regulation 16 Code of Practice puts even less of an onus on public authorities to consult with interested third parties prior to disclosure. Interestingly, the position is made (slightly) clearer where both the public authority and the third party information provider are government departments:

No decision to release information which has been supplied by one Government department to another should be taken without first notifying, and where appropriate consulting, the department from which the information originated. (Section 45 Code of Practice, para.29)

Even where a third party is consulted, there is no provision in the Section 45 Code of Practice requiring the public authority to notify it of its final decision, or of any request for internal review or of any subsequent complaint to the Information Commissioner. Further, nothing in the FOIA or the Section 45 Code of Practice obliges the Information Commissioner to consult an interested third party when considering a complaint under s.50 (but see **10.10.5**).

Except in the very clearest of cases, however, where there can be no chance that the public authority has failed to take account of some relevant issue, public authorities would be well advised to do all they reasonably can to consult an interested third party in advance of disclosing information. If they do not, then not only will they risk breaching the Section 45 Code of Practice (and potentially receiving a practice recommendation from the Information Commissioner) but they may find themselves involved in legal proceedings with financial consequences potentially far more severe than a breach of the FOIA or the Section 45 Code of Practice (see **10.10.5**). Liaising co-operatively with third parties will often of course be fundamental to maintaining good relationships with important suppliers.

Under the legislation, then, interested third parties are essentially left to hope that public authorities and the Information Commissioner will consult them at each stage and that authorities will resist requests with the same zeal and effectiveness as they themselves would at the outset, on any internal review and before the Information Commissioner and that they will, if necessary, appeal to the Information Rights Tribunal.

10.10.4   Maximising the third party's chances of being consulted

A third party can improve its position in advance of any particular request being made by its negotiations and relationship development with the public authorities it deals with. As well as ensuring it has an open channel of communication with such authorities (including their FOI officers), it should look to insert confidentiality undertakings in relevant agreements, as well as terms requiring the public authority to notify and consult with it promptly and adequately in relation to any request for information which it receives that relates to or affects the third party in any way. It might also look for a commitment to be consulted in the wake of any decision or enforcement notice of the Information Commissioner requiring disclosure of information affecting the third party, so that it and the public authority could consider the scope for appealing against the notice to the Information Rights Tribunal. Similarly, a third party should review any information it provides, or has in the past provided, to public authorities and draw their attention to which elements it considers as confidential or engaging any of the other exemptions under the FOIA, and it should mark the documents accordingly. With regard to a third party prompting the Information Commissioner to consult it, see **10.10.5**.

10.10.5   Options for direct action open to third parties

Third parties do have options for direct action, but each has difficulties and limitations and although some may in theory be used to obtain an injunction to prevent the disclosure of material, the value of such a remedy is severely limited by practicalities: where a public authority has ignored the Section 45 Code of Practice's provisions on consultation, the first that the third party hears of the request will be after the information has already been disclosed and it receives a call from an interested journalist, for example. Even where the third party is on notice of the request, the window for action may be very narrow because public authorities are under an obligation to respond to requests promptly and in any event within 20 working days. There is the further difficulty that if disclosure has already taken place or cannot be stopped, the right of action, or its value to the third party, may fall away because there are no quantifiable damages to be compensated. Information cases (such as breach of confidence cases) tend to be all about the injunction application, for preventing disclosure is the only valuable remedy to the claimant. Lastly, taking legal action can be costly and exposes the litigant to a court order to pay the other side's legal costs if it loses.

Contract

Where the third party had negotiated a term in an agreement that the public authority would notify and duly consult it over any request for information in which the third party had an interest, it could seek to enforce the contract by applying for an injunction prohibiting disclosure and requiring consultation, in the unlikely event that it discovered this in time.

Judicial review

Alternatively, a third party could seek to enforce consultation by looking to public law for a remedy. The courts (and where appropriate the Upper Tribunal in its judicial review jurisdiction – see **10.8.3**) are likely to find that the Section 45 Code of Practice constitutes mandatory statutory guidance which a public authority is obliged to follow unless it has good reason to depart from it (*R* v. *London Borough of Islington, ex p. Rixon* (1998) 1 CCLR 119). For the uncertainties around the nature of the consultation envisaged by that guidance, see **10.10.3**.

There could also be an implied duty on public authorities to consult third parties before making a decision to disclose information affecting them, as part of their general duty to act fairly in the exercise of their functions. The greater the impact of the decision, the more likely a court would find that there was an implied duty to consult. A third party could also point to the obvious importance given to consultation by the statutory scheme, by reference to: (i) the requirement in s.45(2)(c) of the FOIA for the Secretary of State's code of practice to include provision on public authorities consulting with interested third parties over requests for information which affect them; (ii) the resultant Section 45 Code of Practice, which makes such provision; (iii) the obligation on the Information Commissioner in s.47 of the FOIA to act in a way which promotes the observance of the Section 45 Code of Practice; and (iv) the provisions which allow third parties to be joined to appeals before the tribunals (see **10.7.5** and **10.8.1**). The significance of taking due account of a third party's view was also reflected in the Information Rights Tribunal's practice note on protecting confidential information (paras.19–20), which was available on its website until early 2012.

Guiding principles on the nature of proper consultation have been established by the courts (*R* v. *North and East Devon Area Health Authority, ex p. Coughlan* [2001] QB 213, para.108):

- consultation must take place at a time when the proposals are still at a formative stage;

- the proposer (in this context, the public authority) must give sufficient reasons for the action it proposes to take to permit intelligent consideration and response;
- adequate time must be given for consideration and response;
- the product of consultation must be conscientiously taken into account in finalising any proposals.

The duty to consult does not imply a duty to obtain agreement before acting (*R (on the application of Smith)* v. *East Kent Hospitals NHS Trust* [2002] EWHC 2640 (Admin) per Silber J at [61]), nor will a different outcome necessarily be reached where the reviewing court orders the public authority to reconsider its decision in the light of the third party's views.

Aside from the issue of consultation, a third party could also ask the court or the Upper Tribunal on an application for judicial review to quash a decision of a public authority, the Information Commissioner or the appellate tribunals where the decision failed to give due weight to the third party's interests or evidence, or was flawed by (other) errors of law or fact, substantive unfairness or unreasonableness, unjustifiable inconsistency with earlier decisions, was supported by inadequate reasons, or involved a breach of the Human Rights Act 1998.

Pre-action injunctions are available ancillary to an application for judicial review and the High Court may also grant declaratory relief and award damages (Supreme Court Act 1981, s.31(2) and (4)). The procedure on judicial review applications in England and Wales is set out in Parts 8 and 54 of the CPR and in the Pre-Action Protocol on Judicial Review. As a matter of discretion, the courts will not normally make the remedy of judicial review available where there is an alternative remedy by way of appeal (*R* v. *Chief Constable of the Merseyside Police, ex p. Calveley* [1986] QB 424).

Bringing a successful judicial review will often prove a significant challenge to third parties. In one early example, a US-based gaming company had resort to judicial review in an attempt to prevent Birmingham City Council disclosing details of commercial arrangements between the company, the council and Birmingham City Football Club to try to bring a super casino to Birmingham. A request for this information had been made by a local newspaper, the *Birmingham Post*. Although it was turned down initially, this decision was reversed on internal review on public interest grounds. The judicial review application was rejected and not appealed (*R (Las Vegas Sands Corp.)* v. *Birmingham City Council* (HC, 2 March 2006, unreported)).

Protecting confidential information

A third party could seek to restrain a public authority from disclosing the third party's confidential or private information by applying for a breach of confidence injunction. The third party would need to show that the information was neither trivial nor already in the public domain, that it was communicated to the public authority in circumstances importing an obligation of confidence (whether under a contract or otherwise), that disclosure would be an unauthorised use of the information and that (at least in the context of commercial rather than private information) it would result in the third party suffering some detriment, which can include reputational damage. As public interest is effectively a defence to claims for breach of confidence, the third party's restraint application would fail where the public authority shows that disclosure would be in the public interest and proportionate in all the circumstances (see *Higher Education Funding Council for England* v. *Information Commissioner and Guardian News and Media Ltd* (EA/2009/0036, 13 January 2010)).[53]

On the other hand, if the requested information had been designated confidential under a contract between the third party and the public authority, yet did not meet the test referred to above, the third party would probably not be able to restrain disclosure even on a breach-of-contract basis. This is because the information would not then be covered by the terms of the exemptions regarding confidential information under s.41 of the FOIA or reg.12(5)(e) of the EIR and therefore the public authority would be compelled to disclose it. Often a public authority will have a clause in its contracts permitting disclosures of 'confidential information' where this is required by law.

From the public authority's point of view, where there is a risk of a breach of confidence claim from a third party, it would be advisable for the authority to consult the third party throughout and to be prepared to refuse the applicant's request and appeal against a decision by the Information Commissioner or the Information Rights Tribunal ordering disclosure. It remains unclear whether such a decision notice would provide the public authority with a cast-iron defence to a breach of confidence claim. The question was raised but not decided in *Milford Haven Port Authority* v. *Information Commissioner* (EA/2007/0036, 6 November 2007) at para.24.

Damages are available to compensate losses where disclosure has already taken place, as is an account of the profits made from the disclosure.

Public authorities cannot contract out of the FOIA, since a party may not contract out of a statutory protection which is intended to serve the public interest (*Johnson* v. *Moreton* [1980] AC 37). Further, a third party will fail if it seeks to prevail upon a

---

[53]   To obtain an interim injunction, a claimant may well have to show it is more likely than not to succeed at trial. This is a higher test than that ordinarily required on injunction applications, where the claimant must show it has a 'real prospect of success' or there is a 'serious question to be tried' (*American Cyanamid Co.* v. *Ethicon Ltd* [1975] AC 396). This is because of the effect of s.12(3) of the Human Rights Act 1998 where an injunction is sought in a claim for breach of confidence to prevent the exercise of the ECHR, art.10 right to freedom of expression (*Cream Holdings Ltd and Others* v. *Banerjee and Another* [2005] 1 AC 253). A government claimant will in addition have to show that there is a public interest in keeping the information confidential (*Attorney General* v. *Jonathan Cape Ltd and Others* [1976] QB 752 at 770–771). For a fuller discussion of what constitutes confidential information, see **4.5.8**. Note also that in cases involving private information of the kind protected by art.8 of the ECHR, the relevant defence is that the public interest in the art.10 right to freedom of expression outweighs the art.8 right (see *Ash* v. *McKennitt* [2006] EWCA Civ 1714).

public authority to impose a duty of confidentiality on any recipient of information which it is required to disclose under the FOIA or the EIR. In *S* v. *Information Commissioner and General Register Office* (EA/2006/0030, 9 May 2007), the Information Tribunal held:

> A disclosure under FOIA, is a disclosure to the public (i.e. the world at large). ... Consequently there is no provision for the public authority to create conditions of use pursuant to a FOIA disclosure or to indicate that such disclosure should be treated in confidence. (para.80)

Copyright

A third party affected by information to which access has been requested will in some cases have provided that information to the public authority and will own the copyright in the underlying document or work. However, the question of whether third parties are entitled to seek an injunction against public authorities on the grounds that disclosure under the FOIA would constitute an infringement of their copyright or any separate database right has been answered by the Information Commissioner in the negative. In *House of Commons* (FS50276715, 7 June 2010) the Information Commissioner expressed the view that a public authority would not breach a third party's copyright where it disclosed information under the FOIA, due to s.50(1) of the Copyright, Designs and Patents Act 1988 (CDPA), which provides a defence to infringement where 'the doing of a particular act is specifically authorised by an Act of Parliament ... unless the Act provides otherwise'. This position was affirmed and elaborated in subsequent guidance: *Intellectual Property Rights and Disclosures under the Freedom of Information Act* (ICO, 11 July 2012).[54] The guidance also rejects the argument that by prohibiting copyright infringement the CDPA creates a statutory bar to disclosure of such information for the purposes of the exemption in s.44(1)(a) of the FOIA, again on account of s.50 of the CDPA (para.13).

All is not lost for third parties, however, because the guidance makes clear that even though a public authority is authorised to make disclosures which would otherwise infringe copyright, a third party would be entitled to prevent the recipient of such material from making any use of it which infringed its intellectual property rights. This indeed was the view of the Information Tribunal (and all the parties) in *Office of Communications* v. *Information Commissioner and T-Mobile (UK) Ltd* (EA/2006/0078, 4 September 2007) at para.51, a case involving database rights.

Nevertheless, to prevail in a copyright action against the requester, the third party would need to prove its case in the normal way, including showing that what was copied was a substantial part of the copyright work. Equally, the third party would need to consider any defences which the recipient might have. In this regard, the Information Commissioner's guidance note expresses the view that the various 'fair

---

[54] The Copyright and Rights in Databases Regulations 1997, SI 1997/3032, are in similar terms to CDPA, s.50.

dealing' provisions in Chapter III of the CDPA (in particular the defence of fair dealing with a copyright work for the purpose of criticism, review or reporting current events (CDPA, s.30)) provide 'ample scope for the contents of information disclosed under FOIA to be debated publicly' (para.18).

The Information Commissioner's position that disclosures by public authorities under the FOIA do not infringe intellectual property rights is not particularly surprising since the effectiveness of the FOIA as a means of promoting freedom of information could be significantly undermined if third parties were able to prevent (or recover compensation for) disclosure of their copyright material by public authorities. One might also point to the absence from the FOIA of any express exemption for third party intellectual property rights as suggesting that Parliament did not intend such rights to prevent disclosure under s.1 of the FOIA. The position under the EIR is different as it contains an exception to the duty to disclose environmental information to the extent that disclosure would adversely affect intellectual property rights (EIR, reg.12(5)(e)). Similarly, the Re-use of Public Sector Information Regulations 2005, SI 2005/1515 expressly exclude from their scope documents of a public sector body where a third party owns relevant intellectual property rights in the document (reg.5(1)(b)). Public authorities are also expressly restricted from taking any action under the INSPIRE Regulations, such as making available their databases of geo-spatial information, without the consent of any third party which holds intellectual property rights in the dataset.

As desirable as the ICO's position may be, there is still scope to ask whether it is correct: does s.50(1) of the CDPA (or, for that matter, the similar common law tort defence of statutory authority)[55] really apply to disclosures under the FOIA? The ICO guidance asserts that 'responding to a freedom of information request is an act authorised by Parliament and so disclosures under FOIA will not infringe IP rights.' One could take a narrower view that the FOIA specifically authorises disclosure of (non-exempt) information but not documents themselves. It may after all be possible, though time consuming, for a public authority to convey information from a document to an applicant without falling foul of copyright protection of the original document, such as by summarising it in different words or simply granting applicants the right to inspect the information. (These two options are specifically referred to in s.11(1) as means by which an applicant is entitled to have information communicated to him or her as an alternative to receiving a copy of the information, if reasonably practicable.)

Since extracting the requested information from records is one of the elements that a public authority can consider when assessing whether complying with the request would cost more than the cost limit for the purposes of s.12, such an interpretation could, however, significantly limit the amount of information that was freely available to requesters.

---

[55] 'No liability in tort can arise from acts done in pursuance, and within the scope, of statutory powers where the powers are exercised in good faith, reasonably, without negligence, and for the purpose for which, and in the manner in which, the statute provides' (*Halsbury's Laws of England*, 5th edn, vol.97 (2010), para.457)).

Even if the true position is that disclosures mandated by the FOIA (and voluntary disclosures of exempt information in response to a FOIA request) are subject to intellectual property rights, a third party seeking an injunction would again need to consider whether it could make out a case for infringement and whether the public authority might be able to rely on one of the defences to such actions, which, in addition to fair dealing, include consent (express or implied), public interest and – of specific relevance to many public authorities – the CDPA defences in s.47 (copying of material which is open to public inspection under statute), s.48 (the issuing to the public of material communicated to the Crown in the course of public business) and s.49 (copying of materials which are public records under the Public Records Act 1958).

In any event, applicants may need to obtain the consent of rights-holders (which could include the public authority itself) before publishing material obtained under the FOIA. An applicant proposing to rely on a fair dealing defence would have to comply with the CDPA requirements to provide 'sufficient acknowledgement' to the copyright owner in the copies they make. For their part, public authorities may wish to consider protecting their position by marking disclosed third party materials with a clear warning that reproduction without appropriate consent could lead to liability in damages and that the authority is not to be taken as authorising any such further disclosure. Otherwise, the authority could potentially be liable for authorising the applicant's subsequent infringements, by virtue of s.16(2) of the CDPA. The ICO guidance discussed above similarly advises that it would be good practice for public authorities to state clearly where documents made available through their publication schemes are subject to any conditions on republication, such as Crown copyright or third party intellectual property rights (paras.56–59).

Data protection

Certain personal data are exempt from disclosure under s.40 of the FOIA. A third party concerned that a public authority will disclose information containing personal data about him or her (or has already done so) may serve notice on the public authority under s.10 of the DPA requiring it to stop processing such data if disclosure (which would constitute 'processing' for these purposes) is likely to cause the third party substantial and unwarranted damage or distress. Service of a valid notice would bring the information within the qualified exemption in s.40(3)(a)(ii) of the FOIA (or reg.13 of the EIR). In addition, the third party could potentially apply to court for an order:

(i) enforcing the s.10 notice;
(ii) blocking disclosure, or correcting, erasing or destroying the data (DPA, s.14); and
(iii) awarding compensation where disclosure has taken place (DPA, s.13).

Breaches of the DPA can also be investigated by the Information Commissioner under s.42 of that Act, and may result in his issuing the public authority data controller with an enforcement notice under s.40, specifying similar steps in relation to the data in question, save that he cannot award compensation.

For a more detailed discussion of the workings of the DPA and the interaction between it and the FOIA, see **Chapter 8**.

Defamation

A public authority could potentially be liable to a third party for disclosing information which contained a statement that identified the third party and would have made ordinary, right-thinking people think less of that person or organisation. However, where that information was supplied to the authority by another party and the authority is required to disclose it in response to a request under s.1 of the FOIA, the third party would not succeed in an action in defamation unless the authority acted maliciously in doing so (see s.79 of the FOIA). An authority will be acting maliciously where it knows the defamatory information is untrue or is reckless as to whether or not it is true. Malice will be particularly difficult to prove in the context of a statutory duty to disclose the information. By contrast, where the defamatory material is exempt from disclosure but the authority releases it anyway (perhaps not realising that it is exempt), the information is not 'communicated under section 1' and the authority will thus not enjoy the protection of this statutory privilege. In general, where defamation is concerned an interim injunction to restrain publication is very difficult to obtain.[56]

It is worth noting, however, that the s.79 defence will not protect a public authority where the defamatory allegations were contained in papers generated internally, so authorities could be sued in defamation by third parties in respect of such material. In addition, there is no protection in the FOIA for applicants republishing (i.e. communicating to any third party) defamatory information which they have received from public authorities, and thus a third party which was the subject of such allegations could sue the applicant (and anyone else) in respect of any such re-publication. In any claim, the defendant will have various further defences open to it, such as that the third party had consented to their disclosure or that the allegations were substantially true, or amounted to 'honest comment' (as the 'fair comment' defence has been re-baptised), or were made on a privileged occasion; and a media defendant may be able to rely on the qualified privilege defence for responsible journalism where there is a public interest in publishing the allegations (see *Jameel and Others* v. *Wall Street Journal Europe Sprl* [2006] UKHL 44).

---

[56] Under the rule against prior restraint in *Bonnard* v. *Perryman* [1891] 2 Ch 269 (which the Court of Appeal held in *Greene* v. *Associated Newspapers Ltd* [2004] EWCA Civ 1462 remained unaffected by s.12 of the Human Rights Act 1998), a court will not normally grant an injunction where the defendant publisher of the allegedly defamatory statement indicates an intention to prove it is true, or would be subject to some other substantive defence, unless the claimant can clearly show that none of these defences will succeed at trial.

As a public authority could be liable for subsequent disclosures where these were reasonably foreseeable, authorities might wish to consider marking disclosed materials with a clear warning that re-publication or reproduction without appropriate consent could lead to liability in damages and that the authority is not to be taken as authorising any such further disclosure.

Negligence/breach of statutory duty

Even where a public authority is flagrantly in breach of duties imposed on it by or under the FOIA, it is not open to applicants or third parties to bring a civil action on that account against the authority for damages or an injunction or any other remedy, as a result of the bar in s.56(1). The position is the same under the EIR (reg.18(1) and (4)(e)).

Action regarding the Information Commissioner

Where an interested third party becomes aware that an applicant is seeking an adjudication from the Information Commissioner under s.50(1) of the FOIA on whether the authority's refusal to disclose the information is justifiable, the third party could write to the Information Commissioner with its views on the questions at issue. The Information Commissioner would arguably be obliged under public law to take account of them when reaching his decision, and were he not to do so, he could be open to a challenge from the third party by way of judicial review.

As a separate possibility, where no appeal to the Information Rights Tribunal is made by the applicant or the authority, an interested third party would potentially be able to seek judicial review to challenge the Information Commissioner's decision notice issued in response to a complaint under s.50(1) of the FOIA.

Lastly, if all else fails, a third party might consider drawing any failure to consult on the authority's part to the Information Commissioner's attention. (This could not be done by means of a s.50(1) complaint, which is only available to applicants for information.) The Information Commissioner might look into the matter and issue the authority with a practice recommendation for a breach of the Section 45 Code of Practice. While that will be of no immediate benefit to the third party, it might stimulate a more co-operative response from the authority in relation to future requests.

APPENDIX A

FSA publication scheme

[© The Financial Services Authority. Updated as at 5 October 2012 at **www.fsa.gov.uk/ information/publication_scheme**.]

Who we are and what we do

Organisational information, structures, careers at the FSA, Biographies of our Executive Team and Management Board members, information about the legal basis for our activities, and information about how to contact us is included in this section.

A pound sign (£) is used to indicate material for which there may be a charge – see **administrative arrangements** for more information.

- Who are we
- History of the FSA
- How to Contact us
- What we do – including who we regulate, our regulatory approach, fighting financial crime and supporting consumers
- Statutory Objectives
- Management structure and responsibilities
- The Board and Board Committees
- Organisational structure chart
- Accountability – including relations with HM Treasury, the role of the Complaints Commissioner and Financial Services and Markets Tribunal and the Legal Framework, in addition to the Financial Services and Markets Act, under which the FSA has regulatory powers
- Essential Facts about the FSA
- Careers at the FSA
- Organisations we work with – including HM Treasury, The Bank of England, Financial Ombudsman Service, Financial Services Compensation Scheme and Information Commissioners Office.

    – Links to international websites which may be of interest
    – Links to other websites which may be of interest

- Memorandum of Association of The Financial Services Authority
- Articles of Association of The Financial Services Authority
- Schedule of Matters reserved to the Board
- Governance memorandum
- Financial Services & Markets Act 2000
- Payment Services Regulations 2009
- Company, Limited Liability Partnership and Business Names (Sensitive Words and Expressions) Regulations 2009
- Financial Services Act 2010
- Cross Border Payments in Euro Regulations 2010
- Welsh Language Scheme – sets out how FSA will comply with the provisions of the

Welsh Language Act 1993. Note: parts of the Scheme are available in both English and Welsh. *Cynllun Iaith Gymraeg*

What we spend and how we spend it

Financial information relating to projected and actual income and expenditure, procurement, contracts and financial audit. Our financial statements and budgets, and information about our pay and grading structure is included in this section.

A pound sign (£) is used to indicate material for which there may be a charge – see **administrative arrangements** for more information.

- How we are funded
- Annual Report from 1999 onwards, which includes financial review information, including the report of the independent auditor. Information on the remuneration of senior staff and board members is also detailed.
- Business Plan including the FSA's 'Plan and budget' (1999–2003) and 'Strategic Business Plan' (2004 onwards) including details of planned capital expenditure. Also including FSA's Retail Conduct Risk Outlook and Prudential Risk Outlook (from 2011/12 onwards).
- Employee Handbook detailing: expenses policy for staff including travel and subsistence rates payable
- Procurement at the FSA – including invitations to tender and contracts awarded
- Events
- Careers at the FSA including information on our Graduate Careers Programme
- Job families including pay information
- Performance Management Framework
- Flexible Benefits Plan
- Summary of Allowances and Expenses claimed by FSA's Chairman and Executive Members of the FSA's Board

What our priorities are and how are we doing

Information about our strategies and plans, performance indicators, inspections and reviews. Our corporate plan and annual reports are included in this section.

A pound sign (£) is used to indicate material for which there may be a charge – see **administrative arrangements** for more information.

- Annual reports and Accounts from 1999 – provide detailed statistics on the regulated population and Report of the independent auditors. Also, our responses to the Annual Reports of the Consumer, Practitioner and Small Business Practitioner Panels and the Complaints Commissioner
- Business Plan including the FSA's 'Plan and budget' (1999–2003) and 'Strategic business plan' (2004 onwards) including details of planned capital expenditure. Also including FSA's Retail Conduct Risk Outlook and Prudential Risk Outlook (from 2011/12 onwards).
- Service Standards Portfolio
- Internal Audit Division information pack
- The Performance Account including our latest results and details of How we evaluate our performance
- Corporate responsibility at the FSA – including the Environment and FSA in the Community also how we measure performance and how we have performed
- Response to the National Audit Office's Economy, Efficiency and Effectiveness Review of the Financial Services Authority – Full Report: *The Financial Services Authority: A Review under Section 12 of the Financial Services and Markets Act 2000*

How we make decisions

Decision making processes and records of decisions. Consultations, summary minutes of FSA Board meetings and internal guidance are included in this section.

A pound sign (£) is used to indicate material for which there may be a charge – see **administrative arrangements** for more information.

- Articles of Association of The Financial Services Authority
- Schedule of Matters reserved to the Board
- Governance memorandum
- Consultation papers and responses. Note: public feedback responses to consultations are available on request, except where the respondent has asked that their response remain confidential
- Discussion Papers and responses
- Policy statements
- Consumer research publications
- Occasional Papers – peer reviewed papers in financial regulation extending across economics and other disciplines
- Economic Research
- Retail Distribution Review (this information is only available from our website)
- FSA Board Meetings: Summary minutes
- Board Committees – including the Regulatory Decisions Committee
- FSA's Staff Consultative Committee: Summary minutes
- International and EU work, including the Capital Requirements Directive/Basel2
- FSA Annual Public Meetings
- Policy Delivery Standards – FSA's internal guide to process disciplines for making rules and giving guidance

Our policies and procedures

Current written protocols that we follow when delivering our services and responsibilities. This section includes our policies and procedures for providing our services and for the recruitment and employment of staff, our complaints procedure and our records management policy.

A pound sign (£) is used to indicate material for which there may be a charge – see **administrative arrangements** for more information.

- Welsh Language Scheme – sets out how FSA will comply with the provisions of the Welsh Language Act 1993. Note: parts of the Scheme are available in both English and Welsh. *Cynllun Iaith Gymraeg*
- FSA's Business Continuity management [PDF]
- Careers at the FSA – including information on our selection process and application forms
- Staff Operations and Processes – including job families and pay information. Also the Flexible Benefits Plan and Code of conduct (for staff)
- Employee Handbook containing terms and conditions of employment and general guidance to staff on FSA procedures, other than security matters
- Corporate responsibility at the FSA – including FSA in the Community and our Environmental Practice
- Single Equality Scheme 2010–2013 [PDF]
- Environmental Information Regulations Processes
- The FSA complaint scheme – Complaints about the FSA and our responses.
- Freedom of Information processes – including FSA's Freedom of Information Fees Statement

- Data Protection – including FSA's Processes and Data Protection subject access request form
- Re-use of Public Sector Information Regulations Processes
- Records Management Processes – including FSA's retention schedule criteria
- How FSA regulated firms can calculate and pay their Fees
- Memorandums of Understanding with UK and international organisations
- Policy Delivery Standards – setting out the process FSA goes through developing and implementing Regulatory Policy
- Guidance document on practical cost-benefit analysis for financial regulators

Lists and Registers

Information held in registers required by law and other lists and registers relating to our functions. This section includes our disclosure log.

A pound sign (£) is used to indicate material for which there may be a charge – see **administrative arrangements** for more information.

- Memorandums of Understanding – with both UK and international organisations.
- Register of interests for FSA's Chairman and Executive members of the FSA's Board
- £ The FSA Register (this information is available via our website or in hard copy for individual entries. It is also available in CD-ROM; Magnetic Tape and CD-ROM; FSA's Historic Register)
- £ Mutuals Societies Public Records Section including the Mutuals Public Register (this information is available in CD-ROM)
- A List of Banks
- A List of Building Societies
- £ Disclosure log – which includes responses to some Freedom of Information requests that are of wider public interest
- Information Asset Register – information available for re-use under the Re-use of Public Sector Information Regulations
- Hospitality and Gifts Log – received by FSA's Chairman and Executive members of the FSA's Board
- Diary Engagements of the Chairman and Executive Members of the FSA's Board
- Fines Table – contains information about who FSA has fined each year since 2002 and the level of fine imposed
- A list of Published waivers
- Links with other UK agencies and government departments, which have related responsibilities

  - Links to international websites which may be of interest.
  - Links to other websites which may be of interest.

- A List of reportable instruments
- UKLA Official List (this information is available in CD-ROM). Details of securities currently listed on the Official List of the UK Listing Authority (the competent authority for listing).

  - Main Official List
  - All Suspended Securities

- UKLA Daily Admissions and Daily Cancellations – details of securities admitted to or cancelled from the Official List of the UK Listing Authority today
- UKLA Daily Suspensions and Daily Restorations – details of securities that have had their listing on the Official List of the UK Listing Authority suspended or restored today

The services we offer

Advice and guidance, booklets, leaflets, newsletters and media releases. A description of the services we offer.

A pound sign (£) is used to indicate material for which there may be a charge – see **administrative arrangements** for more information.

- Press releases
- Consumer Information
- Legacy Publications of the FSA's predecessor organisations (this information is available on CD-ROM)
- (£) FSA Handbook, (£) Handbook Material, Handbook Development Newsletters and (£) Guidance Notes (please see Useful Links for further information about ordering a printed copy of the Handbook).
- Information for Smaller Firms (this information is only available from our website)
- Information for Wholesale Small Investment Firms
- How to get Authorised
- Approved persons including our approval process
- How to Apply for a Waiver
- Financial Crime Library – including Press Releases
- Whistleblowing
- Industry Training – to improve the financial service industry's knowledge of and ability to comply with its regulatory requirements
- Events – a wide range of conferences, seminars and lectures on topical regulatory issues
- Market Conduct and Infrastructure issues – Market Conduct Assessment of Market Infrastructure providers against CPSS-IOSCO recommendations. These assessments of LCH.Clearnet Limited and CRESTCo Limited are not full supervisory or oversight assessments, as they do not cover a number of areas that fall within the scope of regulation and oversight in the UK
- Transaction Reporting
- UKLA and UKLA publications (this information is available in CD-ROM)
- (£) Mutual Societies Registration Information (this information is available in CD-ROM) and Public Records Section
- Dear CEO letters
- Enforcing the Law including Warnings and Final Notices
- International Work
- Mortgage endowments and Mortgage endowments library including factsheets and reports
- How FSA regulated firms can calculate and pay their Fees – including our fee calculator to enable calculation of your FSA fees, FSCS levy and FOS general levy for different financial periods and scenarios
- Media Centre including Speeches and Articles
- Environmental Information Regulations Processes
- The FSA complaint scheme – Complaints about the FSA and our responses
- Freedom of Information processes
- Staff Operations and Processes – including FSA's Data Protection Processes and Data Protection subject access request form
- Re-use of Public Sector Information Regulations Processes
- Policy delivery standards – setting out the process FSA goes through developing and implementing Regulatory Policy
- Statistics on mortgage lending
- Building Society Statistics
- Mortgage fraud

- Other Publications – including miscellaneous documents, Pensions Publications and Pensions Reviews
- FSA Library – including our latest publications and publications by date
- Reports by skilled persons (section 166) – information on how often we commission skilled person reports
- FSA Resourcing Metrics

APPENDIX B

FOI resources

The Information Commissioner's Office

For general freedom of information guidance and assistance:

Wycliffe House
Water Lane
Wilmslow
Cheshire SK9 5AF
Tel: 0303 123 1113 (helpline); 01625 545745
Fax: 01625 524510
www.ico.gov.uk

Freedom of Information journal

To subscribe to the Freedom of Information journal and for freedom of information training courses:

PDP Companies
16 Old Town
London SW4 0JY
Tel: 0845 226 5723
Fax: 0870 137 7871
www.foij.com

Ministry of Justice

For updates and guidance on freedom of information:

102 Petty France
London SW1H 9AJ

Tel: 020 3334 3555
Fax: 0870 761 7753
www.justice.gov.uk

Department for Environment, Food and Rural Affairs

For enquiries relating to the Environmental Information Regulations:

Environmental Information
Area 1/B, Ergon House
Horseferry Road
London SW1P 2AL
Fax: 020 7270 8970
Email:
informationrights@defra.gsi.gov.uk
www.defra.gov.uk

Freedom of Information Conference

For information on the Annual Freedom of Information Conference and Workshop Series:

PDP Conferences
16 Old Town
London SW4 0JY
Tel: 0845 226 5723
Fax: 0870 137 7871
www.foiconference.com

Index

Housing records 1.6
Human Fertilisation and
Embryology Authority
(HFEA) 3.3.2

Immigration controls
exemption 5.4.6
Incorporated companies
access to records 3.5
Independent Schools
Inspectorate 1.8
India
proactive publication 1.5.3
Information asset register
(IAR) 2.10
Information audit 6.4.2
Information Commissioner
4.1, 4.4
Code of Practice and 1.2, 1.2.1
complaints about 10.6.4
complaints to *see* Complaints
data protection 8.3.6, 8.3.7
decision notices 10.3.1, 10.4.1,
10.6.1
duties 1.7, 8.3.7, 10.2.1
enforcement notices 10.3.3, 10.4.1
enforcement role 1.7, 3.3.1, 10.2.1
entry and inspection powers 10.4.4
environmental information 1.6
exchange of information with other
ombudsmen 10.4.3
information notices 10.3.2, 10.4.1
internal review following complaint
10.5
investigations 10.6.1
ministerial veto 10.3.5
Model publication schemes 2.6
non-compliance with notices
punishable as if contempt of court
10.4.1
powers 10.2.2
practice recommendations 10.3.6
prosecution of offences 10.4.2
public interest test and 5.2.3, 5.2.4
publication schemes and 2.1, 2.2,
2.3, 2.5, 2.6, 2.11, 2.12
role 1.7, 1.8
third parties and 10.10.5
undertakings 10.3.4
Information notices 10.3.2
appeals 10.7
non-compliance punishable as if
contempt of court 10.4.1

Information requests 3.2.1
advice and assistance 3.2.2
appeals 3.2.5
complaints 3.2.5, 10.6.1
effective requests 3.2.2
fees 3.2.3
formality 3.2.2
guidance for applicants 3.2.2
legal formality 3.2.2
private sector 6.3
refusal notices 3.2.4
repeated requests 3.2.4
response 3.2.4, 3.3.1
timescale for response 3.2.4
vexatious requests 3.2.4
who can make a request 3.2.2
to whom request can be made 3.2.2
to whom request should be sent
3.2.2
Information Rights Tribunal
see Tribunal
Information Tribunal *see*
Tribunal
Inquiries
exempt documents 4.5.3
Intellectual property
access to records 3.5
Internal review following
complaint 10.5
International relations
exemptions 5.3.2, 5.4.3, 9.2.14
Internet 1.1, 1.5, 2.10, 4.5.1,
8.3.2
Investigations and
proceedings
exemption 5.3.3
Ireland 1.1, 1.5, 1.5.1
appeals and enforcement 1.5.7
charging 1.5.5
proactive publication 1.5.3

Japan
appeals and enforcement 1.5.7
charging 1.5.5
third party rights 1.5.6
Judicial review 1.4
application for 10.7.9
in Upper Tribunal 10.8.3

Land registration
access to records 3.5
Law enforcement
exemption 5.4.6

limited rights of intervention under
  FOIA 10.10.1
maximising third party's chances of
  being consulted 10.10.4
negligence 10.10.5
options for direct action 10.10.5
other jurisdictions 1.5.6
rights 1.5.6, 10.10.3
Trade secrets
  exemption 5.3.9, 6.2.3
Transparency Programme
  3.7.2, 3.7.3, 3.8
Tribunal 1.9, 4.1
  appeals against decision of 10.8.1
  challenging decisions of 10.7.9
  data protection 8.3.7

public interest test 5.2.4
see also Upper Tribunal

Undertakings 10.3.4
United States 1.1, 1.5, 1.5.1
  appeals and enforcement 1.5.7
  exemptions 1.5.4
  proactive publication 1.5.3
  publication scheme 1.5.3, 2.3
  third parties 1.5.6
Upper Tribunal
  appeals 10.8
  judicial review 10.8.3

Whistleblowers 5.3.3